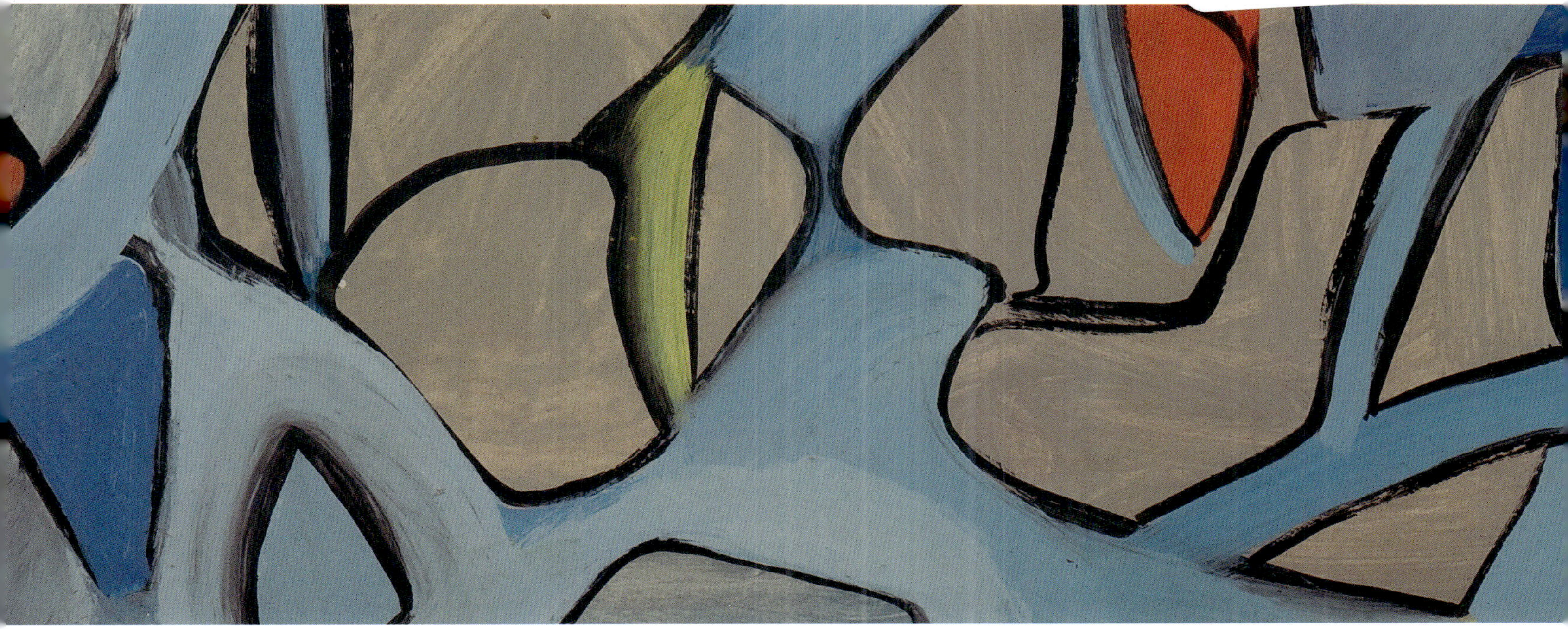

Weatherspoon Art Museum

70 Years of Collecting

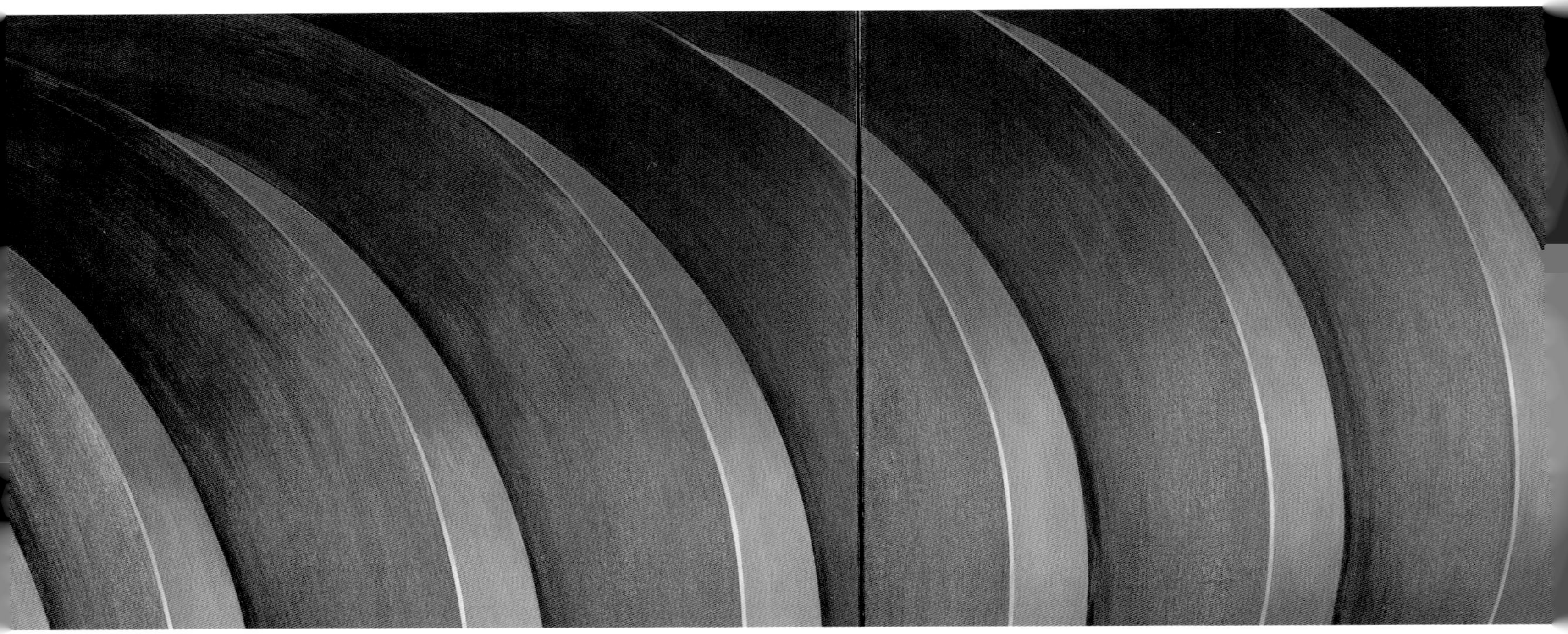

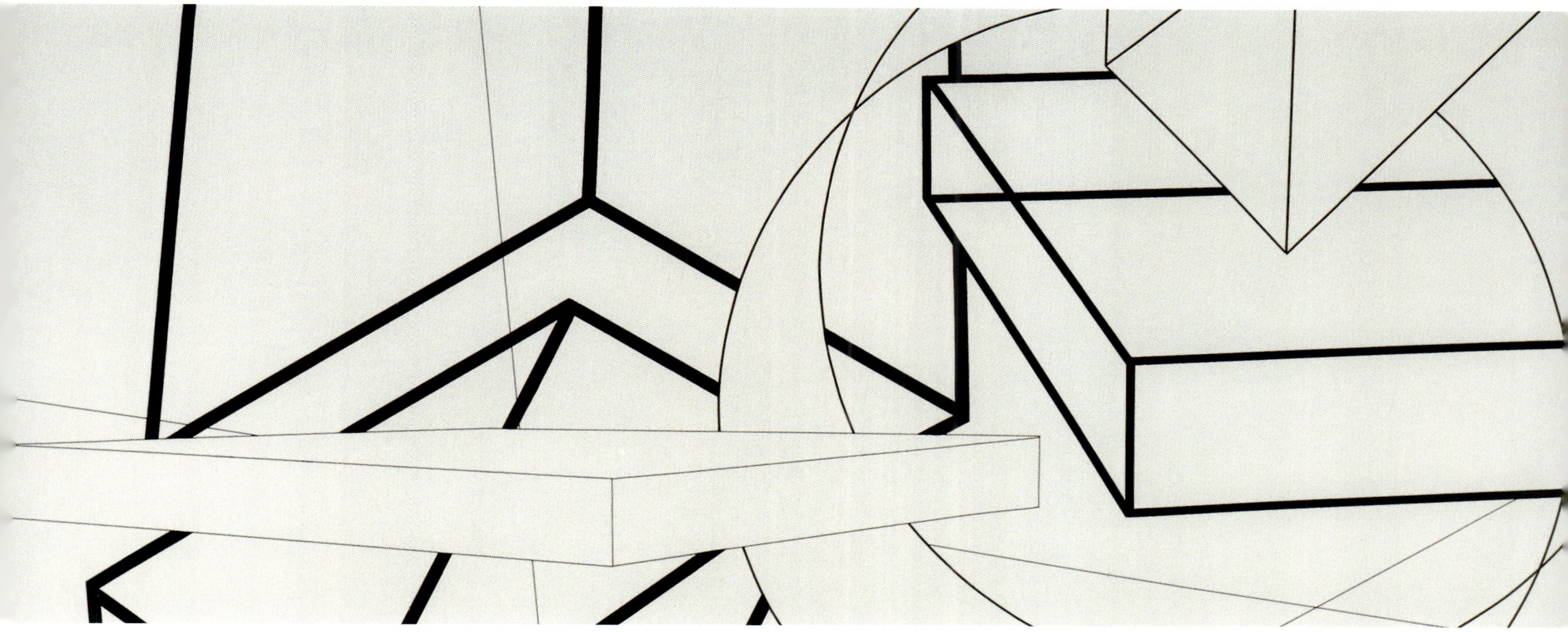

Weatherspoon Art Museum
70 Years of Collecting

Weatherspoon Art Museum, The University of North Carolina at Greensboro

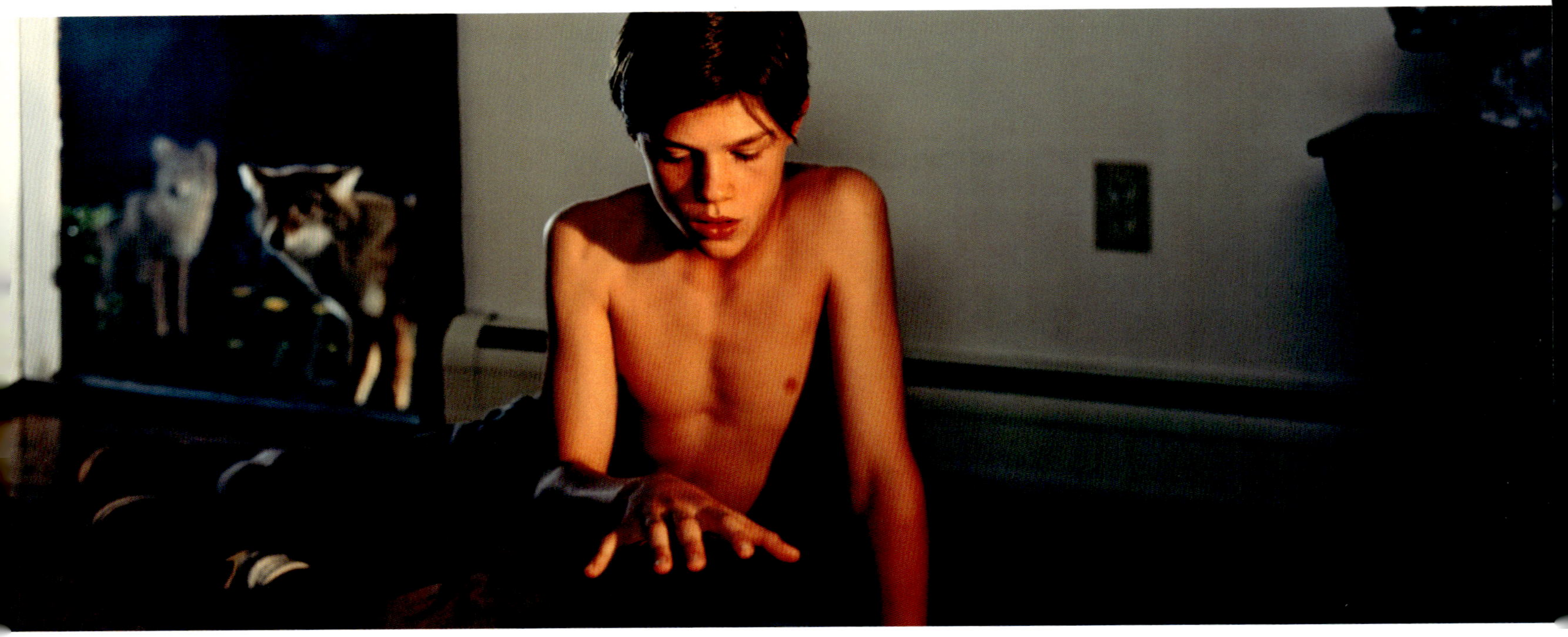

Published in conjunction with the exhibition *Weatherspoon Art Museum: 70 Years of Collecting*, on view at the Weatherspoon Art Museum, February 5–May 1, 2011.

Support has been provided by the Henry Luce Foundation, the Halstead Foundation, the Hillsdale Fund, and the Office of the Provost at UNCG. Additional contributions were made by H. Michael Weaver and Weaver Foundation, Inc., Margaret Gregory, and Evans and Ron Garber.

Library of Congress Control Number: 2010928704
ISBN 978-1-890949-13-6 (hardcover)
ISBN 978-1-890949-14-3 (softcover)

Front cover: Cindy Sherman, *Untitled #85*, 1981

Produced by Marquand Books, Inc., Seattle
www.marquand.com

Copyedited by Fronia W. Simpson
Designed by Zach Hooker
Typeset by Brynn Warriner
Proofread by Ted Gilley
Color management by iocolor, Seattle
Printed and bound in China by Artron Color Printing, Ltd., in an edition of 3,000.

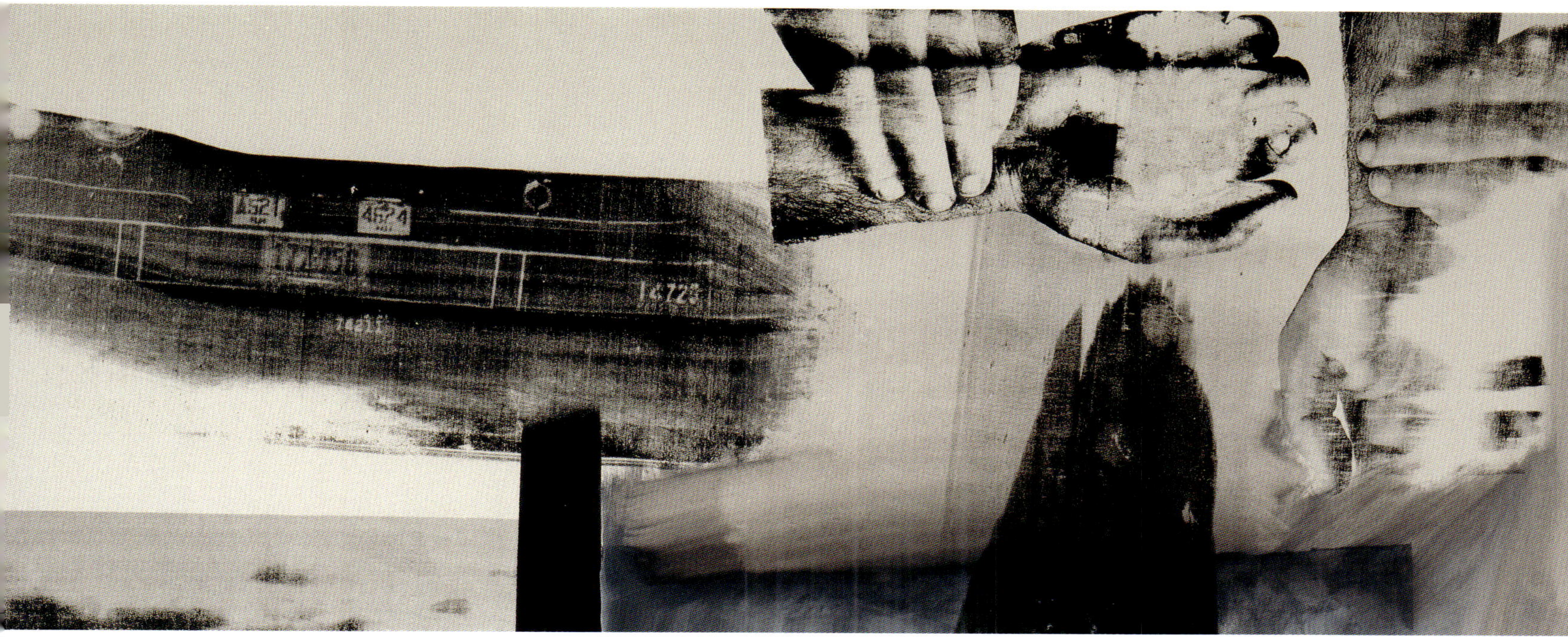

Contents

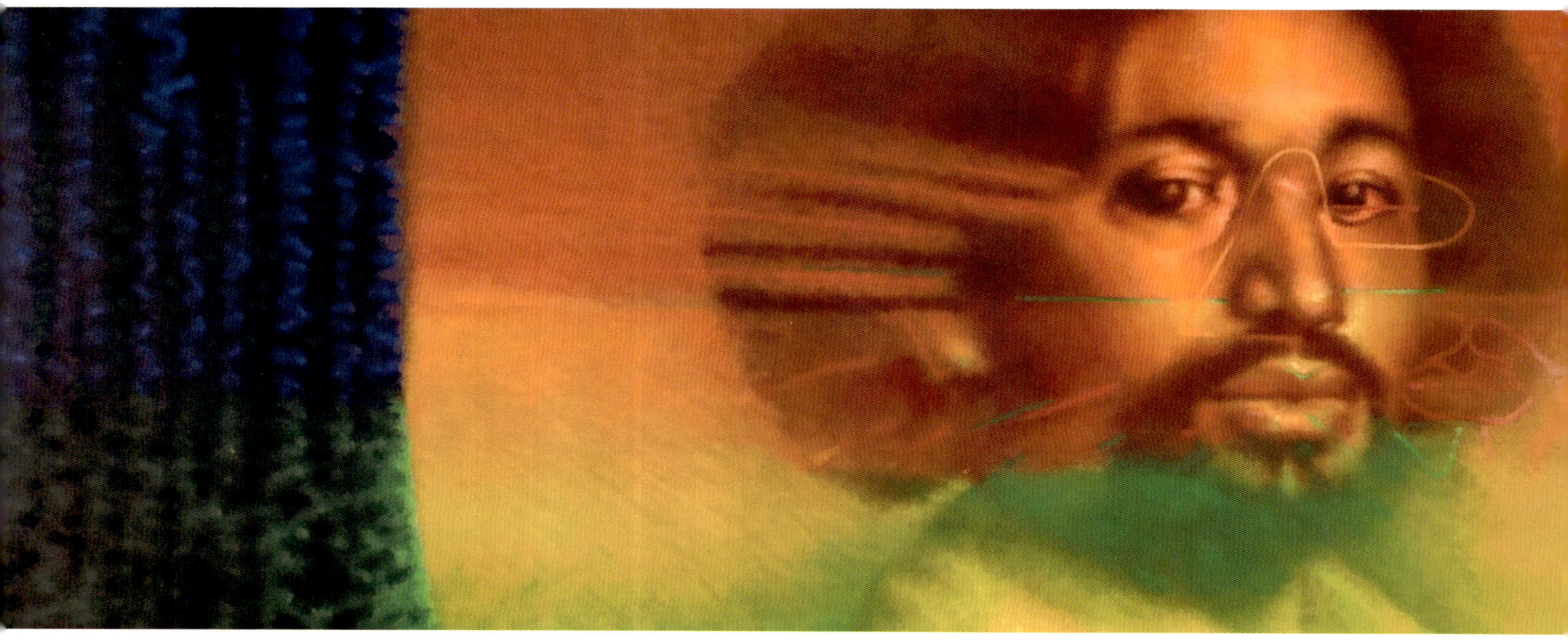

Foreword and Acknowledgments

THE WEATHERSPOON ART MUSEUM: 70 Years of Collecting is published on the occasion of the museum's seventieth anniversary year. The Weatherspoon has a remarkable institutional history, some of which is woven throughout this publication. Underscoring it are a spirit of adventure and risk taking and a chronology of dedicated museum professionals and volunteers. This book is intended to tell the story of the museum's steady growth—from its inception as a small art department gallery to its current position as a university art museum of high national regard—through selected works from the permanent collection and accompanying essays. The artworks were chosen for a variety of reasons but primarily to demonstrate the breadth of the collection and its range from acknowledged masters to younger artists who may one day join their ranks.

Any publication of this scope is an enormous group effort, and I extend heartfelt thanks to the many individuals who made invaluable contributions to it. Foremost among them are those who have provided its content. All six professors of art history in the Department of Art at The University of North Carolina at Greensboro (UNCG) enthusiastically accepted our invitation to participate; for their research, scholarship, and collegiality I thank K. Porter Aichele, George Dimock, Richard Gantt, Carl Goldstein, Heather Holian, and Elizabeth Perrill. Likewise, my gratitude goes to Curator of Exhibitions Xandra Eden, Curator of Education Ann Grimaldi, Curator of Collections Elaine D. Gustafson, and former Curator of Collections Will South for their entries, carved out of time from among their many other projects. Elaine D. Gustafson is to be singled out for taking over the role of production manager within weeks of assuming her position at the Weatherspoon. Her patience and diligence kept us on track and under deadline, and she worked closely with many of the people mentioned below to bring this project to its successful fruition. Other museum staff to be thanked are Registrar Heather Moore, former Registrar Margaret Gregory, Assistant Registrar Myra Scott, Preparators Susan Taaffe and Joel Vander Kamp and former Preparator Jack Stratton, as well as graduate assistant Ashley Boycher and volunteer Maggie Triplette.

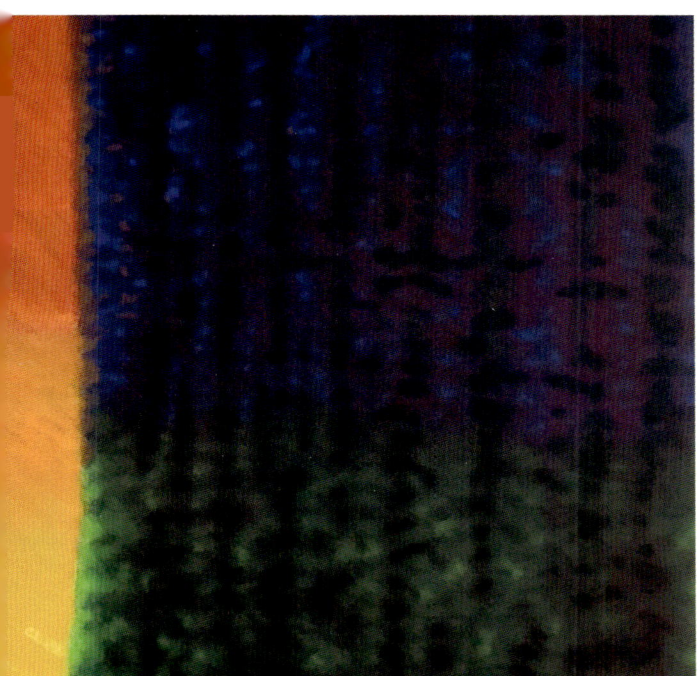

Fronia W. Simpson provided expert editorial help and several individuals at Marquand Books lent their expertise: Adrian Lucia and Jeff Wincapaw to the conception and development of the book, and Zach Hooker to its striking design. Ruth Barach Cox brought her professional experience to bear in conserving selected works for the exhibition. On campus, Mark Schumacher of the Reference and Instructional Services Department at UNCG's Jackson Library promptly and cheerfully answered research questions, while Christine Dorrestein-Schultz in the University Counsel Office assisted with contractual matters. Dan Smith of the University Teaching and Learning Center photographed many artworks for reproduction, and three volunteers interns ably assisted with various research efforts: Ella Yoo, Kyle Cupit, and Julia Piszczak. We are grateful to each and every one.

Primary funding for *70 Years of Collecting* was generously provided by the Henry Luce Foundation, the Halstead Foundation, the Hillsdale Fund in honor of Eloy Doolan, and the Office of the Provost at UNCG. My sincere thanks go to them and to the individuals at each—Ellen Holtzman, Martha and William B. Halstead, Mary L. Scott and the Hillsdale Fund board of trustees, and Provost David L. Perrin, respectively—for their belief in the Weatherspoon and their understanding of the value of the publication. Additional contributions were kindly made by H. Michael Weaver and Weaver Foundation, Inc., Margaret Gregory, and Evans and Ron Garber.

The Weatherspoon Art Museum staff joins me in hoping that you will find this book on our permanent collection a contribution to scholarship in the field, a beautiful picture book, and, most of all, an informative and enjoyable read.

Nancy M. Doll
DIRECTOR

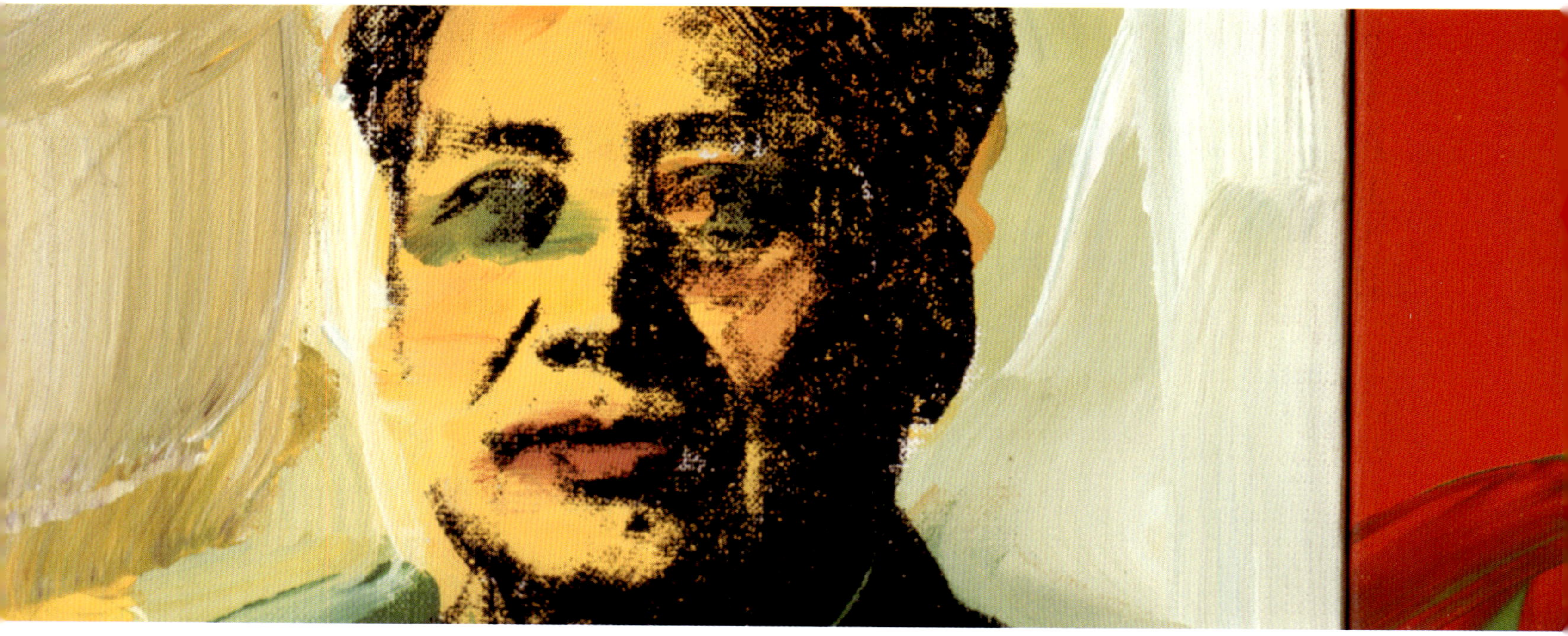

From Classroom to Contemporary Art Museum

Nancy M. Doll, Director

A STELLAR BEGINNING

The history of an organization is at heart a collection of its stories and, over the last seven decades, the Weatherspoon Art Museum has accumulated many. Gregory D. Ivy came to Woman's College, now The University of North Carolina at Greensboro (UNCG), in 1935 to establish a department of art. In 1941 Ivy founded the Weatherspoon Art Gallery, as it was first called. Ivy believed that, to become educated as artists, students needed a solid grounding in art history and the materials and techniques of art making. But as a painter who had studied in New York and was still actively exhibiting there, he also felt they should have direct exposure to the art and artists of their time.

Ivy left little doubt about his convictions by bringing the exhibition *A Brief Survey of Modern Painting* to the college's Students' Building in early 1936. It comprised works from the permanent collection of the Museum of Modern Art in New York (MoMA) and was organized by its director, Alfred H. Barr Jr., one of the most influential people at the time in the world of modern American art. Today, this seems an incredible coup, but it reinforces Ivy's knowledge of, and participation in, the art world of his day and, no doubt, his persuasive determination.[1] Ivy and his faculty made do with presenting exhibitions in the Student's Building (and possibly elsewhere on campus) until 1940. When the Art Department classrooms and studios were consolidated in the original McIver Building, which formerly housed the science departments, Ivy made sure that a space was allocated for exhibitions; the Woman's College Art Gallery opened in a former physics lab on January 7, 1941, making it the first art gallery within The University of North Carolina system. The following year, it was officially named in honor of Elizabeth McIver Weatherspoon, art educator, Woman's College alumna, sister of its late president Charles Duncan McIver, and one of the gallery's most dedicated early supporters. Weatherspoon is to be credited for helping develop the college's interest in the arts.

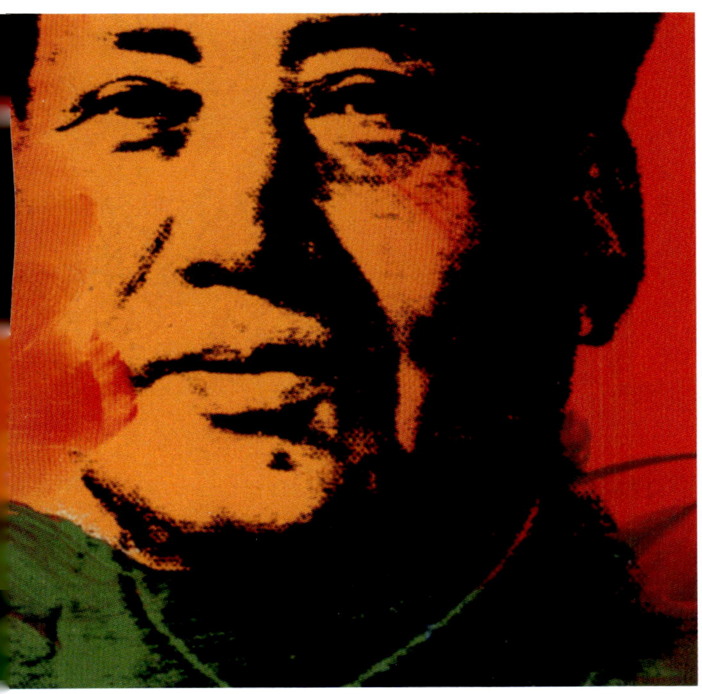

It may have seemed difficult to follow his own success in bringing the MoMA exhibition to his small gallery, but the connections that Ivy and some of his faculty had to the New York art world served his program well. In short order, the Weatherspoon exhibited the work of Maurice Gluckman, Josef Albers, Anni Albers, and selections from the Dr. Claribel and Etta Cone Collection, while the Bauhaus founder Walter Gropius and the painter Robert Gwathmey participated in one of the Annual Arts Forums on campus. Other artists such as Mark Rothko, Philip Guston, and Franz Kline were invited to lecture. Ivy established a summer school in Burnsville, North Carolina, near Albers's Black Mountain College, and a lively exchange of faculty and ideas ensued.

THE CONE SISTERS AND THE START OF A COLLECTION

Ivy also set his mind to building a permanent collection with which to teach. The first works of art to be given backdated accession numbers are a group of prints lent indefinitely to Woman's College by the Federal Art Project in 1936, which remain on loan today through the U.S. General Services Administration. Within the first decade alone, works were added that continue to be hallmarks of the Weatherspoon's collection: *The Flea* (1935, acquired 1945), by John Flannagan; John Marin's *Lake George* (1925, acquired 1948); and *Yellow Sail* (1950, acquired 1951), a mobile by Alexander Calder.

An important gift came in 1950 through a bequest from Etta Cone of works that she and her sister, Dr. Claribel Cone, had collected. Their brothers, Moses and Caesar Cone, established the first textile mills in Greensboro, and their fortune essentially financed the sisters' passion for collecting avant-garde European and American art. Claribel died in 1929, leaving all her artworks to Etta with the instruction to give them to the Baltimore Museum of Art if the city grew in its appreciation of modern art. The city did, and the Baltimore Museum received the vast majority of the sisters' famous and highly sought-after collection. The Weatherspoon Art Gallery, however, was the beneficiary of the second Cone Collection. Laura Weill (Mrs. Julius) Cone, a Woman's College alumna and early advocate for the Weatherspoon, encouraged her sister-in-law Etta to help the fledgling college art gallery. Etta responded by promising in her 1949 will (the year of her death) to donate 242 works from the sisters' combined holdings.

The Cone sisters were well known for their vanguard collection of such modern masters as Paul Cézanne, Pablo Picasso, and Henri Matisse, and, in some cases, each of them purchased a copy of a new print or sculpture by their favored artists, particularly Matisse. Included in the gift to the Weatherspoon is a remarkable group of sixty-seven prints and six bronzes by Matisse, twenty-seven drawings by John Graham, and a complete set of ten color pochoirs by Picasso that were inspired by his work for the Ballets Russes. It was the Cone sisters' spirit of adventure and risk taking in their collecting that further inspired and guided the Weatherspoon's focus on modern and contemporary art.

SUPPORT COMES IN MANY FORMS

In 1942 a group of individuals in the community and on campus formed the Friends of Weatherspoon Gallery to support and advocate for the new endeavor. Among those spearheading the group were Mrs. Frederick Ferguson and Mrs. Roger McDuffie (in whose honor Willem de Kooning's *Woman* painting was purchased later). Dr. Marc Friedlander, professor in the Creative Writing Program and founder of the campuswide Arts Forum, and Greensboro architect Edward Loewenstein also served on the Friends' board. In 1946 the group changed its name to the Weatherspoon Gallery Association.

Later, Louise D. Falk, one of the Weatherspoon's supporters and a Woman's College alumna, persuaded her husband, the prominent Greensboro attorney Herbert S. Falk Sr., to become involved in the burgeoning gallery. As Weatherspoon Gallery Association president from 1963 to 1967, Falk brought tremendous energy and business savvy to his position and persuaded a number of corporate leaders in the community to join him. The textile companies Burlington Industries, Blue Bell, and Wrangler; NCNB (later Nations Bank and now Bank of America); pharmaceutical company Ciba-Geigy; and insurance giant Jefferson-Pilot Corporation made significant contributions, especially toward building a collection of note.

Two other men were instrumental in this mission. James F. Tucker was hired by Ivy in 1959 to serve as the gallery's first curator for the permanent collection. Newly graduated with an MFA degree from the University of Iowa and with no experience as a curator, Tucker evidently made a strong case for the position. As it happened, Ivy wanted someone with no experience and no preconceived ideas about how a college gallery should function. Tucker had his work cut out for him; Ivy had maintained no files, and it was up to Tucker to reconstruct provenance, acquisition source, and other information for a collection already numbering well over three hundred artworks. Following Ivy's retirement in 1961 and the interim appointment of Helen Thrush as department head, Gilbert F. "Bert" Carpenter was hired as professor of art and chair of the department in 1963 from the University of Hawaii, where he

---

OPPER'S FOLLY

As head of the art department, Greg Ivy sent faculty member John Opper to New York to purchase an artwork with funds contributed in memory of Lena Kernodle McDuffie, an art educator at Woman's College and one of the founders of Friends of Weatherspoon Gallery, who had passed away. Opper visited the studio of Willem de Kooning and selected his 1949–50 painting *Woman*, which was purchased from the Sidney Janis Gallery for what was then the significant sum of $1,800. The arrival and unveiling of the painting caused quite a stir in Greensboro, prompting the press to call it "Opper's Folly." Even some of Opper's colleagues were puzzled by the purchase. Today, there is no doubt that this legendary acquisition was the most prescient in the Weatherspoon's history.

had held similar positions. He had studied art at Stanford University and the Chouinard Art Institute in Los Angeles and had done graduate work in art history at Columbia University in New York. Carpenter had also taught at Columbia and led a weekly discussion group on contemporary art, laying the foundation for his approach to teaching and lecturing.

Carpenter also assumed the directorship of the Weatherspoon Art Gallery, and he and Falk became close allies. With Carpenter's enthusiastic support, Falk persuaded his friend and fellow businessman Stark Dillard, president of Greensboro's Dillard Paper Company, to support a national contemporary survey of unique works on paper. Dillard agreed to contribute the considerable sum of $10,000 to finance the exhibition and provide a pool of money for the Weatherspoon to purchase works from it.

ART ON PAPER: A UNIQUE UNDERTAKING

Falk was proving to be a highly influential force behind the Weatherspoon in other ways as well. In 1964 he asked Mary Stephens to develop a group of volunteers to complement the association board by supporting the gallery's activities and helping to foster an appreciation for contemporary art within the community. One of the first projects of the Weatherspoon Guild, as the new auxiliary group was called, was the inaugural *Art on Paper* (*AoP*) exhibition. Undaunted by their lack of experience, Guild members handled countless logistics of the first *AoP*—and numerous others to follow. They sent out hand-addressed entry invitations to artists, museum directors, college art departments, and art journals across the country, and invited C. V. Donovan, director of the Krannert Art Museum at the University of Illinois in Urbana-Champaign, to be the juror. With the help of the Jaycees, they unpacked and registered works as they arrived and assisted James Tucker with installing the final selection of 131 works (from the 1,188 that were submitted). With their social hats on, they hosted the juror and prepared food and refreshments for several parties and receptions. It was a tour de force of organization and dedication, and a wild success.

The Dillard Paper Company name is long gone, replaced by International Paper Company and now *xpedx*, but it is hardly forgotten. The Dillard Fund has continued its extraordinary partnership with the Weatherspoon and its generous commitment to provide funds to acquire works from each and every *AoP*. The acquisition of 25 works from the 1965 exhibition established the Dillard Collection of Art on Paper, which now numbers 549 objects. Carpenter and Tucker made some well-informed and prescient acquisitions in the early years, purchasing a string and ink wash drawing by Eva Hesse in 1967, the year it was made and the first of her drawings to be purchased by a museum, and *The Hypothetical Continent of Lemuria* by Robert Smithson in 1969, also the year it was made. Other early purchases included works by Lee Bontecou, Dorothy Dehner, Jimmy Ernst, Arshile Gorky, Brice Marden, Philip Pearlstein, and Frank Stella, to name a small selection. More recently, purchases of works by Dike Blair, Inka Essenhigh, Andy Goldsworthy, Roni Horn, Ana Mendieta, Donald Moffett, and Pae White have further reinforced the collection's depth and significance. And, following precedent, in 2002 the Weatherspoon was the first museum to acquire a work by the then-emerging artist Amy Cutler.

The first incarnation of *Art on Paper* in 1965 was not only an extraordinary effort, but it also set the stage for a continuing project that, over the years, has brought widespread recognition to the Weatherspoon Art Museum. It remained an annual event until 2000, when, owing to the increasing breadth of the contemporary art world and the increasing complexity of borrowing and shipping works from artists and their galleries, it was made a biennial.

A SPIRIT OF GENEROSITY

Herbert Falk's civic-mindedness and philanthropic spirit manifested itself in many ways. In 1967 he initiated the Benefactor Program, whereby annual contributions of $1,000 or more would be designated for acquisitions. A perk of the program was that participants could borrow works from the Weatherspoon's collection. Although that practice has been discontinued, Friend and Benefactor contributions are still pooled to purchase artwork. In 2001 Benefactors Choice was instituted as an annual event, led by the curatorial staff to engage and educate in a more critical manner those who were contributing their funds to the acquisition process. Following presentations by the museum's curatorial team on three preselected works of art, any one of which would make a welcome addition to the collection, the Benefactors vote on a work to be purchased. Through this process, important objects have further amplified the collection. These have included the photographs *Battleground Point #5* by Richard Misrach and *Nude* by Edward Weston; the early collage *Goddess Because II* by Jess; and the three-part print *Untitled (Red, Yellow, Blue)* by Jasper Johns.

THE PREVIEW PARTIES

Stories about *Art on Paper* abound, and many have to do with the preview parties held the night before the exhibition opens to the public. That evening, attendees have the first opportunity to purchase works from the shows, and *AoP* treasures grace many Greensboro collections. For the party in 1967, a group of docents and hostesses donned colorful paper dresses designed and painted by art department faculty members. A small number have been preserved in the Special Collections Department of Jackson Library and were resurrected for the exhibition's fortieth anniversary in 2004—this time, however, displayed, not worn. In the early years, a cocktail party at the chancellor's house preceded supper in the gallery. In 1970 a ticket price—of $4.00—was first charged for the preview party; a report on the event also mentions the *candlelight* buffet. Times have changed, both financially and in museum practice, but the preview parties are here to stay.

THE CARPENTER-TUCKER YEARS

The Woman's College of The University of North Carolina became coeducational and was renamed The University of North Carolina at Greensboro in 1963, the same year Bert Carpenter was appointed head of the Art Department. In 1969 the department and the Weatherspoon Art Gallery were placed under the administration of the College of Arts and Sciences. The art world was a far different place then than it is today. In the museum's files are handwritten notes and typewritten letters, checks written by the treasurer of the Weatherspoon Gallery Association to purchase works of art, onionskin copies of invoices, and confirmed shipping arrangements, often for someone from Greensboro to drive to New York and pick up works for exhibition and acquisition purposes.

To say that these practices attest to a different world in which art was much more of a practice and pursuit than a business in no way takes credit away from the two men who initiated an ambitious program for the Weatherspoon Art Gallery. The calendar included solo exhibitions of artists visiting campus, group shows of works borrowed from New York galleries and private collections, regional surveys, and student and faculty exhibitions, shows that were tied to the techniques and processes of particular media, and—of course—*Art on Paper*.

As an artist and art historian, Bert Carpenter had friends, colleagues, and other connections in New York and elsewhere across the country. James Tucker had established a reputation as a respected curator with his own contacts. During their coincident tenure, works by many of the foremost artists of the time entered the collection. In addition to those already mentioned were Romare Bearden, Louise Bourgeois, Alex Katz, Sol LeWitt, John Marin, Louise Nevelson, Robert Rauschenberg, and Andy Warhol, among more than two thousand others. A collection of Asian art was begun in 1979 with gifts from Dr. Lenoir C. Wright. And, when Donald Droll joined Carpenter and Tucker in 1983 as assistant director of the Weatherspoon Art Gallery, his gifts and those of his friend and colleague Virginia Dwan further enhanced the rapidly growing permanent collection.

Bert Carpenter was a charismatic teacher who offered lectures on contemporary art to eager learners in the community. In addition to his welcome talks and seminars were those by Tucker, art department faculty members, and prominent artists and critics invited to campus. The availability of this informal but substantial education in modern and contemporary art led to the Guild's establishing a formal docent program in 1971. The docents benefited from a Tuesday study group, and their members conducted research on works in the collection and wrote short articles that appeared in the Sunday issue of the *Greensboro Daily News*. The growing importance of the Weatherspoon Art Gallery as an educational resource for town and gown was confirmed when George Keck was hired in 1976 as its first education coordinator to lead the docent training program.

In 1979, at the invitation of the Greensboro United Arts Council, the Weatherspoon took over a second location in the former *Greensboro News and Record* building, where the Green Hill Gallery and Greensboro Artists' League were housed at the time. Members of the Guild again rose to the occasion, staffing the space and offering docent-led tours. This satellite operation, simply called the Downtown Gallery, afforded new audiences an opportunity to see exhibitions from the permanent collection and to be introduced to the cultural resource the community had in the Weatherspoon. To help fund the space, Carpenter suggested that a limited-edition print series be sold, the first of which was by Peter Agostini, a UNCG art faculty member and insider of New York City's art scene. Along with *Art on Paper*, these prints provided the public an opportunity to purchase contemporary art at affordable prices.

To supplement contributions from corporate and benefactor members of the Association, the Guild also put aside funds from its many activities, ranging from trips to selling Christmas cards with images from the Weatherspoon's collection, as a purchase fund for art. Among their early acquisitions were paintings by Bert Carpenter and James Tucker. In addition to augmenting the small gallery staff with their labor, Guild volunteers organized an impressive roster of programs, trips, and special events. Clearly, these two organizations—the Weatherspoon Gallery Association and the Weatherspoon Guild—were critical to the growing success of the gallery.

A CURATOR'S CONTRIBUTIONS

Donald Droll, onetime director of Fishbach Gallery and later a partner in Fourcade, Droll Gallery, joined the Weatherspoon staff as assistant director in 1983. While in New York, Droll formed close relationships with a number of artists and developed a personal collection, from which he donated 22 works to the Weatherspoon. Among his gifts were *Clash*, a significant painting by Lee Lozano, *Untitled (Floor Painting)*, a characteristically compelling canvas by Sylvia Plimack Mangold, and an early Cindy Sherman color photograph, *Untitled #85*. Tragically, Droll died of a heart attack barely three years into his time at the Weatherspoon, the morning after the opening of the 1985 *Art on Paper* exhibition, which he had curated.

VISITING ARTISTS ON CAMPUS

The names of Herbert and Louise Falk appear again in the history of the Weatherspoon and the UNCG Department of Art, further underscoring their remarkable patronage. The Falk Visiting Artists (FVA) program was launched in 1982 with an endowment established by the couple to support the department's tradition of bringing artists to campus to teach. Still vigorous today, the program is a collaboration between the Art Department and the museum: each semester the Weatherspoon presents an exhibition of work by an artist selected by the FVA Committee, and the artist comes to campus for several days to offer critiques for the MFA graduate students and to give a gallery talk and public lecture.

Since its inception, the program has brought to campus the likes of Lynda Benglis, Jeremy Gilbert-Rolfe, Martin Puryear, David Reed, Laurie Simmons, and Anne Truitt. To date, more than seventy-five artists have visited. The FVA program also has fed into the Weatherspoon's collection; purchasing work by artists who exhibit here has long been an objective, and the museum has acquired works by Falk artists Dike Blair, Mel Chin, Anne Chu, and Pat Steir, among others.

AN EXPANDED BUILDING AND AN EXPANDED STAFF

Like many university galleries, as its parent organization expanded and grew more structured, so did the Weatherspoon. Two notable events took place in 1985. The first was the closure of the Downtown Gallery, when Green Hill Gallery wanted to expand its space. While this marked the end of an era, the next was close behind. The Weatherspoon's gallery in the McIver Building was becoming increasingly inadequate, and the permanent collection was rapidly outgrowing the available storage space. The state legislature responded to the advocacy efforts of Weatherspoon supporters and appropriated funding for a new art building that would house the gallery. Anne Cone, one of the Weatherspoon's foremost proponents at the time, and her husband, Benjamin, former Greensboro mayor and son of Caesar Cone, contributed a lead gift of $2 million; museum supporters raised an additional $1.5 million; and the combined sum was matched by the state. Plans for the building were approved in 1985, and a groundbreaking ceremony took place on September 9, 1987.

The physical and organizational metamorphosis of the Weatherspoon unfolded quickly. To say that the Cones' gift was transformative is the proverbial understatement. Two other important transitional events were the resignations of curator of collections James Tucker in 1986, after more than twenty-six years of dedicated service, and that of Bert Carpenter in 1989, after twenty-five years at the helm. In what could have been a time of instability, Ruth Beesch, the young acting director of the university gallery at the University of Florida in Gainesville, took Carpenter's place. She adeptly oversaw the completion of the new building and the move into it of the Weatherspoon Art Gallery and the art history program of the UNCG Art Department.

Internationally acclaimed Romaldo Giurgola of Mitchell/Giurgola Architects in Philadelphia and New York was engaged as design architect, and Leslie Boney's firm in Wilmington, North Carolina, executed the plan and oversaw construction. Conceptualized at the height of postmodernism, the building contextually reflects its surroundings. A tower at the northeast corner echoes that of the College Place United Methodist Church directly across on Tate Street. On the Spring Garden Street side, where the Weatherspoon's main entrance from campus is located, a series of windows mimics those of Aycock Auditorium opposite. From the parking area to the south of the building, a brick courtyard reminiscent of an Italian palazzo with a loggia leads to the building's second entry. Columns on either side of the back gate and supporting the loggia repeat larger, two-story columns at the campus entrance. The new building was dedicated in November 1989, and the first exhibition held there was, most appropriately, *Art on Paper*. The grand opening of the

---

A NEW YORK–GREENSBORO CONNECTION

Virginia Dwan was one of the first women gallery dealers in New York and one of the most influential forces in the art world there during the 1960s and 1970s. She represented artists working in the Abstract Expressionist mode and was a pioneer in commissioning and exhibiting many Postminimalist, earthwork, and Conceptual artists. Also an avid collector, she donated more than 100 works of art to the Weatherspoon in 1982. It is tempting to speculate that Dwan admired the Weatherspoon's early acquisition of some of the artists she represented. Among the key works coming from Dwan were a 1954 drawing by Willem de Kooning, *Woman*, Louise Nevelson's *Night Plant VI*, and *Straw-Boss* by Robert Rauschenberg. She also contributed multiple works by Alan D'Arcangelo, Sol LeWitt, and Larry Rivers.

Anne and Benjamin Cone Building was celebrated with a preview party on September 21, 1990, and a public reception was held the following day.

The Weatherspoon Art Museum occupies the majority of the 42,000-square-foot Cone Building, with six galleries, a sculpture garden, atrium, two storage vaults—one for paintings, sculpture, and framed works, the other for unframed works on paper—areas for matting, framing, and woodworking, and three small meeting rooms. Museum administrative offices share a second-floor corridor with the art history faculty. A 150-seat auditorium is utilized by the Art Department, primarily for art history classes, and by the Weatherspoon for many of its educational programs. A classroom and a visual resources room further support the Art Department's program.

In 1990 Sarah and Jack Warmath contributed funds, in honor of Sarah's parents, for the first public work of art commissioned specifically for the Cone Building. The artist Tom Otterness was engaged to install a permanent re-creation of an earlier piece, *The Frieze*, which he first exhibited at the Brooke Alexander Gallery, New York, in 1983. When he visited the new Weatherspoon location, Otterness immediately chose the lower perimeter of the atrium's elliptical opening as his site. A continuous ring of white cast figures narrates the artist's version of the story of human civilization from its dawn to its destruction. *The Frieze* enlivens the vast space in an eye-catching manner without compromising its architectural integrity.

From the days of Gregory Ivy to the present, education has been central to the Weatherspoon's activities. This core function and role of the gallery as an educational arm of the university was further reinforced in 1989, when it was moved under the jurisdiction of the provost and executive vice chancellor for academic affairs. Twelve full-time staff positions were allocated to the gallery's operation, including the positions of curator of exhibitions, curator of education, registrar, public relations coordinator, and museum administrator. Under the direction of Beesch, this new professional staff developed the policies and procedures required to earn accreditation from the American Association of Museums in 1995. This award recognized that the Weatherspoon met the highest standards of museum practice and positioned the gallery for growth in new directions, including successful fund-raising efforts at the national and regional levels.

A BRILLIANT AND VISIONARY IDEA

The Weatherspoon Arts Foundation was the inspiration of several members of the Gallery Association; particularly involved were the Greensboro attorney and former state senator Hubert B. Humphrey; Sarah D. Warmath, Association president and later the first Foundation president; businessmen Charles W. Cheek and Sion A. Boney; and Weatherspoon supporter Frances Loewenstein. With the promise of a new building, questions arose about who owned the collection and who should take care of it. All gifts of art and acquisition funds had come from private sources, and this group felt that it was crucial these donations be honored according to their original intent to build the permanent collection and that it be professionally managed. Following innumerable meetings and negotiations, Chancellor William Moran endorsed the idea, and on February 20, 1985, the Gallery Association approved the creation of the Arts Foundation as a body to hold legal title to works of art in the permanent collection. In January of the following year, the articles of incorporation were signed and the nonprofit foundation was chartered.

The purpose of the Weatherspoon Arts Foundation is to acquire works of art by gift, purchase, or loan that will maintain and enhance the collection for teaching, research, and public service purposes for the use and benefit of The University of North Carolina at Greensboro.[2] The university and the Association (for the Foundation) worked out a binding agreement specifying the roles and responsibilities of each, which was signed on November 3, 1988. Implicit in the intentions of the newly formed body and in the spirit of the agreement was the extension of the use and benefit of the collection to the community in the broadest sense of the word.

ANNE WORTHAM CONE

Although Anne and Benjamin Cone took the financial lead on the new building to house the Weatherspoon, that was hardly their only contribution. Anne also was dedicated to improving the permanent collection, and her name and Ben's appear on numerous credit lines for artworks they generously donated. Tales abound about the many acquisitions committee meetings during which Anne would end lengthy deliberations as to whether the gallery could afford a particular acquisition. Cigarette in hand, she spoke up to pledge additional funds or the full amount of a work if she felt it was something that would bolster the gallery's holdings.

CONTINUING GRASSROOTS SUPPORT: THE GALLERY ASSOCIATION AND THE GUILD

The supportive roles played by the Weatherspoon Gallery Association and the Weatherspoon Guild in the gallery's development continued, and both found new ways to lend needed support. With the move into the new building, the Guild restarted a docent program. And, with funds raised from its sales of limited-edition prints, it opened a museum shop in 1990. Staffed totally by volunteers led by Barbara Boulton, The Inside Corner generated a new line of revenue from which the Guild allocated an annual contribution to the gallery.[3]

The following year, the Association fostered another auxiliary group, the Contemporaries, aimed at attracting younger members to the gallery through trips, lectures, and other opportunities to learn about contemporary art. Now re-formed as the Contemporary Collectors Group, members enjoy special lectures, private receptions with artists, studio visits, and trips to art capitals around the country, where they visit galleries, museums, and private collections.

Volunteers remain at the heart of the Weatherspoon Art Museum today. In 2007 the Guild and Association boards voted to merge into a single volunteer base to avoid overlapping or duplicating efforts. Members of both groups continue to serve as dedicated docents who offer hundreds of tours to school and community groups each year and serve as gallery greeters for major exhibition openings. Committees host *Art on Paper* parties and special exhibition receptions, as well as the biannual *Art from the Heart* fund-raiser. They also lend their time and energy to the annual Summer Solstice Party, Community Days, and a host of other projects.

CONTINUING TO MOVE FORWARD

Ruth Beesch resigned as Weatherspoon Art Gallery director in 1997, with a record of impressive achievements. During her eight-year tenure, she oversaw the development of an exciting special exhibition program that kept alive the institution's risk-taking spirit and offered stimulating, thought-provoking art to UNCG's campus and the community alike. *Hannah Wilke: Intra-Venus*, *Sally Mann: Still Time*, and *It's about Control: Two Installations by Beth B* respectively looked at the devastating effects of chemotherapy on the artist's body, controversial photographs by a mother of her nude children, and female body-altering practices and the questionably redemptive purpose of confinement. Other exhibitions, such as surveys of Ida Applebroog and Dennis Oppenheim and installations by Jessica Stockholder and Meg Webster, brought major work by leading contemporary artists to the campus and the community.

The permanent collection expanded further as Beesch worked closely with the museum's curators of collections, private donors, and galleries on gifts and purchases. Among annual purchases from *Art on Paper* were works by William Beckman, Jimmy Ernst, Nancy Grossman, Yayoi Kusama, Charles Long, Theodore Roszak, and William Tucker. These were supplemented by gifts of works on paper by artists including Dorothy Dehner, Robert de Niro Sr., Blanche Lazell, Ed Ruscha, and Sean Scully, among others. *Family Portrait*, a significant early sculpture by Richard Stankiewicz, was purchased in 1994 in memory of Cordelia Penn Cannon, who had provided funds for sculpture acquisitions over the years. No doubt one of the most important acquisitions during Beesch's tenure was *Uncle Charlie* by Robert Colescott. Shortly after its purchase in 1997, it was shown that summer at the Venice Biennale, where Colescott was the first African American to represent the United States. After Beesch's departure to become deputy director at the Jewish Museum in New York, curator of collections Douglas Dreishspoon served for a year as interim director.

MORE THAN A NAME CHANGE

Changing the name of the Weatherspoon had been broached on more than one occasion over the years. In the early 1980s there was debate about calling it the North Carolina Museum of Modern Art, but this fell by the wayside. By 2001, however, it seemed time to adopt the name Weatherspoon Art Museum. The word *museum* more fully represented what the Weatherspoon was: a multifaceted, accredited, and well-respected institution with an ambitious exhibition schedule in six galleries, a fully professional staff, a growing budget, and an important collection. Further, the new name would help dispel any lingering identification of the Weatherspoon with the one-room gallery it once had been, and the occasional assumption that it was a commercial enterprise. The name change was approved in 2001 by the Weatherspoon Gallery Association and by Provost

Edward Uprichard and was endorsed the same year by the UNCG board of trustees.

A strategic plan developed by museum staff and members of the Weatherspoon Museum Association and adopted in 2003 prepared the staff for the work required to be successfully reaccredited by the American Association of Museums in 2005. The budget continued to grow, audience numbers rose, and the Weatherspoon took on an even more visible role in the community and across campus. Outreach and collaboration with area organizations became key to expanded educational programming. The unique, ongoing program New Art/New Audiences was instituted in September 2003 as a way to introduce small groups of adults at a time to contemporary art, to museums in general, and to the Weatherspoon in particular. The program seeks to demystify museums and help people overcome any intimidation they may feel about the art of their own time.

DIGITAL AND PHYSICAL IMPROVEMENTS FOR THE COLLECTION

For well over a decade, museums around the world have adopted electronic databases to manage their collection records. Not only does this technology allow for the assimilation of information into a single record, but it also enables sorting collections by different categories and provides for the inclusion of digital photographs. Museums can now make their collections available online to colleagues in the field, scholars, researchers, and the general public.

The Weatherspoon Art Museum was quick to move toward implementing an electronic collections management program, made possible beginning in 2000 with $50,000 in funding from the Office of the Provost and a $100,000 American Collections Enhancement grant from the Henry Luce Foundation. After purchasing the necessary software and licensing and having the database housed on the university server, the museum contracted for two years to have the collection records vetted and transferred to the new system.

The next major project was renovation of the main vault to provide safer storage and improved access to paintings and sculptures in the collection. The original painting storage racks had been built and installed by the university's Physical Plant Department during construction of the Cone Building. Fashioned from steel fencing, they served well until wear and tear caused them to stick and create vibrations when moved in and out of the tracks. A successful matching grant in the amount of $150,000 from the Institute of Museum and Library Services in 2004 enabled these racks to be replaced with new, state-of-the-art equipment. Through careful planning on the part of museum staff and the company engaged to provide and install the new racks, the Weatherspoon approximately doubled its square footage for storing paintings in half the original space and created a new area for consolidated sculpture storage.

SUCCESSFUL FUND-RAISING CAMPAIGNS

In 1994 The University of North Carolina at Greensboro launched the Second Century Campaign, in which the Weatherspoon's primary goals were endowment funds for art acquisitions and monies for a redesign of the museum's courtyard. Judy Proctor, chair of the museum's campaign steering committee, worked closely with Association presidents Sally B. Cone, Barbara Boulton, and Edward F. Cone and the university Development Office to successfully raise more than $3.1 million in gifts, pledges, and bequests by the end of the campaign in 1998. Of that, approximately $2.2 million was designated for eleven art acquisition endowment funds.

The Weatherspoon Guild contributed to the campaign with two highly successful art auction events, Spring for Art/Art for Spring. The goal was to raise matching funds for a $100,000 National Endowment for the Arts Challenge Grant toward the Weatherspoon's goal. Very able chairs, Mary Berkelhammer in 1997 and Judy Kapanka in 1998, were assisted by a large group of Guild and Association volunteers to successfully meet the match.

The positive impact of the campaign was seen in the naming of two Weatherspoon galleries for prominent members of the community and steadfast museum supporters. The first was appropriately the Louise D. and Herbert S. Falk Sr. Gallery, named in the couple's honor for their years of patronage and service. The second gallery was dedicated in honor of Leah Louise Tannenbaum, recognizing a major gift from the

Tannenbaum-Sternberger Foundation to purchase for the collection a significant sculpture, *DYBY* by Magdalena Abakanowicz. In addition, a visiting lectureship was established in honor of Ruth Beesch.

In 2004 UNCG embarked on the ambitious Students First Campaign, with the goal of raising $75 million over ten years; to everyone's enormous pride, the university raised more than $135 million in five years. The Weatherspoon shared in the success. In this campaign, co-chaired by Sally B. Cone and Jane Levy and again aided by the University Development Office, the museum sought to provide foundational support in the form of endowments for its four core missions: exhibitions, education, publications, and conservation. Carried over was the goal of renovating the courtyard, and added was that of a lecture fund for visiting artists, critics, and curators. By the campaign's conclusion, the Weatherspoon had quadrupled its five-year goal of $1.1 million.

Funded by a major gift from Michael and Katherine Stern Weaver, the courtyard was redesigned by Lappas + Havener, PA, Landscape Architects in Durham, North Carolina, into a welcoming and aesthetically pleasing space of plantings and sites for sculpture that prepares visitors for the experience of the museum itself. Three more galleries were named: the Gregory D. Ivy Gallery with a gift from Sarah and Jack Warmath; the Weatherspoon Guild Gallery, funded by Seymour and Carol Cole Levin; and the Robert and Lissa Shelley McDowell (Class of 1968) Gallery, whose testamentary gift of $1 million was the largest of the campaign.

THE FIRST DECADE OF THE NEW MILLENNIUM

The success of the recent campaign is only one of the ways in which the Weatherspoon has moved forward during the past ten years. The decade began with the first major exhibition of the paintings of Dona Nelson. Other survey shows with major catalogues contributing new scholarship to the field followed: Tom Knechtel's paintings and works on paper, *Inside the Floating World: Japanese Prints from the Lenoir C. Wright Collection*, Jessica Stockholder's studio works, and Jim Hodges's sculptures that engage with light. The latter two were, respectively, co-organized with Blaffer Gallery, the art museum at the University of Houston, and the Tang Teaching Museum and Art Gallery at Skidmore College, Saratoga Springs, New York. Another solo show with catalogue, *Gregory D. Ivy: Making North Carolina Modern*, surveyed and paid homage to Ivy's work as an artist.

Several group exhibitions organized by Weatherspoon curators and accompanied by award-winning catalogues felt the pulse of artists responding to topics of social and political interest. *Borne of Necessity* featured ten artists or artist teams whose work addressed facets of the complex issue of economically marginal existence. *Uneasy Nature* examined matters of global warming, biotechnology, medical engineering, and other potential threats to our future. *The Lining of Forgetting* considered the sphere of memory and its loss, a timely, far-reaching subject. In addition, *Transactions: Contemporary Latino and Latin American Art*, a traveling exhibition hosted by the Weatherspoon, offered audiences an overview of the stylistic and conceptual interests of artists from both North and South America. *Art on Paper* 2008 marked the fortieth anniversary of this cornerstone of the Weatherspoon's program. Support for these exhibitions came from the National Endowment for the Arts, the Rockefeller Foundation, the Andy Warhol Foundation for the Visual Arts, the Weatherspoon Museum Assocation, the North Carolina Arts Council, the Firestone-Graham Foundation, and additional private and public sources.

The year 2000 launched the new millennium with the proverbial bang when the museum acquired by purchase and gift more than 221 works of art. The reputation of the Weatherspoon's Dillard Collection prompted the drawing collector Wynn Kramarsky and his wife, Sarah-Ann, to give works on paper by Carl Andre, Sol LeWitt, and Alan Saret, among others. Toward the end of the decade, in 2008, the Weatherspoon was honored to be selected as the North Carolina museum to receive work from the Dorothy and Herbert Vogel Collection: Fifty Works for Fifty States. Through this project, which is documented in the film *Herb and Dorothy*, the Vogels distributed fifty works in their extraordinary collection to one museum in each of the fifty states.

Significant purchases have included *Compton Nocture*, a seminal sculpture by Alison Saar; four unique color photographs taken in 1969 by Robert Smithson and printed posthumously

---

A MAN WITH A PASSION

Dr. Lenoir C. Wright, a professor emeritus at UNCG before his death in 2003, was an exceptional man and an exceedingly generous friend of the Weatherspoon. While stationed in Japan during World War II, he developed a great interest in Asia. When he came to Woman's College in 1953, he taught classes in Asian history and culture, effectively offering an Asian studies program before the concept was popularized. During a trip to Japan that summer, Len purchased a few Japanese prints to supplement his teaching. Over fifty subsequent years, he studied countless books on Japanese woodblock prints and developed an unstoppable drive to collect them. In his later years, a retirement home left him with little wall space, and so Len periodically would have galleries send a small group of prints to the museum for his consideration. His excitement in seeing the works was palpable, and he often purchased several exquisite works at a time, as many as he could afford by "shaking the money tree." The Lenoir C. Wright Collection of Japanese Prints is a superb resource of more than 450 prints, primarily from the eighteenth and nineteenth centuries. Len's generosity was celebrated with the exhibition *Inside the Floating World*, which featured 100 highlights of the collection in the fall of 2002, just months before his death.

in 2001 that document the site of his drawing for his hypothetical continent of Lemuria; a sculpture by Deborah Butterfield; and *Lost Hat*, a large, multipart painting by Elizabeth Murray. A bequest of Anne Wortham Cone provided funds to purchase *To Be*, a sculpture by Mark di Suvero, and another generous gift from the Tannenbaum-Sternberger Foundation brought *Urban Francis* by Judith Shea into the collection. Grants from the National Endowment for the Humanities and the Institute for Museum and Library Services provided crucial funding for the care and maintenance of the collection.

A wide variety of works on paper, both from *Art on Paper* and other gifts and purchases, including those by Elliott Hundley, Walter Murch, Kiki Smith, and Nancy Spero further enriched the museum's holdings in this area. Intentional focus has been placed on expanding the photography holdings, and works by Gregory Crewdson, Yasumasa Morimura, and Vik Muniz are helping to meet this objective. At her death in 2004, a bequest from Maud Gatewood of ten of her paintings and eight drawings gave the Weatherspoon a substantial representation of one of North Carolina's most popular and well-known artists.

CONCLUSION

Over its seventy years, the Weatherspoon Art Museum has meant many things to many people, as it has educated students, challenged and enlightened audiences, presented critically acclaimed exhibitions, and cared for an important collection of art. The stories behind these efforts weave a fabric from past to present and most assuredly into the future. Behind all of these stories is a host of incredibly generous, enthusiastic, and dedicated individuals who have nurtured and sustained the museum's growth for seven decades. As the fourth and current director of the Weatherspoon, I am indebted to all of these people, to Greg Ivy for his vision, and to my predecessors who so successfully carried the adventurous spirit of the early Weatherspoon forward.

Notes

1. For a comprehensive study of Ivy and his work, see Will South, *Gregory D. Ivy: Making North Carolina* (Greensboro: Weatherspoon Art Museum, The University of North Carolina at Greensboro, 2005).
2. Charter of The University of North Carolina at Greensboro Weatherspoon Arts Foundation, 1990.
3. An invaluable resource for the history of the Weatherspoon Guild, Weatherspoon Museum Association, and the museum is *The Weatherspoon Guild: Growth and Change, 1964–2000* (Greensboro, NC: Guild Historical Review Committee, 2003). This committee was chaired by Mary Lee Copeland and cochaired by Barbara Boulton and Joan Gregory.

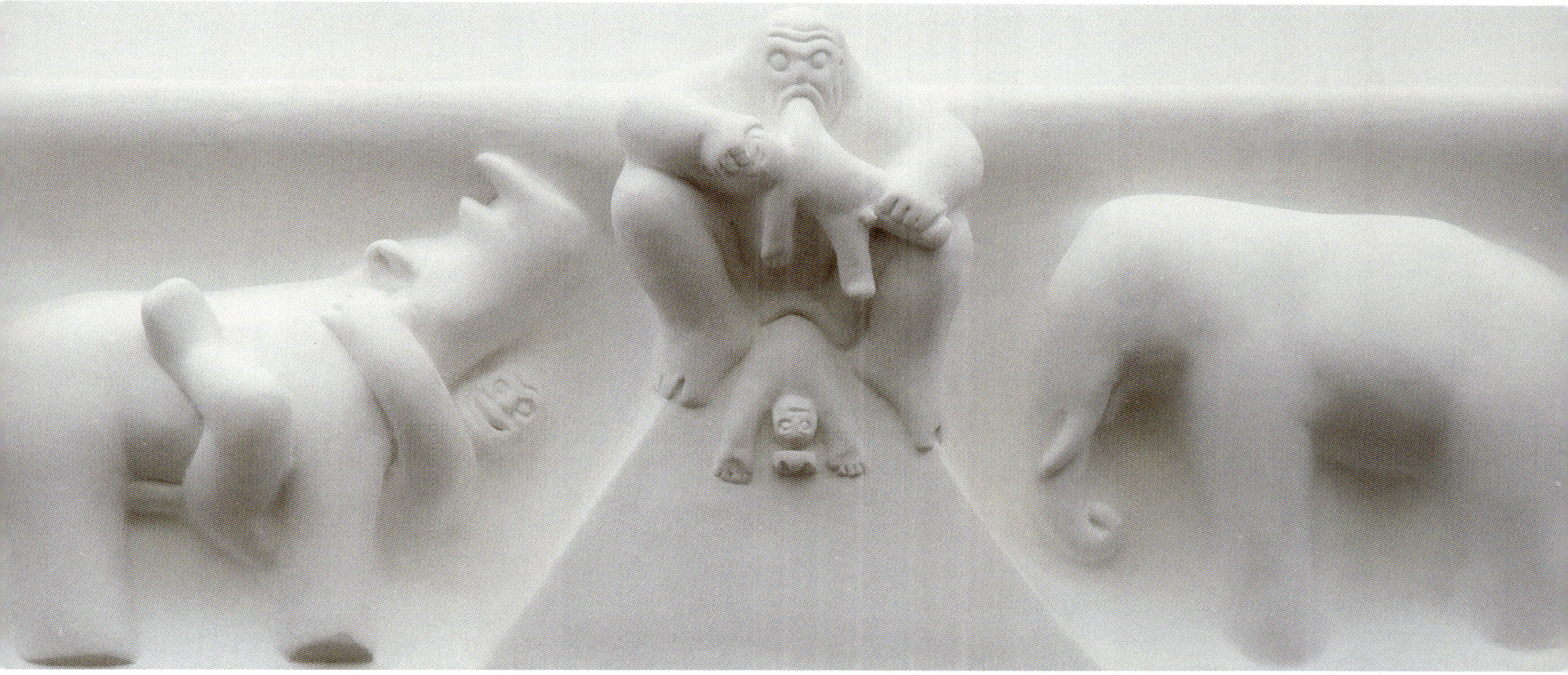

Selected Works

CONTRIBUTORS

K. Porter Aichele	KPA
George Dimock	GD
Nancy M. Doll	NMD
Xandra Eden	XE
Richard Gantt	RG
Carl Goldstein	CG
Ann Grimaldi	AG
Elaine D. Gustafson	EDG
Heather Holian	HH
Elizabeth Perrill	EP
Will South	WS

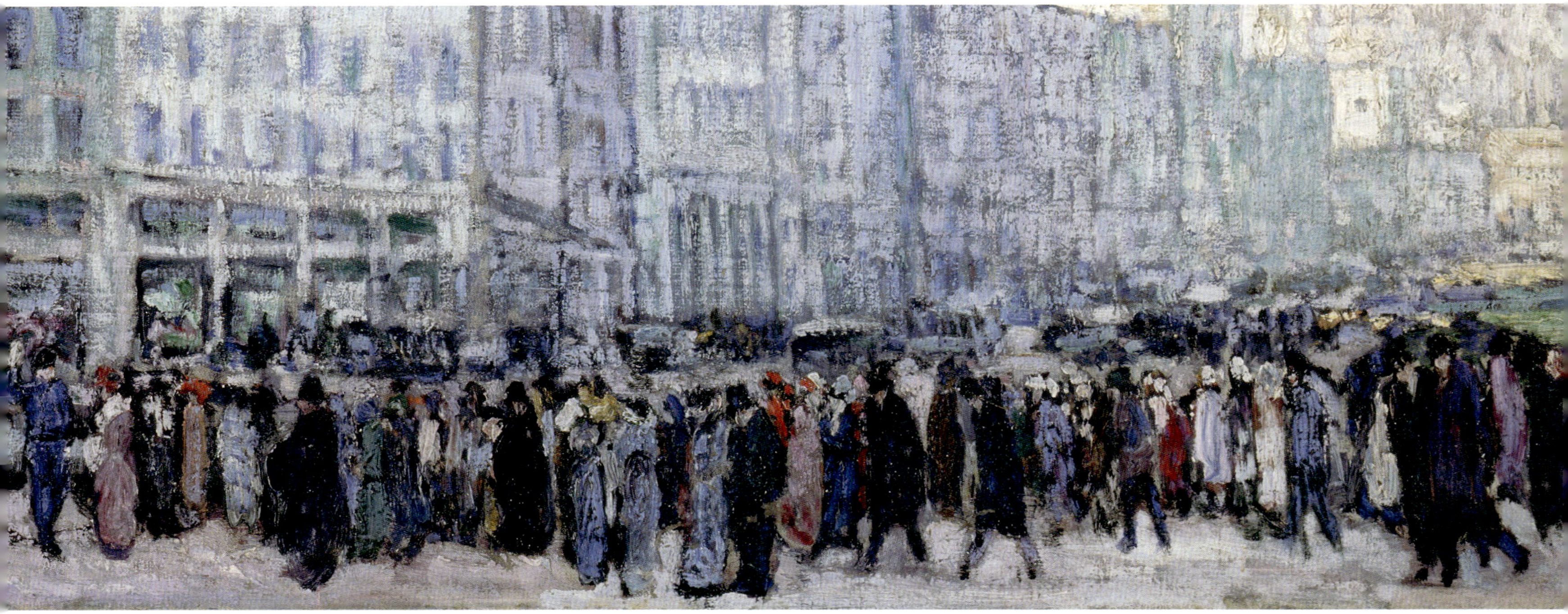

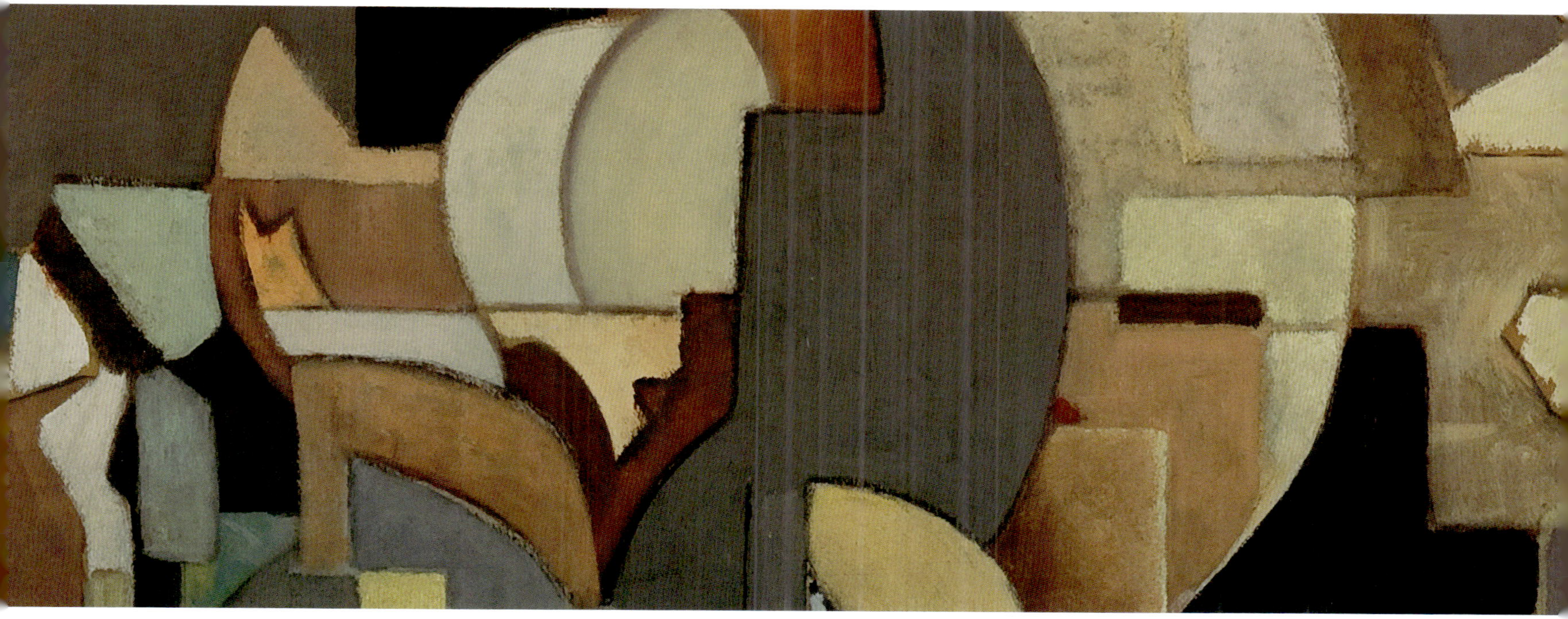

Selected Works: 1900–1920

HENRI MATISSE French, 1869–1954

IN PUBLIC, HENRI MATISSE maintained the appearance of bourgeois respectability. In the privacy of his studio, he was a radical innovator. Even before making a name for himself as an avant-garde painter, Matisse was challenging the long-established conventions of figurative sculpture. Beginning in 1899, he experimented with studies based on the work of such celebrated sculptors as Antoine-Louis Barye and Auguste Rodin. *Madeleine I*, which dates from 1901, is the first of Matisse's early sculptures that anticipate his own innovations rather than paying respectful homage to his predecessors.

When he was twenty-two, Matisse abandoned the legal profession to pursue what would have seemed a less promising career in art. After failing the entrance examination for the École des Beaux-Arts in Paris, he prepared for a second successful attempt by drawing from plaster casts of antique sculpture in the courtyard of the prestigious art school. This exercise introduced him to contrapposto, a pose that shows how the human anatomy responds to a shift in body weight. Originally intended to make representations of the human figure more naturalistic, contrapposto can have the opposite effect when it is exaggerated, as in *Madeleine I*. Matisse's female nude is not naturally aligned but instead traces a sinuous S-curve that spirals from the top of her chignon through the raised heel of her right leg. The fluid pose lends mannered elegance to a body that is otherwise strangely configured, and intentionally so. With her truncated arms, Amazonian breast, and massive left hip, *Madeleine I* looks ahead to the expressive anatomical distortions of figures in Matisse's later work.

As the numerical modifier in the title indicates, *Madeleine I* is the first in a series of studies of the same model. (There were two in all.) Rather than giving his nude model the fictional identity of a mythological goddess or historical femme fatale, Matisse specified her name in the titles *Madeleine I* and *Madeleine II*. Ironically, neither figure is the physical likeness of an individual. It is clear from related drawings and oil studies that Matisse had another objective in mind from the outset. By eliminating the model's facial features and taking considerable liberties in rendering her anatomy, he created figurative abstractions. From some points of view, the solid masses of *Madeleine I* are dynamically counterbalanced by spatial voids. Other angles of vision shift the viewer's focus to emphatically curved contours or subtle modulations in surface planes. Because Matisse seamlessly integrated these multiple points of view, *Madeleine I* is entirely convincing as a coherent sculptural form.

Despite his formal innovations in representing the female nude, Matisse's process and materials were traditional. Matisse began *Madeleine I* by constructing a metal armature to which he added clay as he shaped and modeled the figure. Visible mold lines confirm that the original clay figure was used to create a plaster piece mold from which the sculpture was cast in bronze. Later in his career, when he could afford professional help, Matisse hired a mold maker. In the case of *Madeleine I*, he may well have made the piece mold himself.[1] Like his prints, Matisse's sculptures were issued in limited editions. The Weatherspoon's *Madeleine I* is the second in a numbered edition of ten casts. Numbers one through eight were cast in 1925, shortly after Matisse began using the Claude Valsuani foundry, which is identified by the stamp next to the artist's signature on the base.

A characteristic feature of Matisse's bronze casts is that they retain visible traces of the artist's touch. Instead of smoothing the surfaces of *Madeleine I*, Matisse left the imprints of his fingers, as if to confirm that his knowledge of the female body was acquired from touch as well as observation. These tactile signs stimulate the viewer's sense of touch and, by implication, the sensation of pressing into human flesh. Not coincidentally, the intimacy of touch is reinforced by the familiarity implicit in a title that gives only a first name. Whether Etta Cone, who once owned *Madeleine I*, resisted the temptation to touch is not known. Reportedly, she insisted that anyone else who handled the works in the Cone Collection do so with white gloves.[2] *Madeleine I* receives similar treatment at the Weatherspoon.

KPA

Notes

1. Ann Boulton, "The Making of Matisse's Bronzes," in *Matisse: Painter as Sculptor* (Baltimore: Baltimore Museum of Art, 2007), 75.
2. Barbara Pollock, *The Collectors: Dr. Claribel and Miss Etta* (Indianapolis: Bobbs-Merrill Company, 1962), 237.

Madeleine I, 1901, cast 1925. Bronze, edition 2/10, 23⅜ × 8⅜ × 7 in. Bequest of Etta and Claribel Cone, 1950

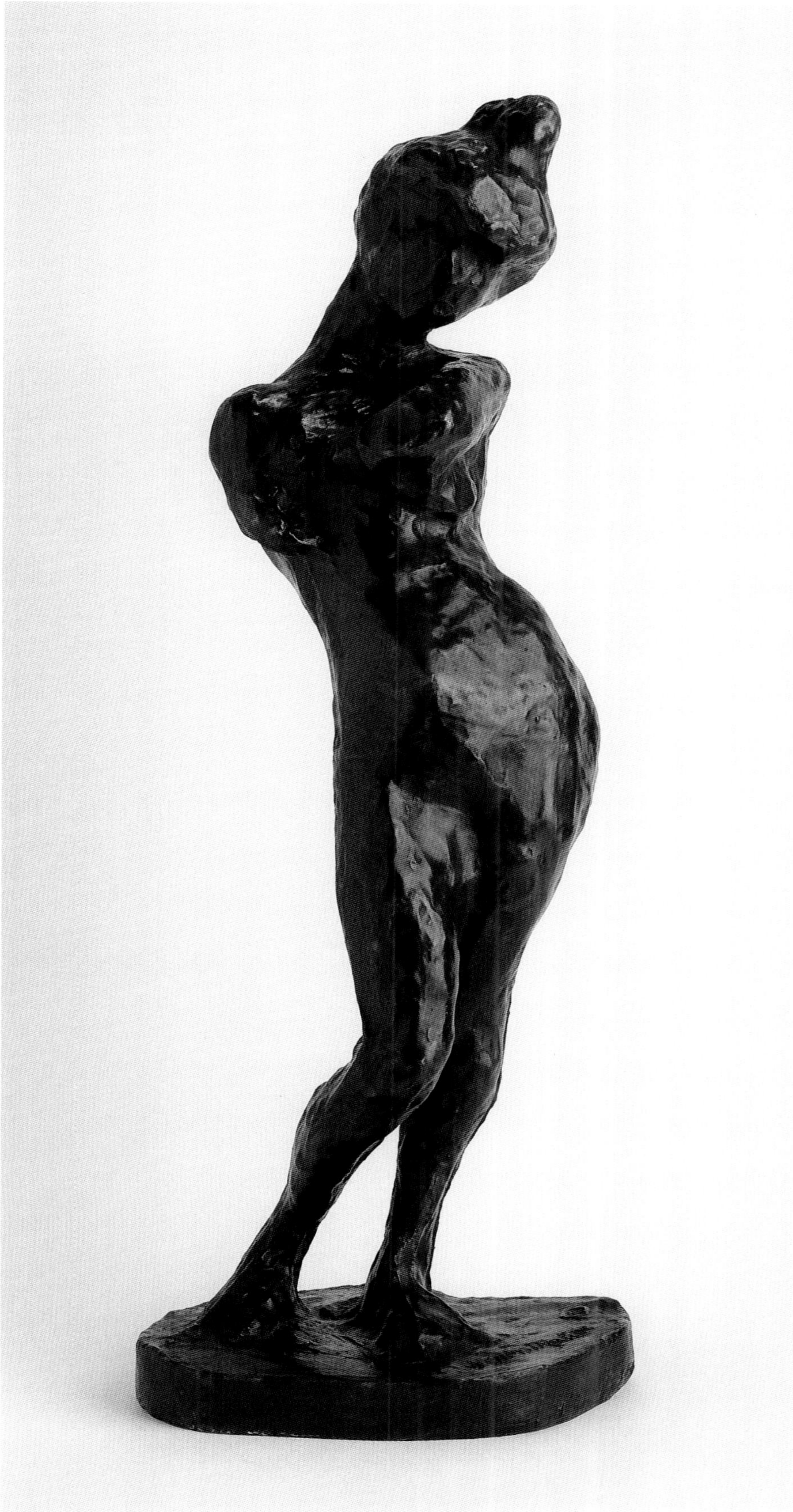

ELIE NADELMAN American, born Poland, 1882–1946

IN THE YEARS BEFORE WORLD WAR I, many early modern artists found inspiration in the art of antiquity. The smooth, clear forms of classical Greek sculpture demonstrated how abstract ideas of rhythm, harmony, and ideal form could be pursued independently of a strict imitation of nature. Using forms from antique art—which promised to be timeless and at the same time universally accessible—was liberating for artists who sought an art of simplicity unencumbered by complex academic narratives. One of these artists was Elie Nadelman.

Born Eliasz (Polish for Elijah) Nadelman in Warsaw, Poland, the artist was encouraged by his parents to pursue a career in the arts; by 1904 Nadelman was studying in Munich. There, he came under the sway of Jugendstil (the German form of Art Nouveau) with its simplified curvilinear designs, while simultaneously steeping himself in the classical statuary of the Bayerisches Nationalmuseum. His earliest sculptures show, too, that he was heavily influenced by the sensual energy of Auguste Rodin, the French sculptor whose example was inescapable at the turn of the century.

Barbara Haskell has persuasively argued that Nadelman's first three years in Paris were spent struggling to reconcile his interest in a simplified classicism with the expressive vocabulary of Rodin.[1] That Nadelman was soon successful in this struggle was evidenced by his acceptance into the 1905 juried Salon d'Automne. His work, especially his extraordinarily minimalist drawings, caught the attention of luminaries in modernist art circles, and before long Nadelman met Leo Stein, who in turn introduced him to his sister, Gertrude. Nadelman became a regular visitor at the famous salons held by the Steins at their apartment at 27, rue de Fleurus.

In the Weatherspoon's *Standing Female Figure (Gertrude Stein)*, Nadelman recasts the notoriously immodest Gertrude Stein in the guise of a modest Venus, keeping her short-cropped hair and substantive physical girth intact. The original plaster for this bronze was in Nadelman's first show in Paris at the Galerie Druet, was purchased by Leo Stein, and can be seen in a photograph from about 1912 of the Stein apartment. In *Standing Female Figure (Gertrude Stein)*, the artist achieves a sought-after sense of sensual immediacy along with a stylized distortion that summarizes the modernists' creative adaptation of the past to the present: this work may have been inspired by Praxiteles, but it is fully modern in its conscious reduction of forms. In 1914 the poet and critic André Salmon wrote the following in *L'Art décoratif*: "Here is someone equally removed from the Academy, from realism, and from insipid symbolism. Here is how Nadelman is connected to the Greeks: in order to be positioned for new departures."[2]

In 1914 Nadelman moved to New York with the help of his patron, Helena Rubinstein, who in 1911 had purchased the entire contents of the artist's one-person show in London. In 1915 he exhibited new work at Alfred Stieglitz's gallery 291 that expressed his interest in both American popular culture and folk art. Nadelman married a wealthy widow in 1919, and throughout the 1920s the couple collected folk art, eventually opening a museum of the material at their estate in Riverdale, New York. These were years of wide critical acclaim for the artist, along with a presumed financial security.

The great stock market crash of 1929, however, ended Nadelman's cosmopolitan lifestyle. The folk art collection was sold, as was the couple's Manhattan residence. Nadelman lived in near seclusion in Riverdale, refusing even to exhibit his work. Remote, increasingly ill, and depressed in the 1940s over World War II and its effect on his native Poland (which included the death of family members), Nadelman finally took his own life. At the time of his death, his home was full of hundreds of small sculptures —intended for people of limited financial means—that had never been shown.

WS

Notes

1. Barbara Haskell, *Elie Nadelman: Sculptor of Modern Life* (New York: Whitney Museum of American Art in association with Harry N. Abrams, 2003), 28. The Whitney's cast of Nadelman's *Standing Female Figure (Gertrude Stein)* is reproduced on 26.
2. Quoted in Suzanne Ramljak et al., *Elie Nadelman: Classical Folk* (New York: American Federation of Arts, 2001), 114.

Standing Female Figure (Gertrude Stein), ca. 1908–9, cast ca. 1926. Bronze, 30¾ × 10 × 9⅜ in. Gift of Anne and Benjamin Cone, 1972

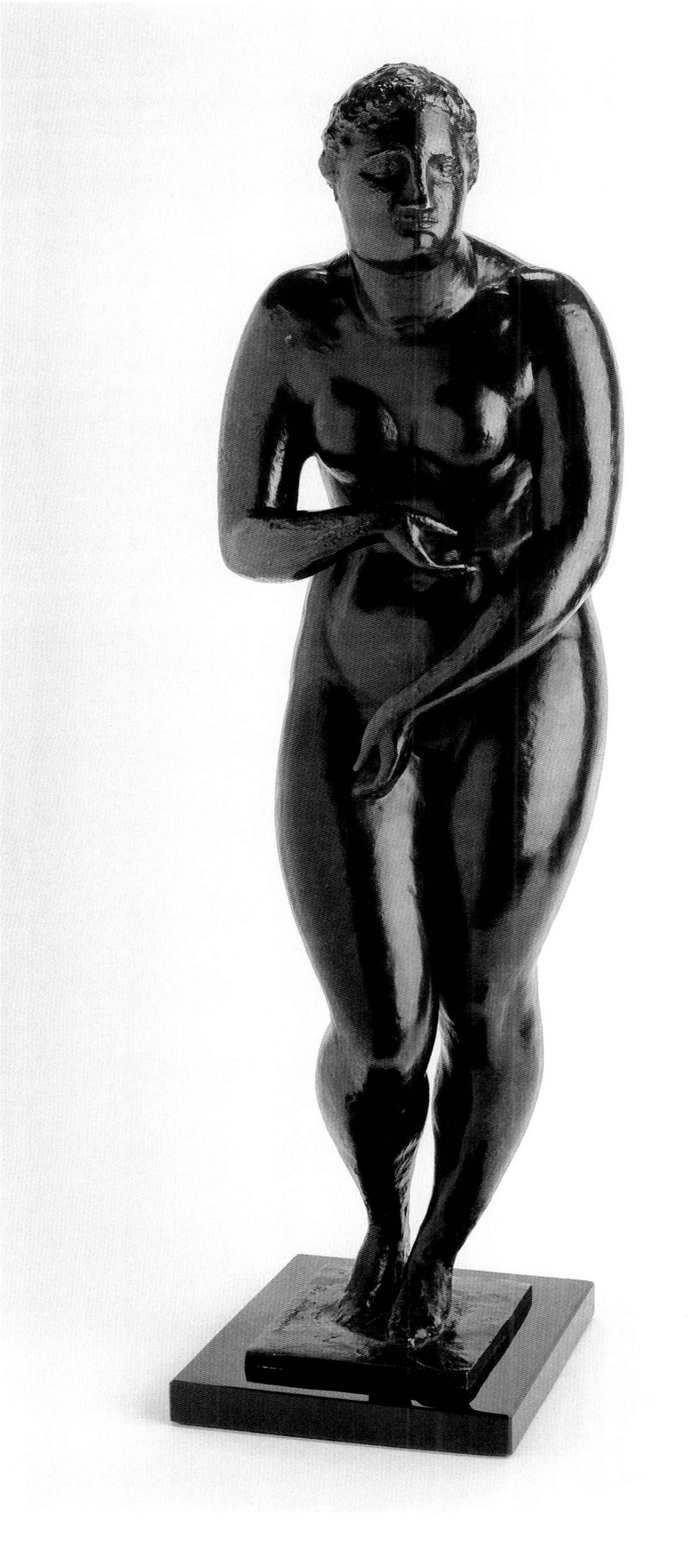

HENRY OSSAWA TANNER American, 1859–1937

A WOMAN SITS, absorbed by her domestic task, in an interior of calm and quiet. The mood is completely at odds with the journeys across time and space that characterized the illustrious career of its maker, Henry Ossawa Tanner. By 1909–10, when the painting left his easel, he had studied at the Pennsylvania Academy of the Fine Arts under the great Thomas Eakins. Tanner moved to Paris in 1891 and enrolled at the Académie Julian. Within three years he had a painting accepted at the Salon de la Société des Artistes Français, where he exhibited each year thereafter through 1914. Tanner garnered consistently good reviews and received notable awards. Numerous exhibitions in the United States followed his success at the Salon. Among these were his first major solo show in New York at the American Art Galleries in 1908 and another solo exhibition at the Thurber Art Galleries of Chicago in 1911. It seems likely that *Mary* was one of several paintings about the life of Christ and the Holy Family featured in the Chicago exhibition. Further distinguished recognition had come to Tanner in 1909 when he, along with another Philadelphia-Parisian painter, Mary Cassatt, was inducted into the National Academy of Design. France would later award the artist the Legion of Honor for his contributions to that nation.[1]

He and his family had endured encounters with American racism, and the tightening grip of discriminatory laws that came to be called the Jim Crow laws effectively promised a difficult future rife with humiliations. When, in 1899, he married Jessie Macauley Olssen, a white American, Tanner had to be increasingly vigilant about avoiding occasions where his family could be subjected to slights and hostilities. From 1891 Tanner found in France an atmosphere less fraught with the issues of race: "There is a breadth, a generosity, an obsolete cosmopolitanism about her [France's] recognition of the fine arts, which bars no nationality, no race, no school, or variation of artistic method. All she asks is that the art shall be true, in other words that it shall set forth life."[2] For the duration of his life, Tanner made his home in France.

The grace, repose, and serene mood of Mary seen in the painting of the Holy Family in Chicago suggest an antidote to the complexities of the artist's life. As was frequently the case when Tanner painted the mother of Christ, the model was his wife. He often depicted spiritual subjects using mundane figures and settings because such a practice suited both his artistic philosophy and his personal religious views. Tanner's religious paintings, such as *Mary*, project ordinary daily experience onto biblical times. The Western tradition of academic idealism is bypassed in favor of presenting religious subjects in a more realistic manner, seen as a way to embody spiritual truths in physical facts. For Tanner, who was from a highly religious, educated family, blending the historic with the contemporary enabled him to represent an ancient religion that was still potent and viable in his own time and in his own life. Contemporary newspaper reviews pointed out the strength of conviction that Tanner's religious paintings conveyed through their reserved simplicity. They function as if they are the testimonies of witnesses.

Evident in *Mary* is the artist's solid command of drawing. The fluid application of the paint is firmly anchored to a rigorous drawing practice, which provides an armature for the figure and a scaffolding for space and light. Tanner chose a palette and tonalities for *Mary* that show he recognized and embraced the new ideas regarding the liberation of color in art. The pinks, violets, and alizarin crimson are balanced by analogous variations of yellow-ochers. The expertly orchestrated color harmonies are supportively warm, natural, intimate, and feminine. Harriet Munroe, in her thoughtful review of the Chicago exhibition that included *Mary* and paintings of the Holy Family, was struck by Tanner's mastery of color. She wrote: "More important from the artistic point of view than the sacredness of the titles is the beauty of the color, the clarity of light and shade, and the serene and lofty poetic feeling which the best of these pictures attain."[3] Tanner's grounding of New Testament subjects in contemporary reality and innovative color updated the venerable genre of history painting and brought it into the new century. Today, after that same century has passed into history, *Mary* still upholds the surety of Tanner's conviction that his life could find significance and unification through his devotion to the pursuit of art and the depth of his faith.

RG

Notes

1. Dewey F. Mosby and Darrel Sewell, *Henry Ossawa Tanner* (New York: Rizzoli, 1991). For details and dates of events in Tanner's career I relied on information in the chronology compiled by Kathleen James and Sylvia Yount, 34–53.
2. Quoted in "Afro-American Artist Who Has Become Famous in Paris," *Current Literature* 45 (October 1908): 407.
3. Quoted in Mosby and Sewell, *Tanner*, 204.

Mary, ca. 1908. Oil on canvas, 32 × 25½ in. Gift of Helen Fondren Lingle in memory of her husband Kendall Ide Lingle, 2002

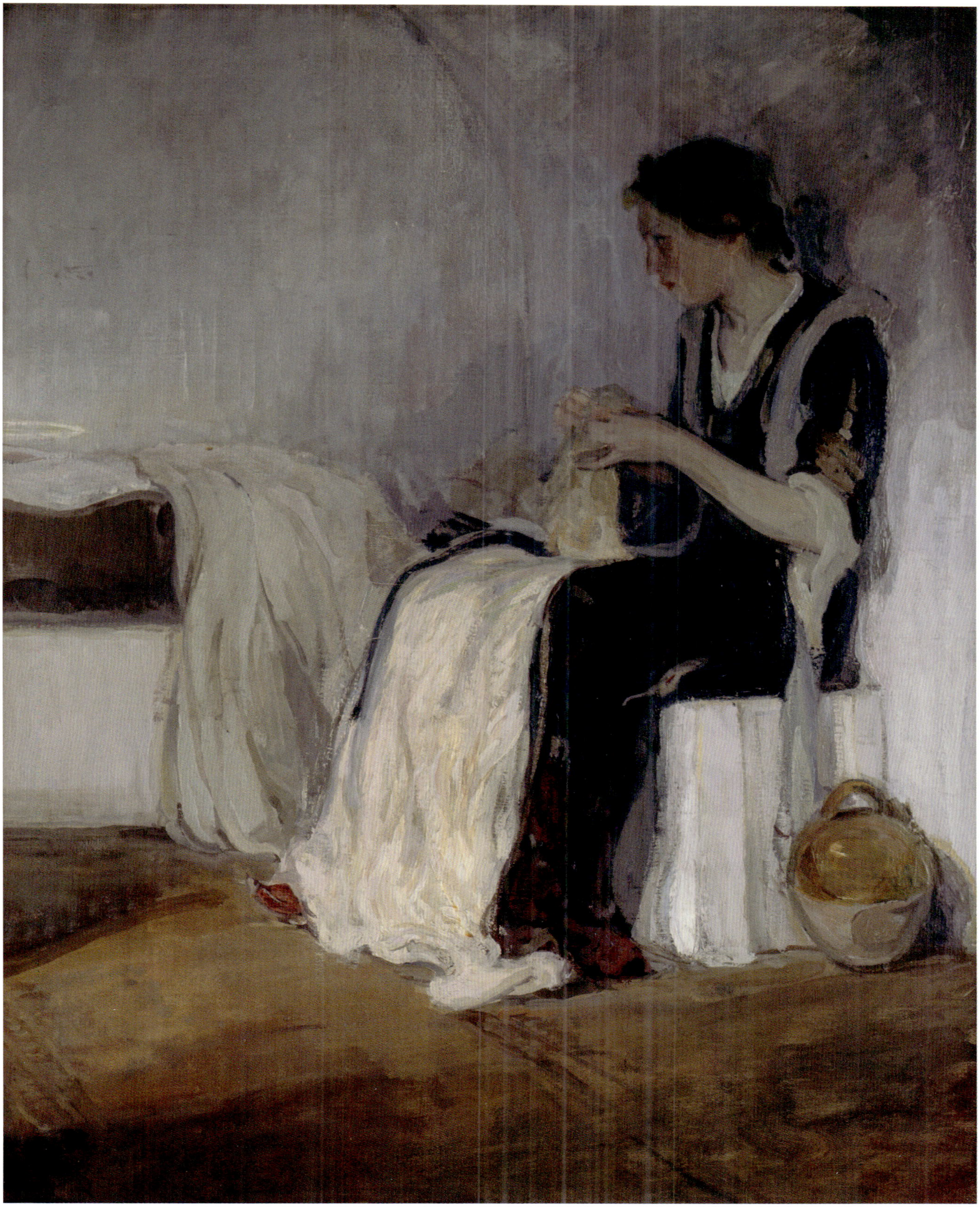

B.J.O. NORDFELDT American, born Sweden, 1878–1955

CHICAGO IS AN early-twentieth-century view of the city's fashionable Michigan Avenue on a cold and blustery winter's day. Newly erected skyscrapers, such as the seventeen-story Railway Exchange Company Building and the twenty-story People's Gas Company Building, tower above the modish pedestrians who hurry about their business in the frigid temperatures. Facing the skyscrapers, at lower right, stands a lone building: the massive, yet low to the ground, smoke-covered, and deeply shadowed Art Institute.[1] Winds from nearby Lake Michigan blow thick clouds of smoke from the nearby railroad tracks into the heart of the metropolis. This dense smoke is both a dynamic element in the painting's composition and as central to its narrative as the tall buildings themselves.

The artist, born Bror Julius Olsson, had immigrated along with his family to densely Swedish-populated Chicago in 1891. In 1899 he began attending art classes at the Art Institute of Chicago while simultaneously working as a printer's apprentice for a local Swedish newspaper. While still a student, he was chosen to assist the New York artist Albert Herter to paint the McCormick Harvester Company's murals for the Paris Universal Exposition of 1900 and was able to travel to Paris to see the project through completion. During his time in Europe Nordfeldt continued his art training, studying for two weeks at the Académie Julian in Paris as well as printmaking and woodblock techniques in London. In 1903 the artist returned to Chicago, where he experienced great commercial and critical success with prints and portrait commissions.[2] It was at this time that he began using his mother's maiden name, Nordfeldt, to distinguish himself from the then well-known contemporary artist Julius Olson.[3]

During the first decades of the twentieth century, American art was divided into two disparate aesthetic camps espousing wildly different viewpoints and styles. While one faction advocated an introspective, narrative approach to art making that emphasized uniquely American experiences, the other embraced formalist ideas that had first been explored in European art. Nordfeldt aligned himself with this latter group and embraced its investigations of form, space, and composition. As a result, the artist embarked on a period of experimentation to a greater degree than any other artist of his time, rapidly absorbing and adapting the lessons of several European-based styles—Art Nouveau (1910), Impressionism (1912), and Fauvism (1914–17)—before finding his voice in the mid-1930s.

Nordfeldt wanted his paintings to be expressive rather than factual and to awaken imaginative responses and distinct ideas in viewers. To that end, he did not paint *Chicago* realistically but rather as he experienced the city. Relying on both sketches and his memory, Nordfeldt painted the universal forms and rhythms that lay within the city. Despite the addition of site-specific, architectural details, the painting evokes mood over place through the artist's deft handling of composition, light, and color. The heavy application of vigorously applied paint, the unexpected compositional arrangement, the treatment of light and shadow, and the misty atmospheric conditions all recall French Impressionism. Using a limited palette of primarily blues and grays, Nordfeldt rendered the smoke clouds with a weightiness and volume nearly equal to those of the buildings. Their swirling energy, combined with the dwarfing of the figures by the buildings and the addition of an automobile in the lower left corner, suggests a thriving metropolis. Overall, a feeling of progress and enthusiasm imbues the painting.

Although *Chicago* was not among them, eight of Nordfeldt's Impressionist-inspired Chicago cityscapes were exhibited in a one-person show at the Roullier Gallery in Chicago in May 1912.[4] These paintings were exhibited again at Thurber Art Galleries in that same city and at the galleries of the Milwaukee Art Society, along with other new paintings by the artist.[5]

By 1913 Nordfeldt felt his art was too radical for Chicago. One year after painting this urban scene, he left for Europe, stopping first in New York to see the controversial Armory Show of recent European art. Although he intended to settle in Paris, the start of World War I cut his stay short. He returned to America in 1914, living and working in New York and Provincetown, Massachusetts, until 1919, when he moved to Santa Fe, New Mexico. In 1937 Nordfeldt relocated to Lambertville, New Jersey, where he remained until his death by heart attack in 1955.

EDG

Notes

1. Both designed by D. H. Burnham & Co., the Railway Exchange Building (now named the Santa Fe Building) opened in 1904 at 224 South Michigan Avenue, while the People's Gas Company Building opened in 1910 at 122 South Michigan Avenue. The Art Institute had been constructed in 1893 as part of the World's Columbian Exposition.
2. An accomplished printmaker, Nordfeldt invented a way to print more than one color with a single impression, called the White Line print, in 1916.
3. Laura Stewart, "The Man, the Work, the Times," in *B. J. O. Nordfeldt: An American Expressionist* (Pipersville, PA: Richard Stuart Gallery, 1984), 57–59.
4. Van Deren Coke, *Nordfeldt the Painter* (Albuquerque: University of New Mexico Press, 1972), 36.
5. Ibid., 37.

Chicago, 1912. Oil on canvas, 42 × 36 in. Gift of Mr. and Mrs. W. S. Weatherspoon in memory of Mrs. Elizabeth McIver Weatherspoon, 1969

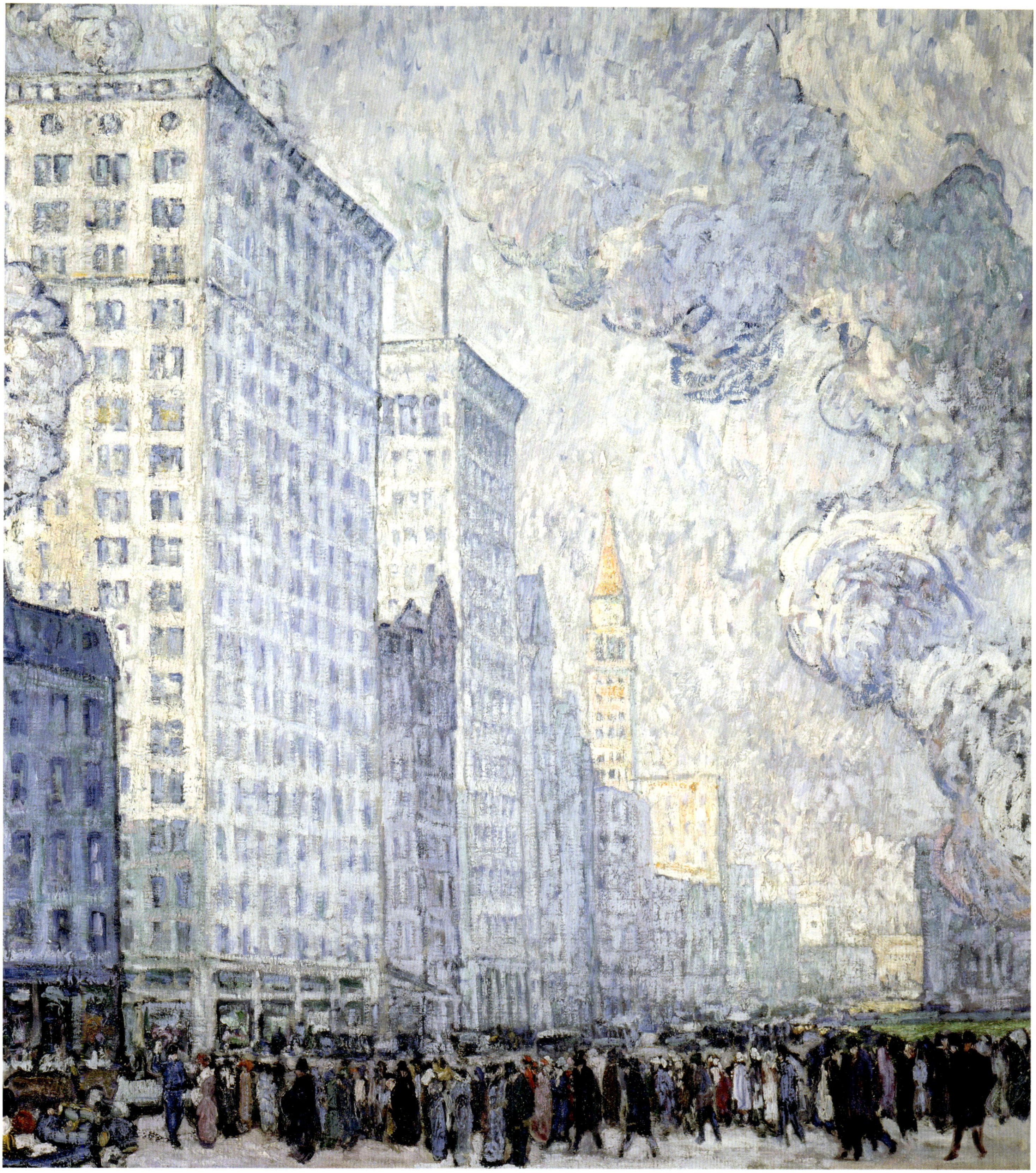

MAX WEBER American, born Russia, 1881–1961

This is a wonderful age we are living in now. Everyone has more creative liberty. The creative mind finds new ways and stops at no law laid down by, or piled upon us by lesser or non-creative minds. The real self is desired that the personal become universal, and a new reaching out from one to all is hoped for, a new contact even with the past. It is great to live now! It is harder, but what of that? The hunger we have now! This new embrace of the universe. This great blending of various forms of expression.

—Max Weber, 1912[1]

JUST BEFORE THE TURN of the twentieth century, Max Weber was a student of the great colorist and teacher Arthur Wesley Dow. From him, Weber learned early to see colors and shapes as visual relationships in and of themselves and not merely as tools to describe objects in the physical world. Primed with this aesthetic awareness, Weber went abroad from 1905 to 1908. No other American of that time steeped himself in as broad a spectrum of theory and practice: Weber discovered and embraced the crucial lessons of Paul Cézanne; he became enamored of the primitive Henri "Le Douanier" Rousseau; he studied the collection of Leo and Gertrude Stein; he befriended Pablo Picasso (and purchased a work from him); and he helped to organize a class taught by Henri Matisse. When he returned to New York in 1909, Weber was well positioned to serve as a pioneer of modernism in American, and he did just that as a painter, writer, exhibition organizer, and poet.

In 1910 the legendary photographer and art dealer Alfred Stieglitz included Weber in the landmark exhibition *Younger American Painters* at his Little Galleries of the Photo-Secession (later called 291). Before his tempestuous relationship with Stieglitz ended in 1911, Weber published an important essay in Stieglitz's influential journal, *Camera Work*, titled "The Fourth Dimension from a Plastic Point of View." In it, Weber described his concept of a fourth dimension as "the consciousness of a great and overwhelming sense of space magnitude in all directions at one time . . . brought into existence through the three known measurements." Further, he wrote, "It is the immensity of all things."[2] Weber's mystical belief in this dimension underpinned his personal researches into the science and mathematics of art as well as the spirituality of art—indeed, Weber, like so many early moderns, earnestly studied Vasily Kandinsky's otherworldly writings.

Weber's aggressively inquisitive approach imbues his 1913 pastel *In the Woods*. The fractured surfaces imply multiple views extending into different directions as one simultaneous visual experience. A sense of nature's restless energy is evoked through the layers of forceful linear intersections and tonal shifts that spill into and over the picture's outer edge. Weber used this strategy in his large abstract oils of New York of this same time to express ideas of speed and movement, prompting the critic Henry McBride to write of Weber in 1915, "at last we have an artist who is not afraid of this great big city of New York."[3] Collectively, Weber's work during the war years was the first manifestation of Cubism in America.

Weber was born in Russia to Orthodox Jewish parents and in 1891 immigrated with his family to America. The art historian Matthew Baigell wondered whether Weber's devoutly religious Jewish background predisposed him to accept the strong spiritual components of early-twentieth-century modernism.[4] Although he remained a modernist throughout his career, Weber increasingly used figurative elements after 1920 to express themes both religious and secular. While Weber's early work like *In the Woods* baffled and was ridiculed by an uncomprehending public, now we see clearly how his genuine immersion in both advanced theory and practice contributed to the foundation of modern art traditions in America.

WS

Notes

1. Max Weber, untitled essay, 1912, reprinted in Percy North and Susan Krane, *Max Weber: The Cubist Decade, 1910–1920* (Atlanta: High Museum of Art, 1991), 96.
2. Max Weber, "The Fourth Dimension from a Plastic Point of View," *Camera Work* 31 (July 1910): 25, reprinted in ibid., 95.
3. Henry McBride, *The Flow of Art: Essays and Criticisms by Henry McBride*, ed. Daniel Catton Rich (New York: Atheneum Publishers, 1975), 94.
4. Matthew Baigell, *Jewish Art in America* (Lanham, MD: Rowan and Littlefield Publishers, 2007), 21.

In the Woods, 1913. Pastel on paper, 23½ × 17 in. Museum purchase with funds from the Dillard Paper Company for the Dillard Collection, 1974

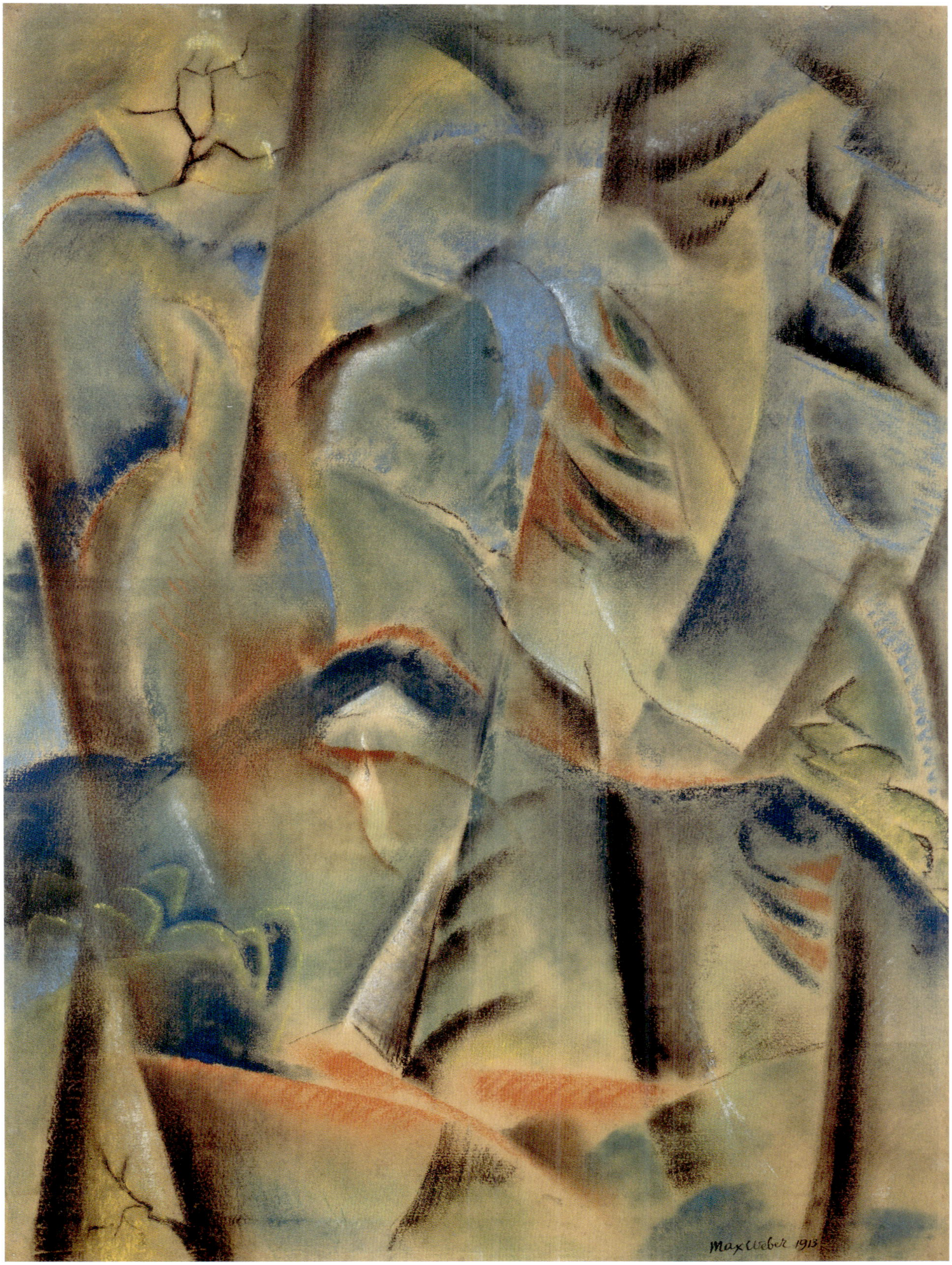
Max Weber 1913

KONRAD CRAMER American, born Germany, 1888–1963

BEFORE IMMIGRATING TO AMERICA, the young Konrad Cramer was in Munich, where he met the radical painter Franz Marc and became acquainted with the ideas of Vasily Kandinsky. It was also in Munich that Cramer met the American artist Florence Ballin, whom he would marry. Ballin had been a painting student in Woodstock, New York, and the newlywed couple settled there in 1911. Cramer soon began articulating the revolutionary ideas he had encountered in Munich and helped organize an art gallery and group of artists whose motto was "Modern Art or Die!"

While not all Woodstock residents were receptive to his vanguard passions, Cramer found sympathetic colleagues at Alfred Stieglitz's gallery 291 in New York City. Stieglitz had purchased Kandinsky's *Improvisation 27* from the 1913 Armory Show, the artist's first painting to be shown in America. Cramer was steeped in Kandinsky's ideas and surely was impressed by the following passage from the Russian's influential book, *Concerning the Spiritual in Art*:

> *The life of the spirit may be fairly represented in diagram as a large acute-angled triangle divided horizontally into unequal parts with the narrowest segment uppermost. The lower the segment the greater it is in breadth, depth, and area. The whole triangle is moving slowly, almost invisibly forwards and upwards. Where the apex was today the second segment is tomorrow; what today can be understood only by the apex and to the rest of the triangle as an incomprehensible gibberish, forms tomorrow the true thought and feeling of the second segment.*
>
> *At the apex of the top segment stands often one man, and only one. His joyful vision cloaks a vast sorrow. Even those who are nearest to him in sympathy do not understand him. Angrily they abuse him as charlatan or madman. . . .*
>
> *In every segment of the triangle are artists. Each one of them who can see beyond the limits of his segment is a prophet to those about him, and helps the advance of the obstinate whole.*[1]

The Weatherspoon's untitled Cramer painting of about 1914 is derived from Kandinsky's writings.[2] The solitary rider depicted at the bottom center of the canvas travels through a harsh world of leafless trees—symbolizing the ravages of war—where emblems of power (the sword) and justice (the scales) appear. Above the clouds and within the triangle the rider is transformed into a cross that nears the sun at the painting's upper edge. Here, Cramer expresses the spiritual journey of man that is, he suggests, one of constant ascent in which the change from our material selves is inevitable.

Kandinsky argued that there are "inner" and "outer" elements to a work of art and that only in aesthetic combination could a "spiritual vibration" be achieved. The physical aspects of a work of art were important only as a step toward that spiritual vibration. Cramer absorbed this theory and explored it in a number of paintings of this time, the Weatherspoon's being the largest.

While Cramer's immersion in both the German and the American avant-garde was significant, he moved away from abstract and symbolic painting after World War I. He wrote, "When the point of contact with the beholder was lost entirely, the painting itself seemed to become sterile."[3] After 1917 he continued to experiment with different media and styles, and by the 1940s photography had become a primary interest. One of the original founders of the Woodstock Artist's Association, Cramer remained a fixture of the artistic life of that community until his death in 1963. Konrad Cramer is best remembered today, however, for his participation in the historical moment when modernism emerged in America.

WS

Notes

1. Vasily Kandinsky, *Concerning the Spiritual in Art*, in the original translation by Michael T. H. Sadler (Munich: Piper Verlag, 1911; Boston: Museum of Fine Arts, 2006), 14–15.
2. The European work of Marsden Hartley, Kandinsky's closest American follower, was also an influence on Cramer. See Gail Levin, "Konrad Cramer: Link from the German to the American Avant-Garde," in Tom Wolf and Franklin Riehlman, *Konrad Cramer: A Retrospective* (Annandale-on-Hudson, NY: Bard College Art Center, 1981).
3. Konrad Cramer, quoted in Gail Levin, "Kandinsky and the First American Avant-Garde," in *Theme and Improvisation: Kandinsky and the American Avant-Garde, 1912–1950* (Boston: Bulfinch Press, 1992), 29.

Untitled, ca. 1914. Oil on canvas, 34 × 34 in. Museum purchase with funds from the Bryan Family Foundation, the Smith-Richardson Foundation and the Blue Bell Foundation, 1977

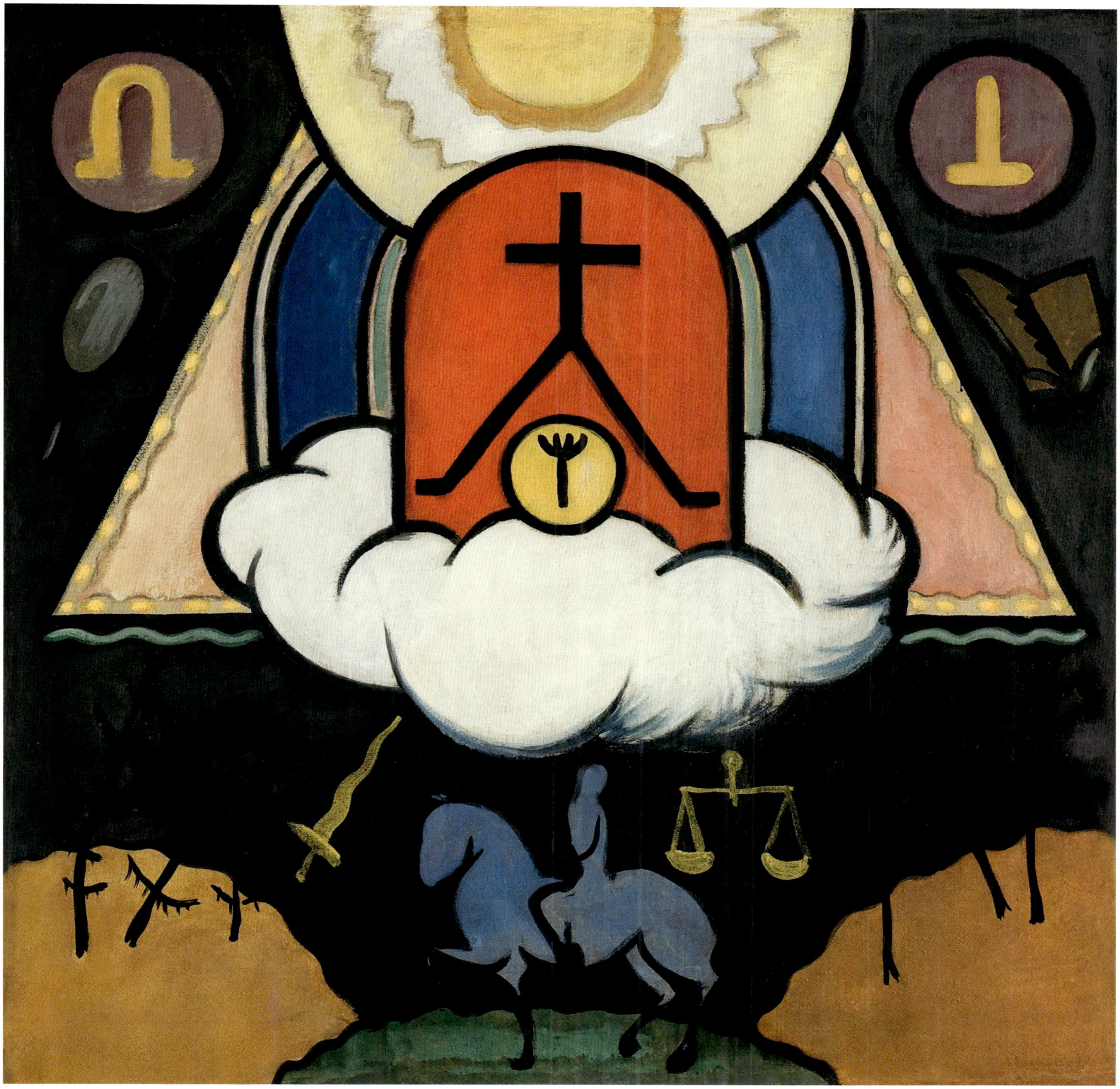

HENRY FITCH TAYLOR American, 1853–1925

HENRY FITCH TAYLOR was a most unlikely modernist. Born in Cincinnati, Ohio, in 1853, he was a good bit older than the first wave of avant-garde painters who came to maturity in the early twentieth century. His initial artistic interest was in theater, and he traveled with Joe Jefferson's theatrical troupe. Jefferson, an accomplished amateur painter in addition to being a stage performer, encouraged Taylor to study art seriously. By the spring of 1884 Taylor was in Paris and enrolled at the Académie Julian. His interest in landscape painting took him first to Barbizon and then to Giverny, where he knew and painted with Claude Monet. When he returned to New York City in 1888, Taylor was a confirmed Impressionist and remained so for the next twenty-five years.

In 1898 Taylor moved to Cos Cob, Connecticut, and there his artistic fortunes shifted. Talented painters and writers congregated at Cos Cob, including such progressive artists as Arthur B. Davies, Walt Kuhn, and Elmer McRae. Taylor met Clara Davidge, member of a prominent New York family and a supporter of the arts, and she hired him to direct the Madison Art Gallery that she had founded. There, the couple helped organize a society to support the liberal artists they knew. Out of early discussions with Davies, Kuhn, McRae, and others, the Association of American Painters and Sculptors was born. From that organization, the Armory Show emerged.

At the age of sixty in 1913, Taylor married Davidge, who had encouraged his renewed interest in the arts since they first met. In the wake of the Armory Show, Taylor explored the suddenly greatly expanded range of artistic options available to the American artist. Living in an era of artistic changes not accepted or even understood by artists half his age, Taylor avidly studied the works of Paul Cézanne, Cubism, Futurism, Synchromism, and color theory in general. Indeed, Taylor wrote and published a treatise entitled "The Taylor System of Organized Color." The result of his immersion in new ideas and styles was an astonishing departure from Impressionism and an embrace of abstraction.

Influenced most profoundly by Cubism, Taylor experimented with the possibilities of overlapping, flat planes of muted color and how these compositions might evoke themes of time and transformation. The Weatherspoon's untitled abstraction of 1915 was arrived at just two years after the Armory Show, and its formal complexity prompted the art historian William C. Agee to write: "In terms of pure painting and total balance, this is one of Taylor's most successful works." Agee further noted that the Weatherspoon's picture is based on a series of color planes expanding outward in a dynamic circular movement, a compositional solution Taylor had observed in paintings by Albert Gleizes.[1]

After his conversion, Taylor remained a dedicated modernist. He continued to work for the advancement of avant-garde art via exhibitions and organizations, though after his wife died in 1921, his own studio production declined. When he died four years later, his contributions as both an artist and an administrator were little known and ultimately forgotten altogether. Today, we appreciate the kaleidoscopic origins of modernism in this country and the important role played by Henry Fitch Taylor.

WS

Note

1. William C. Agee, "Rediscovery: Henry Fitch Taylor," *Art in America* 54, no. 6 (November–December 1966): 43, caption.

Untitled Abstraction, 1915. Oil on compressed board, 30 × 25 in. Museum purchase with funds from Burlington Industries, 1969

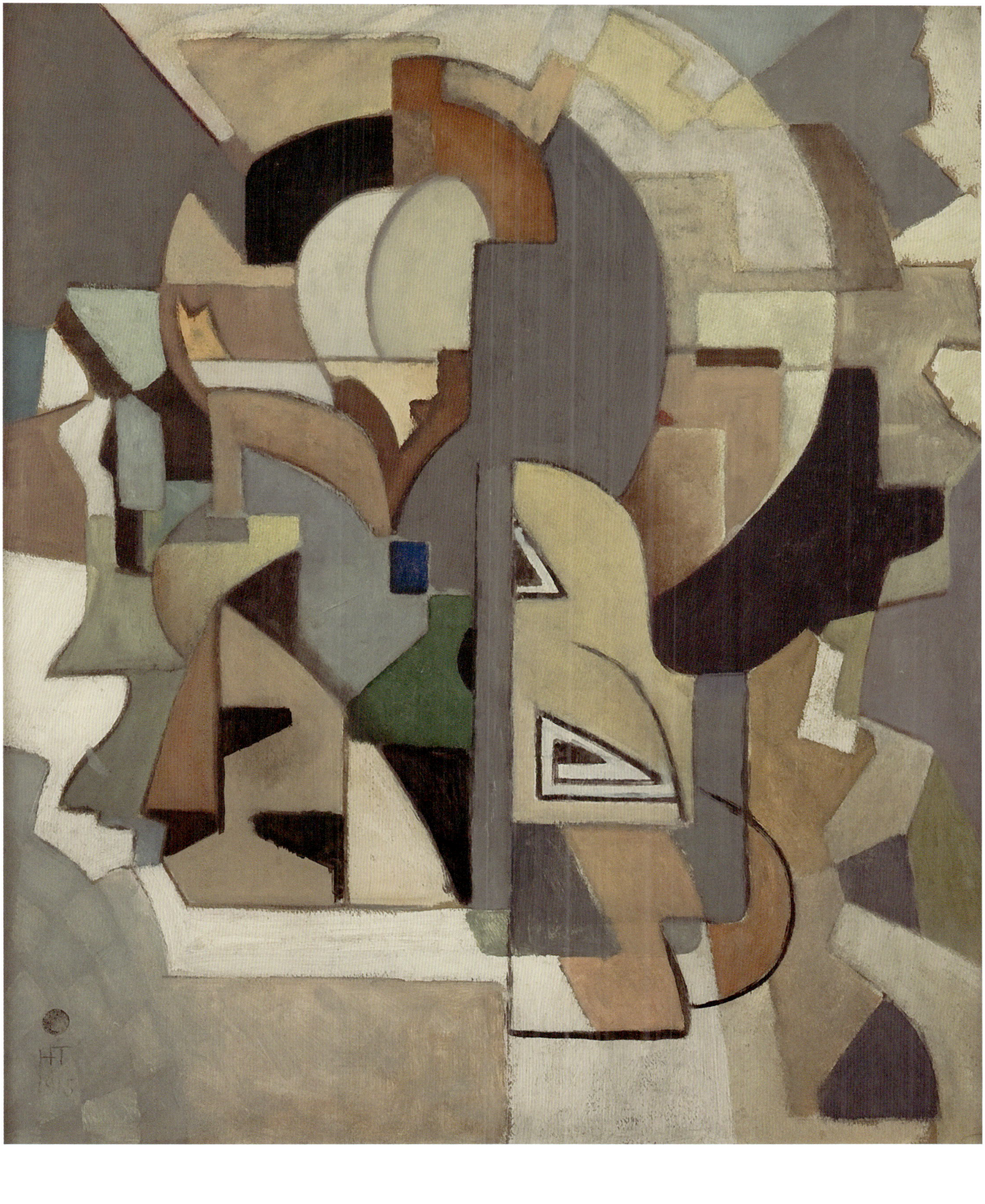

MORTON LIVINGSTON SCHAMBERG American, 1881–1918

It is a real tragedy, therefore, that this young man should have been cut off at the moment when he was about to master his forces. He would surely have been an important figure in the new life that is beginning to find expression, and even as it is his life will make an important chapter in the history that's beginning.

—Henry McBride, 1919[1]

MORTON LIVINGSTON SCHAMBERG died in the great influenza epidemic of 1918 at the age of thirty-seven. As the critic Henry McBride so astutely noted, Schamberg's career, despite its brevity, was a key contribution to the radical directions that had been taken in American art. Schamberg was one of the first artists in this country to explore mechanical imagery as subject matter and also one of the first to understand the political implications of Dada, the art movement that critiqued social conventions, beliefs, and assumptions.

Like the careers of other pioneer modernists born in the nineteenth century, Schamberg's began before the advent of Cubism, Futurism, and all the other "isms" that were to come. After training as an architect at the University of Pennsylvania, he studied at the Pennsylvania Academy of the Fine Arts. Critical to his development was his study there with William Merritt Chase from 1903 to 1906. Chase's liberal impressionistic brushwork showed his students an alternative to the academic approach of strict outline and conservative palette. It was also at this time that Schamberg developed a close friendship with the artist and kindred spirit Charles Sheeler.

Schamberg made various trips to Europe between 1907 and 1909. Joined by Sheeler, he toured the great museums and eventually visited the private collection of Sarah and Michael Stein in Paris. Schamberg was impressed with the thinking of Leo Stein, who advanced Paul Cézanne's idea that Impressionism needed the solidity of classicism to make something "permanent" of it. Back in America in 1909, Schamberg was experimenting with vivid color and interlocking planes that revealed his recent European immersion in the art of Cézanne, Henri Matisse, and Pablo Picasso. This work earned him an invitation to the Armory Show in New York in 1913, an exhibition that essentially introduced modernism to America.

After the Armory Show, Schamberg more fully explored the revolutionary possibilities of Cubism, but he also responded to the philosophical implications of Marcel Duchamp's *Nude Descending a Staircase*. In 1915 Schamberg met Duchamp and Francis Picabia, both radical innovators in the use of objects and ideas. In that year, Picabia made a graphic image of a camera and called it a portrait of Alfred Stieglitz. The intellectual enthusiasm for both the found object and the machine as symbols and arbiters of human experience infected Schamberg, and he soon began his own forays into industrial images.

Schamberg's *Composition*, a drawing of wires and wheels, was made in 1916 and paralleled but did not copy the advances of his colleagues. Schamberg employed a sensitivity to color that had never left him since his studies with Chase. He continued to value the traditional expressive properties of art at the same time he embraced the machine, a subject that could convey the shifting values of a new century and, indeed, a new role for art and artists. In essence, *Composition* evokes an admiration for the concepts of organization and harmony in and of themselves, independent of any purpose to which they might be applied.

In the brief time he would live after creating *Composition*, Schamberg organized Philadelphia's *First Exhibition of Advanced Modern Art*, which included examples by both American and European artists. Perhaps his most arresting work was made shortly after that—a construction made with a wooden miter box and a plumbing trap that he entitled *God*. This Dada-inspired piece, made in collaboration with Elsa Freytag-Loringhoven, conjoined machine and manifesto, that is, it targeted America's obsession with technology as salvation. To the end, Morton Livingston Schamberg was a vital voice for intelligent and well-crafted work that could contribute to a world in flux.

WS

Note

1. Henry McBride, "Posthumous Paintings by Schamberg," *New York Sun*, May 25, 1919, reprinted in Ben Wolf, *Morton Livingston Schamberg* (Philadelphia: University of Philadelphia Press, 1963), 35.

Composition, 1916. Graphite and pastel on paper, 7½ × 8 in. Museum purchase with funds from the Dillard Paper Company for the Dillard Collection, 1992

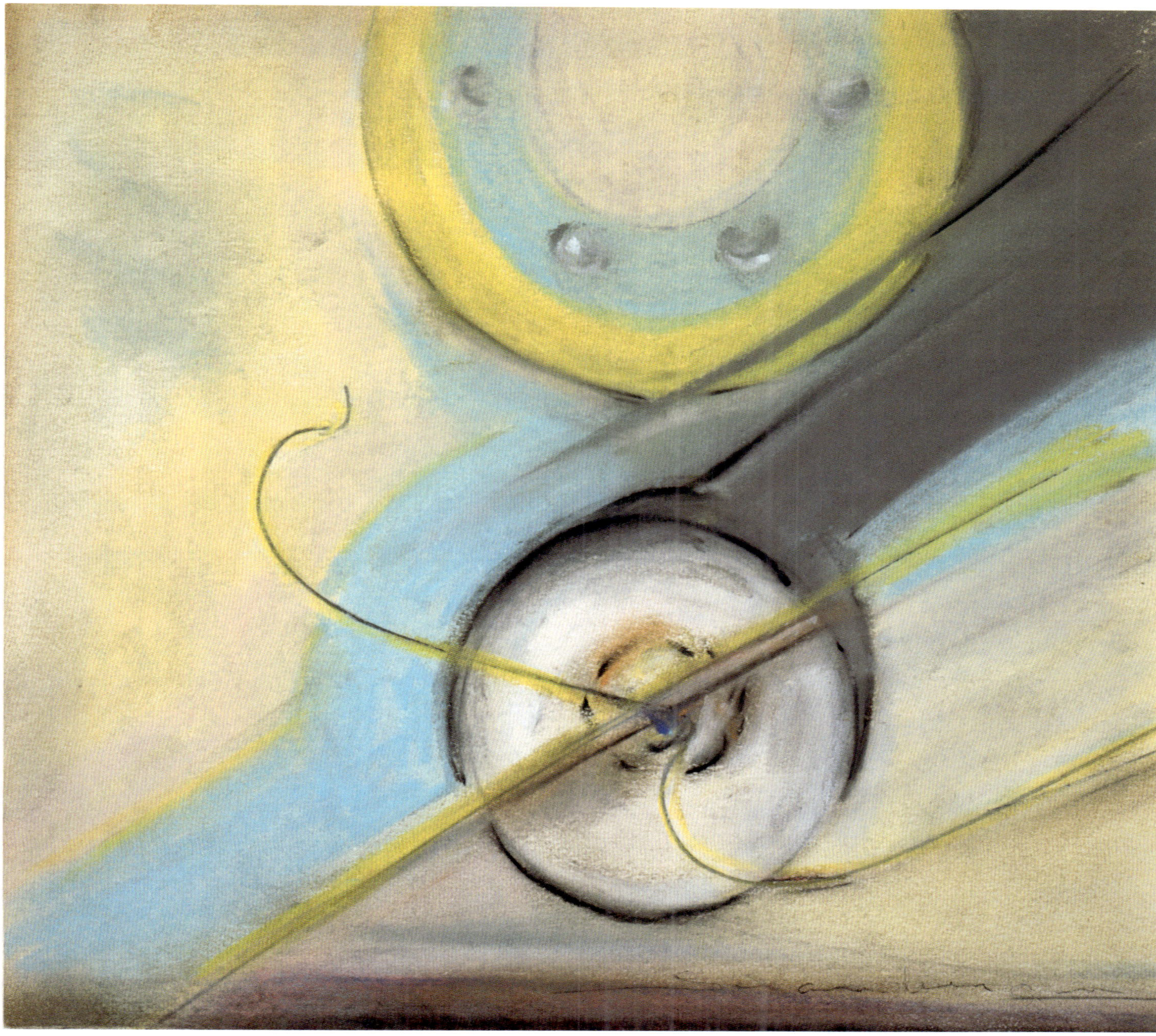

ALFRED HENRY MAURER American, 1868–1932

ALFRED MAURER was a rising star as a traditional painter at the turn of the twentieth century, when he abruptly and confidently embraced the radical styles of painting being pioneered abroad. Maurer was in France during the years of dazzling innovation before World War I: in 1905 he saw the work of Henri Matisse and the Fauves (French for wild beasts) and in 1907 the vastly influential retrospective of Paul Cézanne. He befriended Gertrude and Leo Stein and became immersed in the language and attitudes of modernism at their apartment on the rue de Fleurus, where vanguard writers, poets, and painters gathered. So early and effective was Maurer in his experimentation and exploitation of new developments that the claim, however combative, could be made that he was America's first modern painter.

Maurer's father was an artist who had been employed by the printmaking firm Currier & Ives. At sixteen, Alfred worked as a lithographer for his father before entering the National Academy of Design in 1885. He studied in New York until 1897, when he made the near-requisite trip to Paris for advanced study. Once there, he enrolled at the Académie Julian, remaining just weeks. Working primarily on his own, Maurer evolved a fashionable figurative style indebted to James McNeill Whistler and William Merritt Chase. These paintings garnered favorable reviews, and he could easily have stayed that career course. Instead, Maurer's imagination was captured by the brilliant and intense surfaces of Fauvism with its often arbitrary and purely intuitive (as opposed to Impressionism's fluidly descriptive) color. He began to layer his work with highly saturated hues, abandoning the gray tonalities of Whistler at a time when the art world was freshly experiencing the shock of high-keyed color. Maurer exhibited his Fauve landscapes at the 1907 Salon d'Automne in Paris and in 1909 was part of a two-person exhibition with John Marin at Alfred Stieglitz's 291 gallery in New York. He was included in the legendary 1913 Armory Show, which introduced modernism to America. Before leaving France, Maurer acted as an unofficial art adviser and agent for Dr. Albert C. Barnes, who built a now-famous collection of modern art.

At the onset of World War I in 1914, Maurer returned—as many modernists did—to America. Shortly thereafter, he began traveling to Marlboro in New York's Hudson River valley to paint landscape. Maurer dated very few works, and his New York scenes of this era resemble those he had made in France. The Weatherspoon's untitled and undated landscape is stylistically close to those now identified as having been made while Maurer was staying at the Shady Brook boardinghouse in Marlboro.[1] It is a work of visceral intensity, shot through with unmixed red, blues, and greens. The entire composition of this otherwise bucolic woodland scene is covered with vibrant, broken strokes. Following the example of Matisse and Cézanne, untouched white primer shows through, forcing the surface of the image to assert itself emphatically. Indeed, the Weatherspoon Maurer is a premier example of the artist's immersion in the modernist idea that a painting was an experience first, not a representation of something else.

In 1916, about the time he painted the Weatherspoon landscape, Maurer was included in the important *Forum Exhibition of Modern American Painters* held at the Anderson Galleries, which was the first large-scale show of the American avant-garde. In 1924 the dealer Erhard Weyhe purchased the entire contents of the artist's studio and gave Maurer regular exhibitions until 1932. It was in that year that the artist, deeply troubled, tragically took his own life.

Throughout the 1920s and up until his death, Maurer remained a prolific and powerful painter of still life, landscape, and the figure. He experimented with Cubism along with highly personal hybrid styles, often enigmatic in character. Today, Alfred Maurer's contribution to the rise and dissemination of modernism in America is recognized, as is the still-startling quality of his art.

WS

Note

1. For a detailed account of Maurer's life and career, see Stacey B. Epstein, *Alfred H. Maurer: Aestheticism to Modernism* (New York: Hollis Taggart Galleries, 2000). The wood hand railing, sloping hills, and architectural elements depicted in the Weatherspoon's painting all appear in Maurer's *Bridge over Shady Brook*, illustrated in Epstein, color pl. 39.

Untitled (Fauve Landscape), ca. 1916–20. Oil on board, 22¾ × 18 in. Museum purchase with funds from the Benefactors Fund, 1981

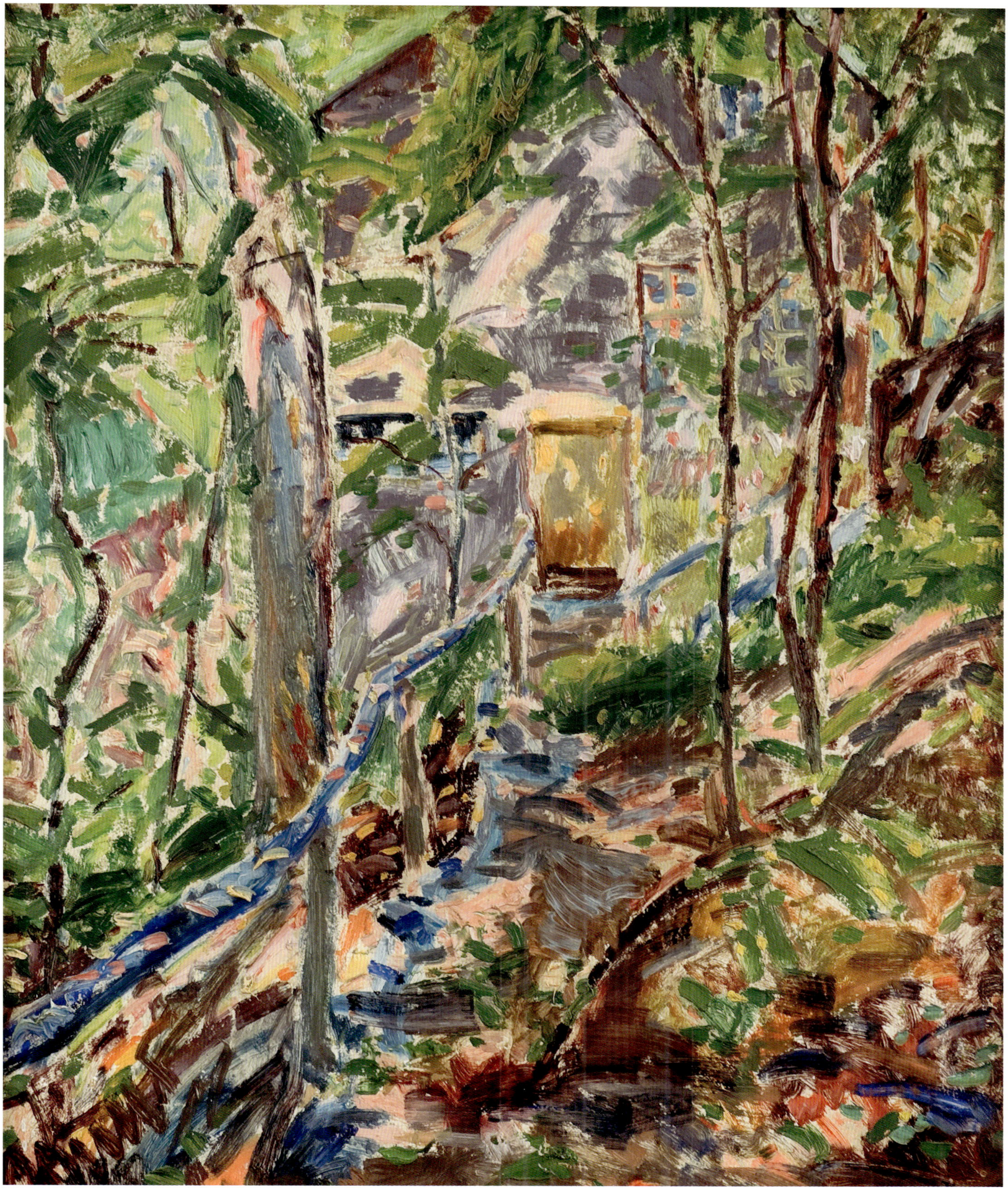

JOHN STORRS American, 1885–1956

As I look around my studio the statues are in bronze or stone or plaster and the paintings are on canvas—you can touch and feel their reality—but their reality for me is still the quality of life and beauty I tried to put into them—not always with great success. A reality I thought I saw and felt and which I can never forget, but for which I have not found forms and color to adequately express.

—John Storrs, 1951[1]

JOHN STORRS WROTE these words five years before his death at his château at Mer, near Orléans, France. Over the course of his long career, he had participated in the birth of modernism and experienced the wonders of the Machine Age, and, like so many others, he also witnessed the devastation caused by two world wars. His early and lasting search for "quality of life and beauty" led him to a deep admiration for native, folk, and ancient art traditions at the same time he saw the future, especially in America, as a field of promise, assimilation, and change. The art of John Storrs reflects the international quality of his education, the breadth of his eclectic interests, and the intensity of his ongoing efforts to find the forms to express his reality.

Storrs was born in Chicago, where his father was an architect and his mother an amateur painter. As a child, he was taken to the enormous World's Columbian Exposition of 1893, a dazzling display of art, architecture, and technology. He studied sculpture first in Berlin, then back home at the School of the Art Institute of Chicago, where the prominent academician Lorado Taft was one of his teachers. In Paris from 1912 to 1914, Storrs studied with and became the favorite student of Auguste Rodin, whose rough, summary treatment of forms influenced Storrs to see the beauty in the stone itself.

During World War I, Storrs volunteered, along with his wife, in French hospitals. Shortly thereafter, the artist began to produce his first mature works that combined his knowledge of architecture with an enthusiasm for the variety of avant-garde movements around him in Paris that extolled simplicity and pattern. *Abstract Forms #2* dates from this era.

The flat planes of Cubism and the artist's own penchant for architecture are suggested in *Abstract Forms #2*. Skyscrapers, specifically, are often connected to this and his later stone sculptures. However, the scholar Noel Frackman identified the primary source for the carved patterns here as Native American art. Storrs had seen and greatly admired Indian ceramics, blankets, and baskets in Chicago's Field Museum, and he collected fine examples himself. The complex angles and facets in *Abstract Forms #2* are derived in large measure from the squared-off and zigzag motifs found in a variety of Native American art forms, including Navajo blankets of the type Storrs owned. Writing on *Abstract Forms #2*, Frackman concluded that "It was in fact at this point in Storrs' career that primitivizing and nature motifs merged with architectural elements to establish his definitive vocabulary of forms."[2]

Throughout the 1920s Storrs explored skyscraper forms as well as machine-inspired works. The streamlined symmetry of Art Deco affected him, as did an ever-evolving appreciation of classical art. He received a number of large-scale commissions in the 1930s and by the end of that decade was well known and respected in the art world.

In 1941, while living in France, he was arrested by Nazi soldiers and interned in a concentration camp. Released after six months, he was later interned again. He survived, but his view of humanity had been wounded. In 1948 John Storrs carved elegant versions of Adam and Eve from a single block of limestone, suggesting, perhaps, that a new beginning was possible.

WS

Notes

1. Diary entry for August 25, 1951, John Bradley Storrs Papers, roll 1549, frame 495, Archives of American Art, Smithsonian Institution.
2. Noel Frackman, *John Storrs* (New York: Whitney Museum of American Art, 1986), 46.

Abstract Forms #2, ca. 1917–19. Granite, 19¾ × 9⅜ × 5¾ in. Museum purchase with funds from the Jefferson-Pilot Corporation, 1968

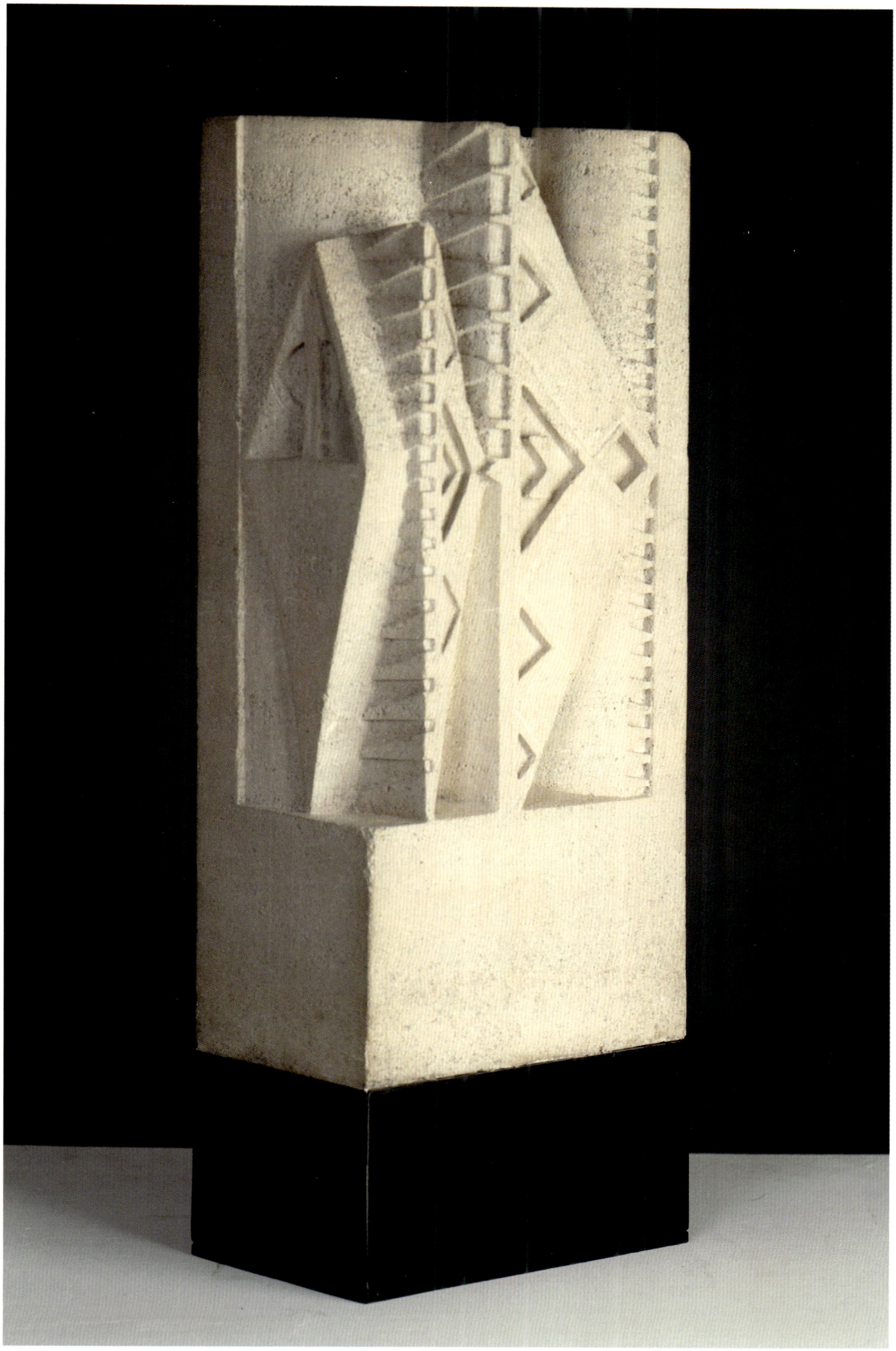

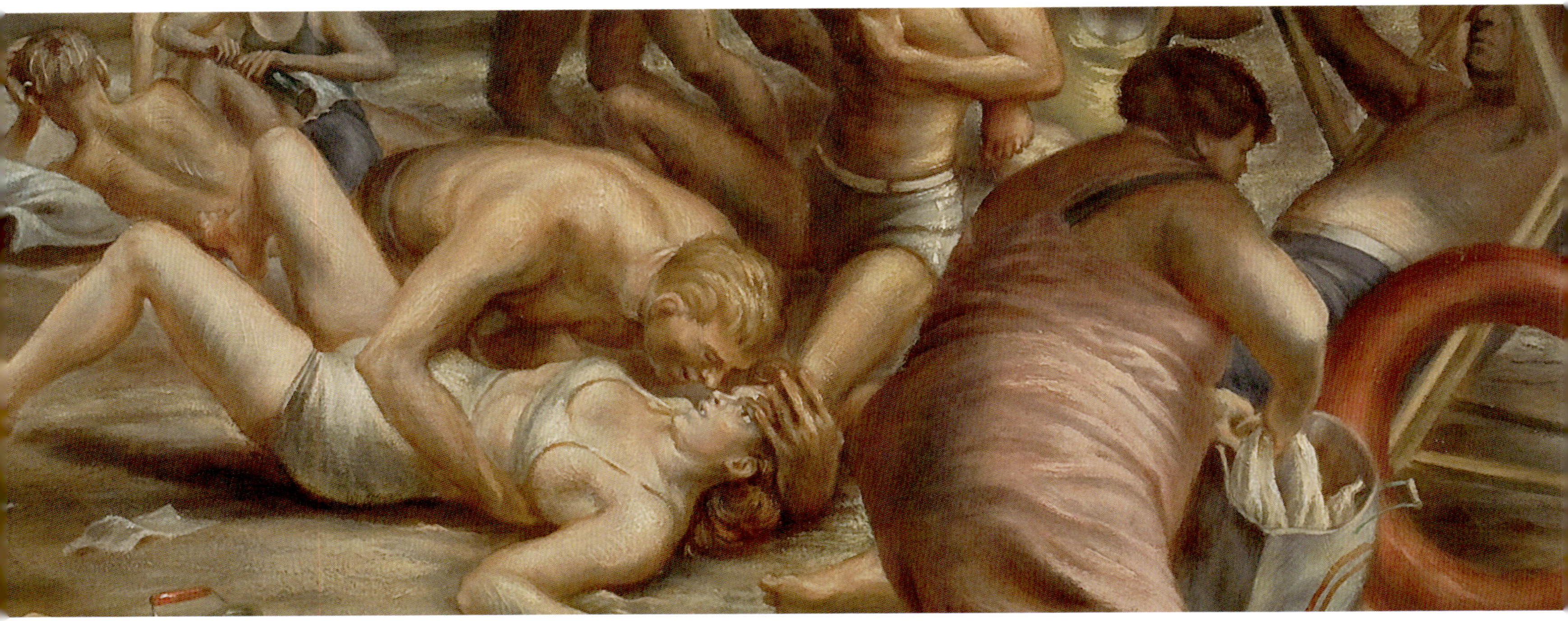

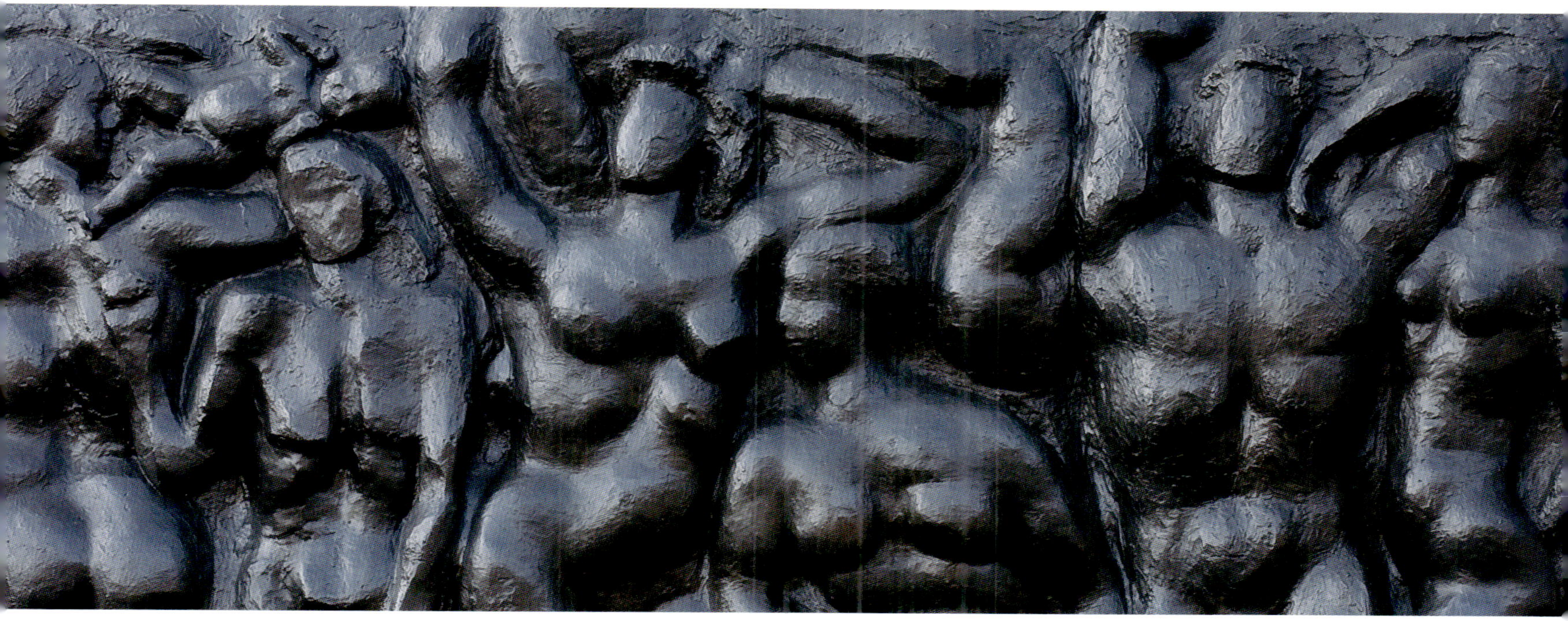

Selected Works: 1921–1945

PAUL MANSHIP American, 1885–1966

ALTHOUGH HE WON nearly every existing award for sculpture during his lifetime, Paul Manship entered the field largely because he was color-blind, not because of a passion for the medium. Originally wanting to be a painter, Manship studied at the St. Paul Institute in Minnesota, then took anatomy and modeling classes at the Art Students League of New York in 1905 and at the Pennsylvania Academy of the Fine Arts in Philadelphia from 1907 to 1908. Between those years he worked as an assistant to the sculptor Solon Borglum and in 1908–9 to the sculptor Isidore Konti. In 1909, at twenty-three, he entered and won the highly competitive contest for the coveted Prix de Rome, an award that provided artists with studio space at the American Academy in Rome. This three-year fellowship also allowed awardees the opportunity to travel through Italy and Greece to study original works of art firsthand.

While Manship was in Europe (1909–12), he became interested in the stylistic features and subjects found in Egyptian, Assyrian, and archaic Greek sculpture, which were then being excavated. Manship became one of the first artists to incorporate these forms, as well as those of classical sculpture from India, into his developing art. When he returned to the United States, he discovered that his distinct style was attractive to both modernists and traditionalists alike. The playfulness and stylized details of his sculptural forms appealed to collectors who wished to move beyond the classical realism of the prevalent Beaux-Arts style, while his incorporation of ancient themes and forms derived from nature made his works attractive to more conservative art patrons.

Directly inspired by classical athletic figures, Manship's *Spearthrower* shows the same attention to detail and awareness of how the body moves and balances as the works of the fifth-century B.C. Greek masters, particularly Polykleitos.[1] With his weight on his back foot, Manship's muscular figure leans back, preparing to throw his spear. The taut athlete displays the inherent proportion and symmetry found in classical Greek art and, as a result, appears timeless and universal. Reduced to essentials, this depiction of male beauty clearly and harmoniously emphasizes form over surface details. Minimally stylized, the figure's slightly almond eyes and patterned hair recall Egyptian or archaic Greek art, while his stern expression and intense concentration are appropriate for athletes or warriors of any period. Despite the fact that the sculpture was cast in the round, its primary vantage point is profile, emphasizing the figure's sinuous contours.

Although Manship's unique mode of sculpture broke from past tradition and paved the way for Art Deco's decorative and streamlined conventions, by the 1940s, as more abstract styles came to dominate the art scene, his work was considered academic. The artist continued to create sculptures that are considered masterpieces and to receive important public commissions, but he did not gain widespread recognition for these achievements. Manship is perhaps best known today for his 1934 gilt-bronze statue of Prometheus (the Greek god who brought fire to mankind) located at Rockefeller Plaza in New York City.

EDG

Note

1. Polykleitos revolutionized sculpture by depicting male figures in naturalistic, relaxed poses, with most of the weight placed on one foot and the shoulders and arms twisted off-axis from the hips and legs, a stance that has come to be called contrapposto.

Spearthrower, 1921. Bronze, edition 8/12, 20 × 32⅝ × 7½ in. Gift of Anne and Benjamin Cone in memory of Herbert S. Falk, Sr., 1976

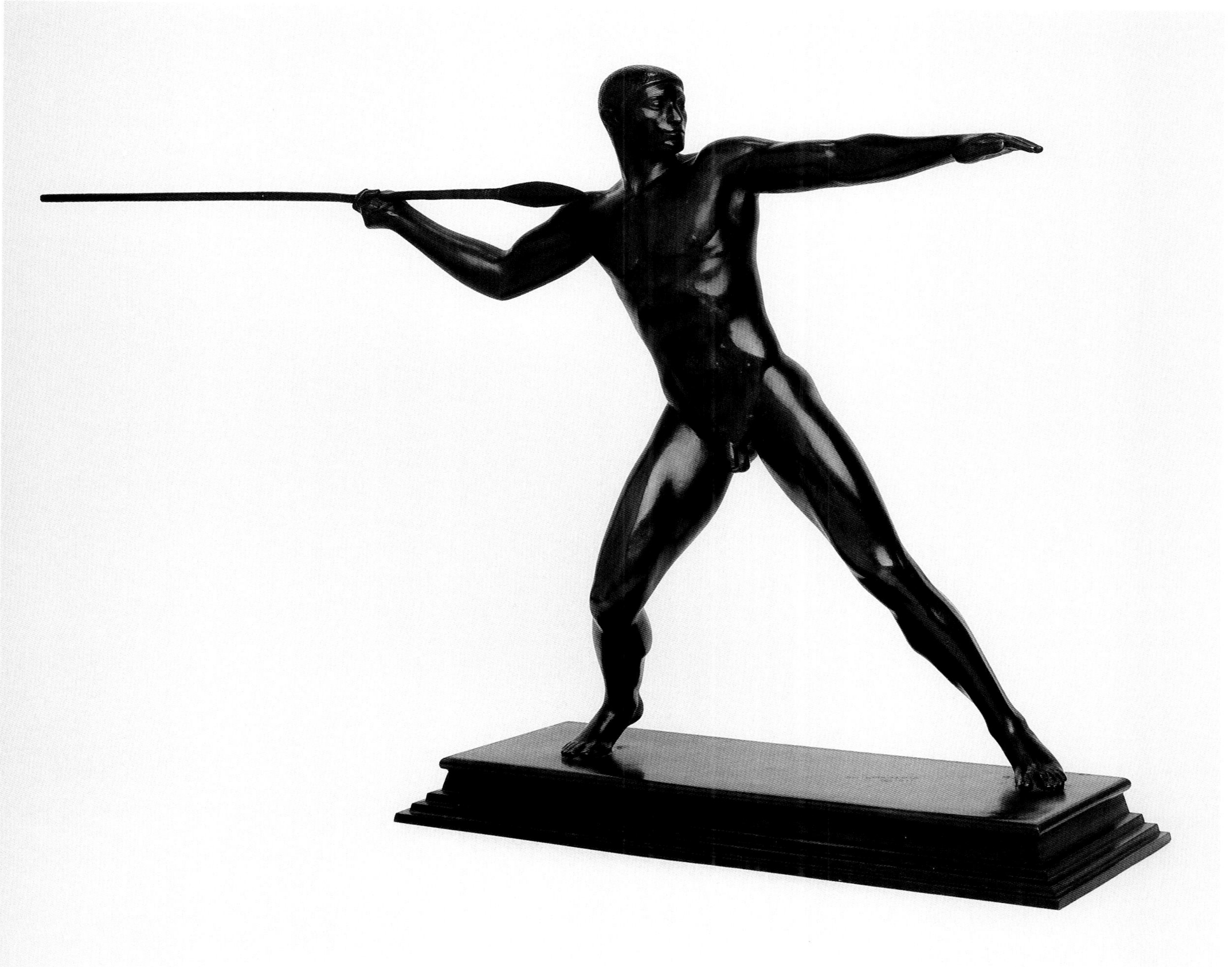

GEORGE BENJAMIN LUKS American, 1867–1933

GEORGE LUKS PARTICIPATED in the 1908 exhibition of the Eight at the Macbeth Gallery in New York City, a show that was a milestone in American art for its rejection of the conventional academic styles that dominated the National Academy of Design. These eight artists, led by Robert Henri, were rebellious in spirit and—although they each painted in distinct personal styles—unified in their goal of portraying urban life as they saw it. Gregarious, funny, hard-drinking, and full of gusto, Luks was the most colorful member of this group that pushed American painting toward a new realism.

The son of well-educated parents, Luks grew up around the coalfields of southern Pennsylvania. His mother and father were sympathetic to the plight of miners, and their example may have been the wellspring of Luks's later affinity for the urban poor. He drew constantly as a child and eventually became a student at the Pennsylvania Academy of the Fine Arts. His restless, if not reckless, personality emerged early, however, and he dropped out.

Luks traveled abroad for study but again found the formality of traditional art schools not to his liking. Instead, he studied works of art in museums directly, discovering his spiritual mentor in Frans Hals. This Dutch master's confident and flamboyant use of thick, buttery paint to depict often highly animated subjects thoroughly appealed to Luks's own boisterous personality. Back in the United States, Luks worked as an illustrator for the *Philadelphia Press*, and there he met John Sloan, William Glackens, and Everett Shinn. They in turn introduced him to Henri, who more than anyone else inspired Luks—and hosts of other artists—to engage the contemporary world through art.

Luks and his fellow artists migrated to New York, where he continued to work as an illustrator. Painting and sketching when he could, he made gritty views of city dwellers that caught the attention of critics, and soon Luks was able to support himself from the sale of his art. He exhibited regularly, won awards, and for a brief time taught at the famed Art Students League. A magnificent storyteller, Luks convinced others (though perhaps not everyone) that he had been a middleweight boxing champion in the Midwest by the name of "Chicago Whitey."

Society Girl is unlike the rougher subject matter that gained fame for Luks in that it portrays a beautiful young socialite. He made a number of such portraits that hark back to Hals via the verve and dash of their brushwork. The artist achieves a striking contrast between the highlighted face and the dark background, making the sweeping curve of the sitter's elegant hat all the more pronounced and dynamic. Luks's considerable skills in summarily defining the differing texture of creamy skin and the thick fur collar and cuffs are complemented by his keen ability to capture a likeness quickly and confidently.

In the 1920s paintings like *Society Girl* show how untouched Luks was by the radical developments in modern art around him. He continued to interpret the visible world in frankly recognizable terms and with the reportorial honesty that defined the Eight. Speaking of his own style (and revealing the influence of Henri's philosophy), Luks said, "Who taught Shakespeare technique? Or Rembrandt? Guts! Guts! Life! Life! That's my technique."[1]

He also continued to struggle with alcohol, and during the 1920s he went through a divorce and spent time in a sanatorium. Surprisingly, given his legendary consumption, Luks continued to exhibit, remarried, and painted a number of impressive works, including in watercolor. His erratic lifestyle eventually overtook him, however, and in 1933 he was found dead in the doorway of a speakeasy, the victim of a barroom brawl.

WS

Note

1. *Statistical Abstract of the United States*, 1989, 751, as cited in James Lincoln Collier, *The Rise of Selfishness in America* (Lincoln, NE: iUniverse, 2005), 112.

Society Girl, ca. 1920s. Oil on canvas, 36 × 30 in. Museum purchase with funds from the Jefferson-Pilot Corporation, Burlington Industries, the Mary Duke Biddle Foundation and the Blue Bell Corporation, 1978

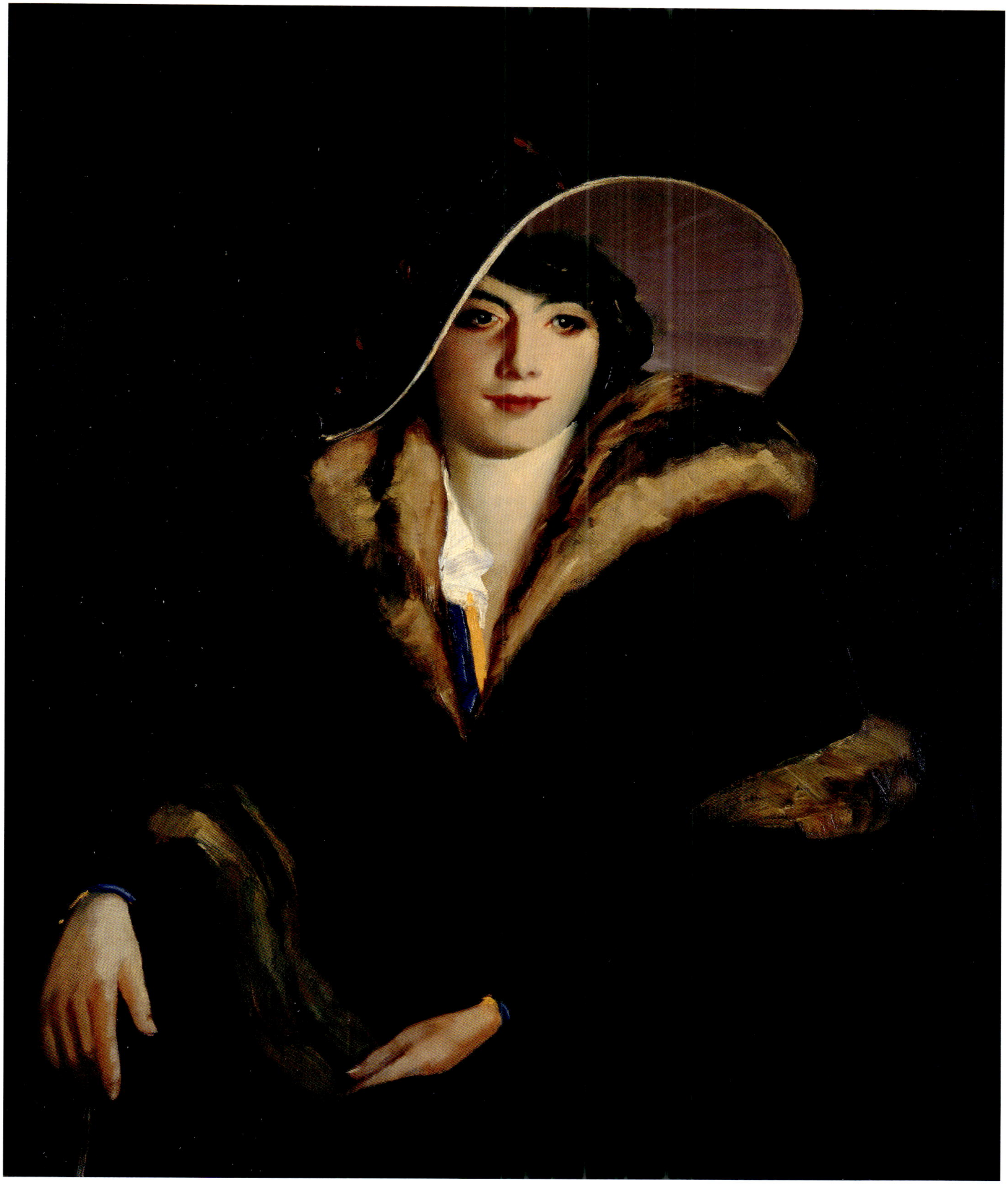

GUY PÈNE DU BOIS American, 1884–1958

THE AMERICAN 1920S are recalled as culturally and economically "roaring," and the stereotypical party girl of that era was the flapper—a boisterous, dancing denizen of the nightlife. Guy Pène du Bois's 1922 picture evokes no sound at all, nor is its solitary figure a gyrating jezebel. It is a pictorial contradiction of popular clichés of the era, one that suggests a physical and psychological isolation from the environment or other people, in which the young woman depicted stands alone, going nowhere, and doing nothing save looking out coldly at the one who looks at her.

Indeed, Pène du Bois's keen ability to critique the social illusions and pretensions of his time lies at the core of his art. His observational skills were derived from and inspired by two equally important sources: his study with the extraordinary teacher Robert Henri and his years as a reporter and eventual art critic. Henri electrified his students with his revolutionary zeal, stressing that mindless virtuosity was not the point of painting; rather, the purpose of art was to grasp a sense of life. Pène du Bois embraced Henri's fiercely democratic views and employed them while writing penetrating examinations of the art world. He became fascinated with the complexities of social interaction, including the seeming chasm between men and women: the artificialities of the bourgeoisie are his signature subject matter.

Guy Pène du Bois was born in Brooklyn, and his father, Henri, was himself a highly literate man (who named his son after Guy de Maupassant) and a full-time reporter.[1] At fifteen Guy was enrolled at the New York School of Art, and he remained immersed in the art life of Manhattan. He wrote for the *New York American*, *Arts and Decoration*, and the *New York Tribune* at the same time he exhibited with fellow contemporary realists—including close friends—such as Arnold Friedman, Edward Hopper, and Rockwell Kent. In 1913 Pène du Bois served on the publicity committee for the Armory Show and showed seven paintings in that seminal exhibition.

But Pène du Bois was no modernist. To the contrary, he felt that undue attention was given to abstraction during the Armory Show. In the late teens, he aligned himself with the Whitney Studio Club (a forerunner of the Whitney Museum of American Art, the largest repository of paintings by Pène du Bois) and in 1920 organized a show of Edward Hopper's works. Pène du Bois's focus coalesced around an articulation of the urban realist aesthetic, and at the outset of the twenties he was poised for his own art to fully mature.

From 1920 to 1924 Pène du Bois taught at the Art Students League (where his students included Alexander Calder, Isabel Bishop, Jack Tworkov, and Raphael Soyer), and he had a one-person show at Kraushaar Galleries in 1922. The Weatherspoon's *Flapper* was painted in that year and is fully indicative of the artist's emerging mature style.[2] Unlike the thick, bravura paint applications of the Eight, the surface of *The Flapper* is smooth. Here, shapes are stylized and architecture simplified: Pène du Bois settled on type, not the specific, to give expression to the malaise that lay beneath the world of Gatsby (the story in F. Scott Fitzgerald's so named novel takes place in New York in 1922). In this flapper's world, there is no movement, no party, and her heavy outerwear is the visual cue that her world is as cold as it is—in this painting—environmentally bleak.

WS

Notes

1. For a biography, see Betsy Fahlman, *Guy Pène du Bois: Painter of Modern Life* (New York: James Graham & Sons, 2004). The artist published his own autobiography, *Artists Say the Silliest Things*, in 1940.
2. *The Flapper* is reproduced as a full-page illustration at the beginning of Guy Pène du Bois, "Guy Pène du Bois by Guy Pène du Bois," *International Studio* 75, no. 301 (June 1922): 242.

The Flapper, 1922. Oil on board, 25 × 20 in. Museum Purchase with funds from Burlington Industries, 1973

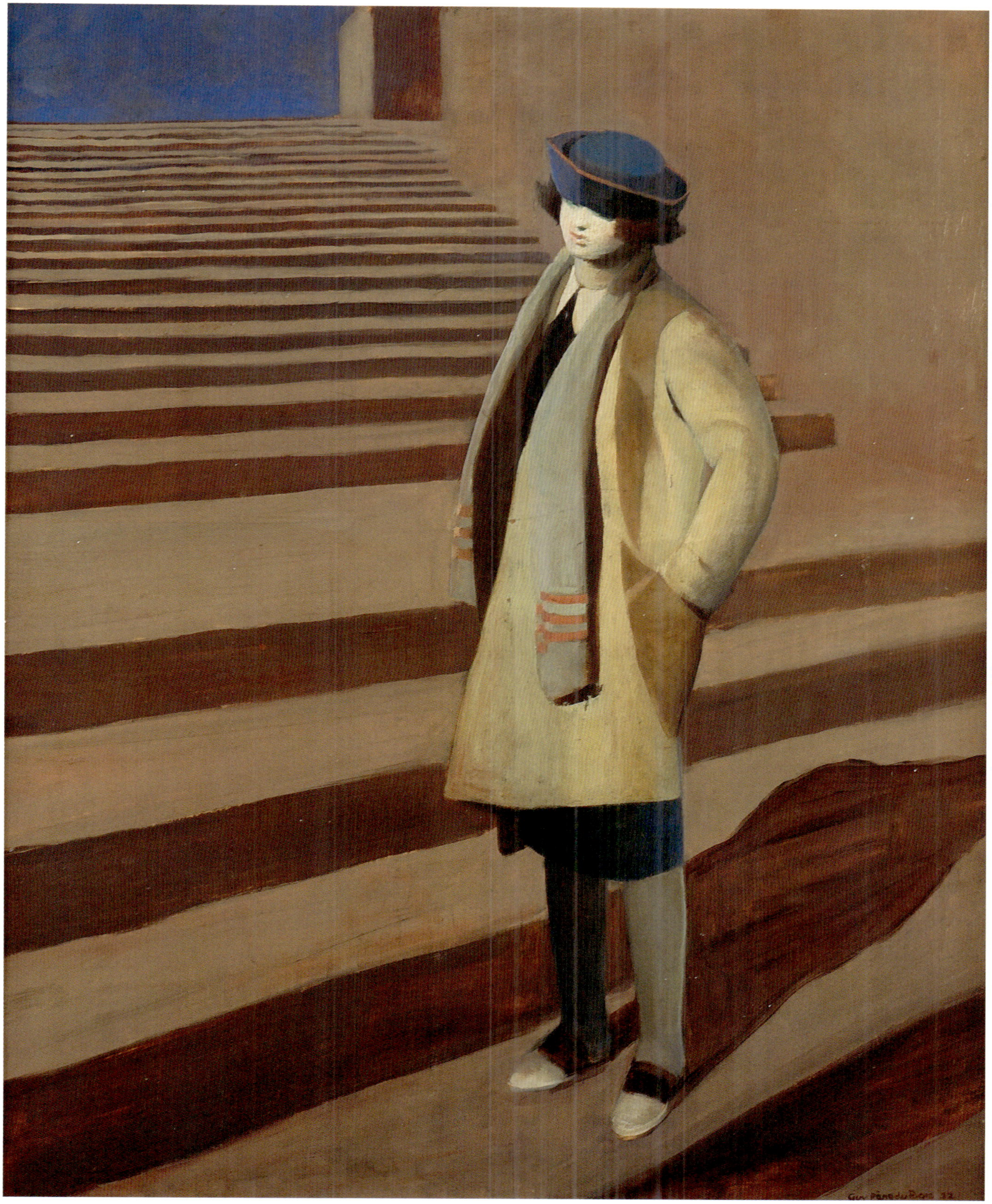

BLANCHE LAZZELL American, 1878–1956

To appreciate art of any period, we must dismiss the idea that painting is a representation of natural form as seen with the eye. Natural form may be used as a means to expression, but never as an end in itself. When we try to paint an object "as natural as life" or as it appears to the eye, our work becomes a literal thing devoid of any poetical feeling. Art is not photography—it is an expression of the inner man. We find in the artist's canvas his conception of life. His philosophy and his religion are revealed to the spectator who is able to read it.

—Blanche Lazzell[1]

LITTLE IN BLANCHE LAZZELL'S early life portended a career as a modern artist. One of twelve children, she was raised in rural West Virginia. She suffered from near-total deafness, a challenge that did not prevent her from pursuing a career in art—a choice in and of itself radical for a woman in those days—but one that surely caused her moments of isolation if not despair. Lazzell was a quiet, socially conservative Christian. What perhaps later disposed her toward abstraction was her openness to seeing the spiritual—as opposed to the verifiable appearance of things—in art. While in college in 1902, she wrote to a friend: "Where can we see God more plainly than in art."[2]

Lazzell studied for a brief time at the Art Students League of New York, where William Merritt Chase was her instructor and Georgia O'Keeffe a fellow student. Another important instructor was the adventurous colorist Augustus Vincent Tack. It was Paris, however, that opened her eyes in 1912 to a more extended art world. There, she attended lectures, visited the Musée du Louvre regularly, and encountered the work of Paul Cézanne and Pierre Puvis de Chavannes.

Not surprisingly, back in the United States in 1915 she was attracted to Provincetown, Massachusetts, where an art colony populated by bohemians was well established. Feeling herself to be "in my element," she moved there permanently in 1918. Provincetown gave Lazzell an artistic identity and a direction. She discovered woodblock printing there, the medium for which she is best known. Carving pine was not the same as painting with oils, and Lazzell learned to work more directly when designing areas of flat, pure color. She became part of a group called the Provincetown Printers, the first woodblock print society formed in America.

In 1923 Lazzell returned to Paris, where she studied with Fernand Léger, André Lhote, and Albert Gleizes. Lazzell, of course, had difficulty hearing and she could not understand French well in any case. Gleizes took the time to write down ideas and instructions for her, and Lazzell absorbed his advanced theories on Cubism. Central to his thinking was that a painting, instead of describing the material world, had its own subjective reality of line, shape, and color. The Weatherspoon's 1924 Cubist drawings by Lazzell date from her time with Gleizes.

In these four drawings, ideas imparted in writing by Gleizes to Lazzell are evident. He taught her to balance shapes not symmetrically but with variety and to take into account how those shapes relate both to the overall picture plane and to the central axis of the image. The organization of visual elements would lead to an experience of space and time not conditioned by an experience of the outside world. According to Gleizes: "That which is *static* belongs to our senses. . . . That which is dynamic belongs to our mind."[3]

As art history has rediscovered the significant contributions of pioneer modernists, Blanche Lazzell once again commands our attention for her singular ability to heed her own maxim that art is not photography but, rather, an "expression of the inner man." And certainly, too, of the inner woman.

WS

Notes

1. Quoted in *Blanche Lazzell: American Modernist* (New York: Michael Rosenfeld Gallery, 2000), 3.
2. Quoted in Robert Ridges et al., *Blanche Lazzell: The Life and Work of an American Modernist* (Morgantown: West Virginia University Press, 2004), 10.
3. Quoted in ibid., 214.

Untitled (Cubist Studies), 1924. Graphite on paper, four sheets, each approx. 10 × 7⅛ in. Gift of Harriette and Martin Diamond to the Dillard Collection in honor of Douglas Dreishpoon, 1996

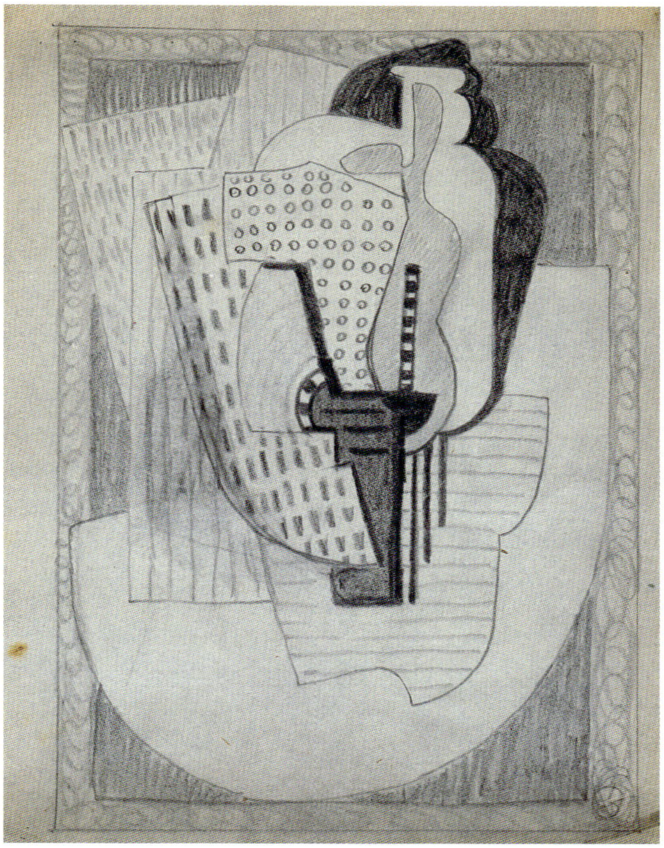

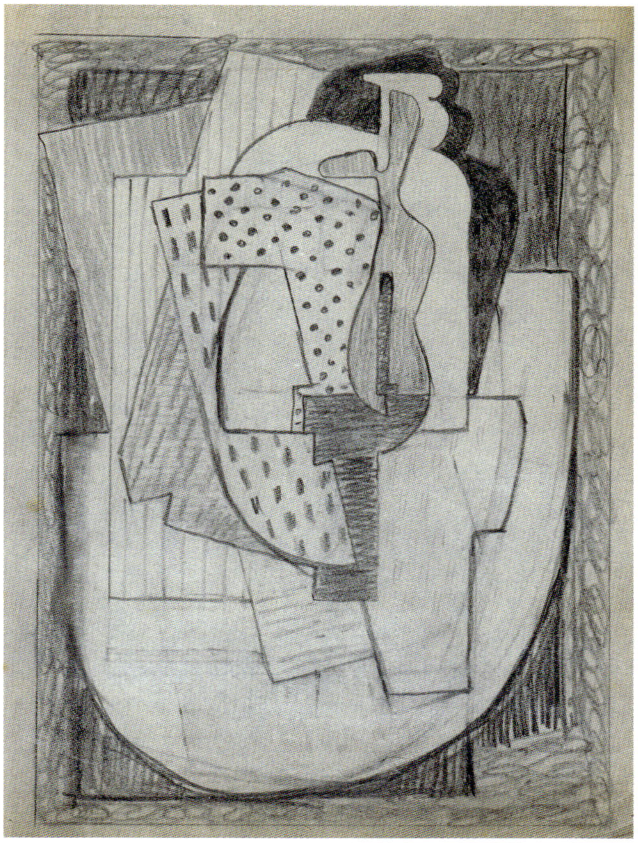

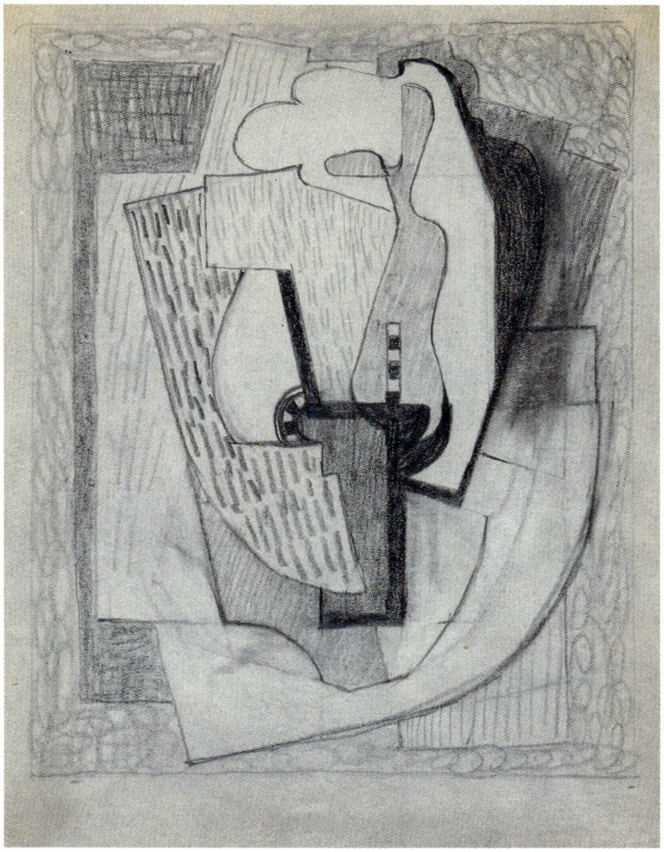

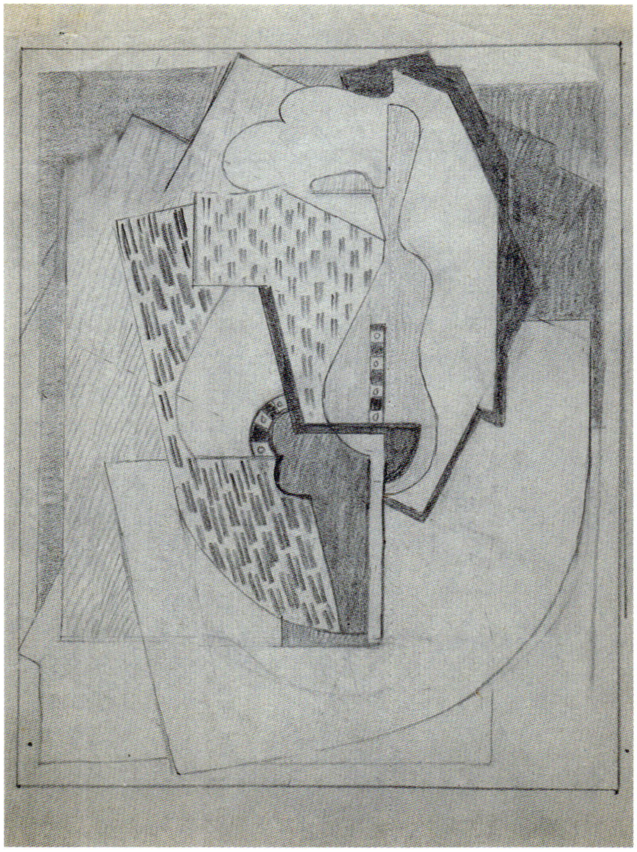

GEORGE AULT American, 1891–1948

BORN IN CLEVELAND, OHIO, Ault moved with his family to London at the age of eight, where his father, a businessman, amateur painter, and active supporter of arts organizations, worked in ink manufacturing. While in London, Ault studied drawing and painting at a variety of schools, including University College, the Slade School, London University, and St. John's Wood Art School, and supplemented this formal training with visits to art museums in both London and Paris. By the time he returned to the United States in 1911 at the age of twenty, he had acquired a firm grounding on which to base a professional career in the arts.

Starting in the 1920s, Ault began receiving critical attention. In 1920 he exhibited with the Society of Independent Artists, a group with modernist tendencies, and in 1923 had his first one-person show at the Bourgeois Gallery, a space sympathetic to Cubist-inspired art.[1] He also began exhibiting regularly at the Downtown Gallery and the Salons of America. It was during this decade that Ault developed the flat, linear approach to urban subject matter that allied him with a group of post–World War I artists known as the Precisionists. Adapting Cubism's formal means of reducing objects to planar components, Precisionist painters such as Charles Sheeler, Niles Spencer, and Ralston Crawford created streamlined, hard-edged views of industrial America and, to a lesser extent, landscapes, still lifes, and interiors. However, unlike his peers, Ault did not idealize modern life and machinery.

Among his early Precisionist works, *Figure Composition (Portrait of Beatrice Hoffman Ault)* is an intimate glimpse into the artist's studio and a portrait of his first wife, Beatrice.[2] Painting directly from life, Ault reduced and simplified the scene into flat shapes and planes that emphasize the underlying geometry of the figure and surrounding objects. Located in the center of the composition within a relatively shallow space, the figure gazes directly out at the artist/viewer, albeit with a slightly vacant look. Shadow and light delineate the contours of her face, while the folds of her dress counter and interact with the diagonal patterning of the wood floor. The solid square shapes of the bookcase, desk drawers, and the frame of the painting on the wall balance the composition and draw attention to the figure. Equally significant is the candlestick that rests on the desktop in the background: it seems as important as the figure herself. An overall feeling of austerity permeates the work, a consequence of its simplified form, spare geometry, and melancholy. Sorrow, fragility, and enigma would become dominant themes in Ault's later paintings, many of which invoke the work of Giorgio de Chirico, an Italian Surrealist.

Unlike the trajectory of his Precisionist colleagues, Ault's impressive professional ascent was derailed by an array of personal problems: his mother died in a mental institution, and each of his three brothers committed suicide, two after the family lost its fortune in the stock market crash of 1929. By 1930 Ault suffered from alcoholism and had become increasingly remote from friends, dealers, and other artists. Although he continued to paint, the tone of his canvases became more introspective and somber. In 1937 he and his second wife, Louise, moved to Woodstock, New York, where they remained year-round until Ault's accidental death or suicide by drowning in 1948.

EDG

Notes

1. Ault's shift toward a modern painting style prompted his father—an academic painter—to stop supporting him financially.
2. Ault and Beatrice Hoffman married in 1914 and were divorced by 1935.

Figure Composition (Portrait of Beatrice Hoffman Ault), 1925. Oil on canvas, 42 × 28 in. Gift of Andrew Tananbaum, 1986

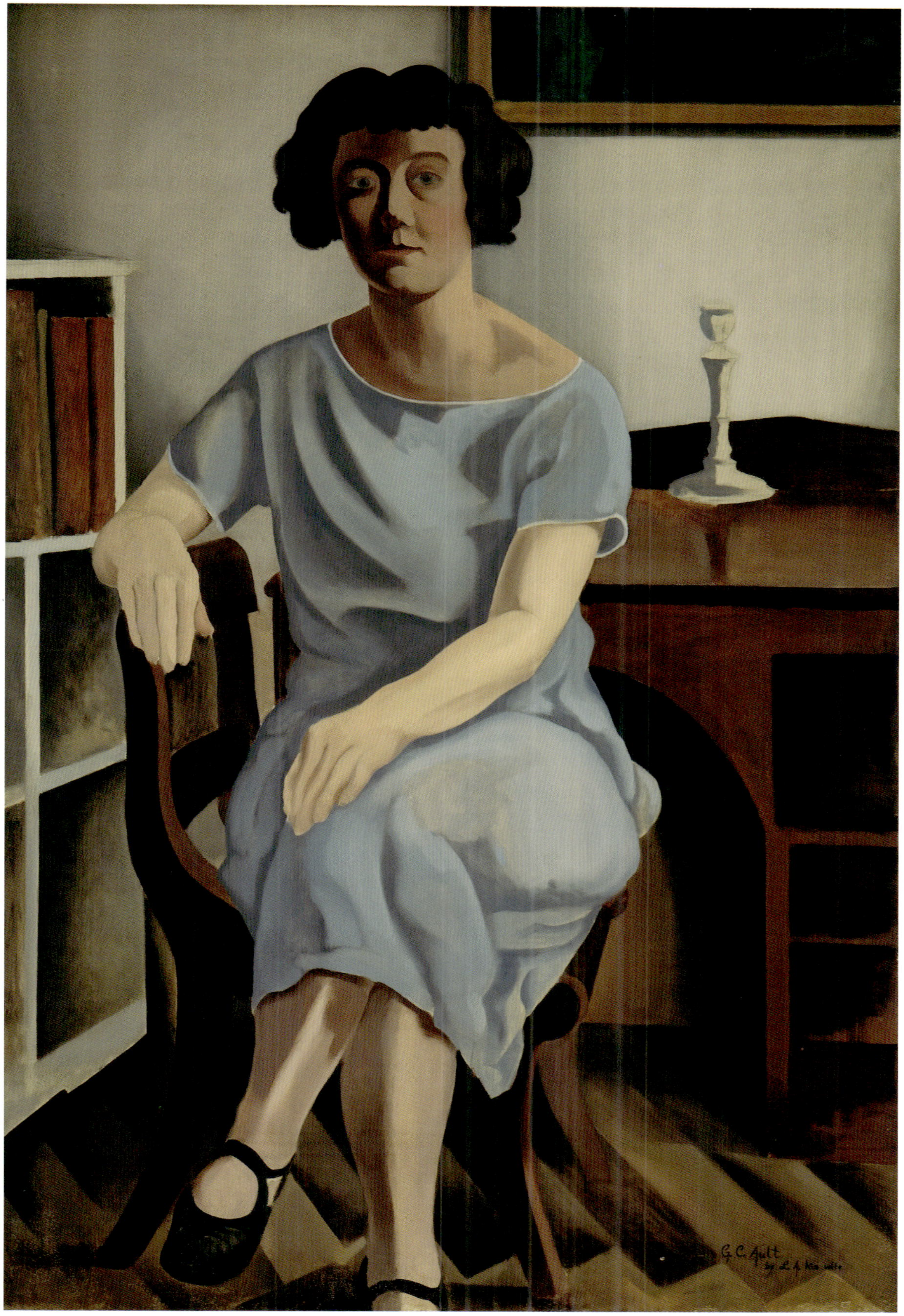
G. C. Ault

JOSEPH STELLA American, born Italy, 1877–1946

The great evil of the city is this: the houses close it off from the sky and countryside, which are furthermore obstructed by thronging crowds from morning to evening. Everyday life is mean and low. In order to have the energy to live one must cover over its cruel wounds with our dreams, with our most intense striving for the highest realms of blessedness, where our weightless soul becomes immersed in the celestial blue. Our father's house is the sole link with the past. It is the solid, firm bridge.

—Joseph Stella[1]

JOSEPH STELLA'S JEWEL-LIKE *Morning (The Hay Stack)* pictures the celestial blue of his dreams. It is a fantastic image of sharp-edged, distant mountains and a silhouetted haystack, where a flowering tree emerges improbably from somewhere between the two. Stella would always be inspired by nostalgia for the Italy of his youth and look for the bridge to that past, but his own art was propelled forward by the energy and dynamism of New York City. His allegiance to the great art traditions of the Old World coexisted—and conflicted—with his immersion in the rapidly evolving metropolis of the New. Indeed, just as Stella lived physically and culturally between Europe and America, so, too, did his art shift between past and present as he made futuristic icons of the city and simultaneously drew fragile flowers in silverpoint.

Stella immigrated to New York in 1896. The next year he studied briefly at the Art Students League and later at the New York School of Art with William Merritt Chase. In 1909 he was back in Italy, where the Italian Impressionist painter Antonio Mancini influenced him with his high-keyed color and dashing, broken brushstrokes. On the heels of this experience, in 1911 Stella visited Paris, where he discovered the work of Paul Cézanne, Pablo Picasso, and Henri Matisse and, importantly, where he saw the work of the Italian Futurists in 1912. Back in New York in 1913, he painted *Battle of Lights: Mardi Gras, Coney Island*, a work of brilliant, fragmented color that answered the Futurists' call for a new art of energy and excitement and that emphatically did not portray, as Stella's earlier work had, "a civilization long since dead."[2] *Battle of Lights* represented the electric future that had arrived.

Opportunities for Stella to deepen his philosophical understanding of modernism came shortly thereafter, when he became a regular visitor to the apartment of Walter and Louise Arensberg. There he befriended Marcel Duchamp, leader of New York Dada and painter of the notorious *Nude Descending a Staircase* that had caused the greatest furor at the Armory Show. Stella's ongoing investigations of the vitality of the city in combination with the innovations of vanguard painting culminated in his Brooklyn Bridge paintings of 1919–20. In these, the artist identified and glorified material prowess and progress, making these large canvases spiritual shrines to the new age.

America was not, however, everything to Joseph Stella. Nor was the abstract concept of the future. Tradition, Catholicism, the Renaissance, Italy, poetry, music, and nature itself mattered as much and more, and the artist drifted from the epicenter of modernism in New York. Into the 1920s he painted and drew a wide variety of subject matter in various styles. Surely a source for his unpredictable creativity was his willingness to reach back into the rich trove of past art and synthesize it with the unrestricted means of modernism.

Morning (The Hay Stack) is just such a hybrid work. Its intense color and simplified forms speak to the legacy of Matisse, while its stiff, frontal composition suggests the modernist preoccupation with primitive and folk art. Its small, shimmering surface, however, recalls a Renaissance panel, and its evocation of a sunrise, replete with a blossoming tree, is an allegory of awakening and regeneration. *Morning (The Hay Stack)* specifically and Joseph Stella's career taken as a whole demonstrate the complicated interweaving of using the past and embracing the present that constituted the rise and practice of modern art.

WS

Notes

1. Quoted in Barbara Haskell, *Joseph Stella* (New York: Whitney Museum of American Art, 1994), 224.
2. Quoted in ibid., 206.

Morning (The Hay Stack), ca. 1927. Oil on canvas, $12\frac{1}{4} \times 9\frac{7}{8}$ in. Museum purchase with funds from Jefferson-Pilot Corporation, 1976

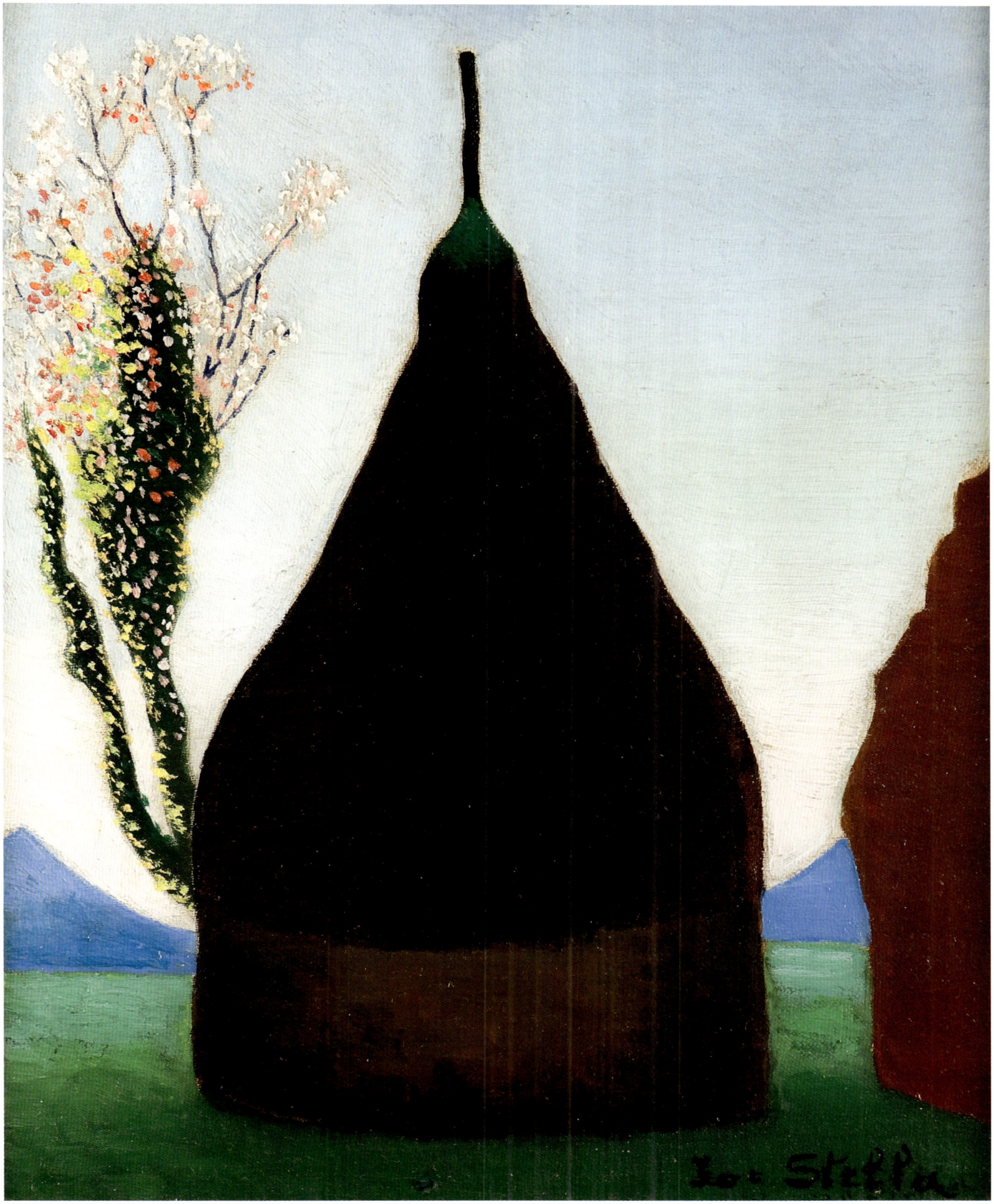

JOHN GRAHAM American, born Russia, 1886–1961

JOHN GRAHAM WAS A PIVOTAL FIGURE in the New York art world of the 1920s and 1930s. He was one of the very few artists with a first-hand knowledge of modern French art, particularly Cubism and Surrealism, about which most American artists had little information and still less understanding. Graham provided both, acting as an intermediary between Paris and New York and helping to lay the foundation for what became known as Abstract Expressionism.

The Yellow Bird of about 1930 is one of his answers to French Cubism in the sense of the works of Pablo Picasso and Juan Gris, the large organic shape recalling the first, and the more literal shapes translating a still life on a table, the second. As in the works of these French Cubists, traditional form and perspective space have given way to flattened shapes vibrating in a shallow space developed in relation to the picture plane. The fundamental two-dimensionality of that plane is further accentuated by a series of similar striations that appear above and below.

That a Cubist grid forms the underlying structure of *The Yellow Bird* is not in doubt. But it relies as well on another, still more recent movement in French art: Surrealism. Under the influence of Sigmund Freud and in reaction against the notion of art for art's sake, Surrealist writers and artists set out to tap the unconscious for forms and images originating in dreams and fantasies. To this end, they developed the practice of automatic writing—or drawing—a process of spontaneous utterances, and they also immersed themselves in the natural world of small and even microscopic organisms, both strategies designed to relax or circumvent the control of the conscious mind over writing, painting, or sculpture. Picasso, a co-inventor of Cubism, was influenced by Surrealism, and his works of the later 1920s are filled with shapes similar to those found in the works of such Surrealists as Joan Miró. The large, opulent shape of *The Yellow Bird* belongs to this vocabulary. Grounded in Cubist principles, *The Yellow Bird* is simultaneously Cubist and Surrealist. All in all, this is an example of the most up-to-date avant-garde painting in New York at the time, equaled only by paintings by Graham's friend Arshile Gorky.

Gorky was only one of the many artists who benefited from Graham's friendship. Others were Willem de Kooning, Jackson Pollock, and David Smith. Well regarded by collectors and dealers, Graham was asked in 1942 to organize an exhibition of modern art for the McMillan Gallery in New York and, for the occasion, gathered together paintings by French and American artists—Gorky, de Kooning, Lee Krasner, and Pollock, together with Picasso and Georges Braque. De Kooning had shown only once before. It was the debut of Krasner and Pollock.

Graham's awareness of developments in modern French art began, according to his own account, when he was hardly more than a boy. Born Ivan Dombrowsky in Kiev, Russia, in 1886, Graham, as he later called himself, claimed that as early as 1905–6 he had visited the Moscow collection of Sergei Shchukin and saw there works by Henri Matisse, André Derain, and Picasso and that he had deepened his knowledge of this art during a stay in Paris, before sailing for New York in 1920. He was no less open to trends in modern American art. The Weatherspoon Art Museum houses an important group of works by Graham in addition to *The Yellow Bird*, among them a portfolio of drawings from the early 1920s. These drawings show Graham looking to works by such artists as John Marin, Charles Demuth, and Marsden Hartley. Evidently, during the 1920s and 1930s Graham was one of the few artists in the New York art world with a keen eye for developments in modern art, both French and American. His unique qualifications appreciated, he was made an agent for American collectors of both African sculpture and modern art, making frequent trips to Paris during the 1930s to stay in touch with the latest developments, particularly Surrealism.

Especially closely related to *The Yellow Bird*, though even more overtly Surrealist, are Graham's *White Pipe* of 1930 and *Blue Abstraction* of 1931, both closely related to contemporary paintings by Gorky and looking forward to paintings and sculptures of the 1930s by de Kooning, Krasner, Pollock, and Smith. Paradoxically, just as these artists were building on the foundation that he had helped to lay, carrying abstract art in new directions, Graham moved back into the history of figurative art, drawing his inspiration, not from modern Paris, but from Renaissance Italy. With this last body of figurative work, of figures, heads, and horses, signed with his newly adopted name, Ioannus Magus, Graham dropped out of the history of modern American art that he had helped to create.

CG

The Yellow Bird, ca. 1930. Oil on canvas, 16⅛ × 20⅛ in. Museum purchase with funds from Jefferson-Pilot Corporation, 1970

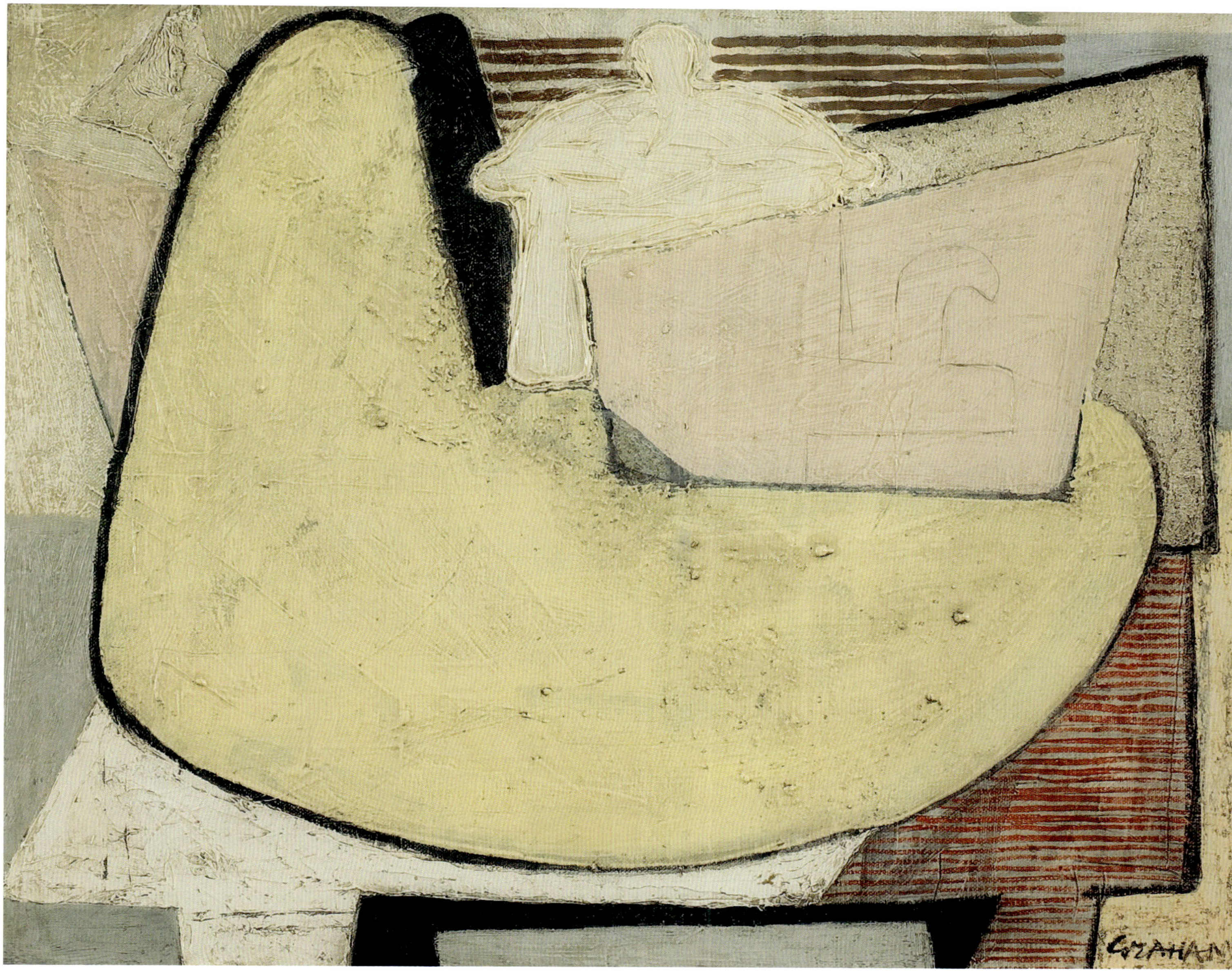

REGINALD MARSH American, 1898–1954

BORN IN 1898 to a family of East Coast artists, Reginald Marsh reveled in city life.[1] One of the most prominent New York painters of the 1930s and 1940s, he was so enamored of the city that he scarcely left the teeming metropolis during the sweltering summer months. Each of the city's moods and social classes found its way into the sketches, watercolors, prints, and tempera paintings of this prolific draftsman.

During his formal education at Yale University, Marsh learned the technical rigor of the old masters. However, it was for his work in the university humor magazine, *The Yale Record*, that Marsh was praised for his insightful sketches of human behavior and the urban landscape.[2] The editors of the magazine were so taken with Marsh's work that they commissioned sketches from him after his graduation.

New York Skyline demonstrates Marsh's ability to capture both the grandeur and the chaos of the city. Completed in 1934, this view features not only the skyscrapers that sprang up in the city during the 1920s and early 1930s but also the lower buildings that form the foreground of Marsh's scene taken from a Manhattan pier. The crisp September sky (the watercolor is signed and dated at lower right) is punctuated with soaring giants, but in the right foreground Marsh provides a hint of the activity that would have surrounded the artist. The vertical smokestacks of a small tugboat, picked out in red and black, remind us of the darker skyline of the older buildings in the midst of the gleaming towers above and the piers that define the New York waterfront.

Although this is a view made during the Depression, we see it from the waterways that were the source of New York's original prosperity as a seaport. There is none of the sentiment of the painters of the Ashcan School, Marsh's predecessors in depicting the rougher side of New York. Instead, Marsh knew the crews of the city's tugboats and sketched frequently in New York's ports.[3] The artist captured the grit and the dynamism of New York so poignantly that he was asked by the New Deal art program to decorate the U.S. Custom House in New York with maritime murals.

Many of Marsh's landscapes are located in the areas between the city and the water: the piers, the ferries, and Coney Island. He is also known for his portraits and types, which he saw everywhere from Fifth Avenue to the burlesque theaters. Marsh was the New York counterpart of the Parisian flaneur. He walked the streets, a well-educated, erudite individual who was sensitive to the social divisions and activity around him, subjects featured in six other works featuring New York by this artist held in the Weatherspoon Art Museum's collection.

Over the years, in both these human studies and in his skylines, Marsh captured the development of the city. To review his sketches and watercolors from the 1920s up to the 1950s is to watch a great American landscape unfurl, an urban scene that was this artist's passion.[4] Although he traveled and studied the drawings of Raphael, Leonardo da Vinci, and Michelangelo, Marsh was always a student of New York. He captured its landscapes and characters and, when he died while away from home on a brief vacation in Vermont in 1954, he left his cramped little studio above Union Square ready for the next scene full of sketchbooks chronicling his favorite subject in all its moods.[5]

EP

Notes

1. Edward Laning, *East Side, West Side, All around the Town: A Retrospective Exhibition of Paintings, Watercolors and Drawings by Reginald Marsh* (Tucson: University of Arizona Museum of Art, 1969), 89.
2. Lloyd Goodrich, *Reginald Marsh* (New York: H. N. Abrams, 1972), 20.
3. Edward Laning, *The Sketchbooks of Reginal Marsh* (Greenwich, CT: New York Graphic Society, 1973), 108.
4. Ibid., 11.
5. Ibid., 17.

New York Skyline, 1934. Watercolor and graphite on paper, 13½ × 20⅜ in. Gift of Anne and Benjamin Cone to the Dillard Collection, 1980

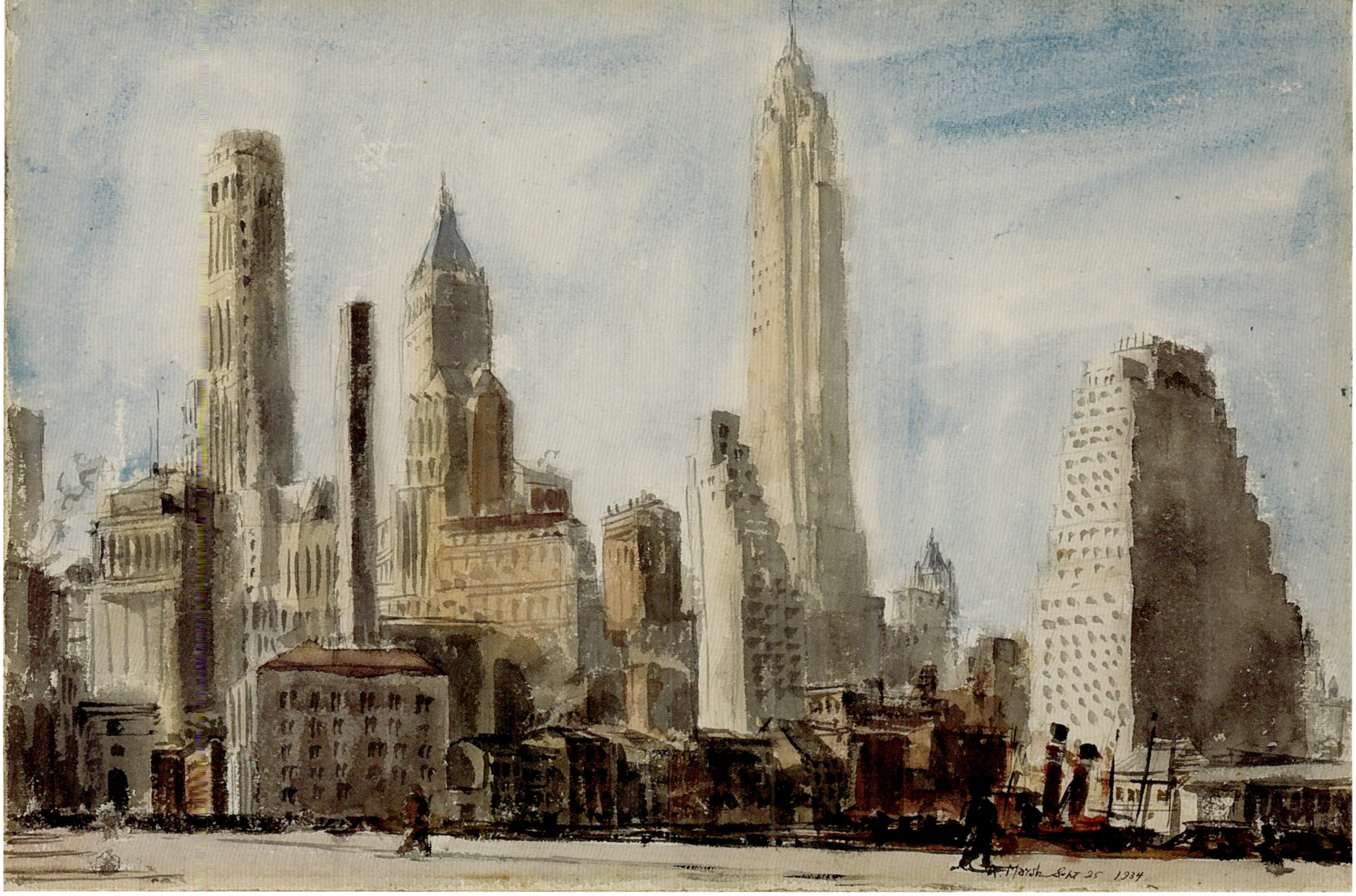
R. Marsh Sept 25 1934

JOHN BERNARD FLANNAGAN American, 1895–1942

I've been meditating a little about sculpture as something of a discovery of the occult fossil as though the form finally realized were all the time just bound up in the particular rock awaiting release.

—John Flannagan[1]

JOHN FLANNAGAN was a modernist for whom many of the primary conceits of modernism—progress, machines, time, speed, the city, the future—meant nothing. Hailed now as one of America's first avant-garde sculptors, Flannagan saw himself deeply attached to the past and the ceaseless cycles of nature. For most modern artists, ancient and so-called primitive art forms were a source of inspiration, yet Flannagan was a true pantheist. He respected the stone first, feeling his purpose as an artist was to mediate between the material and the message that he believed lay within.

Born in Fargo, North Dakota, Flannagan decided as a teenager to become an artist and by the early 1920s was in New York. There, he met Arthur B. Davies, who hired him to work at his country farm. Flannagan was exposed to Davies's considerable collection of folk and primitive art, and Davies urged the younger man to try his hand at carving. In 1927 Flannagan had his first one-man show of wood and stone carvings at New York's Weyhe Gallery, where he would exhibit for the next ten years.

At the Weyhe Gallery, Flannagan saw examples of African carvings that would directly influence his work. He elongated human forms and simplified facial expressions with masklike geometry. The mother-and-child motif became a favorite, as did animals. Both subjects were consistent with Flannagan's belief that the artist's task was to reveal natural laws. His work was well received by both critics and the public, and the Weyhe Gallery sponsored a trip for Flannagan to Ireland in 1930.

After a second trip to Ireland in 1932, sponsored by a Guggenheim Fellowship, Flannagan increasingly focused on animal motifs. In *The Flea*, a dog stretches his right hind leg behind his ear to scratch, while his snout reaches backward. Minimally carved and incised, the clear, bold design conforms to the shape of the rock from which it emerges. The sheer unpretentiousness of *The Flea*, its utter lack of heavy-handed symbolism or theoretical intent, enhances its charm and thus our recognition in it of familiarity and, indeed, connectedness to the animal world. In *The Flea*, a humble and endearing vignette from a dog's life, Flannagan recognized and ritualized the continuity of the shared patterns of existence. Life itself, replete with its mysterious cycles, was his subject.

In 1935, the year *The Flea* was made, Flannagan spent seven months in the hospital after an attempted suicide. He had struggled for years with depression and alcohol. Despite these challenges, the artist found a new love in his life and continued to exhibit, including a one-person exhibition at Vassar College the following year. A serious auto accident left Flannagan with severe brain damage in 1939, and he took his own life in 1942. The year before his death, Flannagan wrote a short yet deeply moving article on sculpture that included the following: "All as part of the profound social purpose of art—communication. We communicate something of the record of the human spirit."[2]

WS

Notes

1. Margherita Flannagan, ed., *Letters of John B. Flannagan* (New York: Curt Valentin, 1942), 57.
2. John Flannagan, "The Image in the Rock," *Magazine of Art* 35, no. 3 (March 1942).

The Flea, 1935. Bluestone, 6 × 17¾ × 10½ in. Museum purchase, 1945

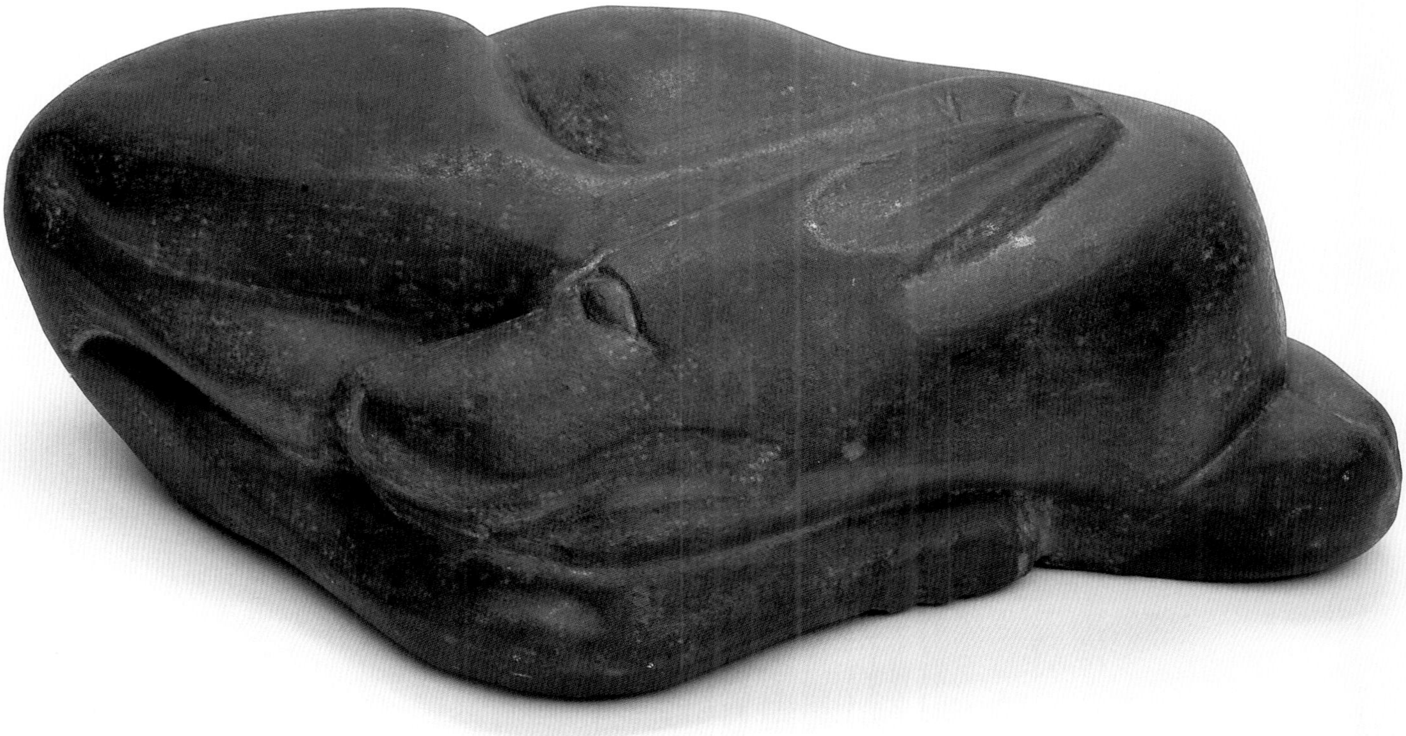

EDWARD WESTON American, 1886–1958

EDWARD WESTON, based on the West Coast, was preeminent among pioneering modernist American photographers whose aesthetic principles and working methods were forged in the 1920s. Schooled in the photographic pictorialism and modernism of Alfred Stieglitz, he devoted himself to rendering the formal beauty of the commonplace. Without hint of irony, he once compared favorably the porcelain grace of his Mexican toilet bowl to the Winged Victory of Samothrace.[1] His best images provoke a moment of startled reevaluation in which the act of ordinary seeing is suffused with a metaphysic of affirmation, in which vision becomes epiphany. His concepts of straight photography and previsualization, coupled with his virtuoso command of photographic technique as manifested in his eight-by-ten-inch contact prints, remained influential touchstones for American art photography through the mid-1960s.

Nude is among Weston's best-known images and exemplifies a famous statement found in his *Daybooks*: "The camera should be used for a recording of *life*, for rendering the very substance and quintessence of the *thing itself* whether it be polished steel or palpitating flesh."[2] The enduring fascination of this photograph lies in the obdurate fidelity of Weston's camera to the bobby pins and wisps of pubic hair of the real body in front of his camera even while the resulting image conforms to the ideals of classical sculpture. The representation exists unstably in the space between ideal beauty and "the *thing itself*," eliding the oppositions between art and life, form and fact, nude and naked, sublimity and contingency.

Charis Wilson, a young model of extraordinary beauty, came into Weston's life in 1934 in the middle of a particularly creative period in which Weston was photographing nudes. (She was nineteen and he was forty-eight.) In what was to be the final entry of his *Daybooks* (except for a brief coda written a decade later), Weston penned the following entry on December 9, 1934: "On 4-22 a new love came into my life, a most beautiful one, one which will, I believe, stand the test of time. . . . Perhaps C[haris] will be remembered as the great love of my life. Already I have achieved certain heights reached with no other love. . . . I must have peace to enjoy, fulfill, this beauty."[3] In a 1977 book devoted to Edward Weston's nudes, Wilson narrates, some forty years after the fact, the circumstantial particularities of this photograph's genesis from the vantage of a vibrantly irreverent and fondly reminiscent lover:

> *I sat in the bedroom doorway [to the sunroof] with the room in a shadow behind me. Even then the light was almost overpoweringly bright. When I ducked my head to avoid looking into it, Edward said, "Just keep it that way." He was never happy with the shadow on the right arm, and I was never happy with the crooked hair part and the bobby pins. But when I see the picture unexpectedly, I remember most vividly Edward examining the print with a magnifying glass to decide if the few visible pubic hairs would prevent him from shipping it through the mails.*[4]

Although the negative of this famous nude study was exposed in 1936, the Weatherspoon print was made some fourteen years later by Weston's second of four sons, Brett, when his father's Parkinson's disease prevented him from working in the darkroom. Brett considered the print to be wholly his father's creation, insisting that he functioned only as an extension of his father's now incapacitated hands. However, Brett's younger brother, Cole, who shared jointly in the project of carrying on their father's photographic legacy, claimed that Brett had influenced Edward's printmaking decisions and that, given the subtleties of darkroom work and the unavailability of Weston's original printing paper, no later print could be considered a "vintage" Edward Weston. In the film *Remembering Edward Weston*, Cole demonstrates how his father's penciled instructions, written in abbreviated darkroom code on the glassine envelope protecting the negative for this print, could be followed to reproduce Weston's original interpretation.[5]

What makes this photograph worth coming back to over time is that specifically photographic quality of the large-format process that Weston treasured and taught the world to see: "the stark beauty that a lens can so exactly render presented without interference of artistic effect."[6] While subsequent critiques of photographic transparency, as formulated by Roland Barthes, Alan Sekula, Martha Rosler, Abigail Solomon-Godeau, and others, have come to make Weston's working assumptions appear antiquated and naïve, his images constitute a bastion of high modernist achievement against which a subsequent generation of photographers and critics defined themselves.

GD

Notes

1. Edward Weston, *The Daybooks of Edward Weston, 1, Mexico, 2, California*, ed. Nancy Newhall, foreword Beaumont Newhall ([Millerton, NY]: Aperture, [1990]), 32.
2. Ibid., 55. Emphasis in the original.
3. Ibid., 283.
4. Charis Wilson, *Edward Weston: Nudes* (Millerton, NY: Aperture, 1977), 12. See also the film *Remembering Edward Weston*, written and directed by David Turner (Santa Fe: Museum of Fine Arts, Museum of New Mexico, 1992).
5. *Remembering Edward Weston.*
6. Weston, *Daybooks*, 147.

Nude, 1936, printed ca. 1950 by Brett and Edward Weston. Gelatin silver print, 9½ × 7½ in. Museum purchase with funds from the Benefactors Fund and the Joseph R. Morton Acquisition Endowment, 2007

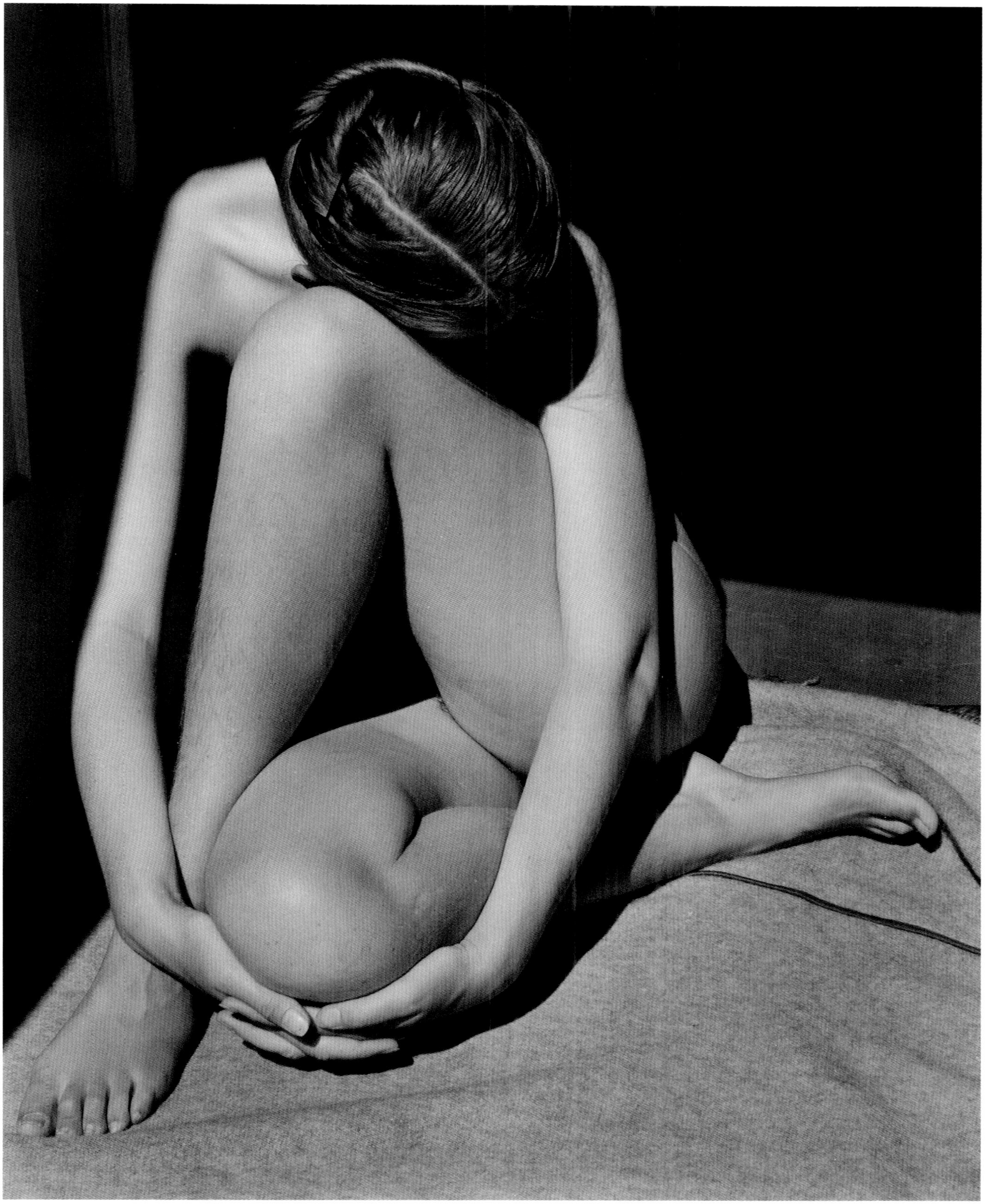

ESPHYR SLOBODKINA American, born Russia, 1908–2002

BORN IN THE SIBERIAN TOWN of Chelyabinsk, Esphyr Slobodkina moved with her family to Manchuria, China, in 1921 to escape the political unrest of the Russian Revolution. There she studied art and architecture until 1928, when, at the age of nineteen, she relocated to New York City on a student visa and enrolled at the National Academy of Design. In late 1930 she met fellow student and expatriate Russian-born abstract painter Ilya Bolotowsky, who became her most important teacher and whom she married in 1933.[1] The marriage lasted three years, during which time she moved from a largely realist painting style to experimenting with abstraction.

Slobodkina embraced abstraction wholeheartedly, becoming one of the founding members of the American Abstract Artists group (AAA). Established in 1937, during the heyday of such narrative styles as Social Realism and American Scene, this group of emerging artists initially gathered in Ibram Lassaw's studio to discuss ways to promote abstraction and nonobjective art to art institutions and the general public alike. A major force in furthering hard-edged geometric art forms, the AAA included such artists as Josef Albers, Ad Reinhardt, Bolotowsky, Willem de Kooning, Jackson Pollock, and David Smith. Slobodkina served as the organization's first secretary and later its president, treasurer, and bibliographer. Even after the group's popularity declined in the second half of the century, she remained a lifelong active member, participating in many exhibitions and contributing to its print portfolios.[2]

Abstraction, from 1936, dates to the beginning of Slobodkina's mature style, when she had fully absorbed the influences of Pablo Picasso and Cubism in general as well as those of Jean Arp, Joan Miró, and Arshile Gorky. Although Slobodkina assimilated the abstract idioms of Arp and Miró, she did not incorporate their anthropomorphic and biomorphic overtones. Rather, as in this example, she created a style of abstraction that utilized irregular geometric shapes of unmodulated color layered one on top of another, as in a collage. This aesthetic was a constant in her work from the mid-1930s on and extended to the illustrations she did for her well-known children's books, such as *Caps for Sale* (1940).

Although Slobodkina relied on observed nature rather than pure imagination to create her paintings, she abstracted it to such an extent that subject matter is often elusive, as here. Her arbitrary use of color and even-handed treatment of forms, highlights, and shadows create shapes floating in space that could equally describe a domestic still life, a landscape, or a fleeting moment in time. However, in keeping with her fidelity to abstraction, she was careful to balance the composition through color and form, favoring a palette of grays and tans.

Abstraction once belonged to Charles Shaw, a fellow abstract artist who, along with Albert Eugene Gallatin, George L. K. Morris, and Suzy Frelinghuysen, made up a group known as the Park Avenue Cubists, so named because of the members' affluent backgrounds. Just as committed to abstract art as Slobodkina, Shaw was the first artist to paint on shaped canvases or, as he called them, "plastic polygons," which he fashioned by abstracting the outline of the Manhattan skyline. The Weatherspoon Art Museum is fortunate to own one of his paintings, also featured in this book.

A prolific painter, Slobodkina was also a sculptor, a children's book author and illustrator, and a designer of textiles, jewelry, and furniture. Through her long and fertile career, she made significant contributions to the establishment and understanding of abstract art in America, from which succeeding artists have benefited.

EDG

Notes

1. As a result, Slobodkina became an American citizen and could thus quit the National Academy of Design (something she could not do while in this country on a student visa), which she found too conservative.
2. The artists who overshadowed the AAA in the 1950s were the Abstract Expressionists, many of whom had studied under and/or were greatly influenced by abstract painters like Slobodkina.

Abstraction, 1936. Oil on board, 9 × 5 in. Gift of Mrs. Herbert S. Falk, Sr., 1982

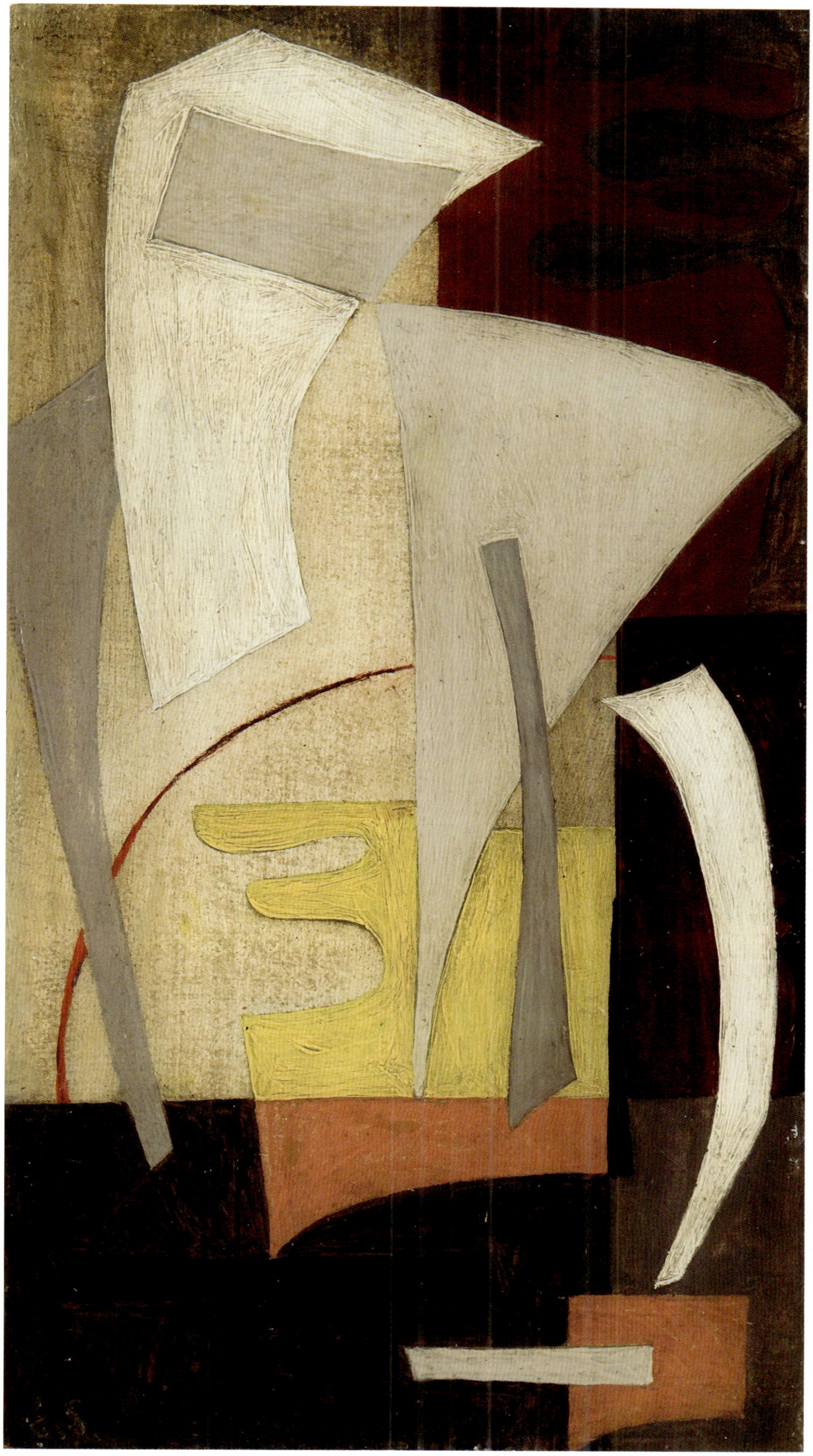

CHARLES GREEN SHAW American, 1892–1974

What I have termed the plastic polygon—a several-sided figure divided into a broken pattern of rectangles—developed in the course of years from certain experiments made by myself in 1933. In the main these experiments were founded upon the New York scene—or rather the Manhattan skyline—treated semi-cubistically. Quite naturally the vertical line predominated.

—Charles Shaw, 1938[1]

MADE THE YEAR BEFORE Charles Shaw wrote the epigraph to this entry, the Weatherspoon's untitled painting is a clear example of the "plastic polygon"—a several-sided figure derived from the Manhattan skyline. Here, the word *plastic* does not refer to the familiar synthetic substance used to make cups but is the word modern artists used when speaking of form. In his polygons, Shaw arrived at an art free of the details of the city, in which his representation of buildings was reduced to pure design and their three-dimensionality collapsed into a single plane. Shaw sought the fundamental structure of the skyscraper, a type he believed to be "solely of America." Like his friend and colleague George L. K. Morris, Shaw believed this type of abstraction was not derived from European precedents but from the energy of American urban life.

Also like Morris, Shaw was born into wealth and privilege. He was also large, over six feet tall: Shaw's friend and Yale classmate Cole Porter called him "Big Boy." A fixture of the elite East Coast social crowd, Shaw also mingled with F. Scott Fitzgerald and George Gershwin. Throughout the 1920s he lived the life of the Manhattan socialite and wrote about its colorful citizens for *Vanity Fair* and the *New Yorker*. One of the few earlier artists he knew and befriended was, not surprisingly, the extraordinarily affable, bar-haunting storyteller George Luks. One might easily imagine these two submerged in the nightlife of the city, boisterously talking art and consuming libations.

Shaw studied privately with Luks and in 1926 took courses with Thomas Hart Benton at the Art Students League. With both of these teachers, the word *abstraction* was never mentioned. Nor was Shaw particularly committed to painting at this time; he wrote a novel in 1927 (which Fitzgerald praised) and a play the next year. Trips abroad in the late 1920s and early 1930s convinced him that he was a painter.

During the Great Depression, Shaw's personal wealth insulated him from financial worry, and he continued to travel to Europe, meeting Pablo Picasso, Fernand Léger, Georges Braque, Jean Hélion, and Jean Arp. All of these artists exerted influence on Shaw's aesthetic thinking as he gravitated toward ever more fundamental shapes and color. He began his series of plastic polygons, which were the first shaped canvases made in America, in 1933.

Shaw had his first solo show in New York at the Valentine Gallery in 1934; it was followed by one at the Gallery of Living Art at New York University. In 1936 he was a founding member of the American Abstract Artists group along with colleagues Morris and Albert Eugene Gallatin. Writing in the American Abstract Artists 1938 yearbook, Shaw denounced critics of modernism and wrote that opponents of abstraction had "not merely failed to *see* abstract art but indeed *any* art."

While he never suffered the economic disadvantages common to so many modern artists, Charles Shaw was no dilettante. He continued to work on his plastic polygons into the 1960s. Those he made in the 1930s, including the Weatherspoon's painting, were among the most sophisticated manifestations of modernism to emerge on this side of the Atlantic for their effective and summary interpretation of a key icon of the American metropolitan experience: the skyscraper.

WS

Note

1. Charles Shaw, "The Plastic Polygon," quoted in Debra Bricker Balken and Robert S. Lubar, *The Park Avenue Cubists* (New York: Grey Art Gallery, New York University, in association with Ashgate, 2002), 83.

Untitled, 1937. Oil on wood panel, 36¼ × 22¼ in. Gift of Mr. and Mrs. Herbert S. Falk, Sr., 1973

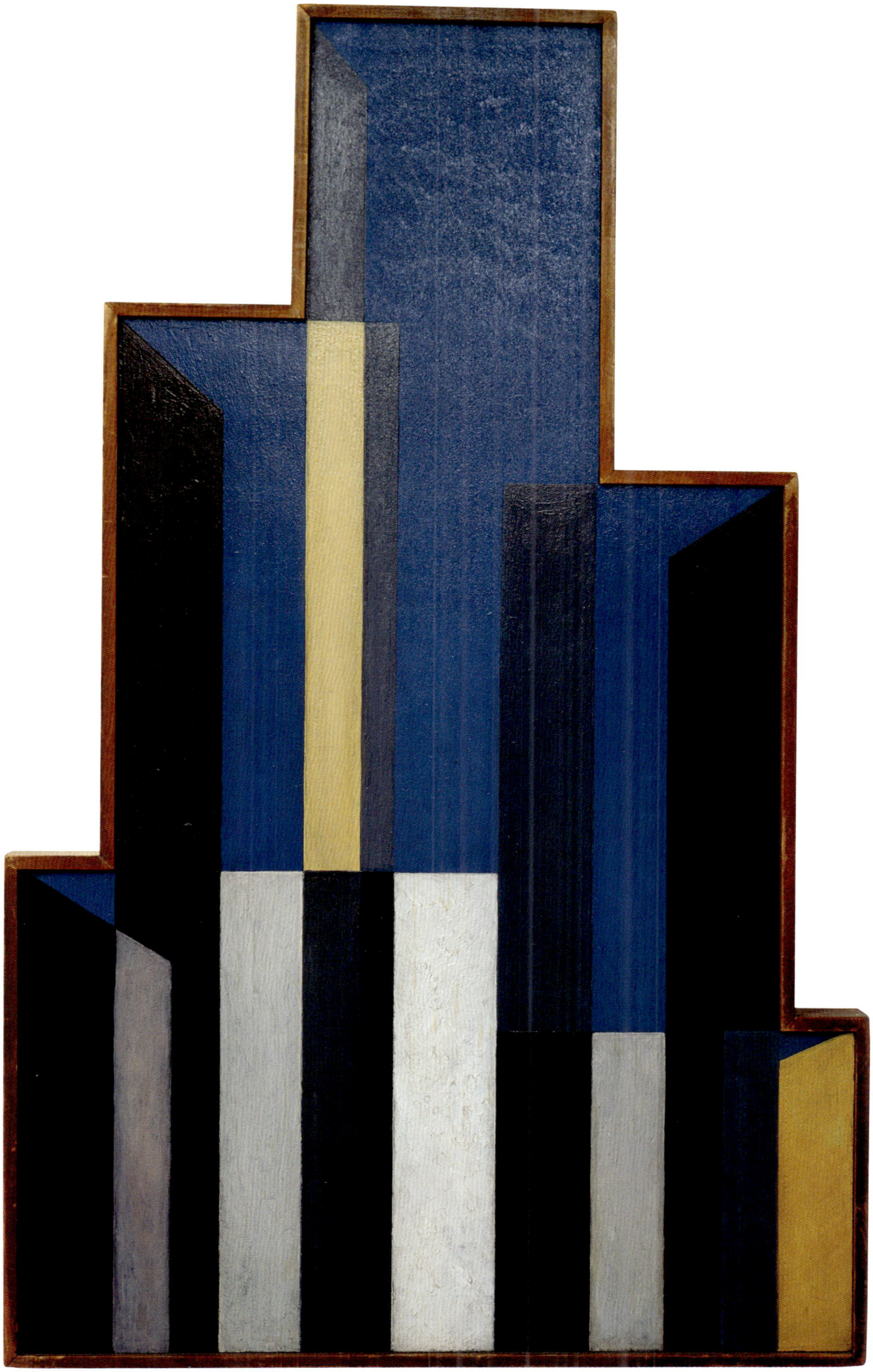

DAVID SMITH American, 1906–1965

THIS CONSTRUCTION IS AMONG the earliest sculptures by an artist who came to be recognized as the most important sculptor of his generation and who was unquestionably the most influential American sculptor of the second half of the twentieth century. Made in 1937 of forged and welded steel, with cast iron, it belongs to a group of direct metal sculptures that David Smith began in 1933, including *Agricola Head* (1933) and *Reclining Figure* (1935), and is sister to *Interior for Exterior* (1939), all of an entirely new kind in the history of sculpture.

Whereas it had always been taken for granted that a work of sculpture must be a monolith, a closed mass, or a form in space, Smith's are open arrangements of metal lines, planes, and forms. These new conceptions of sculpture are often referred to as "drawing in space." Of course, it is not possible actually to draw in space, and these are not drawn lines but steel and iron elements cut, cast, and shaped with obvious physical exertion, but the analogy with drawing is, nevertheless, well chosen. For Smith deploys these elements as if they were on a canvas, just as his friend Arshile Gorky was doing in his paintings at this time with similar and related lines and shapes arranged in pictorial space.

To compare Smith's sculptures to paintings is to suggest that they are pictorial. And indeed they are. *Interior* is relatively flat in the sense that it displaces a shallow space. The arrangement of the elements is essentially rectilinear, the right–left, top–bottom organization reinforced by a base that implies the enclosing rectangle of a painting. *Interior* is a sculpture, in sum, closely related to a painting. This is not at all surprising since Smith began his career as a painter and turned to sculpture only in 1932.

David Smith was born in 1906 in Decatur, Illinois. His only formal training was in painting, which he studied at the Art Students League in New York City between 1926 and 1932, first with the Ashcan School painter John Sloan and then with the Czech Jan Matulka, whose teaching was grounded in Cubist principles. These can be seen in Smith's early paintings, in which large, flat shapes are arranged in a shallow pictorial space. A similar, basically Cubist, vocabulary was used at the time by the painter John Graham, who played a pivotal role in Smith's development. Of all the artists in New York, Graham was the one most closely in touch with developments in modern French art and, about 1930, gave Smith a copy of a French magazine with illustrations of welded metal sculptures by Pablo Picasso and Julio González.

The majority of modern French sculptors, still committed to the traditional stone and bronze, did not fully grasp the revolutionary potential of these works; they did not conceive of a radically new type of sculpture offering new possibilities because of the distinctiveness of iron and steel as sculptural materials. Smith had been applying Cubist principles in his paintings and, earlier in life, had had the real-world experience of forging and welding steel as an employee in a Studebaker plant in South Bend, Indiana. The direct metal sculptures of Picasso and González encouraged him to experiment further with welded steel as a sculptural medium.

Smith's first metal sculptures were similar to those of Picasso and González in both content and form: the constructed human figure and head, strongly linear, incorporating abstract forms and shapes. These works also point to another sculptor who was no less prominent in the Paris art world: Alberto Giacometti. A major figure within the Surrealist movement, Giacometti produced sculptures using a variety of materials and techniques, among them construction. One work that intrigued Smith was a wood construction of 1932–33, *The Palace at 4 a.m.*, re-creating, Giacometti later said, one of his dreams. Smith's fascination with this work was no doubt due at least in part to his own increasing interest during these years in the Surrealist world of dreams and fantasies. But if Smith's idea was to evoke an inner world, he described an outer, physical world in a way that was new to sculpture, even taking into account the revolutionary sculptures of Picasso and González. For their works, no less than traditional sculpture, were more or less restricted to the vertical figure; *Interior*, by contrast, in its horizontality, has the sprawl of a landscape or work of architecture. It opened up entirely new possibilities for sculpture that Smith explored further in *Interior for Exterior* (1939), *Home of the Welder* (1945), and *Hudson River Landscape* (1951). The same principles are behind his great series of the 1960s, Zig and Voltri.

Smith's early works share affinities, then, with the works of different painters and sculptors. Once on his artistic feet, however, he carried modern sculpture in a new direction, only hinted at by others. *Interior* is an important step in that direction.

CG

Interior, 1937. Welded steel with cast-iron balls, 15⅝ × 26 × 6 in. Museum purchase with funds from anonymous donors, 1979

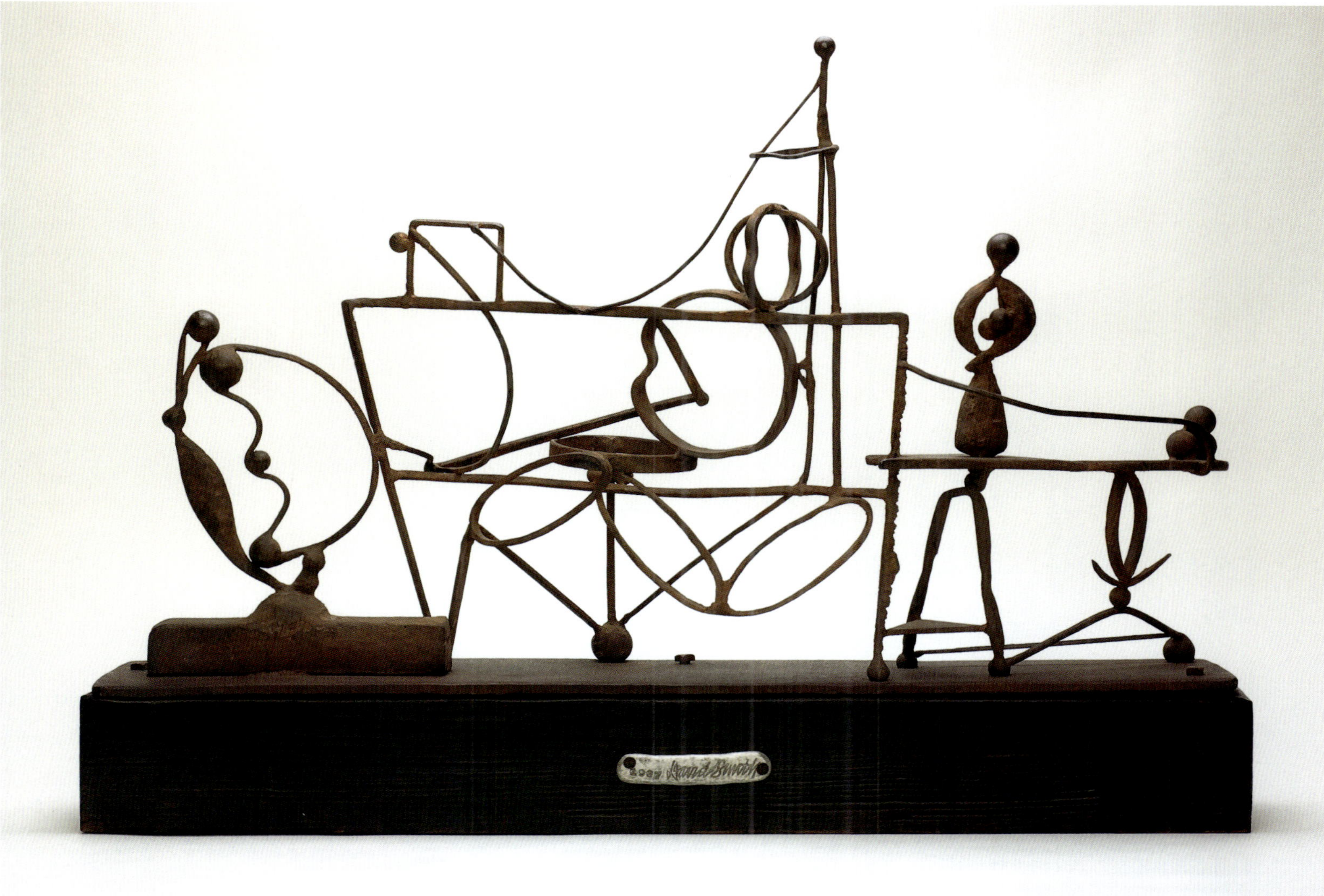

EDWARD LANING American, 1906–1981

RESTLESS BY NATURE, Edward Laning began his studies at the School of the Art Institute of Chicago, transferred to the University of Chicago, then moved to New York. There he enrolled in the Art Students League, taking classes with Kenneth Hayes Miller and John Sloan, both of whose works are also represented in the Weatherspoon's collection. Like other artists of his generation, he survived the decade of the Depression with commissions from the federally funded Works Progress Administration (WPA). Just a year before painting *Coney Island Beach Scene*, Laning and his assistants completed a WPA mural in the dining hall of the Ellis Island immigration center. Although *Coney Island Beach Scene* is not mural size, its composition and figure types could be adapted to the larger scale.

The composition is framed on the left by a potbellied bather whose skimpy trunks are incongruously paired with a homburg hat. Both he and the amply covered woman who rummages in her beach bag at right seem oblivious to the sexually charged struggle that is the focus of the painting. Tilted beach umbrellas and the diagonal supports of a covered lounge chair direct the viewer's gaze to bathers massed in a precariously tipped, asymmetrical pyramid. Since the Venetian Renaissance, painters have intentionally destabilized pyramidal compositions to convey a sense of drama. Like the composition, the poses of Laning's figures were adapted from art-historical models selected to imply that this is a scene of hedonistic good times turned violent. Pinned to the sand by an insistent suitor, the woman with flailing legs looks as unwilling as the victim of Titian's *Rape of Europa*, and the cropped legs in the lower right jut as jarringly into the pictorial space as the limbs of the lifeless bodies in Honoré Daumier's lithograph *Rue Transnonain, April 15, 1834*.

As an American modernist, Laning consciously balanced quotations from the past with details such as the sunglasses and cigarettes that contemporize *Coney Island Beach Scene*. The specificity of the location and the palpable urgency of the action suggest that the event depicted is one that actually occurred. Linked to Manhattan and the other New York City boroughs by the subway, Coney Island offered an amusement park, a boardwalk, and a beach to working-class New Yorkers. Newspaper reports of bathing beauty contests and raucous beach brawls lured artists and writers alike. The unruly crowd pictured in *Coney Island Beach Scene* may include some of the fifty-seven people charged in August 1937 with violations ranging from illegal peddling to undressing on the beach.[1] If Laning witnessed the melee, he would have pulled out the drawing pad he carried in his pocket and scribbled action sketches as the first step in developing a multi-figured composition.

Laning's working process is outlined in *The Act of Drawing*, an instructional manual that synthesizes thirty years of teaching experience. The confident command of the human form that is evident in *Coney Island Beach Scene* resulted from a systematic approach to drawing the figure. Beginning with gesture and contour drawings, he added modeling from light to dark to create the illusion of three-dimensionality. He recommended side lighting as the most effective way to project forms in dramatic relief and mass multiple figures in a dynamic composition. The lighting and placement of the full, fleshy figures in *Coney Island Beach Scene* illustrate his advice. Laning also noted that a great colorist like Peter Paul Rubens drew with red, black, and white chalks on tinted papers to heighten contrasts in drawings intended as studies for oil paintings.[2] The contrasts of tone and hue that maximize the palette of *Coney Island Beach Scene* may well have been established in preliminary drawings.

Laning used a limited range of pigments to give pictorial coherence to the crowded, complex composition of *Coney Island Beach Scene*. Visibly different paint applications distinguish the solidly modeled figures from a windswept sky that reinforces the unsettling narrative content of the painting. Long, parallel strokes flow compulsively toward the upper right, giving the sky an atmospheric turbulence that is mirrored in the rippled surface of the sand and the crumpled beach towels. Like the struggling figures, their stormy setting is a pictorial metaphor of the social turmoil that roiled in the ranks of society where people were slow to benefit from Franklin D. Roosevelt's New Deal.

KPA

Notes

1. "Round Up at Coney," *New York Times*, August 3, 1937, 24.
2. Edward Laning, *The Act of Drawing* (New York: McGraw-Hill, 1971), 50–75, 93.

Coney Island Beach Scene, 1938. Oil on canvas, 36 × 42 in. Gift of his family in honor of Mr. Benjamin Cone's 80th birthday, 1980

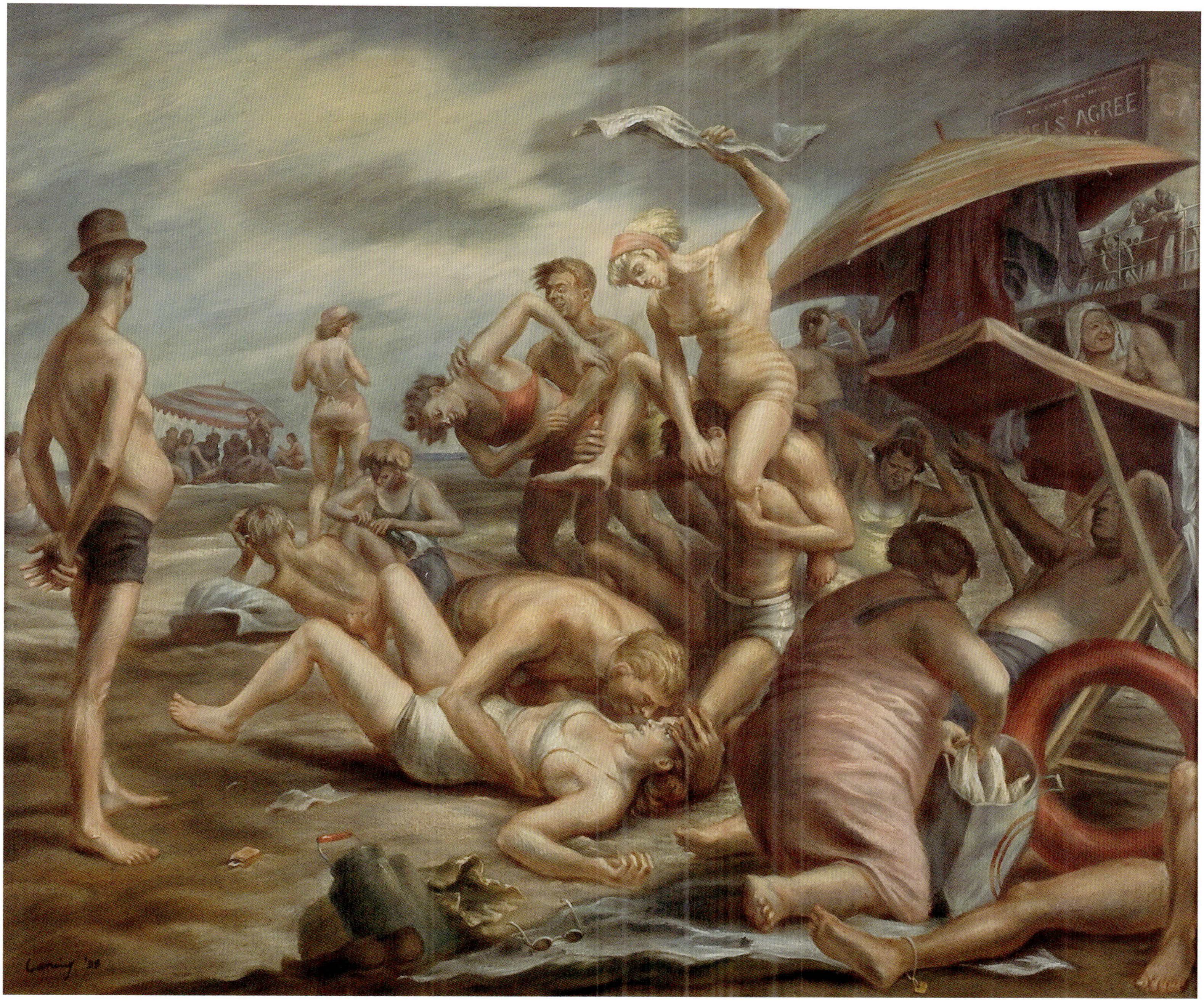
AGREE

SAUL BAIZERMAN American, born Russia, 1889–1957

THIS LARGE BRONZE RELIEF is all that remains of Saul Baizerman's earliest monumental sculptures. Originally modeled in plaster after 1931, it was an attempt to recover something of what had been lost in a fire that had devastated his studio and destroyed all of the works he had made using an innovative sculptural technique: hammering forms into sheets of copper. Before undertaking new work that, because of this laboriousness, would take several years to complete, he felt the need to recover the old. *The Pastoral or Third Sculptural Symphony II*, executed in the easier and quicker medium of plaster, was the result, and it served as a launching pad for the major hammered coppers produced between 1933 and 1939.

Baizerman was born in Vitebsk, Russia, the birthplace also of Marc Chagall, in 1889. He arrived in New York City in 1910 and, shortly thereafter, began studying at the National Academy of Design, from which he moved on to the newly organized Beaux-Arts Institute of Design. The training in these schools was traditional, focusing on drawing and modeling the human figure and, in the case of sculpture, stressing the decoration of buildings and public monuments. For all the differences between his and academic sculpture, he always thought of sculpture basically in the traditional way: as monumental in form and function.

In 1924 Baizerman had a one-man show of his sculptures in London and from there traveled to Paris, where he remained until 1926. While there, he exhibited in the Salon des Indépendants and was drawn to Cubism or Cubisms, as invented by Pablo Picasso and Georges Braque about 1909–10. Although Cubism was interpreted in various ways, all Cubists agreed about the basics, namely, the importance of the plane, of negative as well as positive form, and of opening the form up to its surrounding space.

Back in New York City in 1926, Baizerman slowly put these ideas into practice, increasingly in sculptures made of large-scale hammered copper sheets. The copper sheet, to begin with, is a plane, which he freed from the wall and articulated in space. These hammered sheets were to be viewed from the back as well as from the front, which is to say, as negative as well as positive form. Attached to the sheets were rhythmically shaped steel bands intended to further articulate the forms in space. In question here are the sculptures from 1933 on. But from the evidence of *The Pastoral or Third Sculptural Symphony II*, begun shortly after the fire of 1931, those of the later 1920s would have been similarly conceived and executed, as can be seen in the forms and relations of this work.

The Pastoral or Third Sculptural Symphony II is one large plane covered with figures or partial figures, literally filling the plane from edge to edge. There is no story or narrative, there are no dramatic gestures or facial expressions—or faces—only forms placed in relation to one another on the planar surface. Some of these forms are fully volumetric, others partially so, still others flattened and reduced to planes, echoing and reinforcing the planar organization of the whole. Executed directly in plaster over many years, this work is not as consistently Cubist as the hammered coppers, but it is Cubist nevertheless. (One important difference is that it affords only a frontal view and not the front-to-back views of the copper sheets.)

Of course, this is only a partial explanation. For *The Pastoral or Third Sculptural Symphony II* does not look Cubist in the sense of Cubist sculptures by Picasso or his followers. The reason that it does not has to do with Baizerman's commitment to the human figure. To be sure, this is not the classical and anatomically correct figure of the academy, but it is the traditional figure that Cubists did their best to dismantle and remake as plane and form. Baizerman's project, then, involved combining the methods of Cubism with those of tradition to create a new type of sculpture, modern and traditional at the same time. While unusual, the project was not his alone. Other modern artists felt the traditional figure was too precious to be abandoned, and they made it the basis for their art. The standard-bearer of these "traditional modernists" in France was the enormously popular Pierre Puvis de Chavannes, whose American counterpart was Arthur B. Davies, a leading artist among the New York avant-garde and one of the organizers of the famous Armory Show of 1913 that introduced Americans to modern French painting and sculpture.

If the modern figure and Cubism were the sources on which Baizerman drew for *The Pastoral or Third Sculptural Symphony II*, it is a sculpture that is more than the sum of its parts. Baizerman channeled into his uniquely personal vision whatever he thought might strengthen it. *The Pastoral or Third Sculptural Symphony II* represents an early stage in the formation of that vision.

CG

The Pastoral or Third Sculptural Symphony II,
1933–57, cast 1971–73 at UNCG Foundry by Harold (Herk) Van Tongeren. Bronze relief, 96 × 120 × 11 in. Gift of Carl and Emma S. Avery Jeffress in memory of Edwin B. and Louise Adams Jeffress, 1973

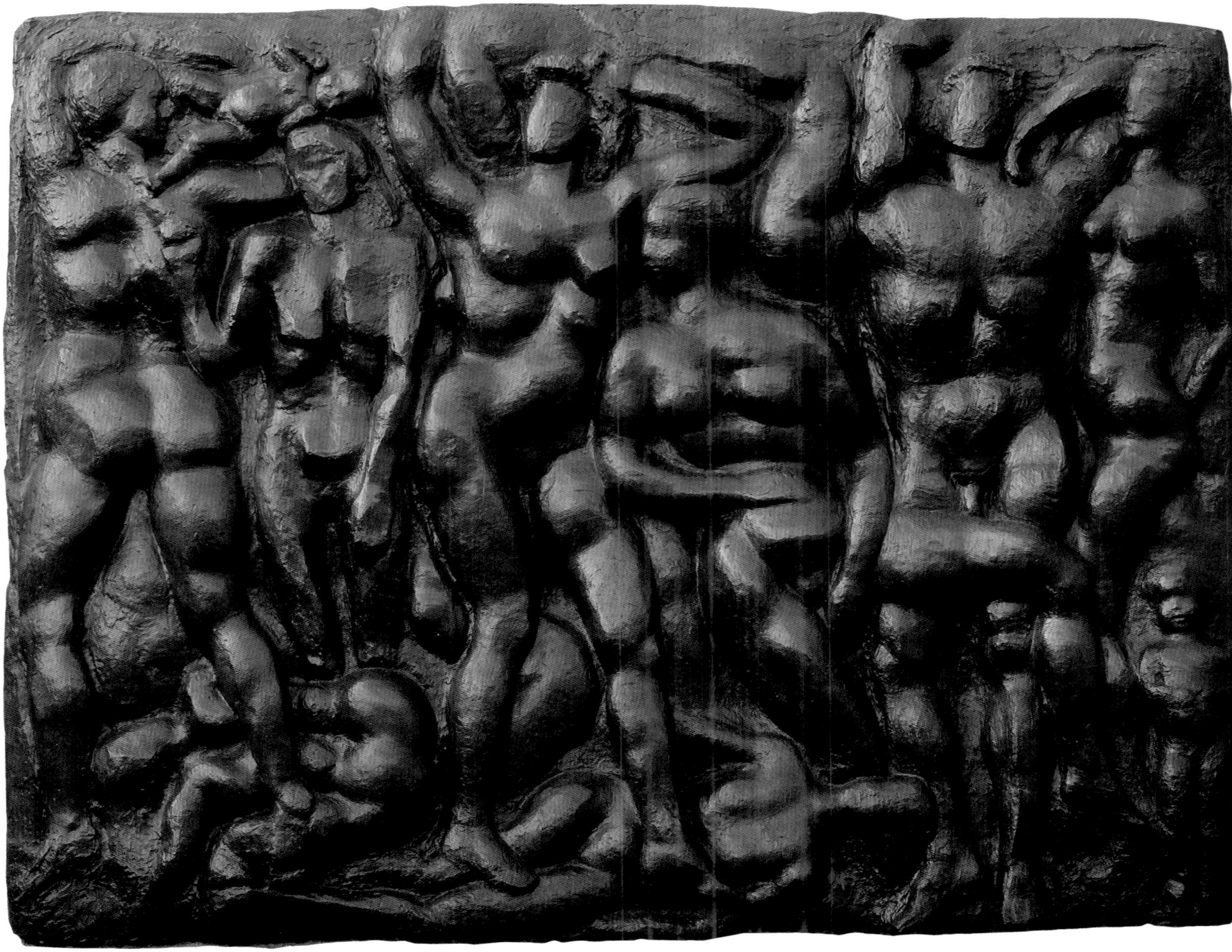

JACKSON POLLOCK American, 1912–1956

AT THE TIME JACKSON POLLOCK made this drawing, he was an unknown artist in his late twenties, violently alcoholic, desperately inarticulate, and in treatment with a Jungian analyst, Dr. Joseph Henderson. He was also an immensely ambitious, talented, and courageous painter on the threshold of a career that was to transform the visual language and conceptual underpinnings of modern art in the twentieth century. *Untitled* was one of sixty-nine drawings Pollock took to his weekly sessions over a period of months in 1939–40 to facilitate a therapeutic process threatened by the artist's inability to talk about himself or his feelings. The image is composed of sixteen (or eighteen, depending on how one groups them) symbolic motifs evenly distributed across the page.[1]

These archetypal forms, derived from ethnographic illustration and Surrealist invention, have no preconceived, programmatic meaning. They derive from the latent content of the artist's unconscious as mediated by his intense preoccupation with the European masters, Pablo Picasso chief among them.[2] A female head that appears psychically deranged (as in a dream) anchors the lower center of the page. Presenting simultaneously frontal and profile views in the manner of Synthetic Cubism, it is surrounded by an array of biomorphic and geometric forms set down according to the dictates of free association and the experimental promptings of a young artist looking for a subject to latch on to. Along the upper left edge, a crowned and circumcised phallus, demonstrating all the explicit crudity of bathroom-stall graffiti, is balanced across the page by a fetal, rabbitlike creature lying beneath an equivocal, two-eyed, hybrid abstraction adjoined to a juvenile rendition of a conical grid. The hermeneutic opacity and arbitrary juxtaposition of these motifs frustrate the expectation of referential specificity and narrative coherence that underlies the drive to interpret.

At the time Pollock made this drawing, he was busily engaged in assimilating a wide range of sources, ranging from African masks and Navajo sand painting to Surrealism and geometric abstraction. Yet it is the influence of Picasso's *Guernica*, which Pollock saw in New York in 1939, that holds sway as the aesthetic force to be assimilated and transformed in the course of getting these figures down on paper.

Compared with Pollock's signature drip paintings of the later 1940s and the archetypal symbolism of such Jungian works as *Moon Woman* (1942), *She-Wolf* (1943), and *Guardians of the Secret* (1943), the technique of this drawing appears conservative: Pollock seems to be "coloring in" with red, yellow, and blue pencil the hard-edged graphite contours demarcating forms derived from the recent history of art. *Untitled* constitutes a "before" by which to measure the achievement that was Pollock's discovery of automatic drawing and allover painting on a horizontal surface—practices that freed his hand and his mind from symbolic imagery, enabling him to create a new, prodigiously generative kind of picture.[3]

While this drawing, among others, helped to facilitate an analytic exchange with Dr. Henderson, it was conceived and executed, not as a therapeutic exercise, but as part of Pollock's practice as a professional artist. (This understanding was argued explicitly when Lee Krasner, Pollock's widow, contested the later sale of the drawings given to Henderson as a violation of doctor-patient confidentiality.) With hindsight and in light of Pollock's psychic unraveling under the pressures of celebrity and his homicidal-suicidal car crash in 1956, it can be argued that Pollock's Jungian therapy was more efficacious for his work than for his life in the world.[4] The self-contained and isolated forms presented in *Untitled* were to become transformed over the next decade, when Pollock worked his way toward increasingly abstract, improvisatory, allover compositions. These later works constitute his greatest achievement: the integration of drawing and painting, line and color, figure and ground, into a pictorial practice in which the artist's subjectivity was rendered spontaneously, intuitively, immediately present.

GD

Notes

1. The final total depends on whether one reads the upper right-hand corner as one composite image or three separate but contiguous figures.
2. Pollock once remarked, "The source of my painting is the unconscious." Claude Cernuschi, *Jackson Pollock: Meaning and Significance* (New York: Icon Editions, 1992), 74.
3. Bernice Rose, *Jackson Pollock: Drawing into Painting* (New York: Museum of Modern Art, 1980), 13.
4. Steven Naifeh and Gregory White Smith, *Jackson Pollock: An American Saga* (New York: C. N. Potter, 1989), 336.

Untitled, 1939–40. Graphite and colored pencil on paper, 12¾ × 10 in. Museum purchase with funds from a bequest by Hubert Humphrey and memorial gifts from his friends and Jacqueline Humphrey, 2005

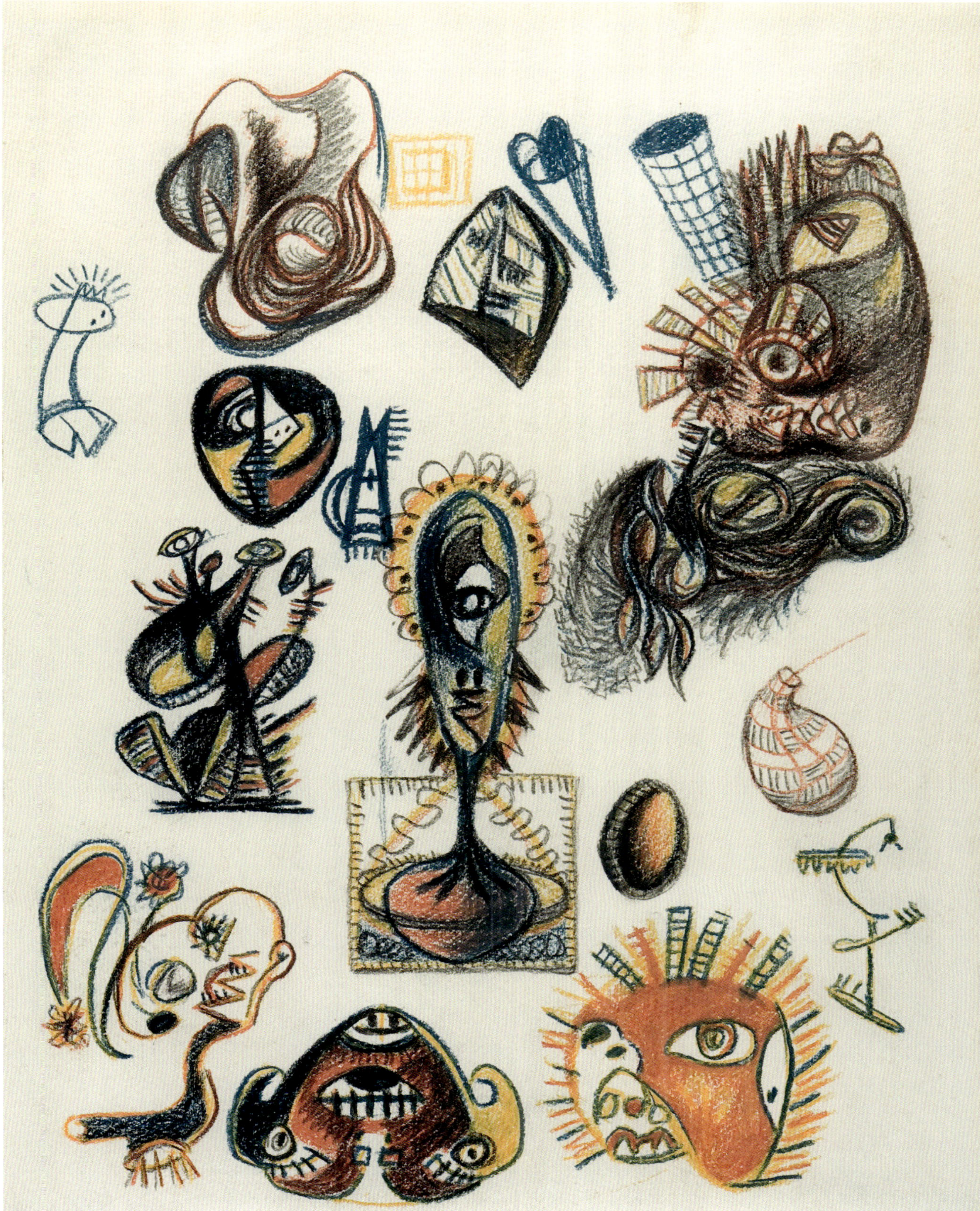

ILYA BOLOTOWSKY American, born Russia, 1907–1981

A CHARTER MEMBER of the American Abstract Artists, a group founded in New York City in 1936, Ilya Bolotowsky was a leading representative, along with Burgoyne Diller, Harry Holzman, and Fritz Glarner, of the type of geometric abstraction that originated with Russian Constructivism and Piet Mondrian's Neoplasticism and that flourished in the United States before the advent of Abstract Expressionism during the 1940s and 1950s. As a teacher at Black Mountain College near Asheville, North Carolina, from 1946 to 1948, together with Josef Albers, Bolotowsy was a formative influence on a generation of artists that came to maturity during the 1960s, among them Kenneth Noland.

Born in Petrograd, Russia (now St. Petersburg), in 1907, Bolotowsky came to this country in 1923 and, between 1924 and 1930, was a student at the National Academy of Design. The curriculum of the academy was organized around drawing from the live model, the dominant "modern" approach in New York Social Realism in the sense of the Ashcan School and American Scene painting. Neither the figure as such nor American styles in general made a lasting impression on Bolotowsky. During a trip to Paris in 1932, he came under the influence of Cubism, particularly Pablo Picasso's, and began to put what he had learned into practice as part of a group of abstract painters known as the Ten, which included Adolph Gottlieb and Mark Rothko. More important than all these early influences was that of Mondrian, especially when that artist was in New York City during the 1940s. At that time he was the single greatest influence on abstract artists, including Stuart Davis, Glarner, Diller, and many others.

Mondrian, a pioneer of geometric abstraction, was one of the founders of De Stijl (The Style) in Amsterdam in 1917. Idealist in approach, De Stijl was underpinned by a universalist philosophy that equated art with life itself. In this philosophy, the vertical line signifies the active, vitalistic principle of life, the horizontal line, tranquillity, rest, and ultimately death. Hence the conjunction of horizontal and vertical in the right angle expresses nothing less than the highest possible tension between positive and negative forces in the universe.

By 1920 Mondrian had reduced his means to the straight line, right angle, square, and rectangle, and the three primary colors of red, yellow, and blue—with white and black. His commitment to this reductive system never wavered. American abstractionists, even those most strongly influenced by Mondrian, however, tended to admit a greater range of geometric elements and a repertoire of strong, vibrant hues. All these qualifications can be found in Bolotowsky's works. Whereas Mondrian's color planes are flush with the surface of the painting, Bolotowsky's typically overlap and tilt back in space. The light intensity, or value of the colors, is so close, however, that the plane inevitably asserts itself, negating the space in a way consistent enough with Neoplasticism. All in all, Bolotowsy's art is freer and more improvisational than Mondrian's but is no less representative of a commitment to geometric abstraction.

Small Diamond is a characteristic work in Bolotowsky's abstract mode. A geometric abstraction in a diamond format (a square set on one corner), it consists of small and large squares, rectangles and triangles, in colors ranging from red, blue, and yellow to green, lavender, and others, arranged within a black grid. The diamond configured with a black grid was one of his recurrent formats; others were the more conventional rectangles and, at times, tondos and oddly shaped canvases.

Produced within the orbit of Neoplasticism, *Small Diamond* is indebted to Mondrian in clear and specific ways. The use of many small units consisting of two or more bands of color was suggested by Mondrian's works of the 1940s, particularly his *Broadway Boogie Woogie* and *Victory Boogie Woogie*, both of which in fact depart from Mondrian's earlier and more usual arrangements of only a few large color planes. In defiance of Mondrian's doctrinaire aesthetic, *Small Diamond* consists of a mix of large and small planes, including triangles, and a range of colors and hues that fly in the face of Mondrian's insistence on using only straight lines and right angles and the colors red, yellow, and blue. If these are departures from Mondrian, they fall well within the agreed-to parameters of Neoplasticism as interpreted by Mondrian's own De Stijl colleagues such as Theo van Doesburg and Georges Vantongerloo and by other members of the American Abstract Artists such as Glarner and Diller.

All the above artists accepted the same basic principles, all influenced by the dominant personality of Mondrian. All used these principles individually and creatively, yet none more so than Bolotowsky.

CG

Small Diamond, ca. 1945. Oil on canvas, 22½ × 22½ in. Museum purchase with funds from the Benefactors Fund, 1990

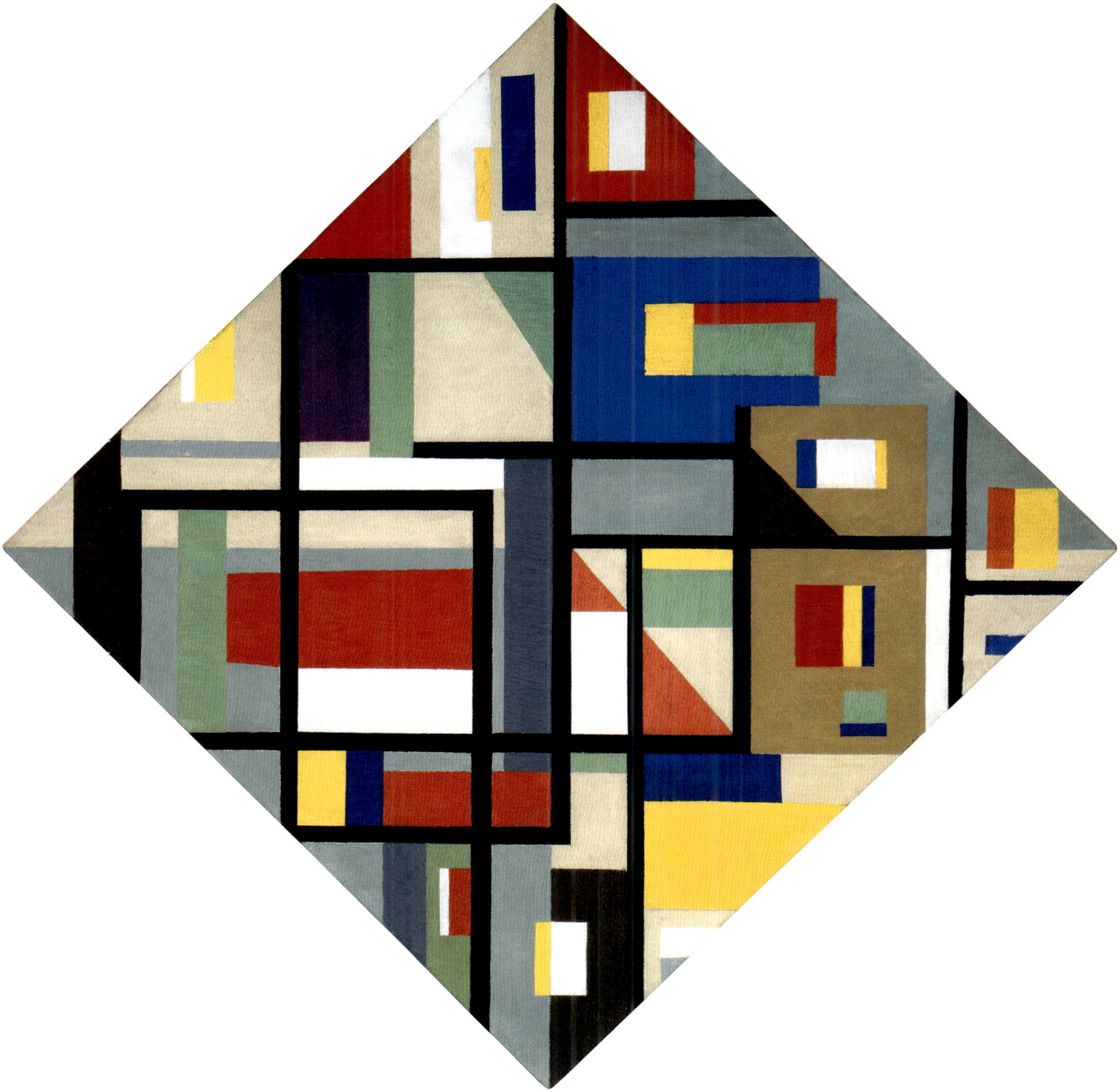

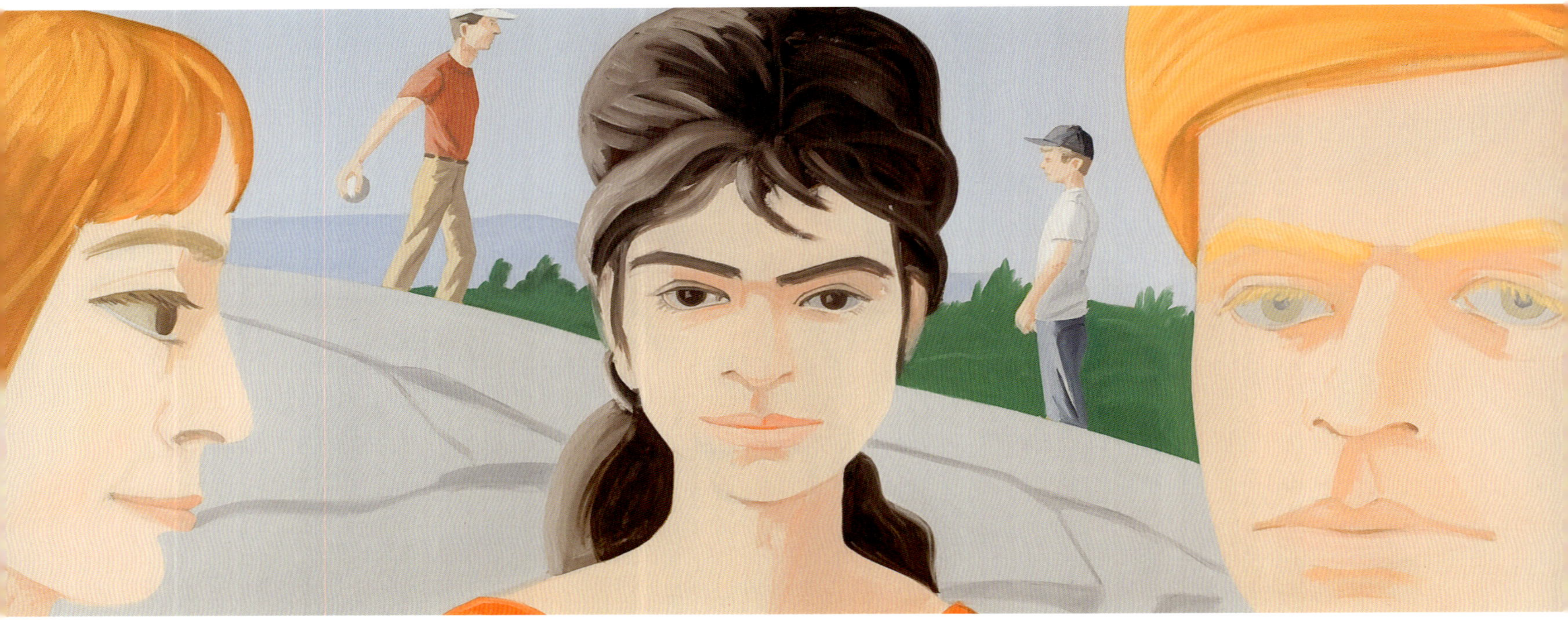

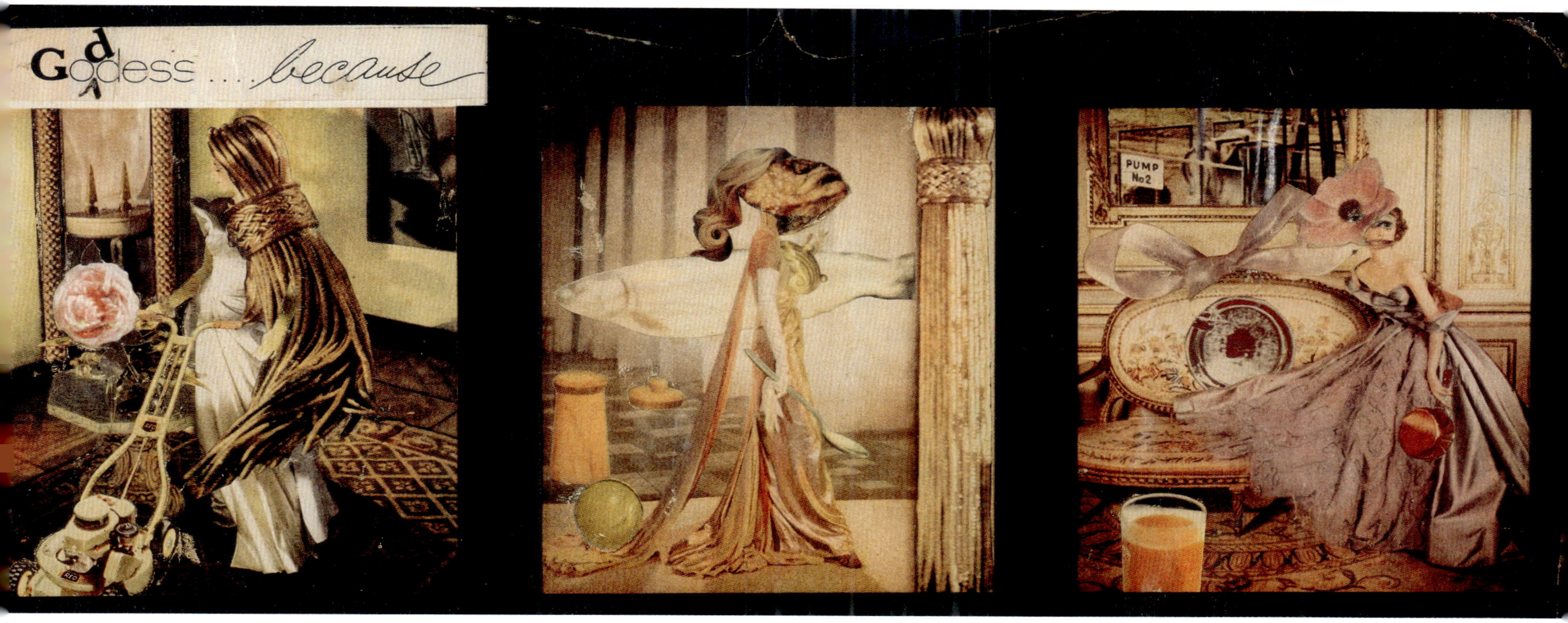

Selected Works: 1946–1969

ARSHILE GORKY American, born Turkish Armenia, 1904–1948

ARSHILE GORKY PLAYED an important role in turning New York City into the mecca of modern art. In tandem with the mysterious John Graham, he served as a mentor and guide to a generation of artists of the future New York School, most importantly such Abstract Expressionists as Willem de Kooning and Jackson Pollock. Though a hero of Abstract Expressionism, Gorky was not himself an Abstract Expressionist. Indeed, his work does not fall neatly into any one category. It was the result, rather, of a succession of dialogues with the works of leading French modernists, all contributing to the highly personal and original style recognizable as "Gorky."

Born in 1904 in Turkish Armenia and originally named Vosdanik Manoog Adoian, Gorky arrived in the United States in 1920 and adopted a new name combining the Russian form of the Greek hero Achilles with that of his literary hero, the celebrated Russian writer whose pen name was Maxim Gorky. Having re-created himself as a cultured individual, he set about creating Gorky the artist. He moved from Boston to New York City in 1926 and enrolled in the Grand Central School of Art, soon graduating from student to a member of the faculty. He also gave lessons in his studio, where his pupils included Ethel Schwabacher, Betty Parsons, Walter Murch, and Hans Burkhardt. Unlike other artist-teachers in New York, however, he rejected American Scene painting and Social Realism, looking instead to developments within European modernism.

Whereas American models dominated the New York art world, others were available, both through art magazines and a few radical art galleries such as Alfred Stieglitz's 291 and Katherine Dreier's Société Anonyme. The Museum of Modern Art opened in 1929 with an exhibition featuring works by Paul Cézanne, Paul Gauguin, Vincent van Gogh, and Georges Seurat. During the mid-to-late 1920s Gorky looked to Cézanne's paintings for an understanding of modern conceptions of space, form, and light. Later he turned to Pablo Picasso, whose many styles he emulated, from the Blue and Rose Periods to Synthetic Cubism, and, finally and ultimately, combining lessons learned from Picasso with the Surrealist strategies of Joan Miró and Matta. With its interest in automatism and preoccupation with psychoanalysis and the erotic, Surrealism, promoted by members of the group who took refuge in New York during the 1940s, made a lasting contribution to American art. In Gorky's case, Surrealism helped him break the habits he had acquired as a "student" of the modern masters. That the language he then developed was broadly Surrealist was never in doubt; the "pope" of Surrealism himself, André Breton, claimed Gorky for the movement. But nor was there any question about the works of the 1940s being original and deeply personal. Stimulated by Surrealism, Gorky came into his own.

An inveterate and superb draftsman called by his onetime student and later biographer Ethel Schwabacher "the Ingres of the unconscious," Gorky invariably explored and tested forms before introducing them into his paintings. He created these forms principally with line (color and shading were secondary). Surrealist automatism freed his line further, giving it an unusual mobility and spontaneity.

Untitled, a pencil and crayon drawing from Gorky's maturity, is such a work, filled with clusters of fanciful and spontaneously drawn shapes, suggested to the artist on his walks through the woods as he scrutinized the insides of flowers. Definite and yet ambiguous, the shapes hint at weeds and flower clusters, stamens and petals, a botanical garden strangely suggestive of human skeletons and internal organs. Drawn separately and as though independently, they nevertheless combine to make up a whole, distantly referring to nature but as a metaphor for the artist's inner life. In the paintings that followed, the vision would be clarified, the feelings further intensified.

The drawing at the Weatherspoon is one such study made in connection with some of Gorky's most important late works, especially *Diary of a Seducer* (1945), *The Plough and the Song* (1947), *Betrothal* (1946), and *Betrothal, II* (1947). Automatism is the basis of the drawing and the means of creating linear structures, which are then either reinforced or canceled out with shading to open up the space to a greater illusion of depth. Indebted in a general way to Matta, the drawing is original in its sheer audacity, something that Gorky would temper in full-size cartoons for the paintings. *Untitled*, representing an early stage in this preparatory process and exploring and testing shapes and forms to be clarified in these paintings, provides direct insight into an extraordinary sensibility at work.

Always committed to the old masters and, like them, carefully planning his paintings with studies such as *Untitled*, Gorky stands apart from the Abstract Expressionists with their stress on immediacy and spontaneity. Different, too, are the sketchbook and easel scale of his works, as opposed to the monumental scale of Abstract Expressionism. If not as radical as some of the works of the Abstract Expressionists, drawings such as *Untitled* are right at home alongside those by de Kooning, Pollock, or Philip Guston.

CG

Untitled, 1946–47. Graphite and crayon on paper, 20 × 13 in. Museum purchase with funds from the Dillard Paper Company for the Dillard Collection, 1967

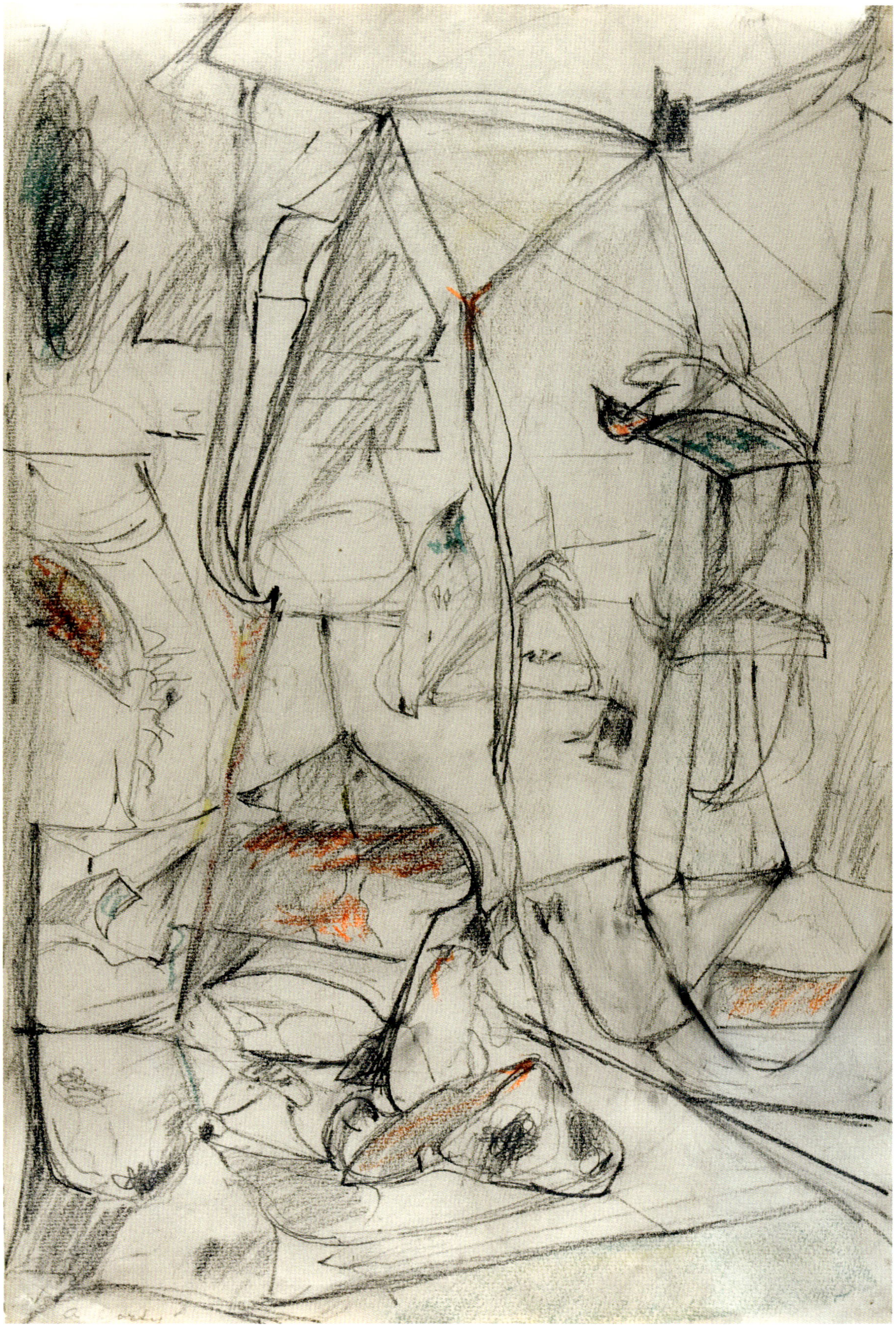

ELAINE DE KOONING American, 1918–1989

AFTER NEARLY SIXTY YEARS, Elaine de Kooning's *Untitled (Black Mountain Painting)* returned to North Carolina. Probably created during a two-month period in the summer of 1948, it is most likely part of a series de Kooning completed while in Asheville with her husband, Willem de Kooning. Willem taught at Black Mountain College while Elaine made a group of bold, biomorphic works on paper in her studio. "Despite all of the unaccustomed student and social activity, I still managed to come away with a roll of enamel paintings on wrapping paper—a testimonial to the durability of paint, if nothing more," de Kooning later recalled.[1] Although the dire financial straits of the couple compelled de Kooning to use paper rather than canvas as a support, the making of series of paintings would become part of her trademark method.[2]

The discovery of Elaine de Kooning's Black Mountain series in the late 1980s, rolled up in her basement, was a critical art-historical find; it allowed her to be more accurately considered within the context of Abstract Expressionism.[3] The Black Mountain works clearly document the interests of this group of New York artists while demonstrating de Kooning's shift away from the more representational mode of her earlier portraits, cityscapes, and still lifes. Indeed, *Untitled (Black Mountain Painting)*, like others in the series, records de Kooning's experimentation with positive and negative space, color, and form. However, here, more so than in other Black Mountain pictures, the comparatively expansive background creates the impression of a fractured stained-glass window rather than a complicated tangle of organic and geometric forms.

De Kooning's application of paint in the example at the Weatherspoon reveals her further investigation of the physical properties of the material and its expressive, gestural possibilities. In some areas the paint is built up, layer over layer, creating thick passages, while in an adjacent form the paint is thinned to a glaze, enabling the paper to become a visible element of the work. Brushstrokes, apparent throughout, enliven the surface, while the calligraphic black outlines describing the boundaries of her abstract forms further emphasize the hand of the artist. Another reminder of her creative presence is to be found along the extreme edges of the paper, now affixed to canvas, where the paint at times recedes from the boundaries of the support, exposing but also incorporating it into the composition. Like the rest of the series, *Untitled (Black Mountain Painting)* also preserves the physical evidence of de Kooning's process in each of its four corners, where the paper was repeatedly pinned to and unpinned from the wall of her studio, as she painted and evaluated her progress.

Despite its undoubted affinity to the other works of the series, *Untitled (Black Mountain Painting)* is unique among the North Carolina group in a few notable ways. First, it was not among the paintings discovered in the 1980s, since at that time it was owned by a private California collector who received it as a gift from the artist probably sometime in the early 1950s.[4] As such, it does not bear a numeric designation within its title like the seventeen works found among de Kooning's belongings. Second, the painting at the Weatherspoon is executed in oil on paper, while the others were done in enamel, as described above by the artist. Despite these singular qualities, it fits easily within the size parameters of the others, which range from approximately 13 by 16 inches to 32 by 44 inches. Before the Weatherspoon work was publicly known, the previously discovered Black Mountain paintings were exhibited in New York City for the first time at the Washburn Gallery in 1991, when most were sold to museums and collectors. One of the largest of the series, *Untitled #15*, was purchased for the Museum of Modern Art, New York.

Not only is *Untitled (Black Mountain Painting)* an important record of the early explorations of a young artist who would become one of the most significant female painters, critics, and educators of twentieth-century America, but it also prompts a multilayered dialogue with another Abstract Expressionist work in the Weatherspoon's collection: *Woman*, which was painted a year later by her husband.

HH

Notes

1. *Elaine de Kooning: Black Mountain Paintings from 1948* (New York: Washburn Gallery, 1991), 5, citing Elaine de Kooning, "de Kooning Memories," *Vogue*, December 1983, 352–53, 393–94.
2. Lisa Mintz Messinger, "Elaine de Kooning, 'Untitled, Number 15,'" in *Abstract Expressionism: Works on Paper; Selections from the Metropolitan Museum of Art* (New York: Metropolitan Museum of Art, 1992), 14–16.
3. Ibid., 13.
4. Weatherspoon Art Museum object file.

Untitled (Black Mountain Painting), 1948. Oil on paper mounted on canvas, 13¾ × 16¾ in. Museum purchase with funds from the Louise D. and Herbert S. Falk Acquisition Endowment and the Lynn Richardson Prickett Acquisition Endowment, 2007

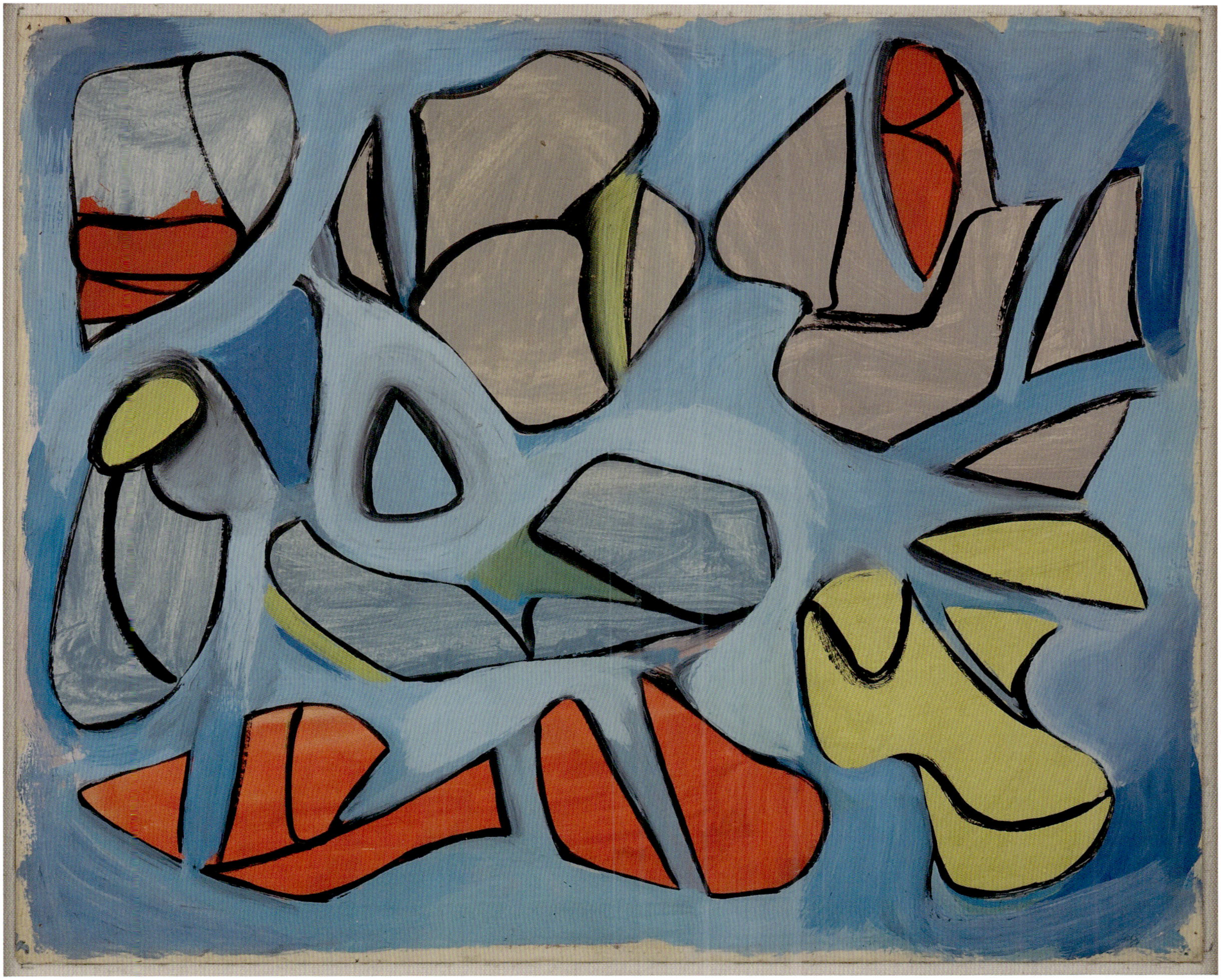

WILLEM DE KOONING American, born the Netherlands, 1904–1997

WILLEM DE KOONING'S abiding commitment to the possibilities of paint in service of a relatively narrow range of subjects—primarily the female form and landscape, with excursions into pure abstraction—has assured his place as one of the greatest artists of the twentieth century. Born and raised in Rotterdam, he apprenticed at age twelve with a commercial art and decorating firm and later worked for the art director of a department store. He concurrently studied in both the fine arts and guild craft traditions in evening classes at Rotterdam's art academy. After immigrating to the United States in 1926, he worked as a housepainter in New Jersey and made his way in 1927 to New York, a city with which he closely identified; he remained there until moving in 1963 to East Hampton.

In New York, de Kooning quickly made friends with other avant-garde artists there: John Graham, Arshile Gorky, and Stuart Davis. He joined the Artist's Union in 1934 and was assigned to the Mural Division of the Works Progress Administration Federal Art Project in 1935. By the time of his marriage in 1943 to fellow painter Elaine Fried, he had become closely associated with other pioneer Abstract Expressionists, among them David Smith, Clyfford Still, and Jackson Pollock. De Kooning has always been regarded as a "painter's painter." His love for the medium expressed itself again and again, and he spoke of his physical and emotional connection to it. "I get the paint right on the surface. Nobody else can do that."[1]

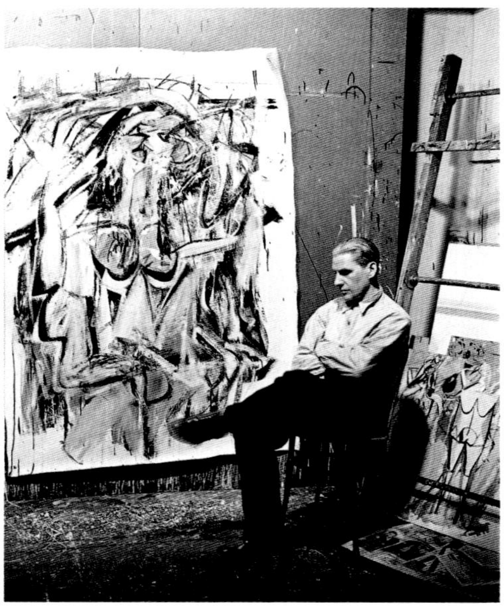

Toward the end of the 1930s, de Kooning produced a first series of paintings of women, which he continued even as he began to create nonrepresentational abstractions. In the late 1940s he incorporated the freedom of pure abstraction into a second round of paintings of the female form that led to his six renowned Woman canvases. The first major extant painting from this precursory group dates from 1948 and depicts a woman gazing at a star in the upper left corner of the composition. The figure seems wrested from an emotional encounter with paint; its aggressive brushwork and figural distortion inspired several related works that include *Woman* of 1949–50.

The Weatherspoon's is the last and largest of the artist's paintings of women of this period; it is also the most abstract. Like the 1948 figure, this one looks upward, and her teeth similarly are visible within her gaping mouth. De Kooning likened these women to Mesopotamian idols, "looking to the sky with this smile, like they were just astonished about the forces of nature, you feel."[2] In this painting, however, the head shows a strongly Cubist influence in that a zigzag black line creates a profile against the full face; this decisive gesture is repeated throughout the image. Figure and ground are completely intertwined, and every inch of the canvas is treated with a high-pitched intensity. Above and behind the seated figure appear three window-like forms, a reference perhaps to the urbanscape of de Kooning's studio at the time.

The photograph below, taken by Harry Bowden in January 1950, shows the Weatherspoon's *Woman* unstretched and tacked to the wall in the artist's studio. The painting was first shown in 1951 in a cooperative exhibition spearheaded by Leo Castelli that came to be known as "The Ninth Street Show" for its eponymous location in a rented storefront there. This was essentially an exhibition about contemporary abstraction, but de Kooning chose to display *Woman* in response to the prevailing taboo of the figure. In fact, the work was exhibited again that year in the Whitney Annual as *Figure*, a title apparently given the work by de Kooning's dealer at the time, Egan Gallery. An undated label from the Sidney Janis Gallery has the term *Figure* scratched out and the title *Woman* written in.

Woman was both a prescient acquisition by the Weatherspoon in 1954 and a pivotal work in de Kooning's oeuvre. It linked the surviving Woman paintings of the early and mid-1940s, which were moving toward abstraction but still distinguished figure from ground, and the six major ones exhibited in 1953 at Sidney Janis Gallery. In the later works, the still discernible but greatly abstracted females are integrated into the entirety of the painted field through the artist's aggressive and expressive brushstrokes. Bridging these two bodies of Woman paintings, the Weatherspoon's work holds a key position in the artist's long and illustrious career.

NMD

Notes

1. Quoted in David Sylvester, *About Modern Art* (1997; New York: Henry Holt, 2002), 334.
2. From an interview with de Kooning by David Sylvester in *Interviews with American Artists* (New Haven: Yale University Press, 2001), 51.

Woman, 1949–50. Oil on canvas, 63¾ × 46 in. Lena Kernodle McDuffie memorial purchase, 1954

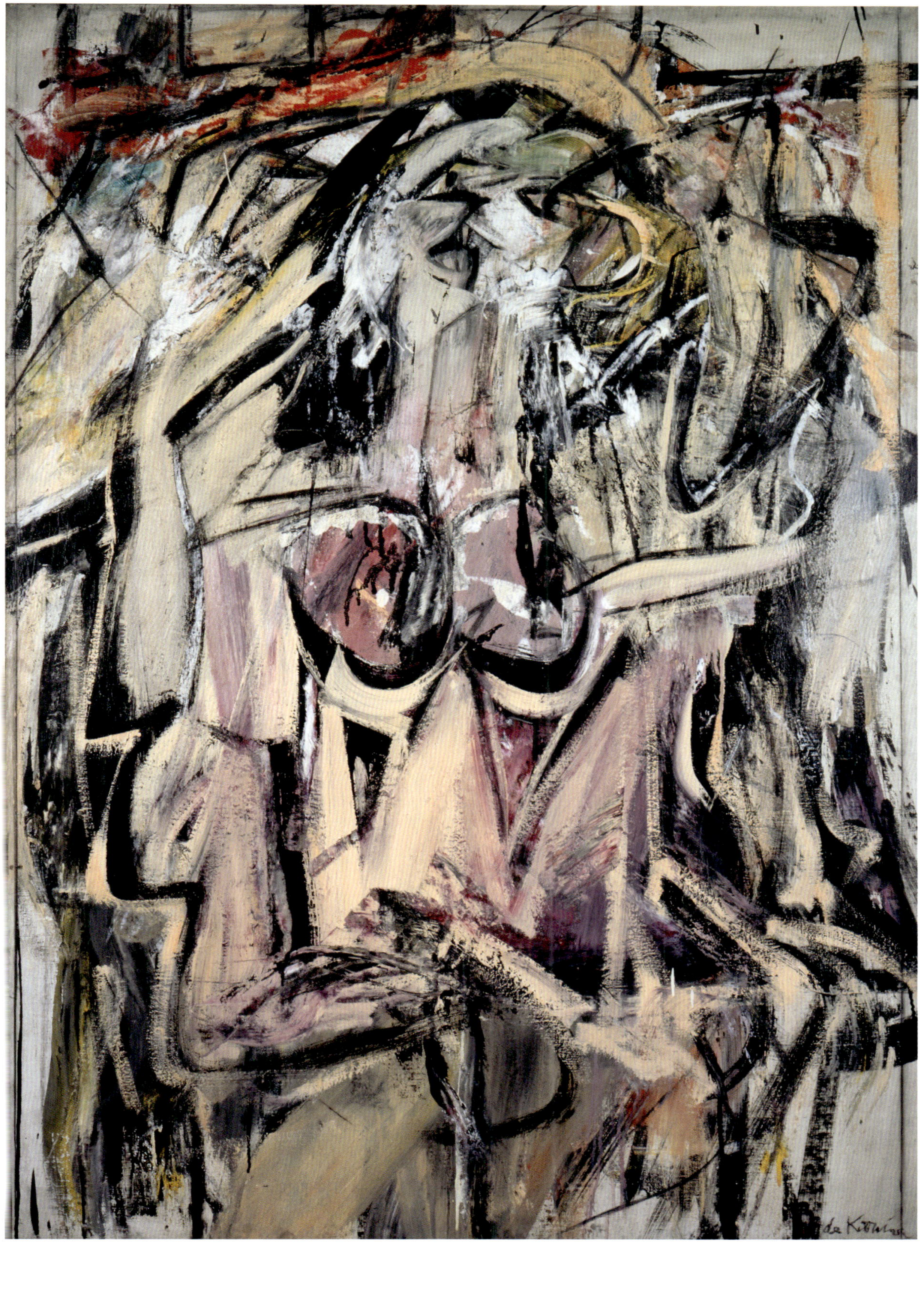

ALEXANDER CALDER American, 1898–1976

HOW CAN A WORK SO APPARENTLY delicate and visually fragile embody such a massive redefinition of the limits of art? Millennia ago, when the artists put down their tools in the cave of Lascaux, bison thundered across the walls and ceilings. In the third century B.C.E., the Winged Victory of Samothrace flew earthward, alighting on the prow of a Greek ship. Umberto Boccioni's 1913 sculpture *Unique Forms of Continuity in Space* surges forward; its fragmented abstract shapes morph into focus and then dissolve. Except they don't. They don't move at all. Not one of them.

These notable works from the long history of art are examples of motion as an element completely governed by appearance, representation, and illusion. They are exceptions only for their fame, for in their methods they join countless other artifacts, united by the tradition of how art was made, how motion was depicted. Such was the rule until the 1920s and '30s, when a few innovative artists, Alexander Calder foremost among them, brought a practical, Machine-Age literalness to the problem by creating works that actually moved. Showing was supplanted by being. At a stroke, history closed and the future opened, revealing a vision wherein art matched modern society: highly mobile, ever changing, and propelled by the progression of flight and time. The salient feature of the new genre was recognized in the name *kinetic art*.

Calder quickly developed from his earliest mechanical explorations to the solution we see in *Yellow Sail*. Geometric and biomorphic abstract shapes are flexibly tethered in fluid suspension and perfect balance. The slightest movement of air from the building's ventilation system, the unseen breeze from displacement by a passing body, the kiss of the viewer's breath, any one or all of these can bring the work to life. A slight shiver, and then segments of the work gracefully retreat while other constellations of shapes move toward the viewer. His fellow artists celebrated Calder's triumph over stasis, and it was Marcel Duchamp who awarded the new species their name, *mobiles*.[1]

Calder clarified the significance of his break from the imprisoning tradition of representation into a liberating existence. He said, "My purpose is to make something like a dog, or like flames; something that has a life of its own."[2] How interesting that Calder would choose two things that we might think quite unrelated but that are in fact joined by their living propensity for unpredictable movement. As the artist and then the viewer relinquish control of the visual experience, the object asserts its autonomy. Calder has realized the famous prayer of the ancient sculptor Pygmalion, that his sculpture come to life. Because of Calder's own understanding of having created a living thing, he termed himself a realist.[3]

Motion incorporates the element of time. As the mobile takes its journey, time is enlisted in the acts of revelation and absorption. As movement continues, the elements of the mobile—their shapes, colors, and positions—realign, and new, never to be repeated compositions emerge, register, and evolve into the future—a state of being as one of becoming. Jacques Prévert noted this crucial fact of Calder's art when he called him the "Sculptor of time."[4]

Duchamp, Jean Arp, Joan Miró, Fernand Léger, Amédée Ozenfant, and Jean-Paul Sartre—giants of European modernism—were colleagues and close friends of the artist. Calder recalled that seeing paintings in Piet Mondrian's studio started him thinking seriously about abstraction as the guiding aesthetic for his own work.[5] However, even with the tidal pull of such formidable Continental talents, in their judgment, Calder remained an essentially American artist. As Léger succinctly put it, "He is 100-percent American / Satie and Duchamp are 100-percent French / Where do they meet?"[6] They met in their shared beliefs in the newly emancipated universal properties of abstraction: form, color, line, space, movement, chance, and time. Like the shapes of *Yellow Sail*, the colors are elemental: black, white, red, blue, and yellow. Abstraction could uphold a chaste virtue of pure design, and it might also, and frequently does in Calder's work, carry a charge of recognition. In *Yellow Sail* the eponymous color and shape/function signal its importance as the sole vertical element. Shape and title make overtures to maritime associations, a recurring theme in Calder's work.

Calder and his European circle diverged in ways that pointed to their cultural origins. Calder's sense of play, subversive antiauthoritarianism, and sheer vibrant physicality embodied American energy and the ceaseless, restless activity that seduced the European modernists into their infatuation with New York City. Calder comfortably inhabited the worlds on both sides of the Atlantic: studios, exhibitions, commissions, themes, titles of works, and close, enduring friendships provided the structure that bridged the division.

RG

Notes

1. Carmen Giménez and Alexander S. C. Rower, *Calder* (London: Phaidon Press, 2004), 88. This extraordinarily comprehensive source provided the information for the present discussion.
2. Quoted in ibid., 87.
3. Ibid., 89.
4. Quoted in ibid., 75.
5. Ibid., 57.
6. Ibid., 65.

Yellow Sail, 1950. Painted metal and wire, 30 × 84 in. Museum purchase, 1951

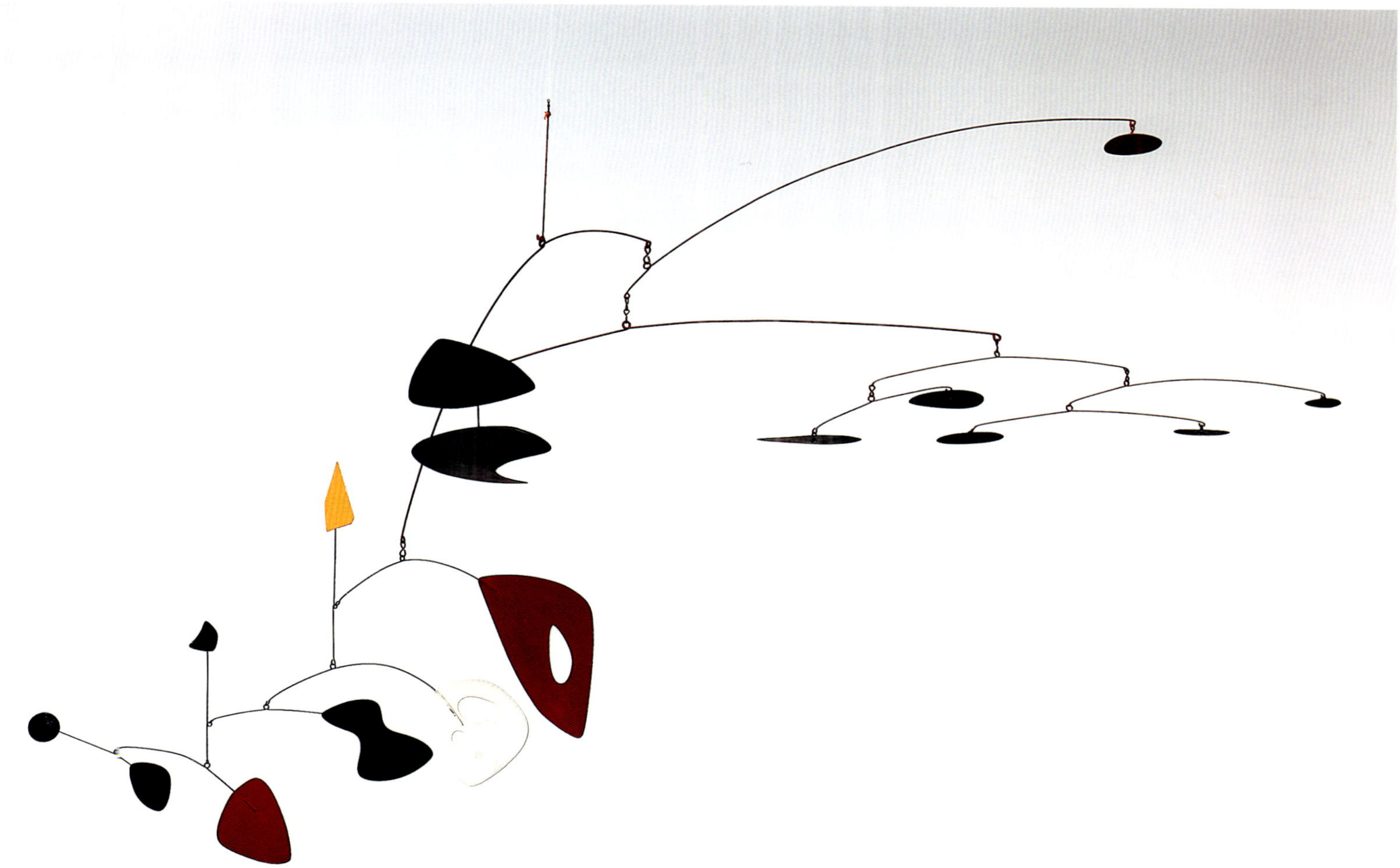

ELIZABETH CATLETT Mexican, born U.S.A., 1915

ELIZABETH CATLETT'S *Sharecropper*, one of her best-known prints, is also one of the great heroic portrait heads in American art. A radiant brown face gazes pensively into the distance. She is a woman of African heritage from the American South: tall, rail thin, dirt poor, and indomitable. *Sharecropper* is a powerful word invoking a history of suffering and exploitation. It denotes a farm laborer who tills the soil in return for only a portion (usually half) of the crop. The remainder goes to the landowner, who is almost always white. A system that perpetuated the exploitation of African American labor in the South, sharecropping is closely tied to the history of slavery and black disenfranchisement following Reconstruction. In response to this legacy, Catlett, a black woman and artist who came of age in the 1930s and '40s under the influence of the Harlem Renaissance, pays homage to her forebear. We gaze upward at her troubled features as if on bended knee, bearing witness to her enduring presence as an ennobled survivor of America's caste system and the Great Depression.

The print embodies Catlett's philosophy of art as social commitment:

> *Art can't be the exclusive domain of the elect. It has to belong to everyone. Otherwise it will continue to divide the privileged from the underprivileged. . . . Artists should work to the end that love, peace, justice, and equal opportunity prevail all over the world; to the end that all people take joy in full participation in the rich material, intellectual, and spiritual resources of this world's lands, peoples, and goods.*[1]

In 1952 Catlett was thirty-seven, highly educated, and technically proficient in both printmaking and sculpture. She had created for herself an expressive realist style in keeping with leftist traditions of politicized printmaking in which figurative drama and the ethical imperative of popular resistance take precedence over the formalist concerns of modernist abstraction. The granddaughter of a woman whose stories of enslavement were a treasured family legacy, Catlett was committed to giving eloquent visual testimony to the sufferings, resiliency, and perseverance of African American women at a time when such overtly political work was rare and courageous.

Growing up in a middle-class, professional household in Washington, D.C. (her father and mother were both educators), she graduated from that city's Dunbar High School and Howard University, where she studied design, printmaking, and drawing. From the 1940s on, Catlett lived and worked amid socially progressive communities made up of fellow artists, performers, intellectuals, and activists, first in Chicago and New York and then in Mexico, where she was to settle, raise a family, and become a citizen. Retiring from teaching in 1975, she continues to be active in the art community of Cuernavaca, Morelos.

Although *Sharecropper* was initially printed in black and white, the Weatherspoon's version has the distinction of being one of a small number of proofs made in 1952 that includes a rich red-brown coloring for the face. It was produced in Mexico City at the Taller de Grafica Popular (Popular Graphic Arts Workshop), an artists' collective dedicated to producing artwork in the service of social change. Both Catlett and her husband, the Mexican artist Francisco Mora, were members until 1966.

Printmaking is an inherently populist medium, given that it produces multiple copies from a single plate. In terms of price and circulation, a print stands in marked contrast to a drawing or painting, those one-of-a-kind luxury items steeped in the aura of originality affordable only by the wealthy elite. *Sharecropper* is one of Catlett's most celebrated linocuts, a medium closely akin to the woodcut but providing a less resistant, cheaper, and more uniform carving surface. The print's meticulous and subtly varied hatchings reveal the artist's technical virtuosity and graphic sophistication in the delineation of the sharecropper's sharply chiseled features, her frizzy white hair, floppy straw hat, and overcoat. The stark rendition of a large safety pin in place of a missing button signals the hardscrabble scarcity that is the defining condition of her material life.

Sharecropper is a characteristic work, one in a long series made over the artist's seventy-year career, that bears witness, in emotionally powerful, graphically compelling form, to Catlett's ongoing championship of working-class black women, who, with immense dignity, integrity, and resiliency, confront a world plagued by hardship and injustice.

GD

Note

1. Melanie Herzog, *Elizabeth Catlett: In the Image of the People* (Chicago: Art Institute of Chicago, 2005), 29.

Sharecropper, 1952. Hand-colored linoleum block print on paper, 25½ × 21½ in. Museum purchase with funds from the Laura Weill Cone Acquisition Endowment, 2004

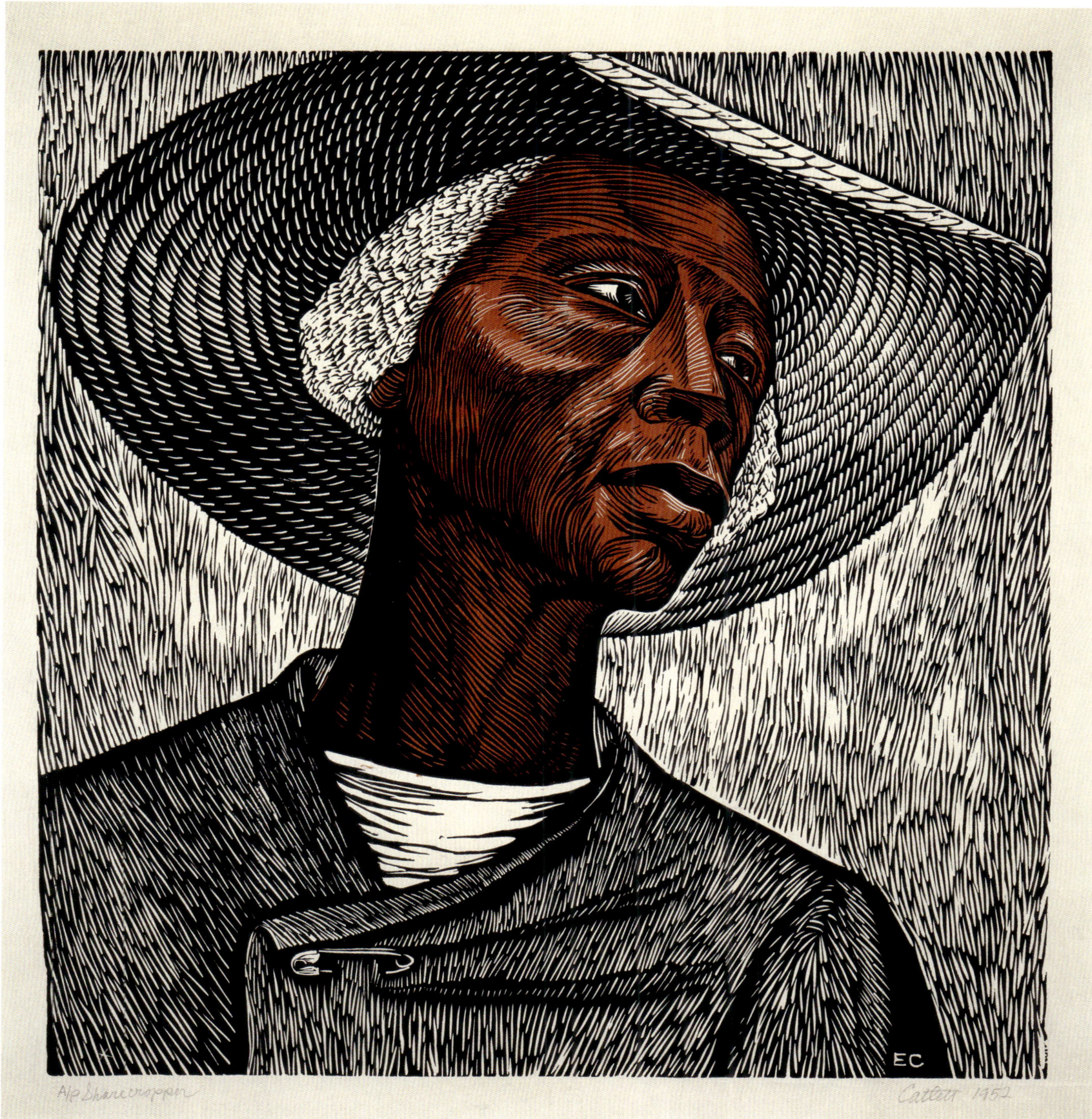
EC
A/P Sharecropper
Catlett 1952

LOUISE BOURGEOIS American, born France, 1911–2010

THROUGHOUT HER HIGHLY DISTINGUISHED and prolific career spanning several generations, Louise Bourgeois fashioned a body of provocative work that confirmed her position as one of the most important artists of our time. Through sculpture, drawings, prints, and installations, she probed the inner reaches of emotional and psychological expression. The symbolic character of her work derived from her personal history but expanded into themes and motifs of universal resonance.

Bourgeois was born to a family of weavers and spent her childhood years along the Bièvre River near Paris, where her parents operated an atelier for restoring and selling tapestries. She recalled watching as skeins of dyed wool were fixed by submersion into the river's cold water and as tapestries were taken off their frames to be washed there. Both operations involved wringing and twisting, visual motifs that appeared early in Bourgeois's work such as *Drawing No. 1*. The artist's drawing skills were recognized by the time she was twelve, when she began to prepare cartoons for missing sections of tapestries. Drawing was always an important part of Bourgeois's oeuvre both as a technique well suited to putting form to psychic expression and also as a journalistic record of particular times and events.

Like other drawings from the early 1950s, the Weatherspoon's sheet shows a complex network of lines that gather and disperse across the limits of the page, with an empty space near the lower right corner. This area serves as a visual escape from the intensity of marks in the rest of the drawing; it may also have been a psychological escape for the artist from the deeply rooted childhood memories that inspired the work. The clusters of line are both semi-literal references to the threads used in restoring tapestries and metaphorical suggestions of hair, waves, and nets.

Louise Bourgeois trained at the Sorbonne, the École des Beaux-Arts, and other art academies in Paris. As a student and practicing artist, she became familiar with Surrealism, overtones of which are notable in early paintings of the 1930s and 1940s. In 1938 she married the American art historian Robert Goldwater and moved to New York, where she studied at the Art Students League with Vaclav Vytlacil (another artist represented in the Weatherspoon's collection). Given her status today, it is hard to believe that a major retrospective exhibition of Bourgeois's work at the Museum of Modern Art in 1982 was the first ever accorded a woman artist. Occupying several floors of the museum with hundreds of artworks, the show was a revelation to the art world. For the first time, viewers could witness the incredible breadth, power, and resonance of her singularly inventive work.

NMD

Drawing No. 1, 1953. Ink on paper, 11 × 14 in. Museum purchase with funds from the Dillard Paper Company for the Dillard Collection, 1973

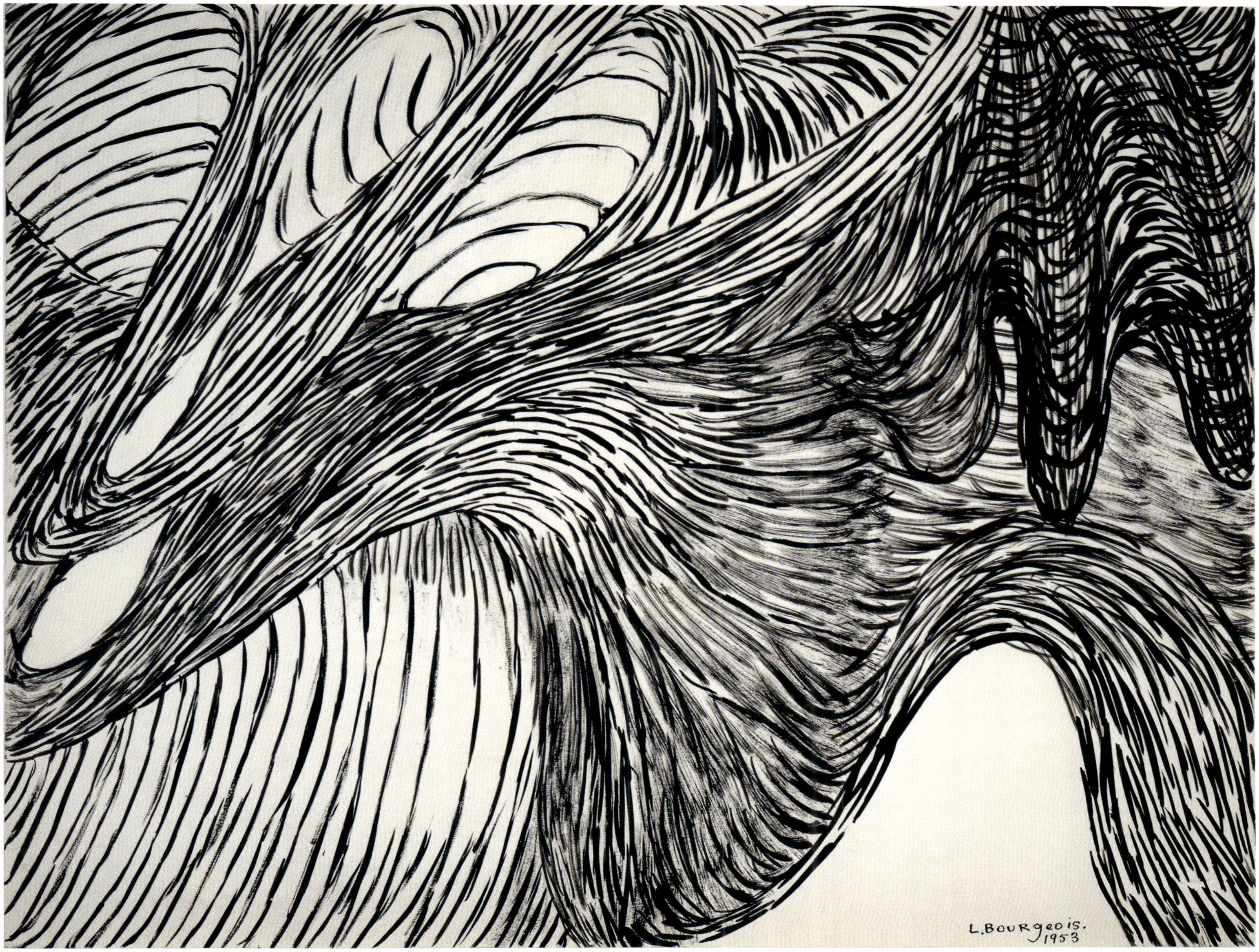
L. BOURGEOIS.
1953

RICHARD STANKIEWICZ American, 1922–1983

[To strike] some taut chord buried below the muck—somehow, no matter how sluggishly, [to] suggest the life in being.

—Richard Stankiewicz[1]

RICHARD STANKIEWICZ'S *Family Portrait* inhabits modernism fully even while it displays the lineaments of an alternative, dissenting art practice just coming into being in 1954. Three terms are often used to locate Stankiewicz's work within the history of art: *assemblage*, *junk art*, and *Neo-Dada*. Such designations are helpful up to a point in giving context to various features of the work: the way cast-off machine parts of rusted iron and steel are conjoined with the remains of various domestic artifacts to constitute a third entity, completely new and spontaneously energized.

In most ways Stankiewicz remained faithful to the tenets and working methods of Abstract Expressionism. From the shards of an American industrial wasteland, the sculptor welded together an open, columnar, rectangular structure in which each discarded machine part is exquisitely, idiosyncratically interrelated to every other in the creation of a balanced whole. *Family Portrait* rises phoenixlike from the junk pile, a radically autonomous pictorial construct. Its achievement is to transcend both function and entropy, giving new and unexpected life to disparate forms.

But *Family Portrait* also points the way out from under the overbearing weight of the New York School consensus of how to make art and what to think about it. Stankiewicz's work shares some of the irreverence and iconoclasm of Jasper Johns's *Flag* and Robert Rauschenberg's *Erased de Kooning Drawing*, two works made at the same time that debunked spontaneous mark-making as the material embodiment of authentic being. Stankiewicz's sculpture has a mordant irony and self-deprecating wit that undercut the philosophical earnestness and humanist grandiloquence of the first-generation Abstract Expressionists.

Family Portrait, for all its elegance, is too funky and whimsical to be taken completely seriously. Its title virtually begs for an anthropomorphic reading even while its wayward forms defy coherent legibility. Yet when taken together with such works as *Two (Potato Eaters)* (1953), *The Bride* (1955), *The Wedding Cart* (1954), *Railroad Urchin* (1959), and *Middle-Aged Couple* (1954), it can be seen to be a rueful meditation on the American family romance. The artist, of Polish Catholic origins, understood himself to have been "from the wrong side of the tracks." A railroad accident caused his father's death before Richard was three. His mother was, in the words of her artist son, "a marrying fool." She went on to have "at least five husbands."[2] Each one, according to family lore, treated her worse than his predecessor. To this must be added the physical violence the artist experienced as a young boy growing up in Detroit at the hands of the man whom his mother married within two years of his father's death. Finally, there was his bohemian disregard for the values of nuclear family life in America at the height of the cold war. In light of this familial and cultural history, *Family Portrait* becomes something of a dysfunctional chimera, a sardonic send-up of American middle-class pieties as chronicled in Norman Rockwell's iconic covers for the *Saturday Evening Post*.[3]

From certain angles, the anthropomorphism of this work is intense. The rusted refuse Stankiewicz transformed into sculpture, he once said, was "us: made, used and discarded."[4] Take, for example, the childlike figure with two nine-inch screw bolts for legs (crossing at the "knees") and a perforated circular metal disk and canister for a "head." The creature "clings" with four "fingers" and a "thumb" to a potbellied "mother" composed of a circular boiler drum from which protrudes a tapering steel wedge with a cyclopean eye drilled through its center. In the fashion of a Picasso found object or a Duchampian readymade, Stankiewicz makes brilliant use of a partially crushed toilet float. Once designed to regulate the level of water in the tank and still bearing an embossed R surrounded by the words *Federal Patented*, it now balances precariously and hilariously on a tiny pedestal of solder at the very base of the assemblage. Its days of ensuring that anything, even itself, can stay afloat, are long since past.

Once the play of figurative allusion begins, it becomes hard to know where to stop. Does the rectangular heating unit from an old gas oven compose the outlines of a family cat or television set—or both? This kind of question betrays the delicacy and finesse of the balancing act that Stankiewicz performs between abstraction and figuration. No element in its transposition from the scrap heap to the gallery pedestal ever gives up its identity as a moribund fragment from a utilitarian past. Nor do the figurative elements ever overbalance the rigorous juxtaposition of abstract shapes.

The rust that envelops *Family Portrait* connotes dissolution and decrepitude, in addition to suggesting the final triumph of entropy in the larger scheme of things. But it also provides the work with a warm, unifying color and a subtly textured surface that gently modulate the light reflecting off its many planes. The toilet float, in all its abject desuetude, along with the other discarded metal fragments that compose this work, have been released from the constraints of functionality and the humiliations of obsolescence. They are arranged now, under the hands of a maestro with an acetylene torch, in harmony with the spheres.

GD

Notes

1. Emmie Donadio, *Miracle in the Scrap Heap: The Sculpture of Richard Stankiewicz* (Andover, MA: Addison Gallery of American Art, Phillips Academy, 2003), 46.
2. Ibid., 13.
3. Ibid., 51 nn. 8, 20.
4. Ibid., 50.

Family Portrait, 1954. Steel, iron, and found objects, 37 × 15 × 21 in. Museum purchase in memory of Cordelia Penn Cannon, 1994

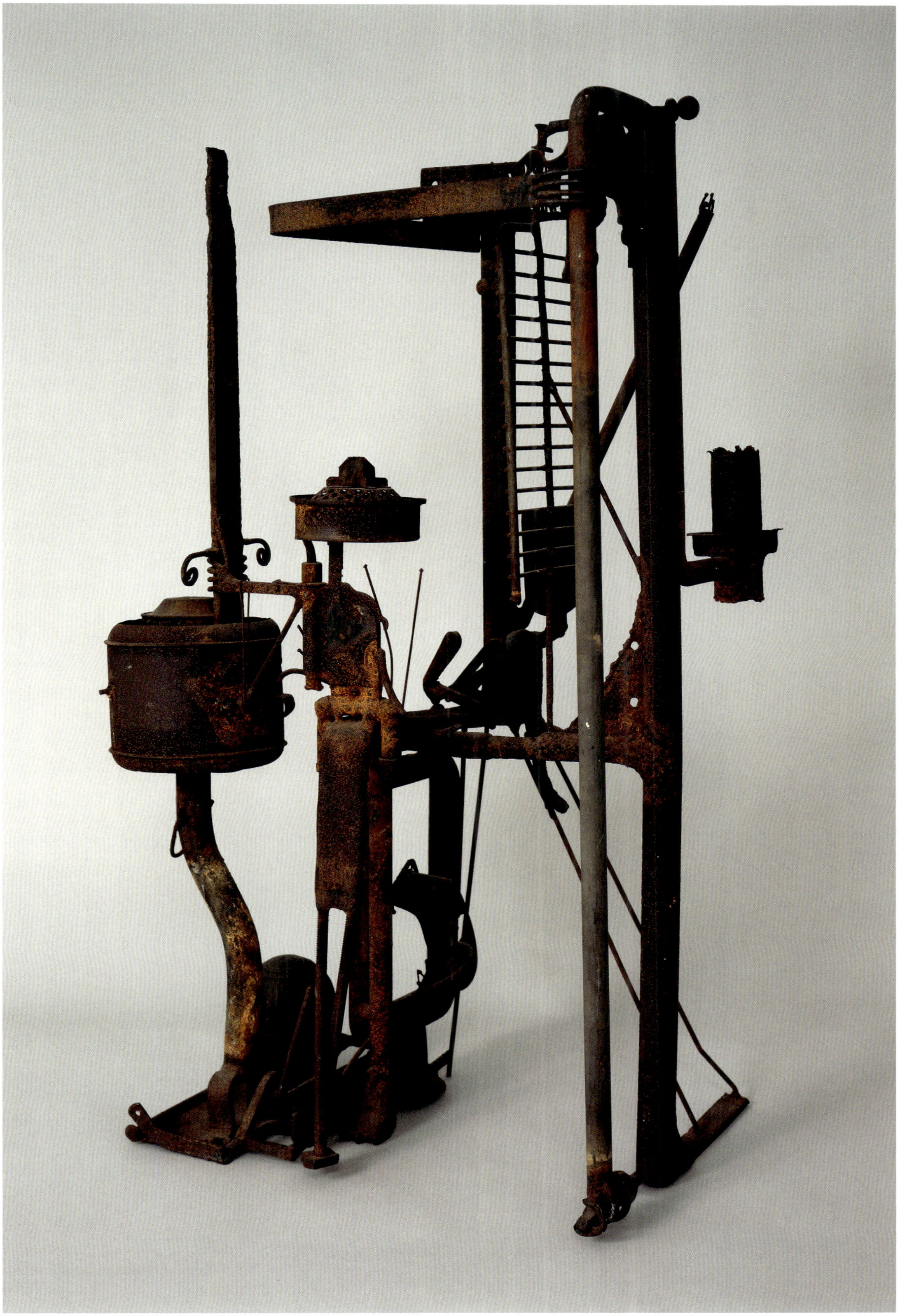

LOUISE NEVELSON American, born Russia, 1899–1988

LOUISE NEVELSON'S *East River City Scape* belongs to a series of "table-top 'landscapes,'" created during the mid-1950s, which anticipate her later large-scale works in terms of technique, material, and color.[1] *East River City Scape* is the first of five acquisitions by the Weatherspoon of the work of this Russian-born American artist, whose prolific production included paintings, prints, drawings, collage, and sculpture in various media and sizes. *East River City Scape* joined the collection in 1965 and was followed over the next two decades by another painted wooden sculpture, *Night Plant VI*, and three prints.

East River City Scape is a wooden construction made through the additive process of assemblage. In 1943 Nevelson began working with this technique, in which an artist selects separate elements and joins or assembles them into a final work. In Nevelson's case, these disparate pieces were found objects, such as architectural elements from demolished brownstones, discarded furniture, broken fruit crates, and scraps of wood from the lumberyards, dumps, and streets of New York City. Nevelson took these worthless castoffs, stripped of their original function, and created sophisticated new forms unified by a single color—black, white, or gold.

Nevelson once famously stated, "Black is the most aristocratic color of all."[2] Indeed, she worked consistently with black, particularly in her early career. When her chosen material was wood, as in *East River City Scape*, each individual piece was coated with matte black paint before she assembled the work with dowels. Painting the pieces before beginning her constructions allowed Nevelson better to "see their form—without any distractions."[3] Nevelson preserved imperfections in the wood of *East River City Scape*, and thus rough end grain, knotholes, and splits in some of the pieces add subtle texture. Nevelson was surrounded by wood scraps at the Maine lumberyard of her father, who was also a builder; it is perhaps not surprising she embraced the material with which she felt a connection.

> *Different people have different memories. Some have memories for words, some for action—mine happens to be for form. Basically, my memory is for wood, which gives a certain kind of form—it isn't too hard and it isn't too soft. I just went to wood. I wanted a medium that was immediate. Wood was the thing that I could communicate with almost spontaneously and get what I was looking for. For me, I think it's the texture and the livingness.*[4]

Nevelson's turn toward wood and away from clay, which she had used in the 1930s and 1940s, was also practical. In the early 1950s the cost of clay went up, which compelled the artist to consider other materials. In addition to the personal preference she had for wood, Nevelson was alone in her use of aged wood as a medium, a fact that no doubt appealed to her sense of artistic individuality and independence.

East River City Scape is more specifically evocative of the urban landscape of New York, both in form and title, than other examples of Nevelson's landscape series from the 1950s. Dominant horizontals are set in front and on top of strong balancing verticals, purposefully reminiscent of a skyscraper's silhouette, while a thin spur of wood dramatically shoots up near the work's center, hinting, perhaps, at a sailboat. This referential reading of the city is possible only from the sculpture's front, which is clearly the primary viewpoint, for, as the viewer moves to either side, the work eventually breaks down into parallel rows of stacked and disconnected forms, and the sense of layering and depth perceived from the front is lost. Further, shadows created by overlapping and attached pieces, which are visible only from the front, intensify Nevelson's use of positive and negative space to create form and meaning. Even the two holes in the topmost horizontal piece, on the front plane of the sculpture, are part of the artist's carefully calibrated monochromatic composition.

Once deservedly called the "Grand Dame" of sculpture,[5] Louise Nevelson saw her career get off to a surprisingly slow start, given the ultimate importance of her position within the history of twentieth-century American sculpture. Born in 1900, she was nearly sixty before she began to receive widespread recognition. *East River City Scape* thus belongs to the beginning of her maturity as a major artist and hints at her trademark large-scale, wall-size constructions that would find their way into notable collections all over America.

HH

Notes

1. Constance Schwartz, *Nevelson and O'Keeffe: Independents of the Twentieth Century* (Roslyn Harbor, NY: Nassau County Museum of Art, 1983), 10.
2. Ibid., 10.
3. Natalie Bober, *Breaking Tradition: The Story of Louise Nevelson* (New York: Atheneum, 1984), 92.
4. *Louise Nevelson: Atmospheres and Environments* (New York: Clarkson N. Potter, 1980), 55.
5. Cover, *Art News*, May 1979.

East River City Scape, 1956. Painted wood, 23 × 30½ × 16 in. Museum purchase with funds from the Benefactors Fund, 1965

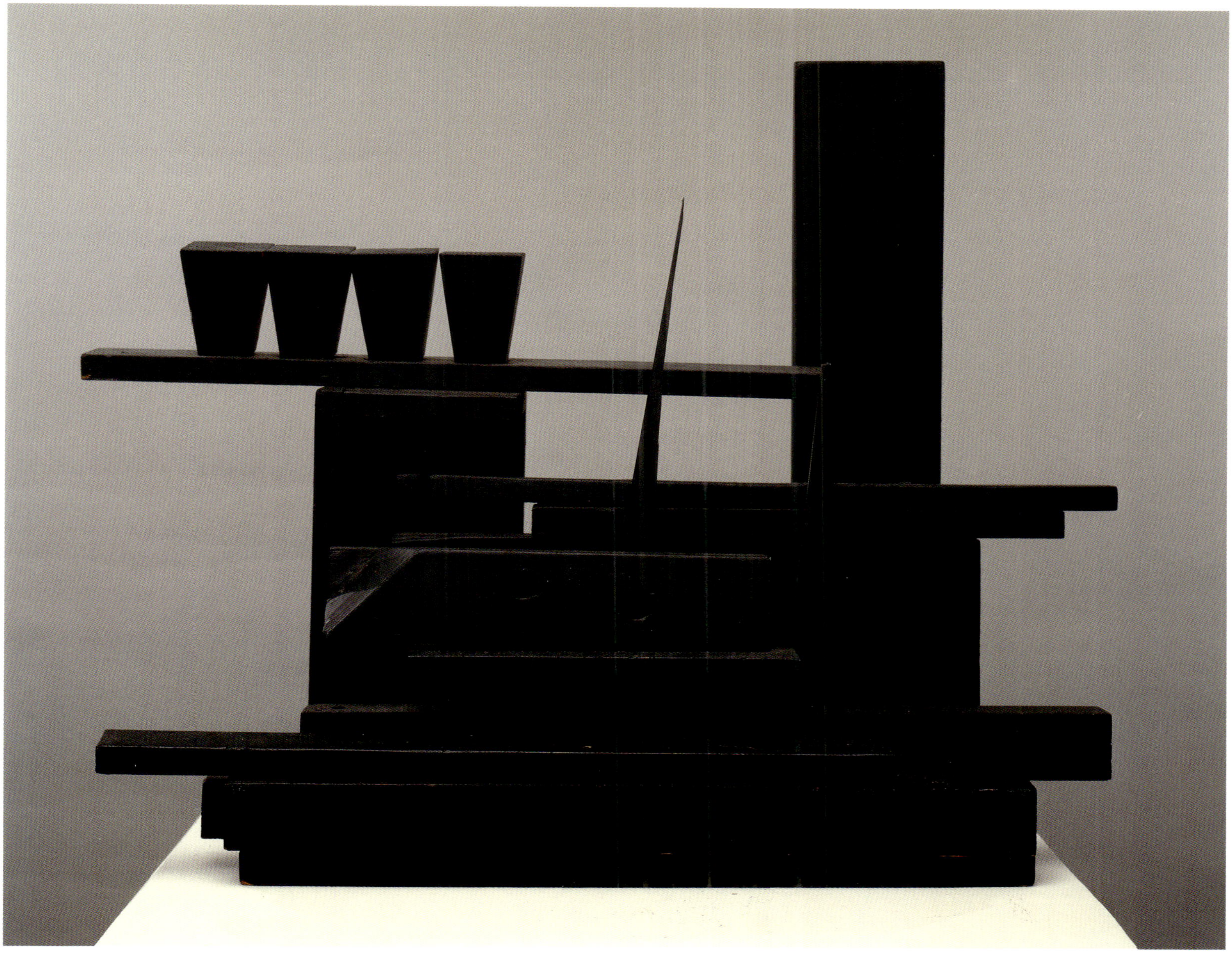

JESS born Burgess Collins, American, 1923–2004

GODDESS BECAUSE II, from 1956, is an early collage by the San Francisco artist Jess, who referred to his paper assemblies, like this one, as "paste-ups." Selecting images and text from magazines, old prints, books, and anything else he might have on hand, Jess carefully cut the desired portion from its original context with the goal of creating new meaning through often fantastical juxtapositions, reminiscent of Surrealist imagery.

Born in 1923 as Burgess Collins in Long Beach, California, Jess originally studied chemistry. He was drafted in 1943 into the U.S. Army, where he worked on the infamous Manhattan Project in Oak Ridge, Tennessee, and afterward briefly produced plutonium at Hanford Atomic Energy Project in Richland, Washington.[1] He drew and painted in his spare time during these years, but a life-changing moment for Jess occurred in 1948, when, after having an apocalyptic nightmare in which the world was destroyed, he shed his name, quit his job, and enrolled at the California School of Fine Arts in San Francisco.[2] There he met the poet Robert Duncan, who had a profound influence on him. The two shared a lifelong romantic relationship as well as a symbiotic creative exchange that informed both men's work and included a mutual interest in mythology, symbolism, and literature.

Like all of Jess's paste-ups, *Goddess Because II* is a meticulously cut and pasted-together work, which demands close inspection to appreciate fully the literal and metaphoric layers of imagery, all seamlessly integrated. This is one of a handful of similarly titled collages Jess made in the mid-1950s, which focus on glamorous women dressed in the latest haute couture. Unusual, however, is this work's division into six individual tableaux featuring a single figure. Each woman is holding or surrounded by attributes, which are often incongruous, humorous, or bizarre. Natural scale is repeatedly violated, and in three of the six scenes the human face is obstructed or oddly modified.

According to Jess, the story of any artwork was of prime interest to him, both as a viewer and as an artist, and he therefore intentionally created paste-ups with multiple narrative and interpretative possibilities, so that, as he put it, "anybody can pick out any story they choose."[3] However, given Jess's reputation for creating imagery rife with "satirical, absurdist views of sexuality,"[4] coupled with the vignettes themselves, it is difficult not to read *Goddess Because II* as a playful commentary on women's roles in 1950s America. Possible clues for such a reading include attributes symbolic of traditionally masculine tasks such as the lawnmower, drill, and large, suggestively placed screwdriver, all taken firmly in hand (literally) by the women in Jess's vision. In addition to flowers, what could be more recognizably feminine in the 1950s than cookware and wedding dresses, all of which appear here. In the lower right panel an enormous white dress bodice entirely obscures the identity of the figure, while dwarfing her and dominating her created world in the process. Although many elements in *Goddess Because II* could be interpreted from the perspective of sexual politics, perhaps the most interesting scene is the center top panel, where an elegant woman stands in profile before a large fish reminiscent of a mounted wall trophy usually caught by men and ultimately found adorning masculine domestic spaces, such as dens or 1950s recreation rooms. Further, the face of this woman is replaced by a fish head, out of which falls long blonde hair, while her right hand holds the domestically coded cooking spoon. As such, her portrayal may be read as a gendered metaphor for the "hunted," the "catch," and the "trophy."

Goddess Because II is mounted in a black mat with a red and gold border, both obviously handmade. Indeed, the handcrafted quality of these elements is juxtaposed with the near-photographic perfection of the collaged scenes, perhaps to perpetuate the ruse that they are printed rather than constructed. Surrounding the whole is an original frame customized by Jess for the work and possibly coming from one of the thrift or secondhand stores he frequented for materials.[5]

Jess continued to make paste-ups through the 1980s. Some of his collages measure as large as four by six feet and are filled with thousands of bits of paper. Despite its complexity and richness, Jess's work is not as well known as that of his contemporaries, owing in part to his reclusive, antisocial nature and his lack of interest in exhibiting. In addition to collage, Jess also pursued painting, sculpture, and drawing, but he stopped making art more than a decade before his death in 2004.

HH

Notes
1. Peter Selz, *Jess: Paintings and Paste-Ups* (New York: Tabor de Nagy Gallery, 2008), not paginated.
2. Ibid.
3. Michael Auping, *Jess: Paste-Ups (and Assemblies), 1951–1983* (Sarasota, FL: John and Mable Ringling Museum of Art Foundation, 1983), 12–13.
4. Jess obituary, *Art in America* 92 (March 2004): 160.
5. Auping, *Jess*, 15.

Goddess Because II, 1956. Collage on paper, 15½ × 19 in. Museum purchase with funds from the Benefactors Fund, 2002

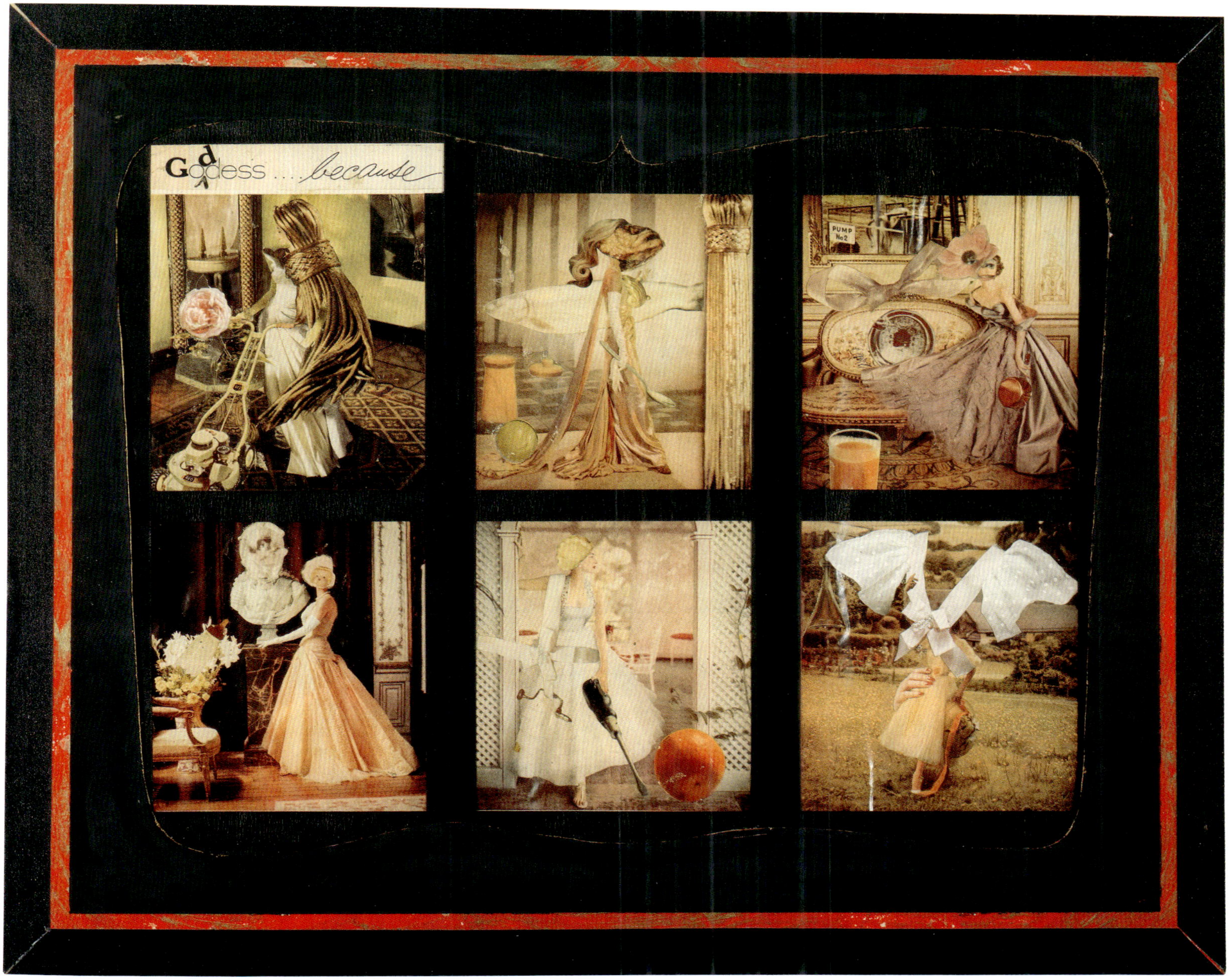
Goddess .... because
PUMP No2

JOSEF ALBERS American, born Germany, 1888–1976

JOSEF ALBERS was one of the important artist-teachers of modern art during the first half of the twentieth century. Born in Germany, he was an early student at the Bauhaus, the first art school established to teach the principles of modern art, with a staff that included such pioneers as Paul Klee and Vasily Kandinsky. In 1925 Albers joined these artists as a member of the teaching staff. After the Bauhaus was shut down by the Nazis, Albers immigrated in 1933 to the experimental Black Mountain College in Asheville, North Carolina, and then, in 1950, to Yale University, where he taught until 1959. Among his students at Black Mountain were Robert Rauschenberg and Kenneth Noland; among those at Yale, Eva Hesse. From the later 1950s on, studio art departments in the United States were increasingly organized along Bauhaus lines, in good part as interpreted and disseminated by Albers and his pupils. While alive, Albers was regarded more as a teacher than a serious painter.

During his Bauhaus years, Albers, surprisingly, did little painting. He worked with colored glass, shards of which he assembled and mounted with chicken wire on sheets of tin, to be hung in front of windows. The choice of medium was made in the context of the curriculum of the Bauhaus, which was organized into workshops exploring the possibilities of different materials, such as stone, wood, glass, and so on. But it was also an early manifestation of Albers's lifelong preoccupation with light and how it affects color. These glass assemblages also increasingly used a language of simple geometric shapes and patterns, typically held within a rectilinear grid. In two important commissions for private houses of the early 1920s, he created such works as real windows. The activity of light diffusion and window structures remained two of Albers's dominant themes from this time on.

A more refined technique for "painting" with glass followed. Called flashed glass, it involved embedding color by means of acid and sandblasting. If the technique was different, the pictorial language was the same, in this case resulting in abstract relief paintings based on varying degrees of transparency and opacity. Albers's oil paintings during these years were by contrast surprisingly monochromatic, in black and white, and gray. It was as though he needed to be uprooted from Germany to clarify his vision.

Once in this country, Albers began to paint on Masonite. His repertoire of forms and shapes expanded, though within the context of a geometric and rectilinear format in the broad Bauhaus tradition. Grounded in the Cubist principles at the core of Bauhaus teaching, these works belong among the geometric abstractions by artists the Bauhaus held up as models for its students, particularly Kasimir Malevich and Piet Mondrian. In its strict rectilinearity, *White Wall A* is more directly related to the tradition of Mondrian's Neoplasticism, but with the difference that whereas Mondrian's means include black lines and bands to activate his red, yellow, and blue squares and rectangles, Albers eliminates line completely.

The configuration was originally suggested to Albers by the adobe houses of the American Southwest with the smaller rectangles understood as windows. Rigorously geometric and rectilinear, with only straight edges and right angles, *White Wall A*, part of a series of the 1950s called Variants, consists of overlapping and transparent planes repeating or reversing one another in a bilaterally symmetrical composition. All relations, whether of light or spatial recession, are created strictly by means of color as value and hue.

Albers continued what was begun in the Variants series in his Homage to the Square series—represented as well in the Weatherspoon Art Museum collection. Seen in the context of his lifelong fascination with the window, these paintings may also be understood as related to windows—windows within windows. But they are still further removed than paintings such as *White Wall A* from the physical world. Gone are possible references to houses; if "windows," they are such unstable optical phenomena that light can be seen, not by means of transparent and overlapping planes, but strictly through the interaction of color, evoking the title of Albers's book of 1963, *The Interaction of Color*.

The Variants and Homage to the Square series are Albers's lasting contributions to twentieth-century American art and art history. While not the only works of geometric abstraction within the history of American art, they were unique at the time in their rigor and simplicity and eventually helped, during the 1960s, to redirect American abstract art away from Abstract Expressionism and into channels feeding what came to be called Minimalism.

CG

White Wall A, 1957. Oil on board, 23¾ × 34⅜ in.
Museum purchase, 1981

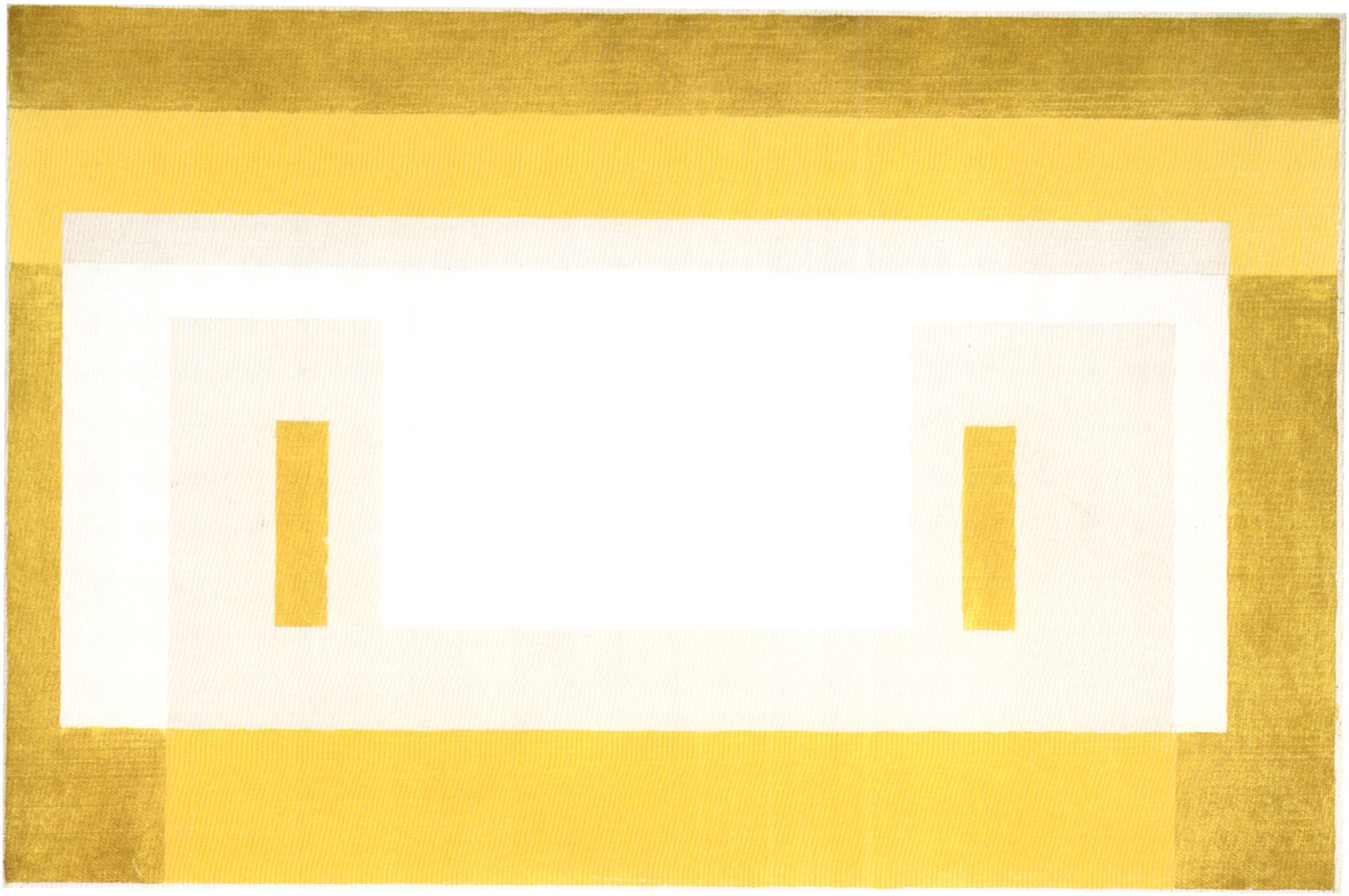

LARRY RIVERS American, 1923–2002

THE AMERICAN PAINTER, writer, sculptor, actor, and jazz musician Larry Rivers was nothing if not a risk taker, in both his life and his art. Artistically, this personal quality produced unexpected and at times dramatic shifts in style or subject matter. *Cozy Cole I*, a large, square, abstract work executed in 1960, is an example of one of these abrupt artistic changes in course and belongs to a group of paintings Rivers completed in New York City in the late 1950s and early 1960s. This body of work followed nearly a decade of portraits and interiors, and preceded Rivers's enthusiastic embrace of popular and commercial subject matter, as well as a return to figuration.

Here, as in other canvases from these years, the paint application is evocative of Action Painting, as exemplified by Franz Kline and others, while the abstraction and general aesthetics of *Cozy Cole I* suggest the tenets of Abstract Expressionism, represented in its purest form by the works of Mark Rothko. Indeed, this period of production, which is unique among his oeuvre, in terms of palette, technique, and subject matter, is the closest Rivers ever came to these contemporary formal concerns of painting,[1] which were shared by several of his friends, including Willem de Kooning.

Close inspection of *Cozy Cole I* reveals it to be a painting made of both additive and reductive mark-making. Thick, impasto passages give three-dimensionality to the surface while boldly declaring the hand of the artist. In other, often juxtaposed areas, Rivers thinned the oil paint to reveal the distinctive texture of the canvas. The result is an assertive work, quite unlike the earlier, more impressionistic portraits Rivers produced in a lighter and more varied palette.[2] Another quality also lacking in these previous works, but present throughout *Cozy Cole I*, is Rivers's emphatic removal of paint to create imagery. This technique is most notable along the vertical axis, just above the center of the composition, where a reduction, perhaps made with the end of a brush, suggests a head in profile. Such paint treatment may be found in other works by Rivers of these years, including *Me in a Rectangle*, from 1959.

Despite the strong abstraction of *Cozy Cole I*, representation is not altogether forsaken. Aside from the profile head, Rivers also included, just below the top edge, an eye facing forward and what appears to be a nose. Could this be the beginning of a body with a flesh-colored torso, bending at the waist? Perhaps. According to Rivers, "Nothing makes an invented shape more moving or interesting than a recognizable one. I can't put down on canvas what I can't see. I think of a picture as a smorgasbord of the recognizable."[3]

When Rivers painted *Cozy Cole I*, he was considered one of "America's premiere avant-garde painters,"[4] and by the middle of the 1960s his reputation and fame were at their zenith.[5] He was creative for fifty years, until his death in 2002, and produced a stunning array of work, ranging from the "vulgar to the lofty," in the opinion of one critic.[6] His legacy within art history continues to be debated. For some, he was the "originator of the imagery of pop art" and critical for the rise of Jasper Johns and Robert Rauschenberg.[7] Others find his contribution in the alternative he provided to Abstract Expressionism.

Born in the Bronx in 1923 as Yitzroch Loiza (Irving) Grossberg to Jewish immigrants from the Ukraine, Larry Rivers (he later changed his name) came to art by accident. A friend and fellow member of the professional jazz band in which Rivers performed was married to the painter Jane Freilicher, who introduced Rivers to painting and encouraged him to attend art school, which he did in 1947. His first solo exhibition followed two years later in New York. Today his work is preserved in more than forty public museums.

Cozy Cole I is one of eight works by Rivers in the Weatherspoon Art Museum collection, which also includes *Cozy Cole II*, a similarly abstract piece from the same year.

HH

Notes

1. Trevor Richardson, "Larry Rivers," in *Changing Perceptions: The Evolution of Twentieth Century American Art* (Greensboro, NC: Weatherspoon Art Gallery, 1991), 64.
2. Sam Hunter, *Larry Rivers* (New York: Rizzoli International Publications, 1989), 28.
3. Jacquelyn Days Serwer, "Larry Rivers and His 'Smorgasbord of the Recognizable,'" in *Larry Rivers: Art and the Artist* (New York: Little, Brown and Company, 2002), 57.
4. Weatherspoon Art Museum, object file, Marlborough Gallery release, 2005.
5. Michael Kimmelman, "Larry Rivers, Artist with an Edge, Dies at 78," *New York Times*, August 16, 2002.
6. Ibid.
7. Ibid.

Cozy Cole I, 1960. Oil on canvas, 48 × 48 in. Gift of Virginia Dwan in memory of Charles and Laura Dwan, 1982

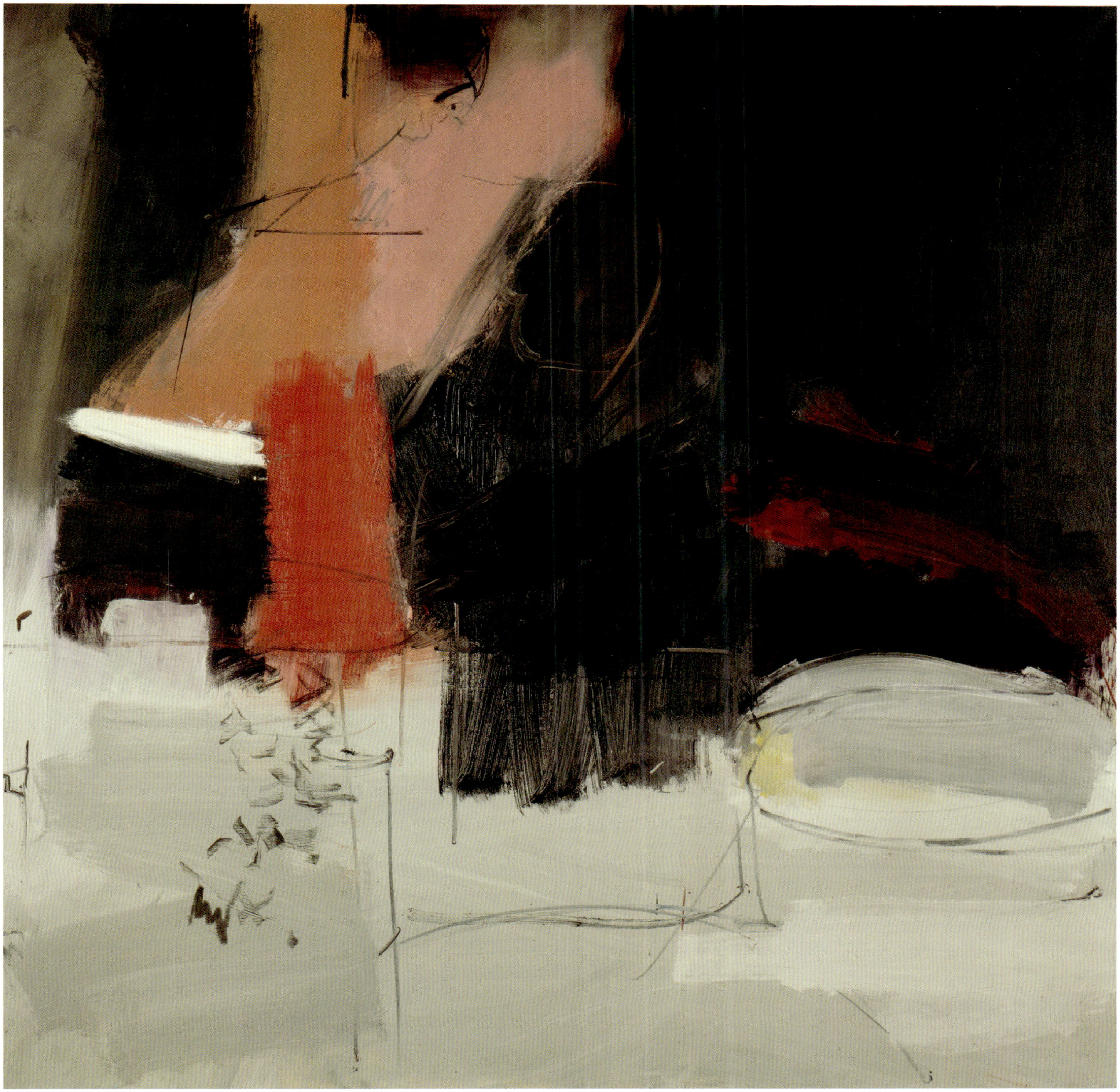

MILTON RESNICK American, born Russia, 1917–2004

MILTON RESNICK was a seminal member of the group of artists who, beginning in the late 1940s, created the New York School of Abstract Expressionism.[1] The new movement sparked excited critical acclaim, altered the path of Western art, and relocated the center of artistic innovation from Paris to New York City. *Queen* exemplifies many of the characteristics of the style. For example, the large size of this canvas insists on the unique physical presence of the artifact as it squares off to face the viewer on its own terms. On this impressive field, materials, formal properties, and process take pride of place over previous, traditional artistic preoccupations such as visual imitation, narrative episodes, illusionistic space, and technique subordinated to description.

The painting might be thought of as a statement concerning integrity, a state attained through Resnick's rigorous distillation of all visual elements to their fundamentals. In this paradigm, for instance, paint is never a vehicle of reference for anything outside its own physical self. Resnick's paint makes a forceful presence; it could not be presented as the expressive medium any more forthrightly than it is here. It inhabits a zone that belongs solely to the surface of the picture and the perimeter of the painting. Space is created by the relations of figure to ground, thinness or thickness of the paint, intensity of the color, its temperature, and the relation of the strokes to each other and the painting's edge. Light stains meet opaquely charged strokes overpainted with impasto gestures. Eyes "feel" both the canvas and the drag of the bristles plowing the pigment. The strokes lie on the surface of the canvas: we see their lengths, widths, directions, color charges, and degrees of viscosity, all irrefutable paint.

Abstract Expressionist artists were known for their instinctual approaches to painting. Finished works were the evolving products of additions and alterations. In the case of Willem de Kooning, for example, much more paint could be found on the studio floor than remained on the painting on the easel. Applications were followed by scrapings, which were replaced by yet more applications of paint. The poet and critic James Schuyler draws our attention to the union of process and product for Resnick when he commented on the "mountainous inundations" on the artist's paint table.[2] Resnick so equated paint as a signification of the inherent honesty of the crucial terms in the contract between the painter, the paint, and the painting—and eventually the viewer—that he once put so much paint on a canvas that the accumulated weight caused it to tear free from the stretcher. Now *that* is a physicality beyond illusion.

Visual "tactility" becomes an element through which the viewer chases Resnick's shifting decisions and mobile hand. It reminds us that among the materials there is another presence always asserting itself, that of Resnick himself. The base elements of the painting, however reductive, nonetheless also contain the artist's individuality. Each stroke reveals the artist's autograph, a signature beyond assigned names pointing to the real individual. Although fundamental principles of form and process were shared among the artists who worked in the Abstract Expressionist mode, their paintings remain uniquely theirs. De Koonings do not look like Jackson Pollocks, Hans Hofmanns are not taken for Robert Motherwells, and Resnicks look like his alone. After years of dedicated, concentrated labor, the process of artistic making becomes so resolved that authorship is firmly apparent.

For Resnick, who was born in Russia, identity was a particularly compelling topic. As a first-generation immigrant to the United States, his name was changed from Rachmiel to Milton, an alteration with which he was never fully comfortable.[3] To Rachmiel Resnick, the success of the artist Milton Resnick must necessarily have been tainted with suspicion. Remarks by friends and associates indicate that the artist possessed little self-confidence. Perhaps this state was heightened by the consciousness that someone else must necessarily share his critical acclaim, someone the artist did not choose. His signature on his paintings is unambiguous, the firmly delineated letters of the sole name of surety, *Resnick*.

In *Queen* the individuality of particular gestures, recurrent marks, painted and repainted areas, the selection of colors, the interplay of the artist's intentions and their subversions by the medium, the endless shifting among emphatic and elusive identities, all conspire to make a work that even with such seemingly spare limits is actually richly complex. Milton Resnick well understood that once a human being acts in the physical world, nothing is truly simple.

RG

Notes

1. Geoffrey Dorfman, ed., *Out of the Picture: Milton Resnick and the New York School* (New York: Midmarch Arts Press, 2003). Dorfman provides a full, detailed analysis of Resnick's position within the New York School.
2. Simon Pettet, ed., *Selected Art Writings: James Schuyler* (Santa Rosa, CA: Black Sparrow Press, 1998), 161.
3. Linda L. Cathcart, *Milton Resnick: Paintings, 1945–1985* (Houston: Contemporary Arts Museum, 1985), 1.

Queen, 1960. Oil on canvas, 114 × 52¼ in. Museum purchase with funds from Burlington Industries, 1966

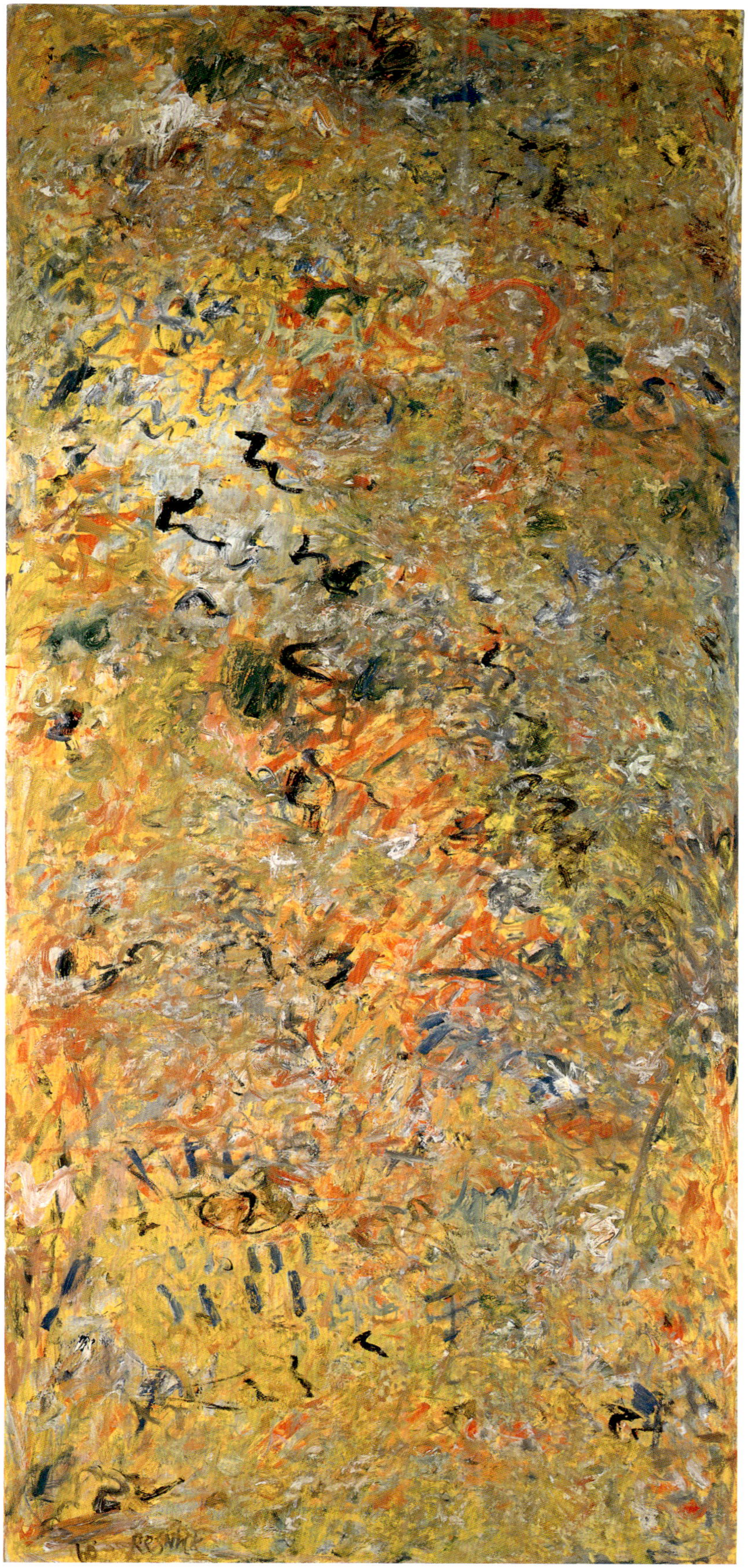

ROBERT RAUSCHENBERG American, 1925–2008

ROBERT RAUSCHENBERG FIRST gained media attention with a series of sculptures he created between 1955 and 1962. Called Combines because they combined aspects of sculpture and painting, these novel works consist of everyday, found objects that the artist painted expressionistically. This unique contribution to the history of art alone would have made Rauschenberg an important figure, but his creativity and inventiveness did not stop there. Concurrently, he explored the techniques of collage and photo-transfer.[1] Thus, by the late 1950s, he had revolutionized printmaking as well.

Driven by a constant desire to try something new and to escape the familiarity of past projects, Rauschenberg began experimenting with the silkscreen process on canvas in late 1962. Although not the first fine artist to try this commercial technique—Andy Warhol had started using silkscreened images in paintings a few months before—Rauschenberg found that silkscreening was an ideal way to adapt his photo-transfer and collage methods to the large format of painting.[2]

Rauschenberg was drawn to commercial images whose meanings were bound to the cultural and sociopolitical climate of the times. After tearing pictures from such popular magazines as *Life* and *National Geographic*, the artist hired a professional screenmaker to make the actual silkscreens, who followed his instructions as to dimensions and quantity. Rauschenberg initially worked in black and white because, like many artists, he did not want color to interfere with his intent.[3] He liked the fact that he did not have absolute control of the silkscreen process, appreciating the interesting and surprising effects that occurred. He stated, "When I get the screens back from the shop, the images on them look different from the way they did in the original magazine cutouts because of the change in scale, so that's a surprise. They look different again when I transfer them to canvas. And they constantly suggest different things when they're juxtaposed with other images."[4]

Working on several paintings simultaneously, Rauschenberg produced seventy-nine silkscreen paintings between the fall of 1962 and the spring of 1964, in addition to spending time on other artistic pursuits.[5] Each canvas has a different intent despite the fact that some imagery is repeated in more than one painting.[6] As is the case with Rauschenberg's work, it is difficult to glean the precise message behind *Straw-Boss*. Rather than pointing to one specific interpretation, it alludes to a broad and topical range of references that together suggest how to find order and connectivity in an apparently random and erratic environment.

With images ranging from the political and social to the scientific and popular, *Straw-Boss* implies a message of American patriotism, specifically through references to baseball and spaceflight. At the time of the painting's creation, both the space program and America's national pastime were receiving significant media coverage. The image of a rocket blasting off was taken from an article in the October 26, 1962, issue of *Life* magazine, which covered the liftoff and descent of *Sigma 7* with astronaut Wally Schirra inside.[7] Other images of rocket ships also dominate the center of the composition. The baseball illustration, seen on its side at lower right, refers to the then-current race between Mickey Mantle and Roger Maris to surpass Babe Ruth's home run record. Also prominent are two overlapping cityscapes, both hand-drawn and silkscreened arrangements of numbers (Florida license plates?), a Ferris-wheel-like contraption, and splotches and drips of paint. The repeated image of two grasping hands suggests that someone is monitoring the pulse of the times.

Reflecting the unpredictable pace of modern life, the multiple images are nonetheless intuitively balanced. Rauschenberg varied the amount of paint he used so that some images are dense while others appear ghostlike. He also combined black and white silkscreen paints to create a whitish gray that he painted on different parts of the canvas to tie the various images together. This expressionistic brushwork also brings the viewer's eye back to the work's surface. In other places, Rauschenberg blurred and dissolved some of the images by scrubbing them with a paint rag soaked in benzine. The artist also chose images that represented varying degrees of spatial depth and that would serve as directional indicators.

Always wanting to be fresh, Rauschenberg destroyed the screens used to create this series of paintings in June 1964, thereby forcing himself to find new subjects and materials to explore. For the rest of the decade, he concentrated on making prints and collaborating in performance and technology-based art before moving on later to other artistic pursuits that promoted world peace and understanding.

EDG

Notes

1. Rauschenberg applied a chemical solvent to a printed image's surface, placed it face down on paper, then rubbed the back of it with a burnishing implement such as a ballpoint pen or stylus. The result was a reverse image of the original, complete with striated markings from the rubbing.
2. Calvin Tomkins, "The Sistine on Broadway," in Roni Feinstein, *Robert Rauschenberg: The Silkscreen Paintings, 1962–64* (New York: Whitney Museum of American Art, 1990), 15.
3. In late August 1963 he began to work in color.
4. Quoted in Tomkins, "The Sistine on Broadway," 16.
5. Rauschenberg was also creating prints at this time and serving as lighting, set, and costume designer for the Merce Cunningham Dance Company, as well as undertaking his first art performances.
6. One of the benefits of the silkscreening technique is that the screen can be reused any number of times.
7. Feinstein, *Robert Rauschenberg: The Silkscreen Paintings*, 79.

Straw-Boss, 1962. Silkscreen and oil on canvas, 96 × 60 in. Gift of Virginia Dwan in memory of Charles and Laura Dwan, 1982

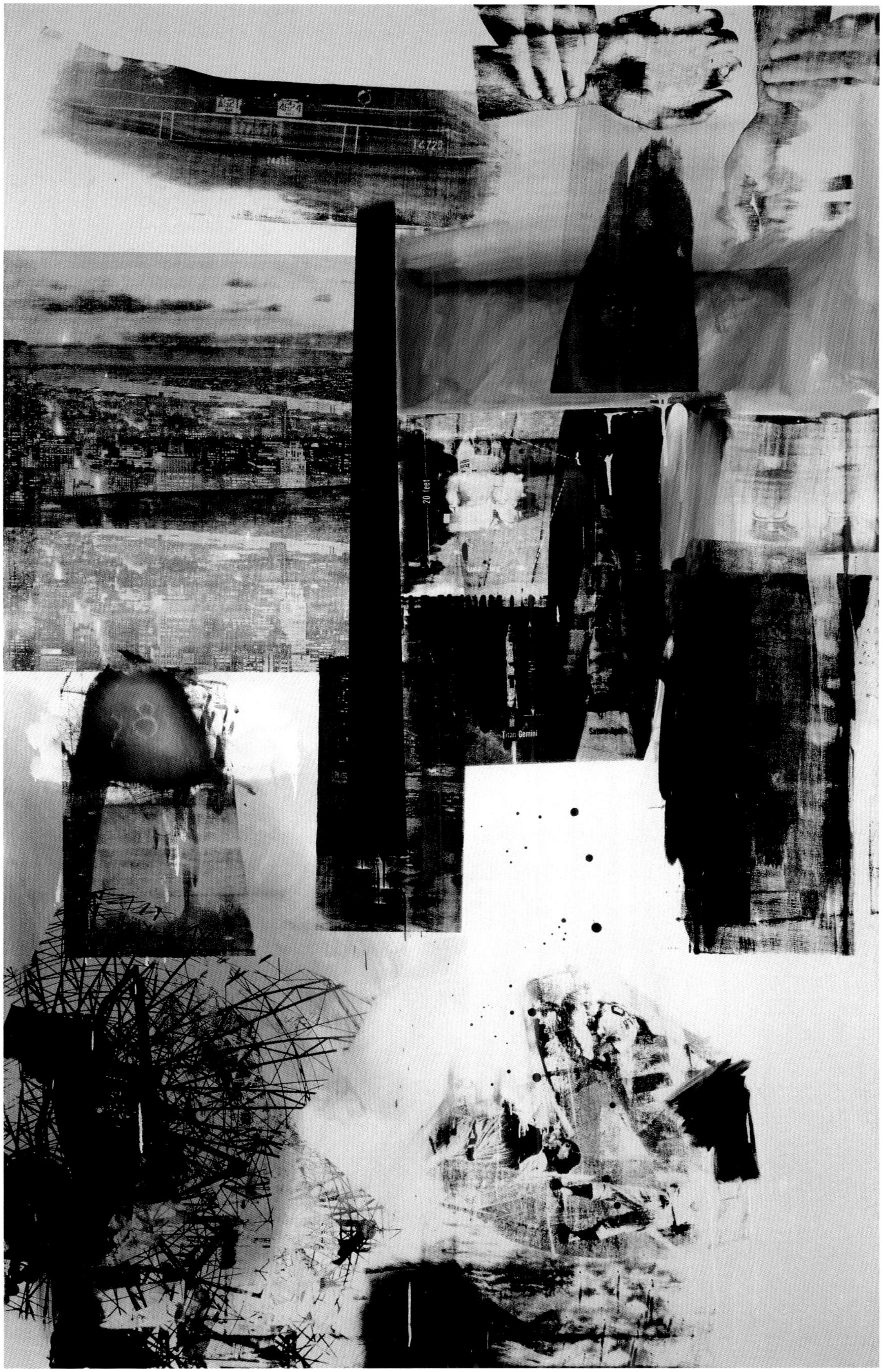
20 feet
Titan Gemini

JOAN MITCHELL American, 1926–1992

JOAN MITCHELL'S PAINTING bridges two generations of abstraction on two continents. A native of Chicago, Mitchell earned a degree from the School of the Art Institute of Chicago in 1947 before gravitating to New York. There she sought out exhibitions of work by Jackson Pollock and Arshile Gorky. Her associations with Willem de Kooning and Franz Kline and exhibitions at prestigious galleries earned her an invitation to join the male-dominated Ninth Street Club. Despite the promise of a successful career in New York, she left the United States for self-imposed exile in France, where she encountered the Parisian cohorts of the New York School painters. By 1959 she had rented the studio in Paris in which she worked for the next nine years. The untitled work from 1962 in the Weatherspoon's collection was painted either there or in one of the houses on the Mediterranean that she leased during the summer months.

In the Weatherspoon painting, the gestural energy of Mitchell's brushwork is confined to the dimensions of drawing paper. In this respect, the work is reminiscent of Vasily Kandinsky's early abstractions, which Mitchell had studied while she was in Chicago and New York. Although Mitchell is best known for her large canvases, throughout her career she also worked on paper, using pencil, charcoal, and pastel as well as oil, which was her medium of choice. The work in the Weatherspoon was painted on colored paper with an evenly textured weave that is clearly visible in passages where strokes of oil paint graze the surface. Some of Mitchell's works on paper were done as exercises or improvisations, whereas others, like the Weatherspoon's, have the character of individual studies in which the artist was intentionally organizing a constellation of specific formal elements. The purchase of this study from the Weatherspoon's *Art on Paper* exhibition in 1986 made a particularly fine addition to the Dillard Collection of works on paper.

The color scheme of the Weatherspoon's work is limited in hues yet subtly varied in density and tonal range. Rich browns are applied in predominantly transparent strokes. Layers of opaque black and deep blue accumulate just off center, demarcating a point of visual focus. Decisive spikes of yellow and a trace of green add vibrant color notes to an otherwise subdued palette. A similar combination of colors recurs in works spanning Mitchell's career, from a gouache landscape painted during her student years to the tangled skeins of oil-based pigment in a painting from 1992, the year of her death.

The Weatherspoon's study is at once painterly and linear. Where Mitchell thinned paint with turpentine, the mixture pools in unpredictable drips. She also applied paint in controlled linear strokes that coalesce in contrasting patterns of sharp angles and sweeping curves. Strong vectors converge in a spiral vortex that deepens an implied pictorial space. Here, as in many of Mitchell's works, space is implicit in the figure-ground relationship between layers of brushwork and the unpainted paper support. In contrast to the dense cluster of interpenetrating trajectories, expansive calligraphic lines hover on the surface, forming spidery webs of paint. These delicate webs are partially framed by unpainted borders designed to reiterate and reinforce the calculated asymmetry of the compositional structure.

Mitchell's titles often evoke her sensory experience of the landscape and occasionally allude to personal relationships. The absence of a title for the Weatherspoon study leaves the viewer to intuit content based solely on the visual components of an abstract painting. Mitchell herself described her paintings of the early 1960s as "very violent and angry."[1] It is tempting to draw parallels between Mitchell's description of her work and the explosive outbursts of a volatile temper recalled by people who knew her. But Mitchell's art is autobiographical only to the extent that it records her relentless effort to claim the process and visual vocabulary of Abstract Expressionism as her own. The violence implicit in the network of projectiles in the Weatherspoon painting is consciously counterbalanced by gossamer linear interlaces. This is a study in opposition and dynamic equilibrium. On a small scale, it exemplifies the same carefully calibrated formal balance that characterizes Mitchell's finest paintings.

KPA

Note

1. Judith E. Bernstock, *Joan Mitchell* (New York: Hudson Hills Press, in association with the Herbert F. Johnson Museum of Art, Cornell University, 1988), 60.

Untitled, 1962. Oil on paper, 15½ × 19½ in. Museum purchase with funds from the Dillard Paper Company for the Dillard Collection, 1986

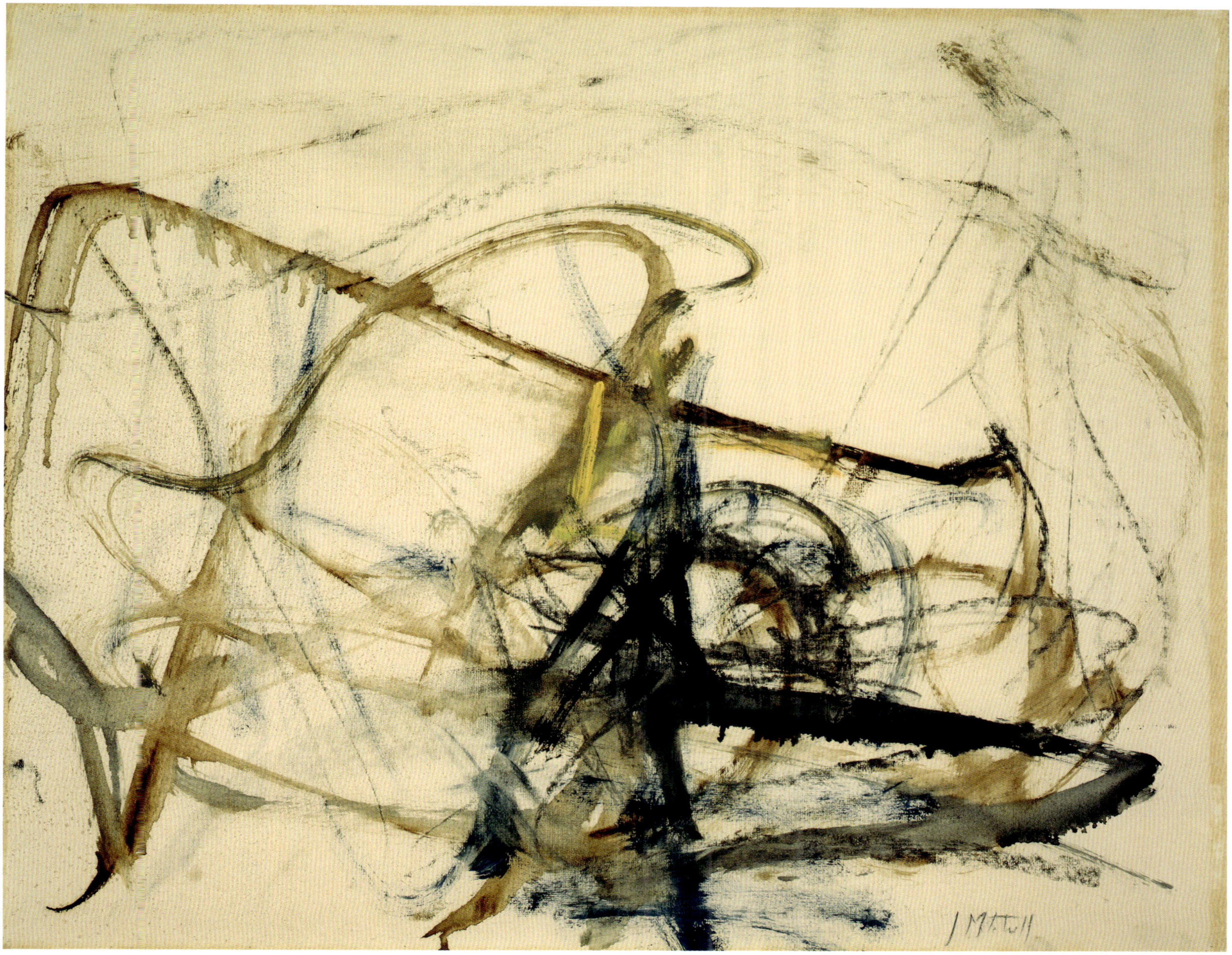

JO BAER American, born 1929

AT TIMES, THE ARTS RADICALLY retune aesthetic criteria, and what emerges is a devotion to profound simplicity. In the 1960s, some artists—among them Jo Baer—produced works that came to be grouped under the term *Minimalism*. From the strong, self-assured, and wholly self-possessed works of that decade, Minimalism developed into an influential mode of expression for many other artists. Recent art criticism and history have judged Minimalism to have as significant a "place in the second half of our century [as] . . . the one held by Cubism in the first half."[1] Executed in 1964–65, Baer's *Grayed Yellow Vertical Rectangle* is a painting that unambiguously punctuated the critical dialogue at the time of its creation, and it has extended its powerful authority into the art of the next century.

As can be the case with almost any stylistic designation, Minimalism could serve as an appropriate descriptor even while some artists resisted their inclusion in the category. Sol LeWitt, for instance, felt compelled to state, "People refer to me as a Minimal artist but no one has ever defined what it means or put any limits to where it begins or ends, what it is or isn't."[2] In the absence of any manifesto or an organized group of artists, critical structures had to be formulated from analyses of the works. Artists shared emphatic preferences for primary geometric shapes, great attention to surface, reductive color palettes, strategic repetition, and works that were related serially or systematically. Selected visual elements meticulously culled from the vocabulary of form were posited as the basis of the work's significance. The goal was to refocus the art encounter toward a recognition of the supremacy of the work of art as an *object*. Minimalism proffered works that must be looked on rather than into; elemental physicality asserted a paramount claim to critical content.

Reflecting on the intentions of these artists while clearly speaking for herself, Baer wrote:

> *The most far-reaching endeavor has been the reordering of subject matter so that the art object itself dominates its particular parts. Figure/grounds and hierarchical arrangements give way to paintings that picture their own shapes and pigments and sculptures that render their own shapes and matter. . . . These new ways have political implications that bear on the sovereignty of the subject and the nature and ramifications of self-determination.*[3]

Grayed Yellow Vertical Rectangle exhibits precisely these properties.

The painting is from a series of twelve in four shapes, four sizes, and four colors: yellow, green, blue, and purple. Baer writes, "They are each constructed equivalent to one another as a color presence."[4] The rectangle announces its shape with a black zone that, due to its narrow proportions, functions within the cultural expectation of a frame. At the same instant, this dimensional reading of the band is contradicted by the fact that it is easily perceived to be only a flat area of paint on the surface of the canvas. This black band is abutted by a thin line of color, a yellow that has been grayed by the admixture of a small quantity of black. The yellow, like the black, conforms to the outline of the canvas. Although differing in color and proportion, it repeats the shape of the black band and restates the dominating shape of the object—a rectangle. These forms introduce the central field of the painting that is yet a third vertical rectangle. The artist has painted it an unvarying warm white. Standing before the work, the viewer is completely conscious that the three areas are uniformly applied paint supported by the flat weave and textures of the canvas—Baer's "matter"—her materials. There is neither allusion nor illusion. Spatial readings rest entirely on the natural properties of value: light advances, dark recedes; the painting rejects any conventional illusionism or figure-ground perceptions.

In the critical literature, the word *radical* has often been applied to the Minimalist works of the 1960s. These artists, their works, and exhibitions were startlingly different from the prevailing artistic modes of expression that had justly garnered such acclaim for American visual art. Each of the characteristics of any Minimalist work of the 1960s offered a point-by-point refutation of the values of Abstract Expressionism. Minimalism also renounced the noisy contemporary images, sources, and colors of Pop art. Jo Baer's assertion that the new ways had political implications recalls the significant status of feminist political and cultural thought of the time, and she has remained an inspiration for American women artists.

RG

Notes

1. Lynn Zelevansky, *Sense and Sensibility: Women Artists and Minimalism in the Nineties* (New York: Museum of Modern Art, 1994), 8.
2. Quoted in James Meyer, *Minimalism: Art and Polemics in the Sixties* (New Haven: Yale University Press, 2001), 3.
3. Jo Baer, "The Artist and Politics: A Symposium," *Artforum* 9, no. 1 (September 1970): 35.
4. "Jo Baer," in *Systemic Painting* (New York: Solomon R. Guggenheim Museum, 1966), 23.

Grayed Yellow Vertical Rectangle, 1964–65. Oil on canvas, 60 × 48 in. Gift of Anne and Benjamin Cone, 1966

LEE LOZANO American, 1930–1999

LEE LOZANO'S CONSIDERABLE and singular contributions to the history of contemporary art have been more or less overlooked until recent years. Some of this oversight is due to her gradual, and then complete, withdrawal from the art world during the early 1970s, and some a result of her oeuvre of hard-hitting, sexually overt drawings and paintings. Even in her lifetime, her work was subject to the vagaries of critical interest: virtually ignored between 1960 and 1965, by 1970 it received regular attention in the leading art journals of the day.

Peel is from a series of paintings from the mid-1960s,[1] a group of works that also has received less attention in considerations of Lozano's art than works that came before and after. Painted between her expressive transmutations of common tools (hammers, razor blades, and screwdrivers, for example) into highly charged sexual objects and her most well-known, conceptually oriented Wave paintings, *Peel* and its counterparts seem to be most comfortably located within the realm of Minimalism. What Lozano achieved in these works was the marriage of cool geometric forms with highly active surfaces. Paint strokes are consonant with the directional shape of each form within a painting; Lozano's use of stiff brushes created ridges within the paint that further reinforce this unity. The modulation of a light sheen often running along the center of each form creates a paradoxical ambiguity of volume and flatness.[2]

Yet Lozano did not leave the emotional and psychological impact of her tool paintings behind in this group of large, muscular works with forceful titles such as *Ram*, *Split*, *Butt*, *Goad*, and *Charge*. The implied action that the titles impart to these paintings is not confined by the boundaries of their canvases. Lozano was interested in the illusionistic possibility that the "details" of the paintings were only parts of monumental forms of unlimited scope. *Peel* shows, in diptych form, a segment of a machine bolt with a stripped thread that moves forcefully and diagonally across both panels. The strokes of paint underscore the roundness of the bolt and sense of movement in its being screwed or unscrewed; the stripped thread suggests the aggression with which the piece of hardware has been treated.

With these paintings, Lozano also demonstrated her interests in visual perception and light. Characteristic of the group is a sophisticated and subtle use of color, often augmented by directional shifts in her brushstrokes. Like some of her male counterparts at the time, Lozano utilized coarse, three-inch housepainter brushes to rake paint with great energy across the surface of the canvas. In this way, she produced a volumetric play of light and dark that causes the appearance of a painting to change as the viewer's vantage point moves. The electric charge resulting from Lozano's process emphasizes her ability in *Peel* and the works related to it to collapse the erotic and the mechanical.

Lee Lozano was born Lenore Knaster in 1930. She studied at the University of Chicago and received her BFA from the School of the Art Institute of Chicago in the 1950s, and then moved to New York City in 1961. She exhibited in several group shows at Richard Bellamy's Green Gallery in the mid-1960s. In 1988 a one-person exhibition, *Lee Lozano: The Sixties*, took place at the Weatherspoon Art Gallery, and a decade later, in 1998, her work was the focus of four simultaneous exhibitions: one at the Wadsworth Atheneum MATRIX space in Hartford, Connecticut, and three in commercial New York galleries, with each representing a different aspect of her work. A large-scale traveling exhibition organized by the Basel Kunsthalle in 2006 brought a surge of new interest to her work.

NMD

Notes

1. The Weatherspoon Art Museum owns another work from this series, *Clash* (1965), as well as preparatory drawings for *Clash*, *Peel*, and *Charge*, and several other works on paper.
2. These paintings are most fully discussed in a text by Jill Johnston for a 1965 Lozano exhibition at Green Gallery in New York City, which never took place. The text is reproduced in *Lee Lozano: Win First Don't Last, Win Last Don't Care*, ed. Adam Szymczyk (Basel: Schwabe AG, 2006), 69.

Peel, 1964. Oil on canvas, each panel, 60 × 66 in.; overall 60 × 132 in. Gift of Mr. Robert C. Scull, 1981

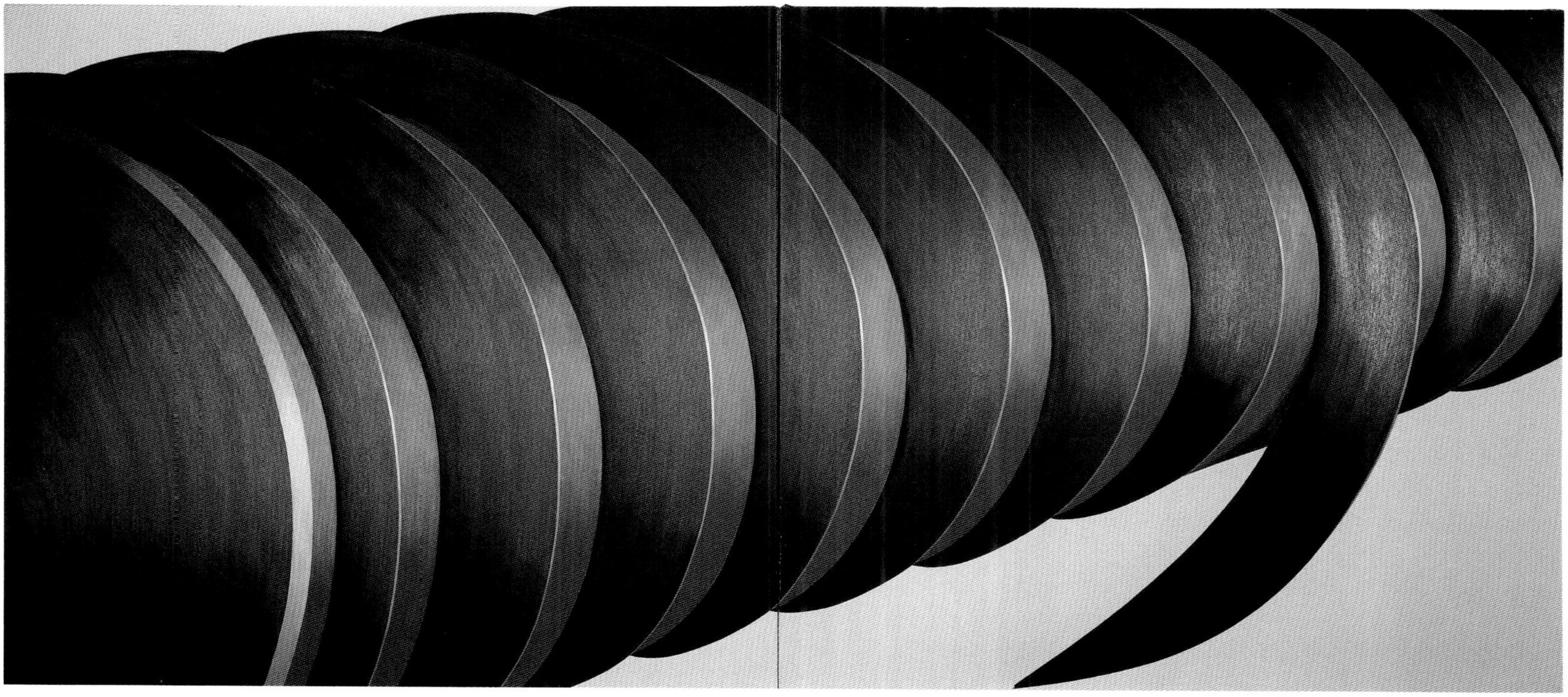

WILLIAM ANASTASI American, born 1933

IN THE LATE 1970S William Anastasi played chess every day with John Cage. That Anastasi followed in the footsteps of Marcel Duchamp, who considered playing chess part of his artistic practice, is not surprising. Born and raised in Philadelphia, Anastasi grew up having ready access to one of the most important collections of Duchamp's work at the Philadelphia Museum of Art. It also then should come as no surprise to learn that Anastasi was one of the pioneers of Conceptualism in the 1960s: his four exhibitions at the Dwan Gallery in New York City between 1966 and 1970 effectively charted the beginnings and apex of classic Conceptualism. In 1967, for the exhibition *Six Sites* at Dwan, he silkscreened photographs of the gallery walls onto canvases just slightly smaller than the walls themselves and installed them in their respective locations around the room. Along with other artists inspired by Duchamp's challenges to the art establishment, Anastasi helped set the stage for today's continued explorations of what constitutes art.

Anastasi became interested in the use of sound as an element of visual art through his long friendship with Cage. In the second solo exhibition of his career—at the Weatherspoon Art Gallery in 1965—Anastasi presented a group of works he called "sound objects." These seemingly simple but conceptually challenging sculptures, which Anastasi referred to as "dumb," were common sound-producing objects displayed with the sounds they produced, for example, an electric fan with a tape of a fan's whirr or a deflated inner tube with a speaker playing the sound of the air being let out. This body of work constituted his first exhibition, *Sound Objects*, at Virginia Dwan's gallery in 1966. *Window on the Airshaft* was exhibited at the same time in another room.[1]

When the Lower East Side building in which Anastasi lived was condemned, he cut out one of the window frames in his apartment. Earlier, in the summer of 1963, he had dropped a microphone down the airshaft outside and, for about an eight-hour day, recorded the sounds of the neighborhood: street traffic, clanking pots and pans, airplanes, fire engines, and crying babies. Anastasi mounted the window on plywood, which he covered with plaster and floral wallpaper. Behind the window, he placed a replication of the airshaft constructed from dark stucco and, out of sight, installed an audiotape edited from his original recording. Giving evidence to the impact of Anastasi's early works and their conceptual vision, *Look* magazine reproduced *Window on the Airshaft* in 1966.

The piece requires visitor engagement: to understand the full intention and effect of the work, one needs to listen to the sound tape. The sensation is one of eavesdropping, of putting an ear not only to private lives but also to a particular place and moment in time. The urban sounds vitalize the somewhat bleak appearance of the window wall and literally and figuratively bring the installation to life. In this way, the work functions like Anastasi's other sound sculptures, reminding us of "how differently each sense contributes to our experience, and, for a moment, metaphor slips in, identifying the objects as dead and the sounds as an echo or memory left behind."[2]

NMD

Notes

1. This piece has been variously dated and has been noted in the Weatherspoon Art Museum's files as 1966. In a conversation with the author, Anastasi dated it to 1964, a date also given by the artist in "William Anastasi and Thomas McEvilley, a Conversation August 1989," in *William Anastasi* (New York: Scott Hanson Gallery, 1989), 12.
2. Eileen Neff, "Anastasi's Presence," in *William Anastasi: A Retrospective, 1960–1995* (Philadelphia: Galleries at Moore College, 1995), 6.

Window on the Airshaft, 1964 Wooden window frame, window shade, plywood, stucco, wallpaper, fabric, clothesline, tape recorder-player, audio tape, and electric cords, 108 × 73 × 33½ in. Gift of the Dwan Gallery, 1968

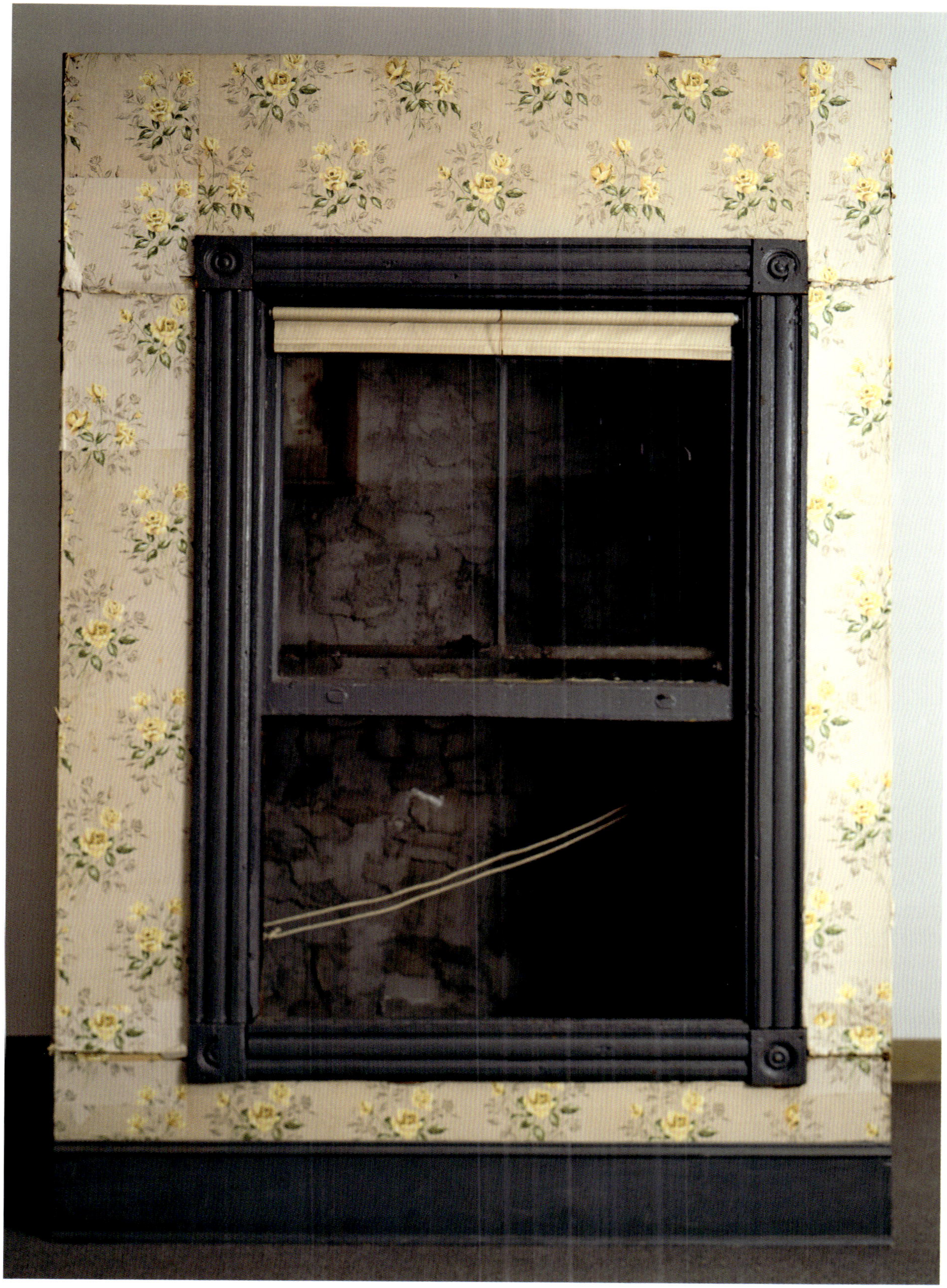

ALEX KATZ American, born 1927

IN 1949 AND 1950 ALEX KATZ attended the Skowhegan School of Painting and Sculpture in Maine to study commercial art. There, after a reappraisal of his interests, he changed his focus to the fine arts and painting. He also developed a strong attachment to the area. He bought a house and established a studio in the small coastal town of Lincolnville, Maine. This is the setting for his painting *Ives Field II*.

As the title's numeral indicates, this painting is the second in a series of large figural compositions.[1] In *Ives Field I* (also from 1964), all the figures are shown full-length, while in Katz's revision, the cropping of the figures yields a far more dynamic composition. Beginning with the left foreground figure, the space punches into the distance, jolts to the central figure, drops again to the distance, and then pops back to the face that dominates the right edge. We can no longer see that originally the women were seated while the man stood, holding a pail. One is reminded of the figural group in Édouard Manet's *Déjeuner sur l'herbe*, the radical painting from the birth of modernism a hundred years earlier. In both works, the figures are linked by spatial juxtaposition but not coherent social interaction.

The central zone of *Ives Field II* is firmly anchored by the central woman's dark hair and red tank top that forms the V of her body, pressing down on the center of the lower edge of the composition. The viewer's roaming eyes are continually refocused here as the painting insistently recovers its balance as if on the apex of an inverted fulcrum. She gazes straight out of the painting, a line of vision perpendicular to the picture plane that meets the inbound examination of the viewer. Gaze pushes against gaze as she checks the viewer's access, and their colliding lines of vision meet and flatten onto the surface of the painting.

The sense of tension created by the cropped figures, the spatial disjunction, and the collage-like relationships within the large canvas suggest a cinematic experience. It is as if we have wandered into a room where a movie is already under way and are glimpsing only a fragment of a narrative in a frozen frame. This new way of seeing evidenced in Katz's paintings of Ives Field from 1964 marks an important development, a "stylistic breakthrough"[2] that encompassed the elements of his "signature style."[3]

The surface of the painting is composed of generous, clean shapes in clear colors. The consistency of the paint, like that of heavy cream, diffuses any sense of hardness, and Katz applied it with a deft touch of masterly confidence. However, the graphic power of the individual motifs and the composition as a whole are uniquely wedded to a fluidity of application that precludes any interpretation that would tend toward the impersonal. After the viewer registers the shapes and their colors, the artist's hand can be discerned. Furthermore, contrary to the frequent characterization of painting in the 1960s as an art that covered the tracks of artistic individuality through a generic application of paint, reinforcing the impersonal nature of the subjects chosen and their source in popular culture, we now recognize that Katz's contemporaries such as Jasper Johns, Robert Rauschenberg, and Andy Warhol imbedded their works with references that were personal signifiers. Katz's paintings are supremely intimate works loaded with the particulars of personalization.

In *Ives Field II*, Alex Katz gathers his friends and Lincolnville neighbors—all from the New York art world. One fine day, Katz asked them to pose in the blueberry field belonging to his neighbor Mr. Ives.[4] The copper hair and smiling profile belong to the artist Yvonne Jaquette. To her right, we meet the eyes of Mimi Gross, an artist married to Red Grooms, the man to her right, with whom she collaborated on notable works that broke down distinctions between painting and sculpture. Both of them survey the view beyond the picture plane with an appraising air. The man in the red T-shirt to the left with the ball is the photographer and filmmaker Rudy Burckhardt, who married Jaquette the year this painting was made, 1964. The boy about to receive the toss is Jacob, Burckhardt's son by his previous marriage. *Ives Field II* frames a tight circle. Yet it must be admitted that all these observations about the "viewer" are true but qualified. The viewer is actually late to the game. Mimi and Red look out toward their friend and fellow artist Alex Katz who is making the painting. He completes the charmed circle.

RG

Notes

1. Ellen Schwartz, "Alex Katz: 'I see something and I go Wow!'" *Art News* 78 (1979): 42–47. In her article Schwartz noted important distinctions between the two versions.
2. Ibid., 44.
3. Ibid., 45.
4. Patricia Krebs, "Katz's Work: 'Elite,'" *Greensboro (NC) Daily News*, July 21, 1974, B12. The identities of the subjects in the painting were recorded by Krebs, who interviewed Katz. Suzette McAvoy, e-mail message to author, October 21, 2008. McAvoy helpfully relayed my questions about the subjects and specific location to Katz's studio. The artist confirmed them and provided the information that the location was a blueberry field that belonged to his Lincolnville neighbor Mr. Ives.

Ives Field II, 1964. Oil on linen, 74 × 120½ in. Museum purchase with funds from Burlington Industries, 1965

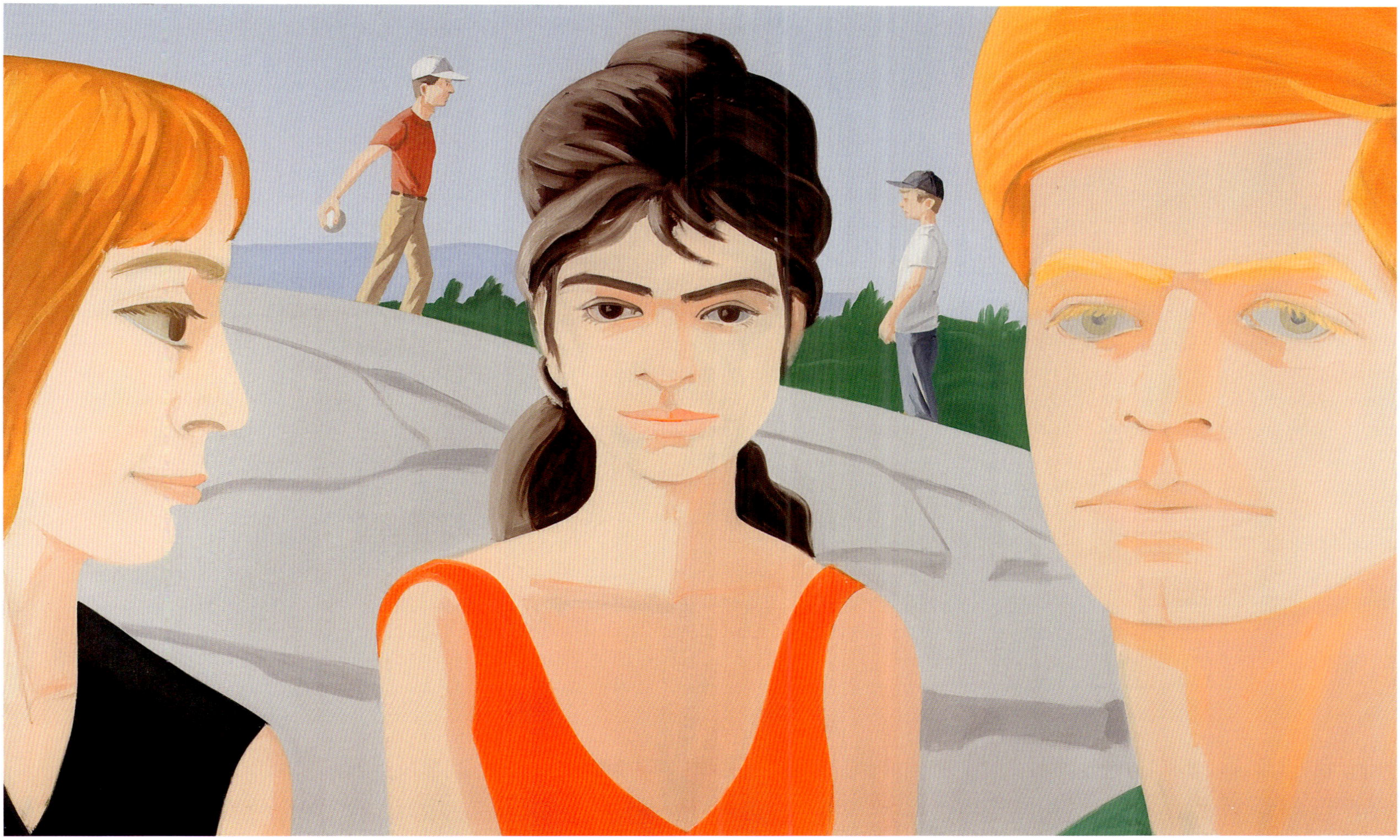

LEON GOLUB American, 1922–2004

AT THE TIME LEON GOLUB painted *Head I*, the popular art forms of the day were the cool commercialism of Pop and the formal and theoretical leanings of Minimalism and Conceptualism. Clearly, Golub's interests were stylistically out of sync with these artistic trends. Yet, in terms of subject matter, his art was au courant, for it focused on the political and social issues of the day.

Born and trained in Chicago, Leon Golub received his BA in art history at the University of Chicago in 1942, then studied art at the School of the Art Institute of Chicago from 1947 to 1949 under the G.I. Bill. As early as the 1950s, Golub aligned himself with a group of Chicago artists called Monster Roster, who favored an observable connection to the external world and to actual events. The group's social awareness remained central to Golub throughout his career. In paintings, drawings, prints, and installations, as well as written texts and public lectures, he advocated that people should abide by universal humanistic values. Believing that all art was political, Golub thus dedicated himself to producing work that was socially and politically engaged. Consequently, his entire oeuvre addresses people's inhumanity to each other.

Golub's earliest paintings from the 1950s focused on the Holocaust and the atomic bombings at Hiroshima and Nagasaki. Through the use of a single totemic figure, he conveyed his personal experiences during World War II as well as critiqued universal systems of power and conflict. Representing the postwar sensibility, the figures also refer to classical mythology and portray kings, warriors, and shamans, as well as hybrid man-beast monsters. Also during this time, Golub developed his lifelong, labor-intensive technique of creating surface texture by applying successive layers of lacquer or acrylic to the canvas surface, then eroding or carving into these layers using solvents and/or scraping tools such as meat cleavers. The resultant images are so heavy with impasto that they appear sculpted.

Head I was made shortly after Golub returned to this country after living in Paris, a time when he concentrated on producing images of generalized aggression.[1] As in his earlier work, a lone figure dominates the composition. With ties to the figural traditions of Greek, Etruscan, and Roman art and more generally to tribal art, the art of the insane, and photography and mass media, the male subject appears both muscular and emaciated. Although no violent narrative is portrayed, aggression is implied through Golub's application of paint and the figure's strained expression. The brushwork is quick and agitated, with areas of paint built up, then physically removed. The dark, limited palette likewise adds to the somber mood of the painting. Centered within a shallow, nondescript space, the figure is meant to disrupt the viewer's complacency.

The creation of this painting corresponded with the escalation of United States involvement in Southeast Asia. Shortly thereafter Golub responded to these political events by producing two specifically anti–Vietnam War series, Napalm and Vietnam. After destroying much of his existing work in the mid-1970s, a result of self-doubt, he concentrated on painting portraits of powerful men. He returned to painting social commentary in the 1980s, investigating incidents of racial tensions, terrorism, and oppression, and in the 1990s invigorated his style by adapting the forms and styles of graffiti art. Golub's work remained out of fashion until the 1980s, when political events and the emergence of Neo-Expressionism in the work of a younger generation of artists helped solidify his reputation. Throughout it all, however, Golub saw his work as more documentary in nature than critique, but hoped his narratives of the abuse of power, cruelty, aggression, oppression, and violence would jolt the world into embracing universal humanistic values.

EDG

Note

1. Between 1959 and 1964 Golub worked in Paris with his wife, the artist Nancy Spero, in part because he believed that Europe would be more receptive to his figural style. When they returned to the United States, they settled permanently in New York City.

Head I, 1966. Acrylic on linen, 32¼ × 36 in. Museum purchase with funds from the Lynn Richardson Prickett Acquisition Endowment and the Louise D. and Herbert S. Falk Acquisition Endowment, 2001

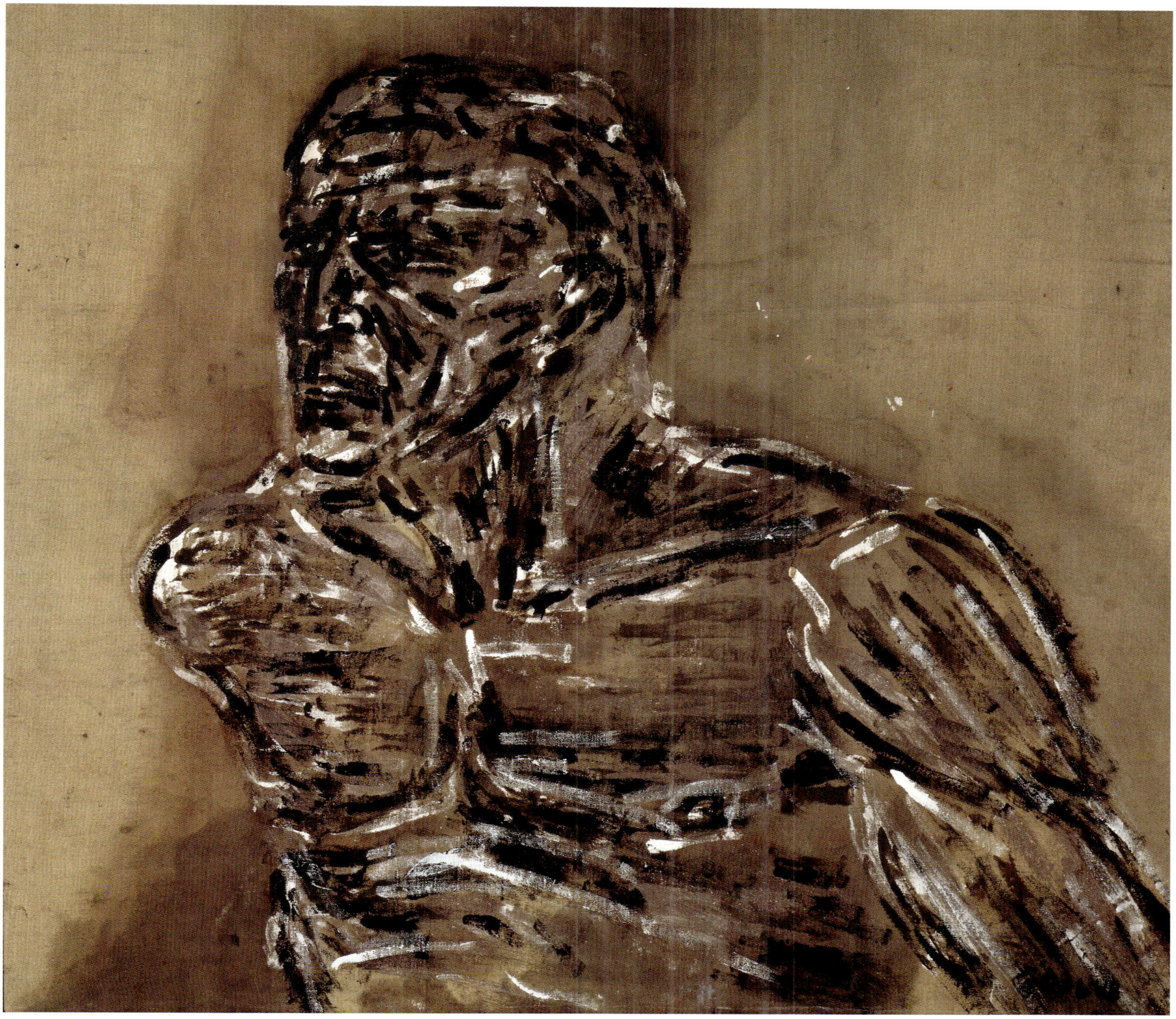

NANCY SPERO American, 1926–2009

WITH HER WAR SERIES of 1966 to 1970, Nancy Spero joined the ranks of artists who have taken up brush, pen, press, or paper in a visceral and intellectual response to the atrocities of war. Francisco de Goya's *Disasters of War* of 1810–20, which documented the barbarities perpetrated by Napoleon's army in Spain, serves as a foundational prototype. One may also compare Spero's protest to the work of the German Käthe Kollwitz, whose personal experiences of loss and the violence of war inspired her antiwar images early in the twentieth century. Spero follows in this tradition and blends it with a first-wave feminist aesthetic.

The War Series features iconographic themes of bombs, bodily functions, and helicopters, which provide both universal and historically specific references to the Vietnam War. The mushroom cloud of *Sperm Bomb* utilizes a less overtly phallic imagery than other works in the series, yet the aggressively smeared paint and dark faces moving toward the base of the cloud transform this iconic form into an explosive male emission.

Throughout the series Spero depicts poison, blood, and victims spewing from the tools of war: bombs, plane fuselages, and helicopters. In *Sperm Bomb* the entire composition is turned into a bodily act, a violent ejaculation. While other works in the series feature the same small heads we see in *Sperm Bomb*, Spero typically shows them vomiting red liquid that may symbolize poison or blood. In *Sperm Bomb* these faces pour out expletives in French and English, the latter spelled both backwards and forwards. Through text rather than imagery, the sexual act and male aggression are implicated in the violence of war.

Sperm Bomb's restrained palette of blue and black is consistent with the aesthetic of the entire series. Spero utilized primary and secondary colors accentuated with stark black or brown outlines. Combined with her aggressive mark-making, this palette ensures the artist's protests are conveyed in both the content and the physicality of her work.

Spero is known to have mixed saliva into her paint and purposefully created marks using her fingers, thereby tying her physical presence into the work. In *Sperm Bomb* this physicality can be seen when one analyzes the text and faces of the black swirling heads, which can be seen as sperm. Spero has smeared and rubbed the black ink and paint that make up these faces to the point that in some areas the paper has started to break down and fray. Anger and frustration are apparent in these physical manipulations.

The artist's frustrations with political and world violence, wars, and the misogynistic art world of the 1960s and 1970s are conveyed in her work. An ardent first-wave feminist, Spero earned a BFA from the School of the Art Institute of Chicago (1949) and was awarded honorary doctorates from that school (1991) and Williams College (2001). In her work the political and the private combine; she has discussed her work as "exorcising demons."[1] Her activism motivated Spero to join WAR (Women Artists in Revolution), an artists' organization that was developed in 1969 when the male-dominated Art Workers' Coalition refused to agitate for equal rights for women, as well as minorities, in the art world.[2]

Spero's art and political activity consistently addressed the place of women in society. In the War Series and later works, she also spoke to the importance of her Jewish identity, equating violent acts such as the My Lai massacre with the atrocities of World War II.[3] Both she and her husband, the artist Leon Golub, balanced their political activism with a strong interest in the study of classical figures and mythologies. Until her death in 2009, Spero was an outspoken commentator on the abuses of power and the violence of contemporary society and featured female archetypes in her work as a means of exploring imagined nonhierarchical social structures.

EP

Notes

1. Barbara Flynn, "Interview with Nancy Spero," in *Paper: Excerpts from the Writings of Antonin Artoud* (Cologne: Galerie Rudolf Zwirner, 1986), cited in *Nancy Spero: A Continuous Present*, ed. Dirk Luckow and Ingeborg Kahler (Düsseldorf: Richter Verlag, 2002), 18.
2. Carrie Ricky, "Illustrated Timeline: A Highly Selective Chronology," in *The Power of Feminist Art: The American Movement of the 1970s, History and Impact*, ed. Norma Broude and Mary D. Garrard (New York: H. N. Abrams, 1996), 305.
3. *Nancy Spero: The War Series, 1966–1970* (Milan: Charta, 2003), 12.

Sperm Bomb, 1966. Gouache and ink on paper, 27⅛ × 33⅞ in. Museum purchase with funds from the Jefferson-Pilot Corporation Endowment, Burlington Industries Endowment and the Weatherspoon Art Museum Acquisition Endowment, 2003

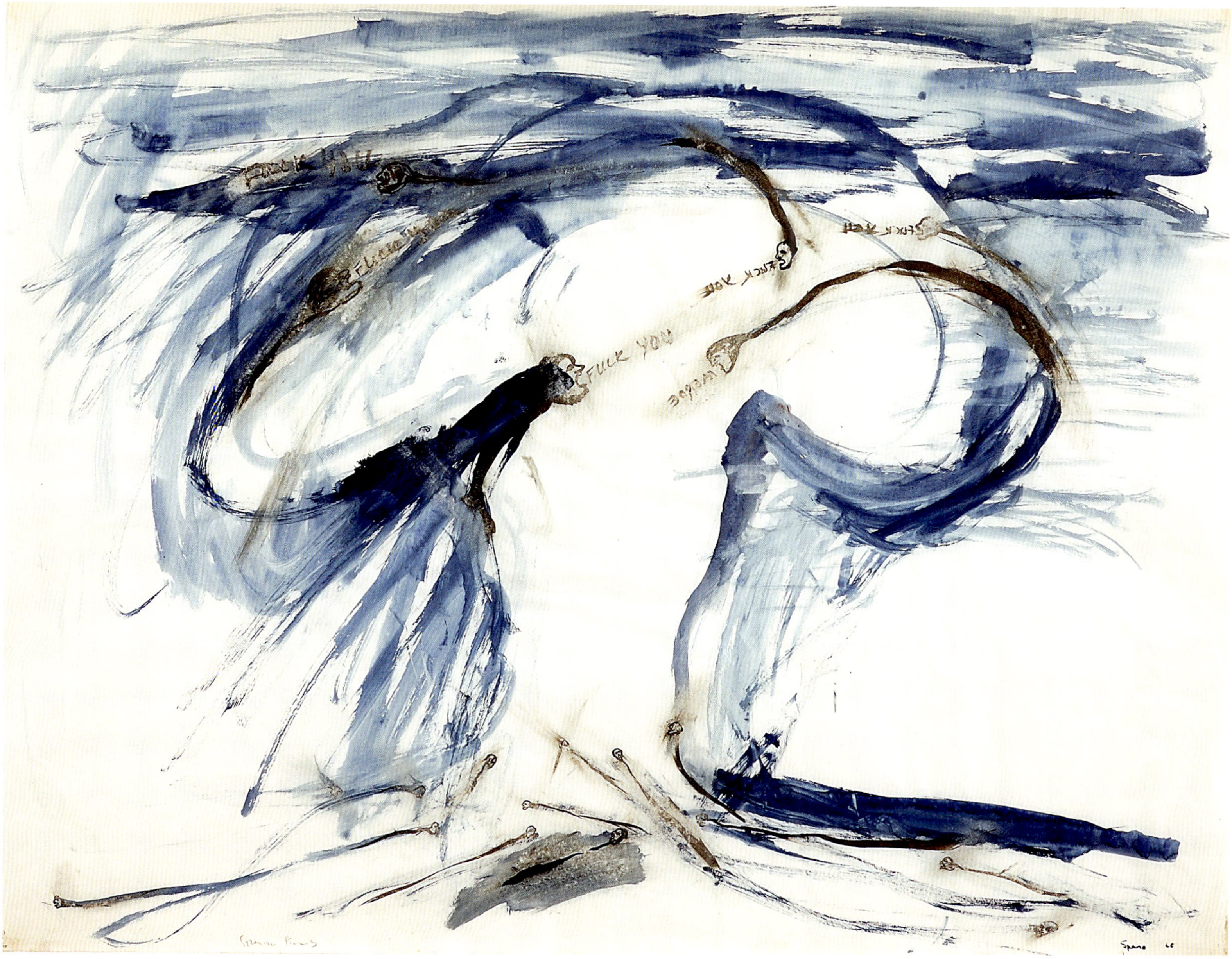
FUCK YOU

DAN FLAVIN American, 1933–1996

DAN FLAVIN'S MEDIUM was light and the architectural space light could occupy. Beginning in the early 1960s he used what were then readily available and inexpensive fluorescent tubes to create arrangements that were neither painting nor sculpture but that evoked aspects of each. He installed lights on floors, on walls, and in freestanding patterns using different colors, all of them commercially manufactured. Flavin's innovations with lines of electric light made him a leader in Minimalism, a broad art movement that included artists who rejected self-expression in favor of revealing the fundamental properties of physical experience.

Born in Queens, New York, Flavin had parents who were not supportive of his early creative efforts. After high school, he and his fraternal twin brother, David, enlisted in the United States Air Force. While serving, he visited art galleries in New York and, once discharged, enrolled at Columbia University. He thought at the time to become an art historian to support himself as an artist. Instead, he became a guard and elevator operator at the Museum of Modern Art, where he met Sol LeWitt and Robert Ryman as well as the art history student Sonja Severdija, whom he would marry.

In 1962 he met Donald Judd, who thought along parallel lines: both envisioned producing art with a minimum of actual "art making." Instead, they would use mass-produced components to make simplified objects that, because of the inherent quality of the materials used (like light), would reconfigure space itself and thus any experience of that space. Both were keenly aware of the legacy of Marcel Duchamp (who would recommend Flavin for a fellowship in 1964) and his pioneering use of the found object. (Duchamp famously stood a common snow shovel up in a gallery and called it *In Advance of a Broken Arm*.)

In 1963 Flavin took a single fluorescent tube and mounted it at a diagonal in his studio. It seemed to him sufficient unto itself as expression: there "was literally no need to compose this system definitively; it seemed to sustain itself directly, dynamically, dramatically in my workroom wall—a buoyant and insistent gaseous image which, through brilliance, somewhat betrayed its physical presence into approximate invisibility."[1] This creative act recalls Duchamp's selection of an ordinary object and calling it art, but at the same time it was quite different, since Flavin used the light to paint the atmosphere around it and change nearby surfaces. From that moment onward, Flavin remained focused on the infinitely variable possibilities of working with fluorescent lights alone.

Flavin dedicated works to friends, fellow artists, and various sources of inspiration. He also carefully controlled the installation of what he called his "proposals" or "situations," and a certificate accompanies this piece detailing the specific angle of the bulb on the floor. Museums or galleries that incorrectly installed his works or—worse yet—misinterpreted them could expect an ornately written and caustic letter in response.

Flavin showed this work in 1967 at the Weatherspoon while he was a visiting instructor for a semester in The University of North Carolina at Greensboro's Art Department.[2] Though an early proponent of the artist, the museum did not acquire *Untitled (for Frank Stella)* in 1967 but, rather, a full twenty-five years later. By then, Dan Flavin's transformative influence on the field of contemporary art was, and continues to be, internationally recognized.

WS

Note

1. Dan Flavin, "'. . . in daylight or cool white': An Autobiographical Sketch," *Artforum* 4, no. 4 (December 1965), quoted in Michael Govan and Tiffany Bell, *Dan Flavin: A Retrospective* (New York: Dia Art Foundation; Washington, DC: National Gallery of Art, in association with Yale University Press, 2004), 33.
2. James Tucker, interview by the author, July 8, 2008. Tucker was curator of collections at the Weatherspoon from 1959 to 1985.

Untitled (To Frank Stella), 1966. Pink and yellow fluorescent light, edition 4/5, 24 × 48¼ in. Museum purchase, 1992

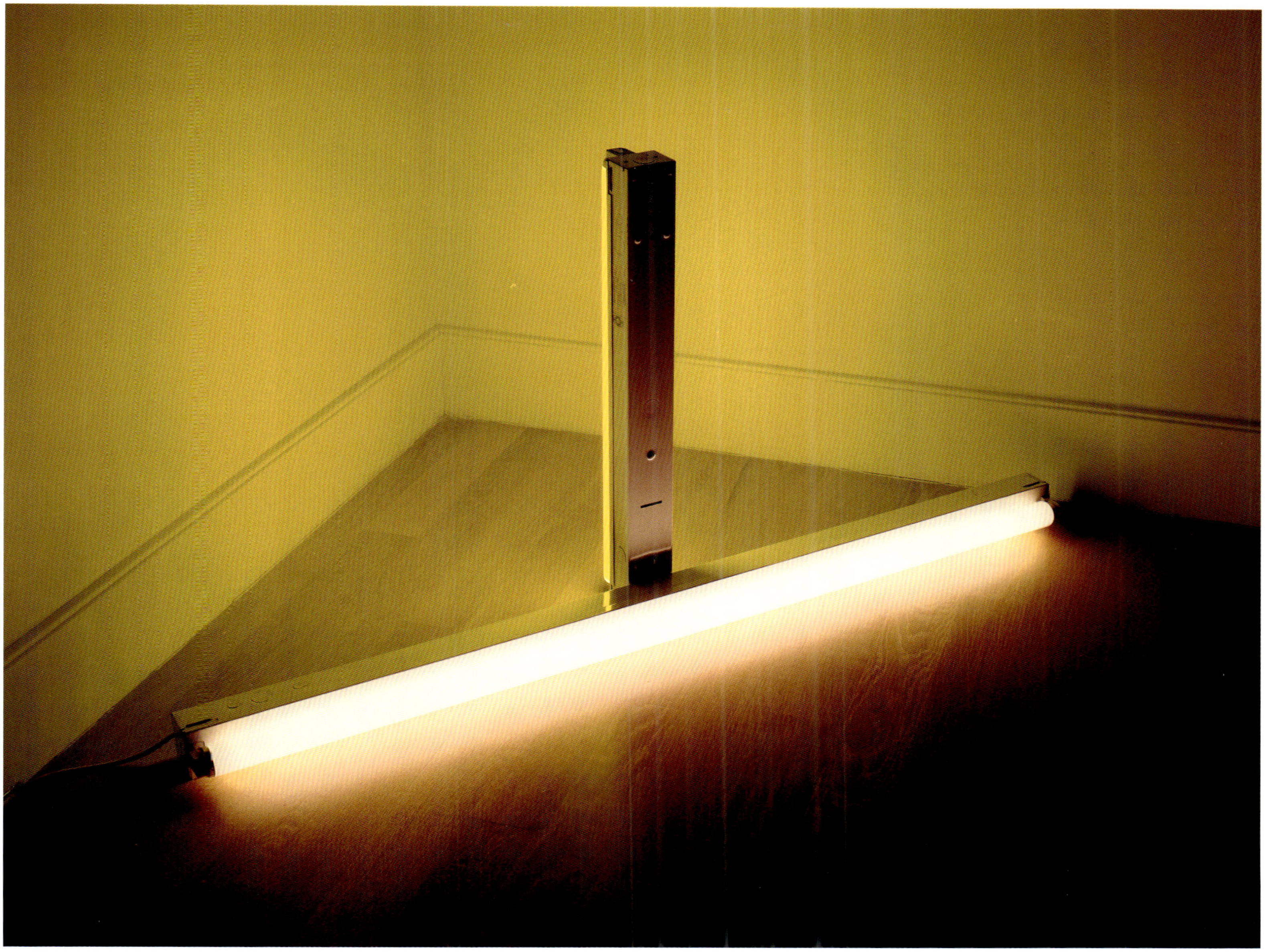

EVA HESSE American, born Germany, 1936–1970

BEFORE HER TRAGIC DEATH at thirty-four, Eva Hesse created a vast number of extraordinary and innovative works that continue to exert their influence on artists today. She is widely recognized for advancing the concepts underlying Minimalism by working with irregular shapes and tactile, organic-looking materials. No Title and No Title No. 1 demonstrate Hesse's inventive approach to drawing and sculpture, which brings together such opposing ideas as chaos versus order, flexibility versus inflexibility, body versus object, and organic versus geometric form.

Born in Germany, Hesse immigrated to New York with her family in 1939 to escape Nazi persecution. As a young woman, Hesse attended Yale University, where she studied under Josef Albers, concentrating on painting and drawing. Willem de Kooning, Jean Dubuffet, and Arshile Gorky were early influences. During a year abroad in Germany with her husband, from 1964 to 1965, Hesse began to focus on sculpture. Her interest was initially spawned by an experiment in which she threaded pieces of cord soaked in plaster through a large mesh screen. Sculpture soon became the generative core from which Hesse produced a remarkable body of work in the span of five years.

Hesse embraced an art-making process that was fluid in manner, responding to the physical qualities of her materials. She possessed an inexhaustible drive to resolve both formal and conceptual issues. Experimentation through models and tests was a vital part of her artistic process, and she considered a number of her sculptural models completed works in their own right. No Title is an early rumination on a concept that Hesse realized as *Accretion* in 1968. A much larger sculpture, *Accretion* consists of a long row of fifty hollow, three-foot-high fiberglass tubes that lean vertically against a gallery wall. Whereas industrial fabricators produced the final versions of this and others of her large objects, Hesse made early and small-scale works such as No Title by hand in her studio. It is made up of twenty cardboard tubes that are stacked horizontally to form a pyramid shape. Each of the cardboard tubes is covered with Sculp-Metal and capped at each end with metal washers. Lengths of gray vinyl tubing are threaded through six of the tubes.[1] The sculpture is shown either on a high base or shelf, with the vinyl cords hanging down on both sides, the ends resting on the floor, or on a low pedestal with the cords arranged along a tabletop or platform.[2] The winding, organic lines of the flexible vinyl that extend away from the stacked forms create a feeling of disorder and fluidity. The instability of the composition evokes feelings of fragility, in part because it seems so open-ended and vulnerable to change. It conveys the imperfectness and absurdity Hesse sought; she once described the overall quality she hoped to achieve to her close friend Sol LeWitt simply as "ick."[3]

Hesse elaborates on the dangling or falling-cord motif in many of her sculptures from the same period, including No Title No. 1, which elegantly intertwines the artist's interests in drawing, painting, and sculpture. It appears, at first, to be a repeated grid, but irregularity is introduced by the faint circles of ink wash in each square and the cotton strings that, rather erotically, protrude from the center of each circle. While the logic of the 15½-by-15½-inch planar grid is respected to an extent, the hand-drawn lines and the unevenness of the ink wash and strings lift the drawing out of the rigid, unchanging geometry of Minimalism to create a subtly shifting field of lines and shadows. No Title No. 1 was acquired from the Weatherspoon's third annual *Art on Paper* exhibition in 1967, when Hesse was still largely unknown outside the New York art world. According to archived documentation from the estate, No Title No. 1 represents the first drawing by Hesse to be acquired by a museum.

XE

Notes

1. It should be noted that one of the twenty tubes in No Title is coated with resin that differs in color from the others and has generally been understood as a test piece that was later added.
2. As in some other works by Hesse and according to the artist's sketches for No Title, the placement of the cords here is open to interpretation and left to the discretion of the curator of the exhibition.
3. From a conversation between LeWitt and Linda Norden as documented in "Getting to Ick," in *Eva Hesse: A Retrospective* (New Haven: Yale University Art Gallery, 1992), 70.

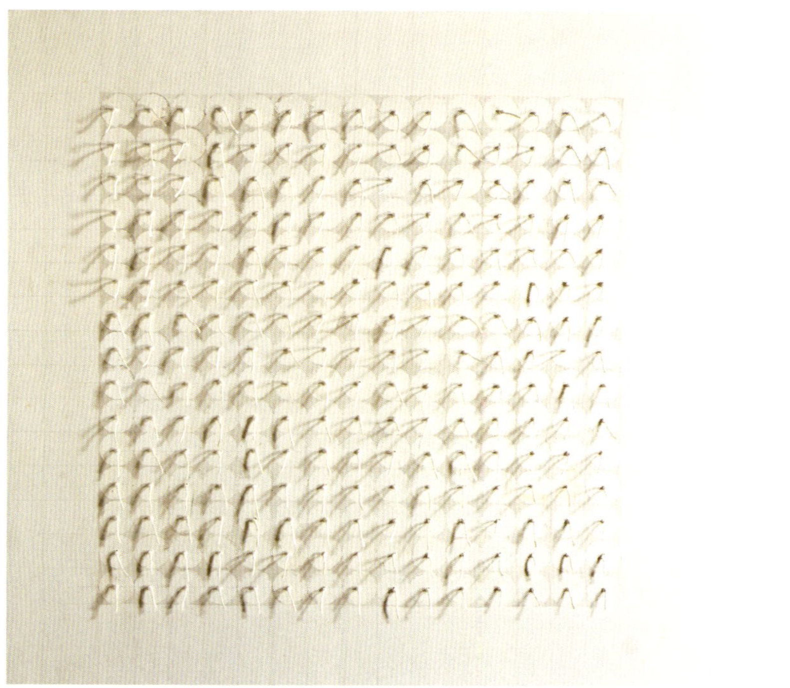

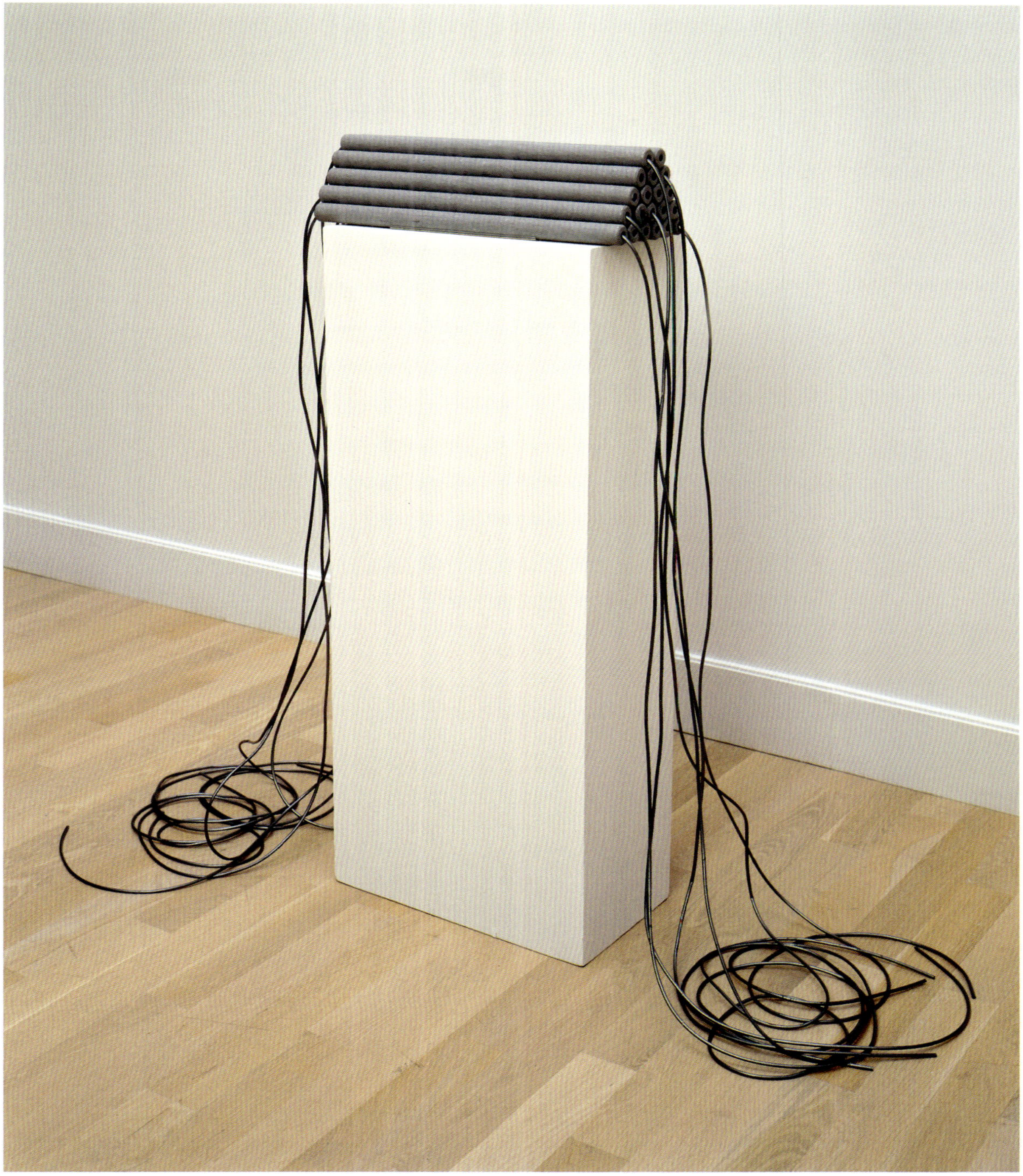

No Title No. 1, 1967. Ink wash, graphite, and cotton string on paper board, 15½ × 15½ in. Museum purchase with funds from the Dillard Paper Company for the Dillard Collection, 1967

No Title, 1967. Sculp-metal, metal, cardboard, and vinyl, 20 tubes, each 20½ × 1 in.; 6 extrusions, each 128 in. Gift of Helen Hesse Charash, 1983

BRUCE NAUMAN American, born 1941

AS A MAJOR FORCE in the Conceptual movement in the San Francisco Bay area, Bruce Nauman advocated the primacy of the artist's ideas over whatever forms those ideas took. His background in mathematics, science, philosophy, music, literature, and Gestalt psychology provided the theoretical impetus for much of his groundbreaking work. A pioneer in materials as well, Nauman was attracted to process-oriented works rather than to traditional media. He was among the first artists to use his body as subject matter and to explore the possibilities of film and video as tools in art making.

Nauman created his first films in 1965 while a graduate student at the University of California, Davis, using an inexpensive 16 mm windup camera that he had bought from a pawnshop.[1] The limits of mid-twentieth-century technology determined the end product: silent and black-and-white, these early films run three minutes at the most, a duration that corresponds to the length of the available film. At this point in his career, Nauman was interested in creating works that investigated straightforward ordinary actions, such as eating and drinking, his personal appearance and skin, gestures, remnants of activity such as footprints and signatures, and simple sounds including spoken words.[2]

In 1968 Nauman began working with low-cost, consumer-available video equipment obtained through his dealer, Leo Castelli, who purchased it for his use and let him keep it in his studio for over a year.[3] With this technology Nauman could now record actions for a full hour. In 1969 he produced *Lip Sync*, a black-and-white video in which he used his body as an expressive tool to explore the relation between words and images in visual and verbal puns.

Lip Sync documents a made-for-camera performance. In it Nauman focused an upside-down camera on his mouth and throat as he says the words *lip sync*, which he hears through the headphones he wears, over and over again in a regular rhythm. Unshaven, the artist enunciates the words so that both the sound and the movement of his facial features are exaggerated. The video records Nauman's attempts to synchronize his lip movements with the utterance of the words that he hears through the headphones. As with many of the tasks Nauman conceived and filmed, the action appears superficially simple but, in fact, was arduous, requiring intense concentration. Nauman noted that he often had problems making the exercises he filmed take up a full hour because the participant(s) would become distracted or bored and their attention would wander.[4] In this exercise, maintaining a perfectly even tempo of repetition was challenging. As a result, the sound of the words alternately goes in and out of sync with the movement of Nauman's lips. The viewer's efforts to anticipate and match the soundtrack with the visual image on the screen sets up a tension analogous to that the artist experienced. The upside-down view of his mouth in action provides a further disorienting quality to the work.

Lip Sync illustrates Nauman's lifelong interest in creating works of art that conveyed messages greater than the sum of their parts. It also expresses the artist's belief that all human activity, no matter how trivial, was worthy of being examined. At the same time, Nauman never intended his films and videos to be viewed from start to finish. Rather, he wanted audiences to be able to come in at any point of the action and to feel grounded. Nor did it bother him that his Conceptual and process-oriented endeavors did not appeal to a large audience. It was the course of pushing his ideas to absurd extremes that most interested him, and which, in turn, has captivated following generations of artists and viewers alike.

EDG

Notes

1. Constance M. Lewallen, *A Rose Has No Teeth: Bruce Nauman in the 1960s* (Berkeley: University of California Press, 2007), 38.
2. Ibid., 45–46.
3. Ibid., 88.
4. See http://www.aaa.si.edu/collections/oralhistories/transcripts/nauman80.htm.

Lip Sync, 1969. Black-and-white video with sound, 60 minutes. Museum purchase with funds from the Benefactors Fund, 1975

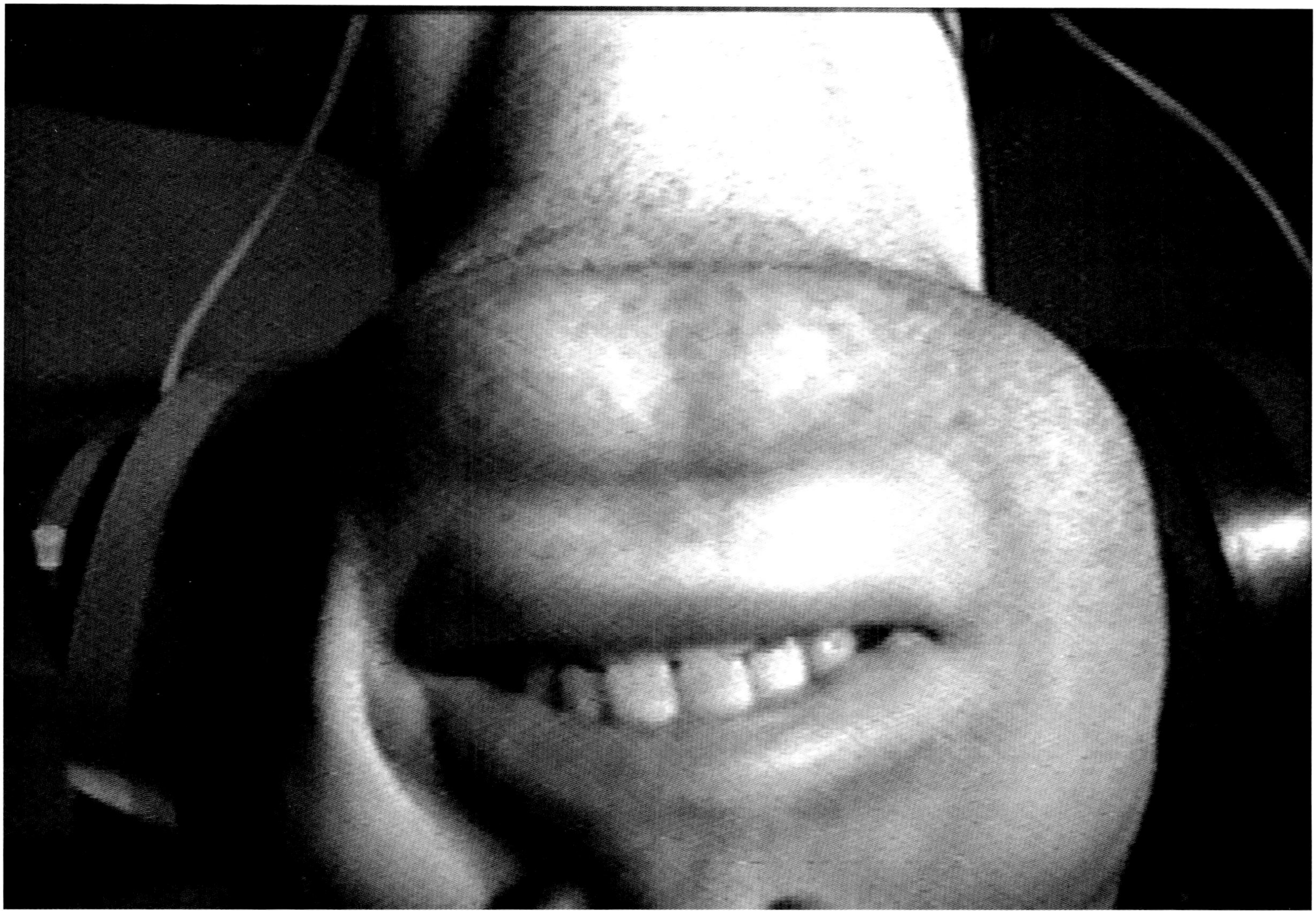

ROBERT SMITHSON American, 1938–1973

ROBERT SMITHSON REMAINS most famous for his enormous work of art in Utah's Great Salt Lake, the *Spiral Jetty*. Made in 1970, the *Jetty* is a 1,500-foot length of black basalt rock, earth, and salt crystals that stretches out into the lake and then curls up on itself like an antique watch spring.

Before he died in a plane crash at thirty-five, Smithson spent years critiquing the relation between art and the institutional world of museums, collectors, and galleries. His interests in time, ritual, the environment, and the future could not be contained by the conventions of the art world as it then existed, and he was a pivotal figure in pioneering earthworks, projects beyond the scale of any traditional gallery space. He chose the Great Salt Lake as a location to build a giant monument of natural materials in part because its instability and progressive decay match the notion of entropy that so fascinated him—everything, he believed, was breaking down and being reordered all the time. Meanings, then, also could shift with the natural decay and rebirth that go on perpetually in the earth and atmosphere.

Smithson also investigated these ideas in a series of works called Nonsites, in which natural materials from expansive sites in nature were brought into the gallery and rescaled to suit its dimensions, and shown with a map of the original site. Similarly, just as he inserted large mirrors into various landscape sites that he then photographed, Smithson reconfigured the concept of spatial displacement for indoor galleries, often as triangular sculptures that endlessly reflect the rooms' interiors.

Smithson's interests in maps, mapping, and geological history are readily apparent in *The Hypothetical Continent of Lemuria*, one of four works he made in 1969 that depict lost continents of legend. The drawing has a pseudo-scientific character, with its images and notations laid out on gridded paper. At the same time, he constructed a three-dimensional map of the continent from seashells he found on the beach of Sanibel Island, Florida. To Smithson, the shells represented some of the deeply buried layers of material that may have existed on the mythical Lemuria.

He documented this ephemeral earthwork in a series of four slides, from which four exhibition photographs have been made. The slides are the only literal record of the earthwork itself. Of his art, Smithson said in 1970,

> *My work has always been an attempt to get away from the specific object. My objects are constantly moving into another area. There is no way of isolating them—they are fugitive. They are things, rather than definable presences. Working with non-illusionistic materials, like opaque materials, breaks down that whole idea of certainty which is in the 'object.'. . .*
>
> *A lot of people are disturbed by my work because it is not within their grasp; it isn't a simple symmetry.*[1]

Robert Smithson's art and philosophy helped to restructure late-twentieth-century thinking about how big art can be, what it can be made of, where it should be located, who can own it or not, and how it relates to the world of change in which we live.

WS

Note

1. Robert Smithson, "Interview with Robert Smithson, 1970," ed. Paul Toner and Smithson, in *Robert Smithson* (New York: James Cohan Gallery, 2001), 31.

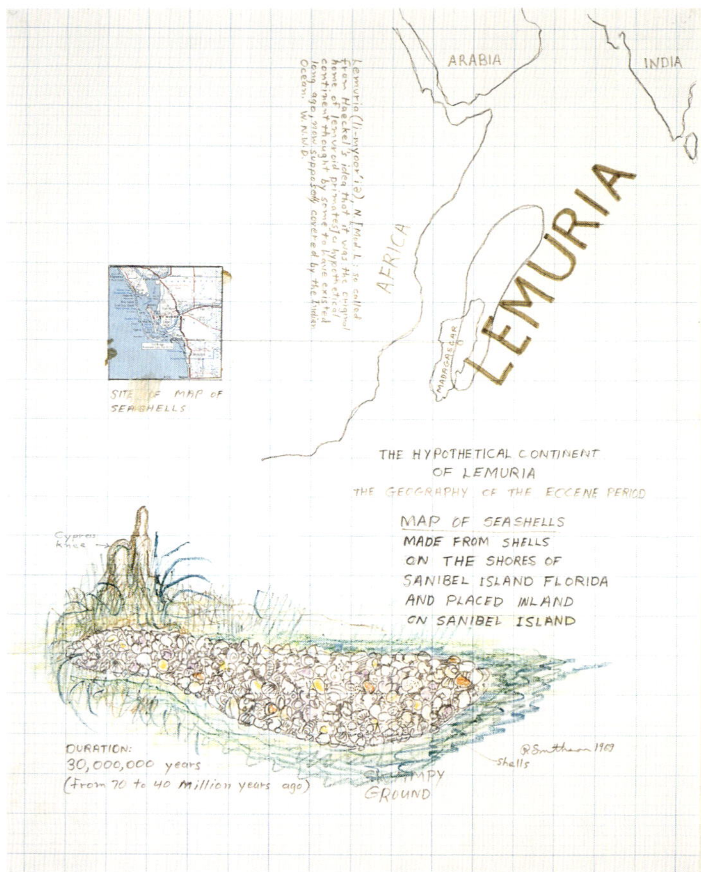

Hypothetical Continent of Lemuria, 1969. Brown ink, crayon, graphite, and collage on paper, 22¼ × 17¼ in. Museum purchase with funds from the Dillard Paper Company for the Dillard Collection, 1969

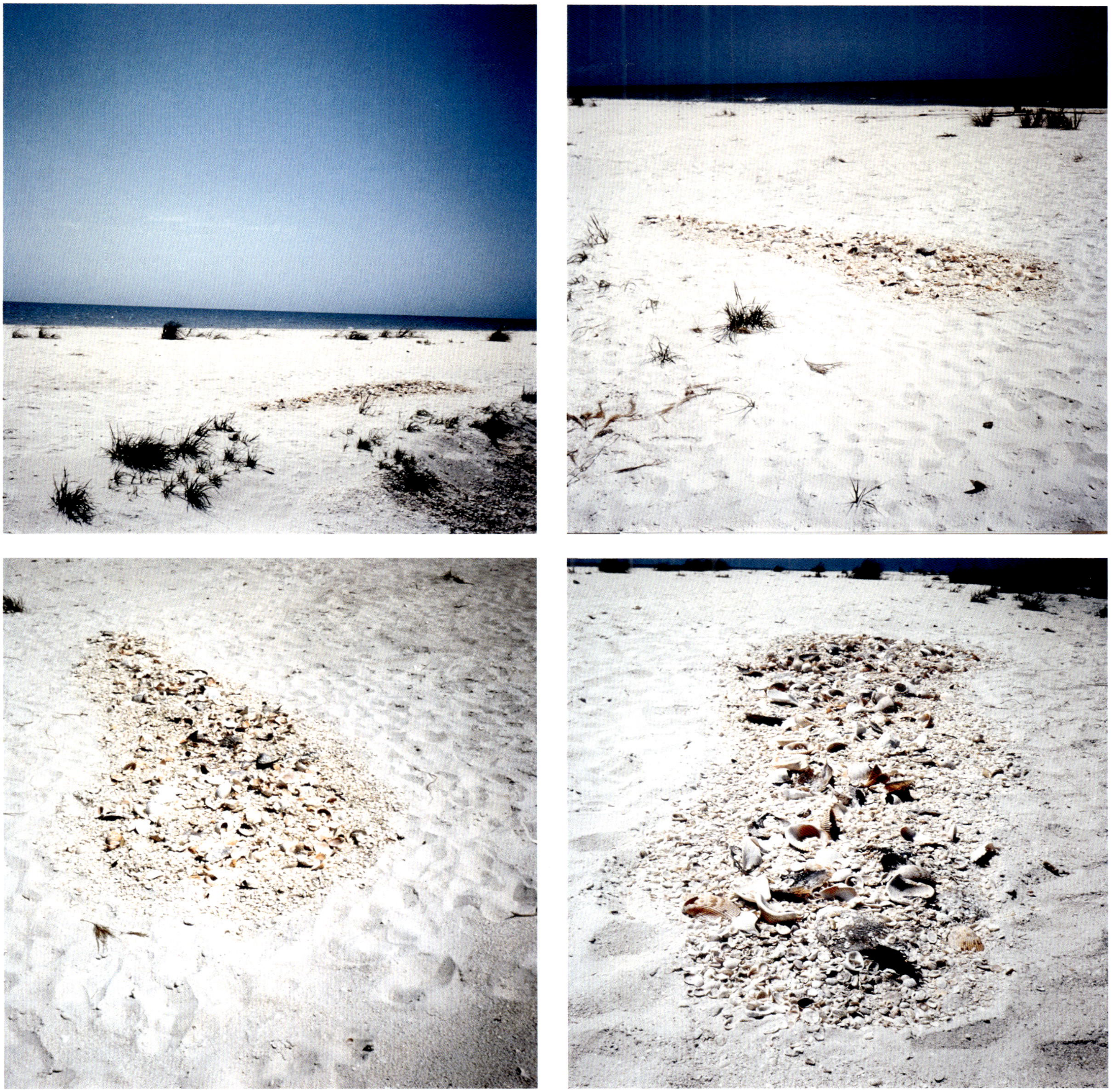

Hypothetical Continent in Shells: Lemuria, Sanibel, Florida, 1969. Four unique exhibition color prints made in 2001 from original 35 mm slides, each 24 × 24 in. Museum purchase with funds from the Lynn Richardson Prickett Acquisition Endowment and the Judy Proctor Acquisition Endowment, 2002

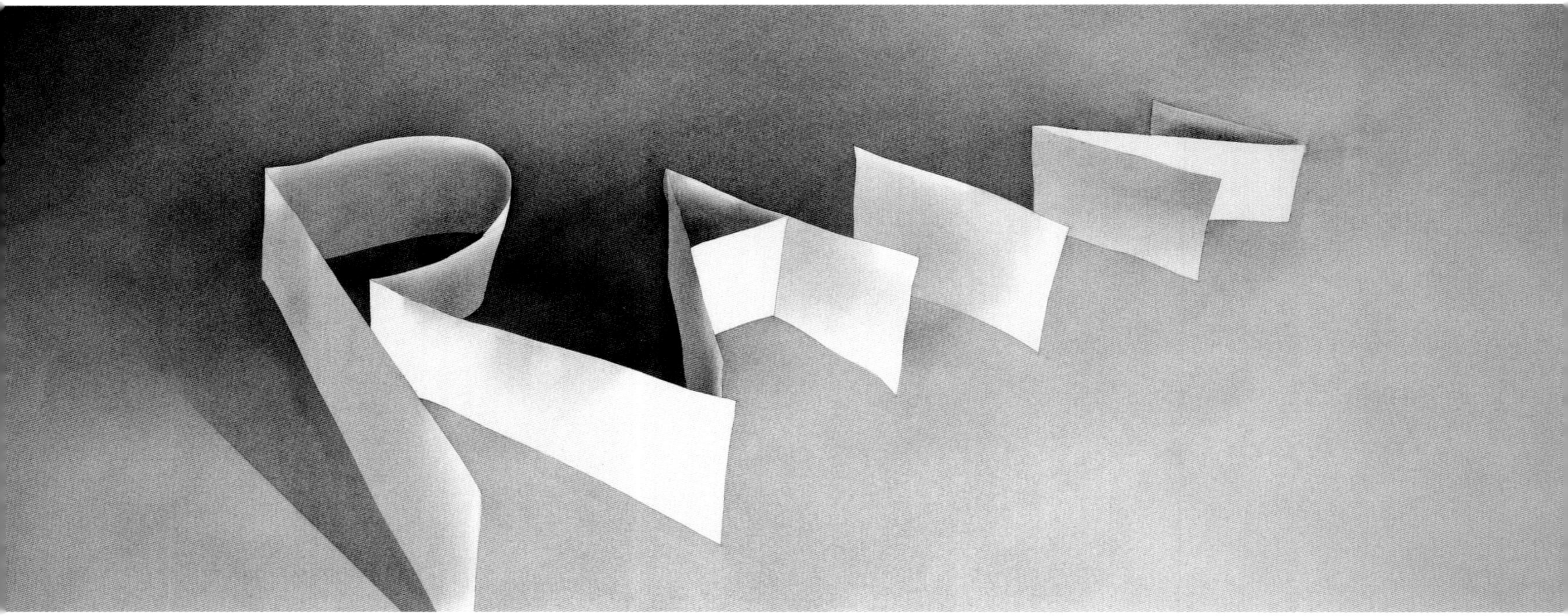

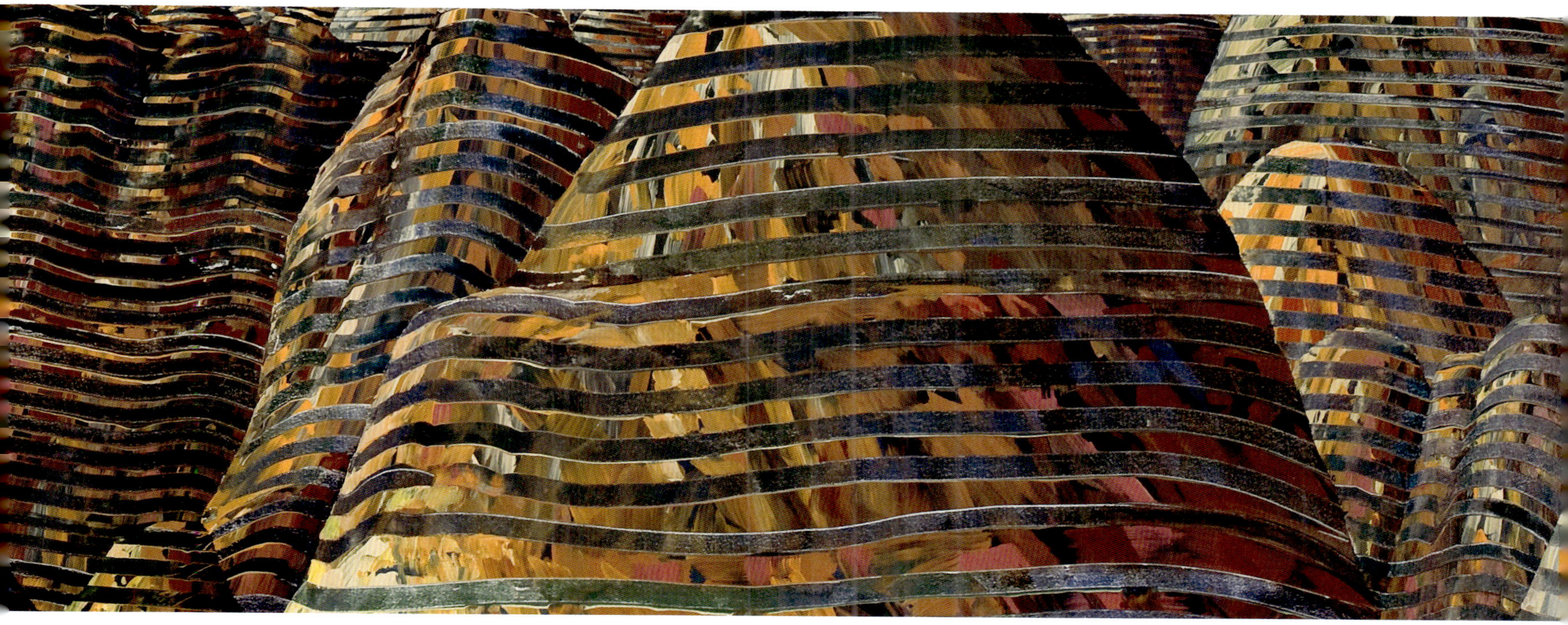

Selected Works: 1970–2010

WILLIAM BAILEY American, born 1930

ALTHOUGH WELL KNOWN as a contemporary realist artist, William Bailey describes his work as abstract, a somewhat startling and perplexing declaration to anyone who has seen the artist's paintings or works on paper firsthand. Despite coming to maturity during the height of Abstract Expressionism and having earned both his BFA and MFA from Yale University under the tutelage of the renowned abstract artist and color theorist Josef Albers, Bailey has never wavered in his commitment to the observable world. So what makes his work abstract?

Still Life with Bottle, Bowl, and Eggs exemplifies one of the genres for which Bailey is well recognized: still lifes of domestic items (bottles, bowls, cups, pitchers, eggs, etc.) that have been arranged on tabletops or shelves and delineated in muted earth tones.[1] Although still lifes have been a stock subject for painters for centuries, Bailey's representations exhibit a decidedly modern quality that has little to do with the date of their completion and more to do with metaphysics and investigations into the nature of reality.

Although variations on a theme, each of Bailey's still life paintings emanates its own tenor and meaning owing in part to the artist's working method. While the objects derive from the real world, Bailey does not paint directly from life or photographic sources, preferring to rely on his imagination and/or memories of observed things. Inventing both the items and their compositional arrangement, the artist stylizes and delineates the objects in such a way that the painting as a whole appears removed from time and place. For example, *Still Life with Bottle, Bowl, and Eggs* contains subtle perspective and lighting "errors" that would not have been made if Bailey had painted directly from life. The shadow that the central egg casts is different in perspective from those of the bottle, jug, and large bowl. Moreover, the edges of the tabletop do not appear to recede in space but rather to tilt up.

The sensibility of Bailey's work, however, does not come solely from the types of objects he portrays or the manner in which he depicts them but from the strangely familiar, silent nature of their setting. The containers and eggs adhere to a highly ordered, architectonic hierarchy that expresses a sense of timelessness and frozen perfection.[2] Unlike conventional still-life paintings where objects spill out of the composition or appear concrete and tactile, Bailey's domestic items are quiet, solemn, and distinct. Made up predominantly of horizontals and verticals, the composition is activated only insofar as the objects are placed near one another, or else only as far as the tilt of the cabinet's top is taken into account. The shallow space and flat, muted expanses of the wall and cabinet further remove the objects from any suggestion of a real-life setting. The artist's meticulous application of paint likewise contributes to the painting's stillness and overall minimalist appearance.

Although based on concrete experiences, Bailey's still-life paintings function as metaphors rather than as factual records. Just as the seventeenth-century Dutch masters offered pearls of wisdom through the inclusion of specific items in their still lifes, so, too, does Bailey offer lessons to viewers who take the time to slow down, look, and disregard the cacophony of modern life.

EDG

Notes

1. Bailey is also praised for his skillfully rendered figurative works.
2. Bailey has said that he sees his still lifes as Italian cities. The artist has maintained a studio in Monterchi, Italy, for more than forty years, so it is not surprising that the colors and feeling of Italy are significant, if elusive, elements of his work.

Still Life with Bottle, Bowl, and Eggs, 1970. Oil on canvas, 36 × 42 in. Museum purchase with funds from North Carolina National Bank and the Smith Richardson Foundation, 1971

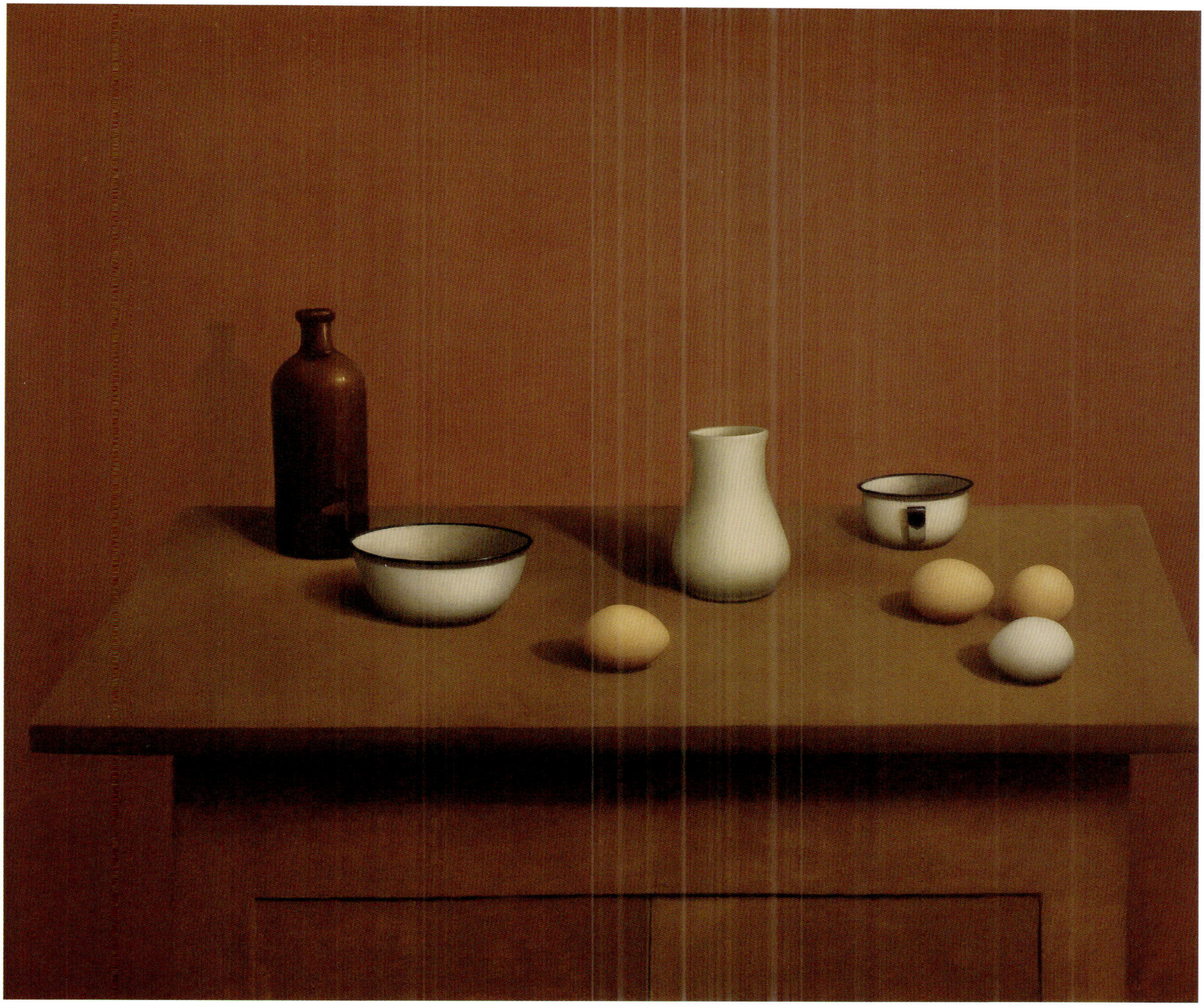

EDWARD RUSCHA American, born 1937

EDWARD RUSCHA SR., a Russian émigré, joined the American middle class working as an auditor for an insurance company in Omaha. His son, Edward Ruscha Jr., was born there, and the family moved to Oklahoma City when Ed was four. In the formative days of the new American republic, John Adams fervently hoped that its citizens would progress from lives of strife, to those of practical concerns, to the pursuit of the arts in three generations. The Ruscha family did it in two.

Ed Ruscha was talented as a child, and his mother encouraged his interests. At nineteen he moved to Los Angeles, having resolved to study at what is now the California Institute of the Arts. He concentrated on commercial art and, after graduating, apprenticed with a printer and also worked in an advertising agency, producing layouts and graphics. Education and employment emphasized elements that would be major properties of his later work in the fine arts: the telling line, the right color, flattened space, economical representation, words and wit, visual impact, commercial objects, subjects and settings, and the excitement of producing multiples rather than the single artifact.

In 1957 he saw a small black-and-white reproduction of Jasper Johns's *Target with Four Faces*. He credits this intersection of the popular image and the art object with prompting him to turn toward fine art. Subsequently, Ruscha's art has been associated with both Pop art and Conceptual art. However, as Kathy Halbreich observes, his work "is more aptly placed in a category that bridges the two, developing independently of any particular art movement."[1]

Ruscha's oeuvre includes drawings, lithographic and screen prints, photographs, and artist's books. He has said, "I love language. Words have temperatures. . . . When they reach a certain point and become hot words, then they appeal to me."[2] In his prints and drawings, a single word often serves as the visual subject. The word may be treated as if it were made from ribbon, paper, or even a liquid.

Rain pulls the viewer into a space wherein a solitary word, *rain*, commands attention. The word is presented as a three-dimensional illusion, as if each letter were formed from strips of paper. The viewer seems to hover above the plane on which the letters stand. Very similar to *Rain* is Ruscha's screen print *Raw* of the following year. The word *raw* appears, again like folded paper; however, the letters are brown in color and the ground is a strong, bright yellow. Colors support associations surrounding the word: reddish brown and hot yellow for *raw*; suffused cool gray and blue for *rain*. If the word were made of paper, nothing would be less welcome than rain. Ruscha is noted for his choices of unexpected media, and *Rain* combines pastel and gunpowder. The most liquid of weather conditions is executed in the driest of media.

Space is curious; the lower edge of the plane feels as if it is vertical, but, as the letters recede, it flattens toward an unseen horizon. Light moving subtly across the surface picks out the letters, imparting an impression of dimensionality. The modulated values gradate toward darker shades at the upper corners, where Ruscha includes areas of cobalt blue pastel. The manipulation of these colors creates a continuing atmospheric space where light cannot reach. The point of view, the space, the light, the delicate shades, and the insubstantial materiality of the letters all conspire to present an image of great delicacy that is paradoxically vast and monumental.

The viewer experiences a pure visualization, something that Ruscha has brought into being, a revelation that could not be seen through ordinary perception. The work retains the character of its conceptual origin; its elemental components engender questions that go unanswered. Where is this? What exactly is it? What does it mean? As a phenomenon of weather, the meaning of rain can be agreed upon. What Ruscha's presentation of rain means, however, is essentially elusive. In *Rain* word and image fuse into an oscillating flicker of possible recognitions not unlike a fleeting glimpse, a half-remembered association, or a fragment of memory. Often remarked on (and frequently denied by the artist), the urban scene of Los Angeles and the landscape of the West are influential presences in Ruscha's work. Indeed, there is about *Rain* a feeling of those western spaces, vistas so vast that the rain from a thunderstorm may be seen falling in the form of curtains.

RG

Notes

1. Kathy Halbreich, foreword to Siri Engberg and Clive Philpot, *Edward Ruscha: Editions, 1959–1999; Catalogue Raisonné*, vol. 2 (Minneapolis: Walker Art Center, 1999), 9.
2. Quoted in Siri Engberg, "Out of Print: The Editions of Edward Ruscha," in ibid., 23.

Rain, 1970. Gunpowder and pastel on paper, 23 × 29 in. Museum purchase with funds from the Dillard Paper Company for the Dillard Collection, 1992

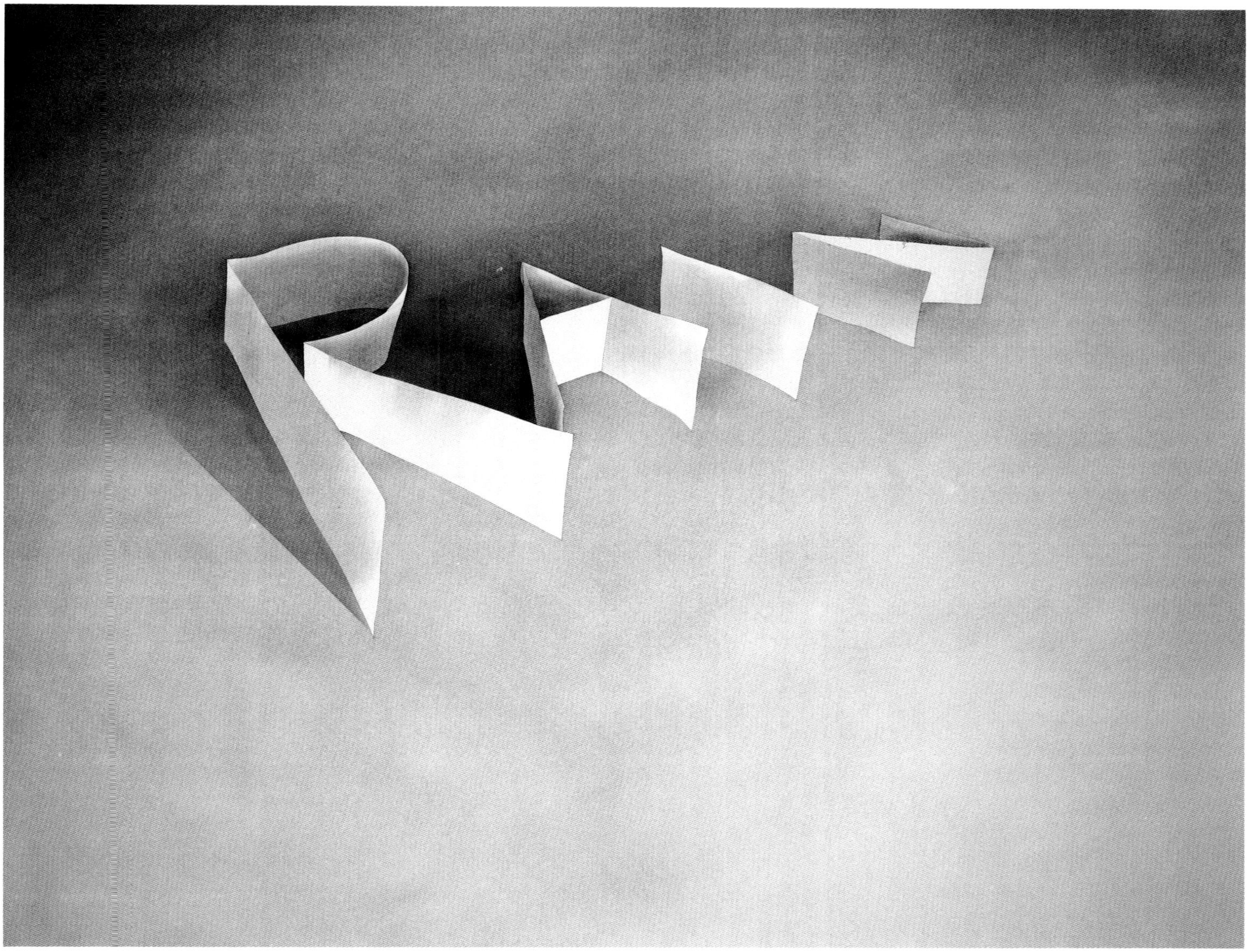

ELEANOR ANTIN American, born 1935

ELEANOR ANTIN EXAMINES the space between art and life by inventing characters and histories that are interlaced with autobiography. She began her career as a Conceptual artist in New York, but, when she moved to California, in 1968, she began to create narrative, performance-based work using a variety of media, including photography, theater, video, and film.

For her seminal work, *100 Boots*, Antin created a time-based, visual narrative through a sequence of postcards that document the life and times of fifty pairs of black boots marching in and around the towns and countryside of Southern California. They end their journey at the Museum of Modern Art in New York City. Antin sent the postcards, one by one, to one thousand artists, writers, libraries, museums, family members, and friends over a period of two and a half years. The work is innovative in structure, collapsing as it does performance, photography, Conceptual art, and issues related to the distribution of artwork.

The adventure of Antin's black boots begins on the ides of March 1971, at the Pacific Ocean in Del Mar, California, with a photograph of the boots standing at attention in a long row facing out to the sea. They are then shown going about their daily business in town, visiting such locations as a church, a bank, and a drive-in movie theater, before perilously venturing onto private property. At this point, the boots hit the road, taking cover in the woods, farmland, and industrial sites on the outskirts of town. Finally, in a postcard sent on May 11, 1973, the boots are shown heading east along the railroad tracks. Five days later, they appear on a ferryboat platform in New York City.

An exhibition of forty-six of the *100 Boots* postcards opened at the Museum of Modern Art two weeks after the boots (and Antin) arrived in the city, and five subsequent postcards in the series were shot in New York and mailed as weekly announcements for the show, which ran from May 30 to July 8, 1973.

Although Antin sent her postcards to hundreds of people from 1971 to 1973, few complete sets survive. The Weatherspoon's is addressed to Antin's sister and brother-in-law in New York, except for one, which is addressed to her niece at the same address. Seven of the postcards include signed notes from the artist to her family, wishing them well.

The humor found in the visual narrative of *100 Boots* belies the seriousness of its political and art-historical context. Antin was a feminist artist working at the height of the movement in the early 1970s. The fact that one of her final postcards shows an army of boots literally marching through the doors of the Museum of Modern Art is not without significance. Antin even refers to *100 Boots* in the masculine singular, writing, "I always knew *100 Boots* would have to end up in a museum—to officially become Art . . . he was installed in his own room, complete with sink and light bulb, mattresses, sleeping bags, and AM radio, along with the postcards and new images of his urban experience."[1] Antin's project also coincided with the antiwar movement in the United States, and many of the recipients of her work considered it an expression of unity among everyday Americans across the country in their efforts to end the war in Vietnam.

100 Boots not only bridges the gap between the realities of the outside world and the inner sanctum of the museum, but, like other Correspondence art of the 1960s, its method of distribution (the U.S. Postal Service) negates any barriers an artist might encounter in showing work within the established art system. Further, the presentation of the postcards at the Museum of Modern Art as documentation of a project that was ongoing, rather than a completed, autonomous artwork, is a radical departure from standard artistic practice and puts Antin in the company of the most progressive artists of the time.

XE

Note

1. Eleanor Antin, "Remembering *100 Boots*," in *100 Boots* (Philadelphia: Running Press Book Publishers, 1999), 9.

100 Boots, 1971–73. 51 offset lithograph postcards, each 4½ × 7 in. Museum purchase with funds from the Weatherspoon Guild Art Acquisition Endowment Fund and the Frances Stern Loewenstein Acquisition Endowment Fund, 2004

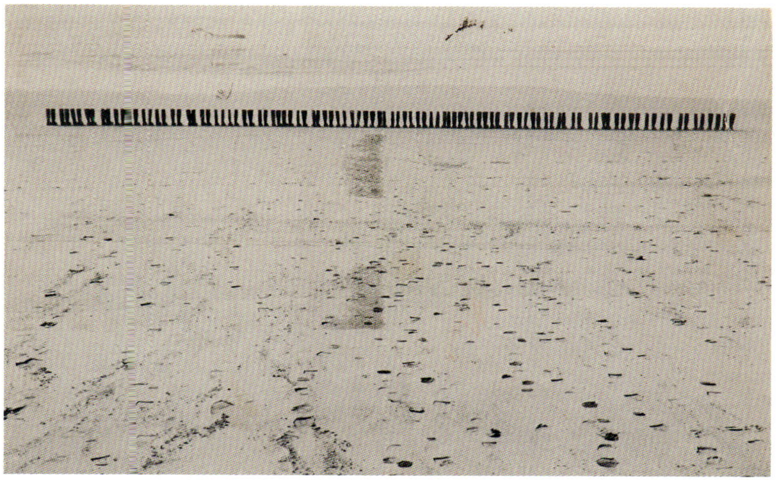

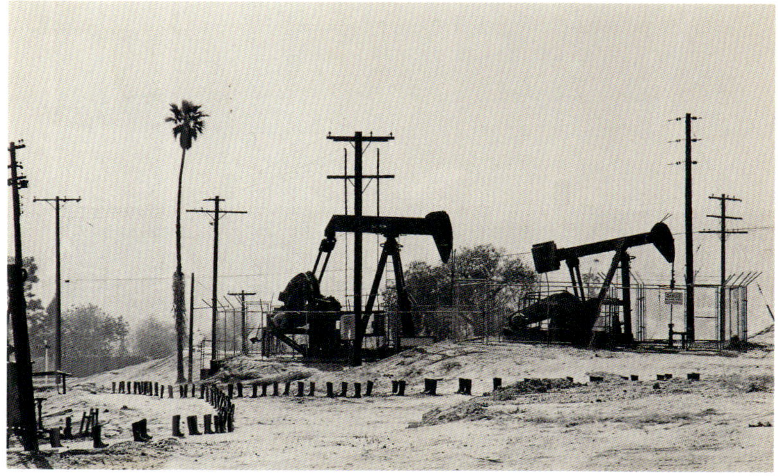

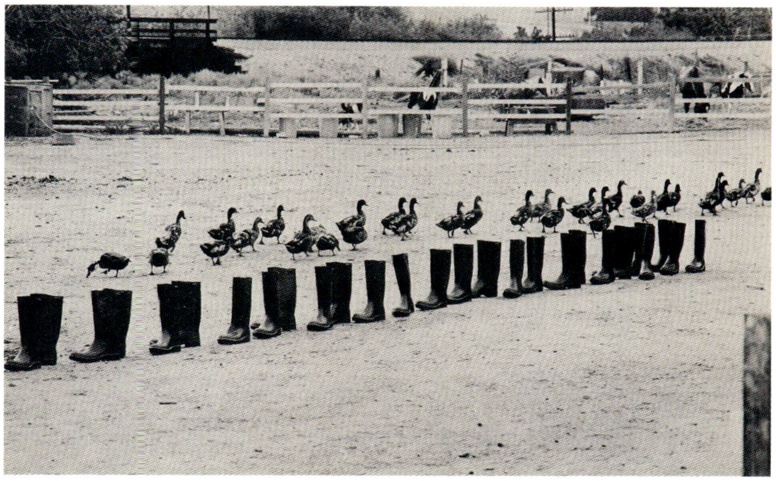

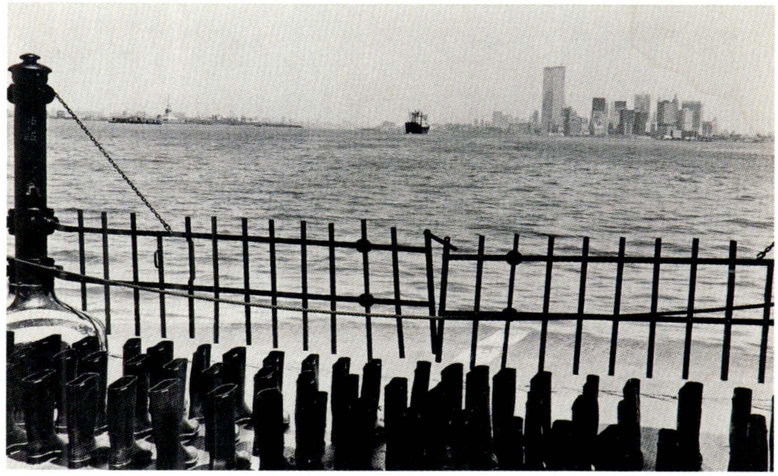

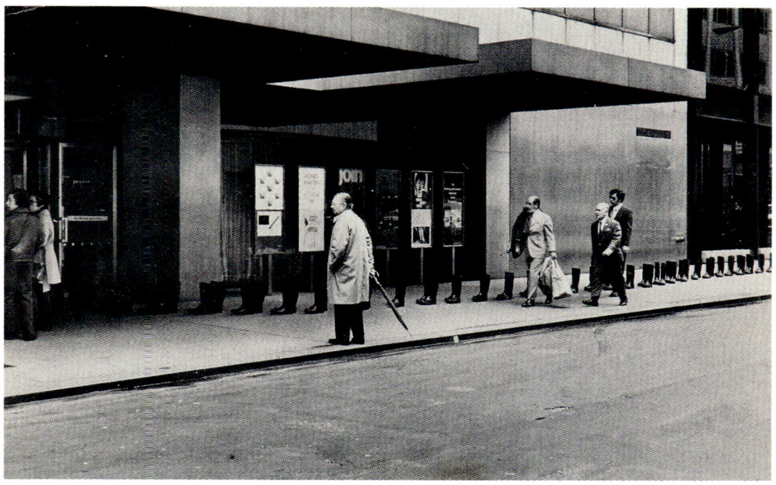

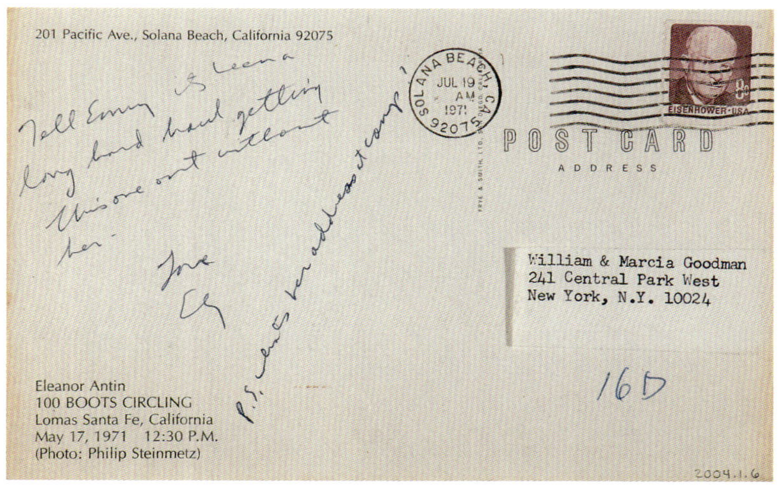

201 Pacific Ave., Solana Beach, California 92075

SOLANA BEACH, CAL. JUL 19 AM 1971 92075

POST CARD

ADDRESS

EISENHOWER·USA 8c

William & Marcia Goodman
241 Central Park West
New York, N.Y. 10024

16D

Eleanor Antin
100 BOOTS CIRCLING
Lomas Santa Fe, California
May 17, 1971 12:30 P.M.
(Photo: Philip Steinmetz)

2004.1.6

ROBERT MANGOLD American, born 1937

I've always had the desire to make the work be a unity, and I wanted nothing to be ahead of anything else. . . . I wanted the elements, which were the periphery line and the internal line, the surface color, etc., to be equal. I wanted them to be so totally locked together that they were inseparable.

—Robert Mangold, 1978[1]

WHILE AT THE CLEVELAND Institute of Art in the late 1950s, Robert Mangold and some fellow art students drove to Pittsburgh to see the Carnegie International exhibition. There, for the first time, Mangold saw works by contemporary painters—including Willem de Kooning, Franz Kline, and Jackson Pollock. He was stunned, inspired, and, perhaps most important, liberated by the experience: abstract art, he discovered, could be profoundly moving.

From Cleveland, Mangold went to Yale University for an MFA and from there to New York City, where, like a number of artists of his generation, he became a guard at the Museum of Modern Art. He continued to immerse himself in the study of contemporary art—reading about, looking at, and painting in the style of artists he found compelling. In the mid-1960s Mangold felt that for him to really know painting he had to start from the beginning and concentrate on the basic elements of making an image. Focusing on line, shape, and single colors alone, Mangold became associated with the Minimalist movement, whose artists shared an emphasis on the essentials of geometric abstraction.

The artist's *Distorted Circle within a Polygon III* features a uniform field of cool blue-gray acrylic paint applied with a roller. This field is broken by a pencil line that circumscribes the inner space and touches each of the outer edges of the painting but does not repeat or reinforce either. Indeed, the curving pencil line, however carefully and mathematically drawn, is evidence of the artist's creative hand and is thus a somewhat Romantic gesture within the broader context of Minimalism's industrial ethos.

Constantly working to explore the possibilities of simplicity, Mangold wound up creating a large body of complex work that is not easily compressed into any movement or "ism." Two years after painting *Distorted Circle*, Mangold was pressed in an interview to divulge what his work was "about," and he responded: "I don't know what to say, really. I am interested in the idea of presenting as simple, economical, and as wholly readable a statement as possible. But at the same time, I really don't know what that means."[2] Mangold, like all artists who work to understand the implications of what they are doing, struggled with the notion of any fixed, clear meaning.

Robert Mangold's art always built on his earlier art and likewise anticipated what he might do next. He embraced the philosophical problem that since an object was produced by an active intelligence it must have meaning, but that meaning might be ultimately elusive. What are certain is the work itself, its materiality—its "thingness"—and the idea that art can be visually experienced, if not always qualified in words. According to the artist, "When all is said and done, I am a maker of images—nothing more and nothing less."[3]

WS

Notes

1. Robin White, "Interview with Robert Mangold," *View* 1, no. 7 (1978): 8.
2. Rosalind Krauss, "Robert Mangold: An Interview," *Artforum* 12, no. 7 (March 1974): 36–38, quoted in Richard Shiff et al., *Robert Mangold* (London: Phaidon Press, 2000), 17.
3. John Gruen, "Robert Mangold: 'A Maker of Images—Nothing More and Nothing Less,'" *Art News*, Summer 1987, 138.

Distorted Circle within a Polygon III, 1972. Acrylic and pencil on canvas, 88⅜ × 83 in. Museum purchase with funds from the Ciba-Geigy Corporation, 1973

PHILIP PEARLSTEIN American, born 1924

DURING THE 1950S AND 1960S, abstract art gained such stature that artists who concentrated on the depiction of the human figure oftentimes were devalued as retrograde, timid, or even lacking in talent and imagination. Despite this negative labeling and the art market's narrow recognition of viable possibilities, several artists who eventually became major forces in the world of contemporary art turned to or continued depicting the human form. Philip Pearlstein was one such artist. His *Female Model in Red Robe on a Wrought Iron Bench* from 1972, as well as paintings by Leon Golub, Alex Katz, and Sylvia Sleigh also in the collection of the Weatherspoon Art Museum, attests that the figurative tradition was deep-rooted and active, if not exactly booming or profitable.

Innovative, original, and at times jolting, Pearlstein's handling of the studio figure is anything but conventional. Unlike his predecessors, the artist emphasizes direct observation over any idealized or psychological nuances. By stripping the figure of its customary associations, such as allegory, mythology, and conventional standards of beauty, and incorporating unusual perspectives and radical croppings of the subject, he single-handedly invigorated the genre.

Having studied art at the Carnegie Institute of Technology in Pittsburgh in 1944 and again in 1947–49 after serving in World War II, in 1949 Pearlstein moved with his classmate and fellow artist Andy Warhol to New York, where he commenced on a career in the graphic arts while simultaneously attending graduate school at New York University.[1] During the early 1950s the artist painted landscapes in a loose, gestural style reminiscent of Abstract Expressionism, but based on observed nature rather than his imagination. A turning point occurred about 1958, when he began attending weekly figure drawing sessions at the studio of Mercedes Matter, a former student of Alexander Archipenko and Hans Hofmann and a founding member of the American Abstract Artists group. In 1961 Pearlstein began painting nude couples based on these drawings and, the following year, turned to painting directly from the model, a method from which he has never wavered.

Pearlstein often hires artist's models to pose for him as a way to minimize the risk of modifying or prejudicing his subject's actual physical appearance with nonvisual information, such as psychological overtones, which might happen with personal acquaintances.[2] His objective is to use his art as a vehicle to understand the processes of visual perception, paying particular attention to the optical distortions and perspective irregularities of binocular vision. Painting only what he sees from a close, fixed viewpoint, the artist depicts each element in the composition in precise focus. Some details are emphasized in part because they are physically closer to him. At other times, Pearlstein chooses to ignore academic "corrections" of perspective to hone in on one aspect of the figure, such as the model's hands here, to which all other parts of the painting are secondary. As is typical in Pearlstein's art, the female figure is depicted clinically rather than erotically but nonetheless is a sexual being, posed in a short robe that barely covers her crotch. Thus, a sexual tension exists between her and the viewer, however much the artist tried to minimize it.

Although coolly detached, Pearlstein obviously was intrigued by the model's angles, volumes, and curves as well as the play of light across her body. Yet he gave equal attention to the bench on which she sits as well as the strong shadows it casts, a result of the artist's penchant for bright artificial studio lighting. The various materials and surfaces of each compositional element are conveyed deftly through restrained color and precise but apparent brushwork, while the complex shadows that fall along the wall and floor assert the composition's shallow space. The cropping of the figure by the edges of the canvas likewise emphasizes the shallowness of the depicted space, bringing the viewer's eye back to the picture's surface. Pearlstein's even-handed treatment of form, light, color, pattern, and composition underscores his belief that one view is as worthy of being described as any other.

In the years following the creation of this painting, Pearlstein continued to produce similar representations of models in staged studio setups through direct observation. However, his compositions grew increasing complex with the addition of exotic or brightly colored props for more surface patterning and a variety of elaborate postures and perspectives. Yet, as always, the artist remains faithful to describing only what his eyes see, saying it best in 1971: "I get my highs by using my eyes."[3]

EDG

Notes

1. Pearlstein received his master's in art history from New York University's Institute of Fine Arts in 1955.
2. Although Pearlstein attempts to exclude his models' personalities, he lets them choose postures that are natural to them and thus reflect their individuality. The poses and the models' vacant expressions induced by fatigue or boredom have the effect of conveying subjective moods despite the artist's intent.
3. Philip Pearlstein, "Why I Paint the Way I Do," *New York Times*, August 22, 1971, Arts and Leisure sec., D17.

Female Model in Red Robe on a Wrought Iron Bench, 1972. Oil on linen, 60 × 72 in. Museum purchase with funds from Burlington Industries, 1972

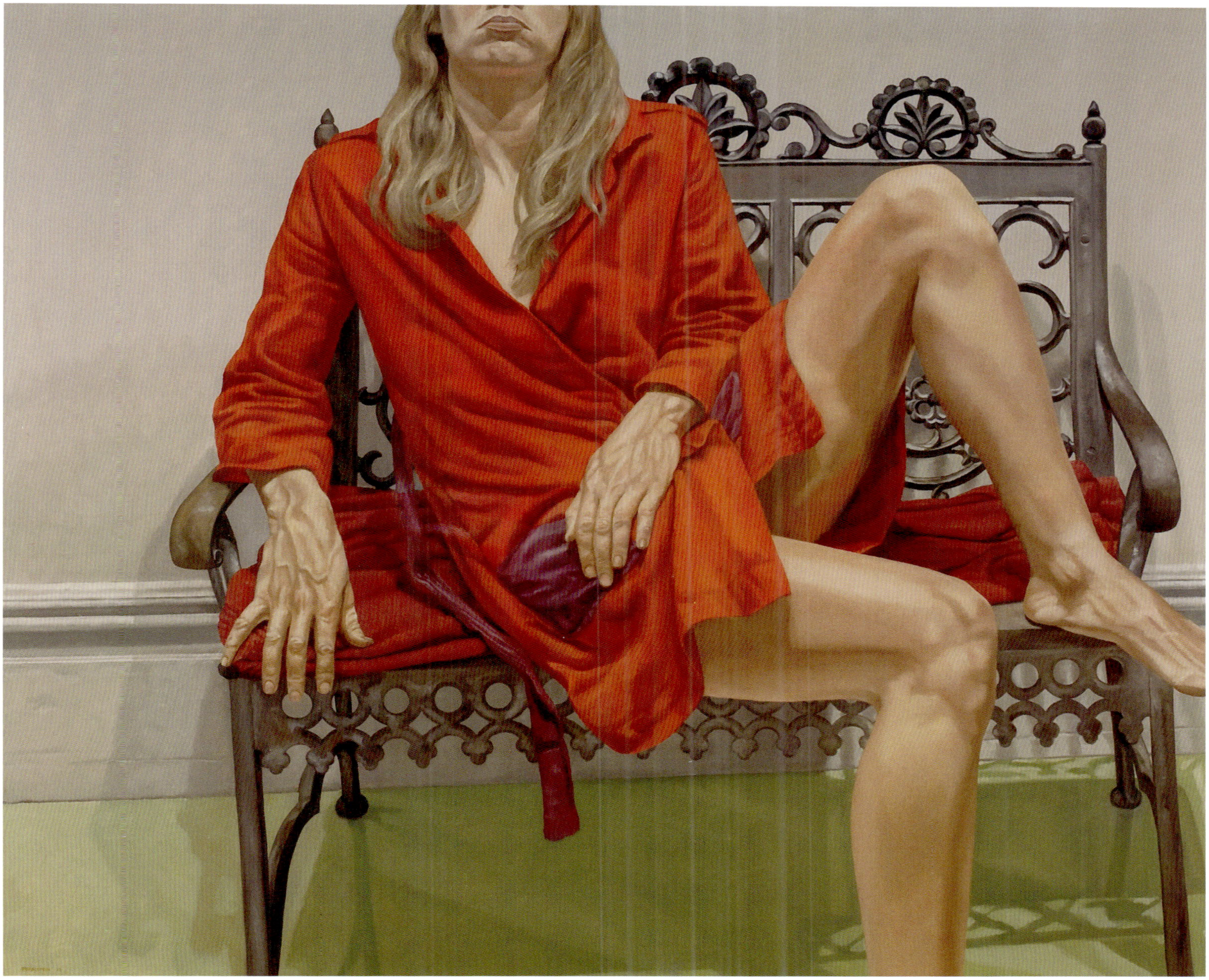

CARL ANDRE American, born 1935

CARL ANDRE IS A PRINCIPAL ARTIST of the Minimalist movement of the 1960s. He is best known for large, grid-based sculptures that adhere to strict systems of repetition of form. However, from 1957 to 1972, Andre created a lesser-known series of more than one thousand works that consist of hand- and typewritten poems in the tradition of concrete poetry.

Andre began the poems shortly after moving to New York City. He met and shared a studio with the painter Frank Stella, who was then working on a series of large, monochromatic, abstract compositions called the Black Paintings. Andre was particularly taken with the bold, geometric simplicity that Stella espoused, which stood in stark contrast to the Abstract Expressionist style of the time. Andre worked to translate his own ideas into a new sculptural form, and, by the early 1960s, he had developed a body of austere, geometric sculptures, first hand-carving them from blocks of wood and later assembling them from prefabricated industrial materials that he acquired in modular units.

In his poems, Andre used another uniform, industrially produced material—typing paper—to experiment with geometric form, but for these works he arranged words, rather than wood or metal, into interlocking patterns and shapes on each page. Some compositions are formed by repeating the same word or group of words over and over again; in other instances, such as the poems from the YUCATAN series, Andre broke up the text into blocks of black and red type, stacking the words vertically, one on top of the other, and dividing them into sections that mingle graphically with other sections.

Many of Andre's poems focus on the lives of great men. He often derived the text for the poems from published sources. *DEPAR TEK from YUCATAN* is the fifth of twenty-six poems Andre wrote based on the well-known writings of John Lloyd Stephens, an explorer who was the first to document and make public the Mayan ruins in the Yucatan Peninsula in Mexico. It is without doubt that Mayan architecture, much of which is built from blocks of cut stone, was of great interest to Andre. However, his YUCATAN poems are not personal ruminations on the ruins, as one might think. Instead, the poems are direct appropriations of text from Stephens's *Incidents of Travel in Yucatan* (1843). *DEPAR TEK* is taken from the first part of the contents for chapter 6, volume 1 of *Incidents*, which reads:

> *Departure from Merida.—Map of Yucatan.—Timucui.—Tekoh.—Human Skulls and Bones.—Church of Tekoh.—Convent—A revolting Spectacle.—View from the Top of the Church.—Cura of Tekoh.*

Study of the structure and source of the poems shows that while Andre may appear to have been working on two distinct branches of work (the sculpture and the poems), they are quite thoroughly connected. Andre's artistic transgression of using preexisting, industrially produced forms to create his sculptures is similar to the act of appropriating the mass-produced, published words of others or to his practice of repeating the same word or similar words to compose his other poems. Andre invites us to understand words less in terms of their meaning than as abstract building blocks toward a greater form. For Andre, words are conceived as predetermined units from which to create complex and visually rich works of art.

A close friend of fellow Minimalist Donald Judd, Andre donated nearly five hundred of his poems to the Chinati Foundation in Marfa, Texas, the site of Judd's studio and home. They are permanently installed in their own room at Chinati, in vitrines Andre designed. Another large segment of his poems is in the collection of the Stedelijk Museum in Amsterdam, the Netherlands. *DEPAR TEK* is one of few original pages from Andre's YUCATAN series available for public viewing in the southeastern United States.

XE

DEPAR TEK from YUCATAN, 1972. Typewriter ink on paper, 11 × 8½ in. Gift of Werner H. and Sarah-Ann Kramarsky, 2000

```
DEPAR   TEK
TUREF TIMOH
ROMME UCU
RIDAMAPOI CON
    FYUC  VEN
    ATANHUMAT
       NSKUL
       LSAND
       BONESC
         HURC ACURI
         HOFT OUSBA
     AREVEKOHCURSIN
     OLTIN  AOFT
     GSPEC  EKOK
    VTACLE
    IEWFR
    OMTHE
    CHURC
    HSTOP
```

ANDY WARHOL American, 1928–1987

BY 1972, WITH CONCEPTUALISM, performance art, photography, and video staking claims in the contemporary art world, Pop art seemed to inhabit a distant past. Andy Warhol, who seven years earlier had declared his "retirement" from painting, was now fully occupied in publishing his magazine, *Interview*, and producing films in the second location of the Factory (Andy Warhol Enterprises) in New York City. It was there in 1968 that he was nearly fatally shot. Whether fueled by recuperative desire or economic necessity to support his filmmaking endeavors, Warhol casually returned to painting commissioned portraits.

President Richard Nixon's historic trip to China in 1972 and the ensuing media blitz provided Warhol with the inspiration for the Mao series. It marked a critical new direction and freedom in the way he handled paint and color in the following decades.[1] In all, Warhol created more than one hundred paintings and drawings of Mao Zedong between 1972 and 1974 in various sizes, including a silkscreen wallpaper version.

Warhol derived his Mao directly from the infamous portrait reproduced millions if not billions of times in the chairman's *The Little Red Book*. If Hollywood celebrities and Campbell soup cans were ubiquitous in American society, it seemed only fair that Warhol would choose this image of Mao to symbolize China's cultural revolution. The concepts of instantaneous recognition and worldwide notoriety were a perfect match for the artist who had made a career of celebrating superstardom.

What made the Mao series different, of course, was the Communist leader himself and the meaning his image held for Western viewers. Despite Warhol's claims that he did not concern himself with politics, it was inevitable that the Mao paintings, in their multitude of color and size combinations, would help, if only through the act of consumerism, usher in the post–cold war era. Warhol had managed to detoxify one of the most threatening political images of the time and make it something anyone could hang in their home.[2] Equally important, he had fused the hands-off mechanical process of printmaking with a return to the gestural and subjective qualities of Abstract Expressionism. The series was met with critical success following its premiere exhibition at the Musée Gallièra, Paris, in 1974, and resulted in numerous commissions from celebrities and socialites around the world for portraits by Warhol.[3]

In the Weatherspoon's *Double Mao*, as in other paintings of similar size in the series, the background colors were applied first, in a loose, painterly manner, and the image of Mao was silkscreened on top.[4] Warhol then added paint to specific areas such as the jacket in the portrait on the left. The silkscreen image and paint nevertheless function as a whole, each balancing the other to the extent that at times it is difficult to separate the two processes. The two unique canvases were not initially created as a diptych but, rather, were the result of a framing choice made between 1975 and 1984 before the Weatherspoon acquired the work.[5] *Double Mao*, so named for its configuration if not also in reference to other Warhol Doubles (e.g., *Double Mona Lisa*, *Double Self-Portrait*), became the first painting by Warhol to enter the Weatherspoon's collection.

AG

Notes

1. Kynaston McShine, introduction to *Andy Warhol: A Retrospective* (New York: Museum of Modern Art, 1989), 19.
2. Arthur Danto, *Andy Warhol* (New Haven: Yale University Press, 2009), 113–14.
3. McShine, introduction, 19.
4. David Bourdon, "The Long March to New Extremes," in *Andy Warhol's MAO* (New York: Christie's, 2006), not paginated; originally published in Bourdon, *Warhol* (New York: H. N. Abrams, 1989), 317–18.
5. Neil Printz, e-mail message to author, December 23, 2009. Printz is editor of the forthcoming *Andy Warhol, Catalogue Raisonné*, vol. 3, *Paintings and Sculpture, 1970–1974* (New York: Phaidon, 2010).

Double Mao, 1973. Acrylic and silkscreen on canvas, each 12 × 10 in. Museum purchase with funds from the Benefactors Fund, 1984

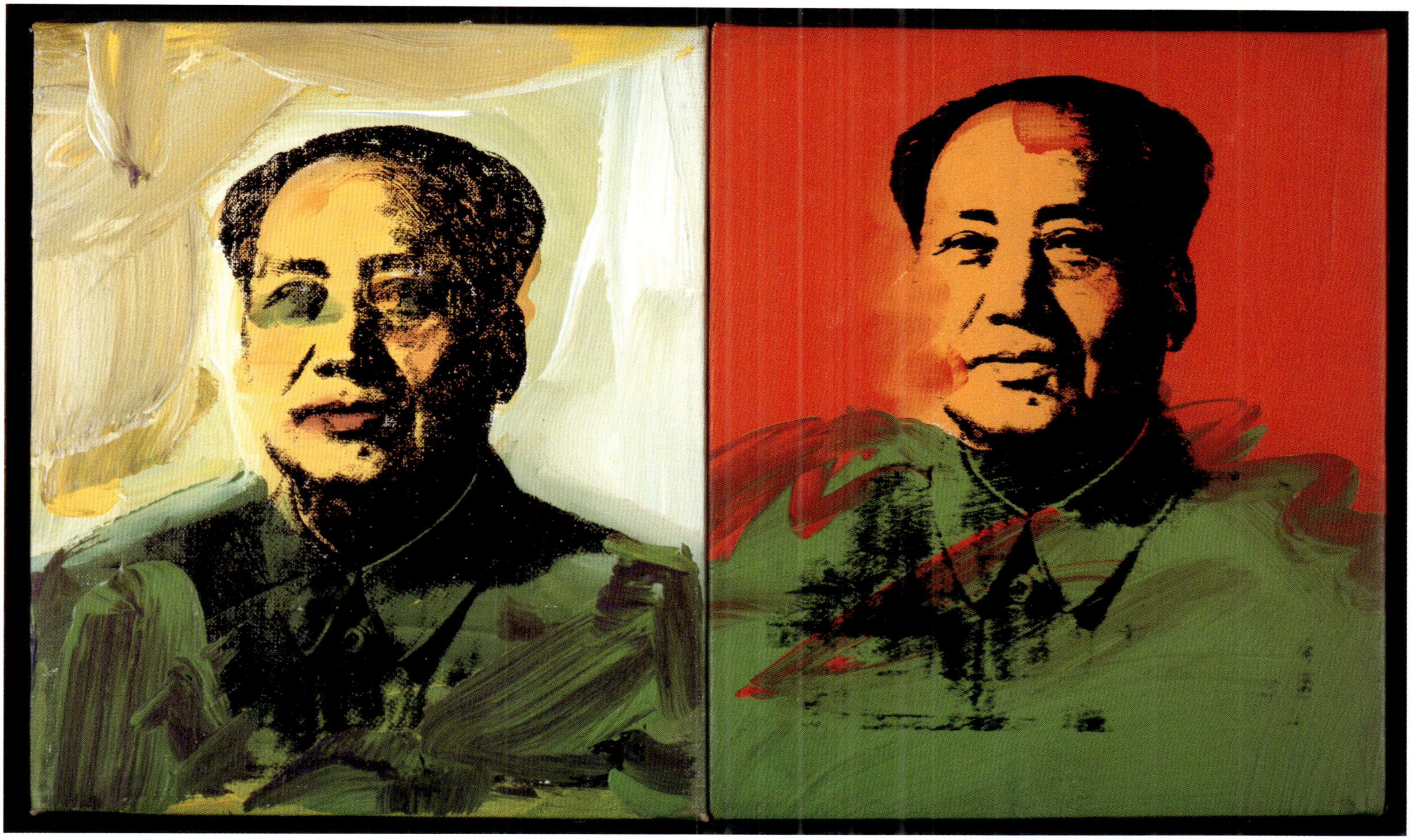

NANCY GROSSMAN American, born 1940

WORKING IN COLLAGE, assemblage, drawing, and sculpture, Nancy Grossman is perhaps best known for her exquisite leather-bound heads. Grossman received widespread acclaim for her work early on, having five solo exhibitions before she reached the age of thirty and, in 1965, being the only woman painter to be awarded a Guggenheim fellowship. Her Head series began in 1968 and by 1972 had grown to a total of forty-three works. It is believed there are approximately seventy-five heads in existence today. The tough, sinister character of the heads may be interpreted to imply contemporary sadomasochist notions of power, sex, and violence. However, a careful consideration of these works shows them to convey a much more complex examination of identity formation, power relations, and social oppression.

The early heads, such as *Brush*, are hand-carved from wood salvaged from telephone poles. Each carved head is tightly bound in leather, which forms a kind of second skin, and is embellished with such things as zippers, straps, buckles, and horns. Facial features formed from epoxy, like lips and noses, peek out from under the leather masks. In some works, glass eyes are visible, though in this particular example, the eyes are completely covered, as are the mouth and ears. Two shaving brushes attached to the back of the head of *Brush* form a crown, recalling a tribal warrior's headdress. The configuration of the straps that cross over the face and buckle at the sides and base of the skull are reminiscent of a horse harness. As in Grossman's other work from the Head series, including *A* (1981), also in the Weatherspoon's collection, it is impossible to determine the gender of the figure. This leather-bound, faceless, sightless head nevertheless expresses a form of identity—albeit one that is highly coded and guarded, for the mask shields and protects the figure within at the same time as it wards off advances through its menacing countenance.

Grossman grew up riding horses on a working farm in upstate New York, and the paraphernalia of equestrian riding, such as bridles and halters, was a clear influence on her later work, as were her parents' involvement in the garment industry and the processes of cutting and assembling this work entails; Grossman worked as a "dart and gusset girl" in her youth. Unfortunately, her early years were also marked by corporeal punishment and abuse, an experience that undeniably played a role in the development of such a large body of work focused on physical restraint and oppression.

While working on the heads in the late 1960s, she became especially interested in representations of the Other as monsters or alien beings, examining, in particular, the latent tale of awakening feminine sexuality in Mary Shelley's *Frankenstein: "The Modern Prometheus."* Some of Grossman's ideas share interesting correspondences with the social and Freudian investigations of the Surrealists, particularly Marcel Jean's *The Specter of the Gardenia* (1936), a black plaster female head adorned with zippered eyes. But, as Arlene Raven writes, "Grossman wanted to exemplify black beauty in her black leather heads, and based the shapes of the first group of head sculptures on the clenched fist of the black-power salute. Yet they were also conceived as self-portraits and looked substantially like the artist."[1] Created in the tumultuous social landscape of the early 1970s, Grossman's carefully crafted heads serve as a fascinating metaphor for the feminist and African American civil rights movements, as well as the devastating events related to the Vietnam War. The tactile quality of her materials and her labor-intensive process further enhance this sense of a body and mind that are restricted and confined. Combining her deep interest in the complexities of the inner psyche in relation to the body with symbols of bondage, Grossman creates a conflicted and fragmented image of identity that simultaneously evokes a palpable strength.

XE

Note

1. Arlene Raven, *Nancy Grossman* (Brookville, NY: Hillwood Art Museum, 1991), 106.

Brush, 1973. Leather-covered wood, epoxy, and brushes, 17¼ × 11½ × 7½ in. Anonymous gift, 1999

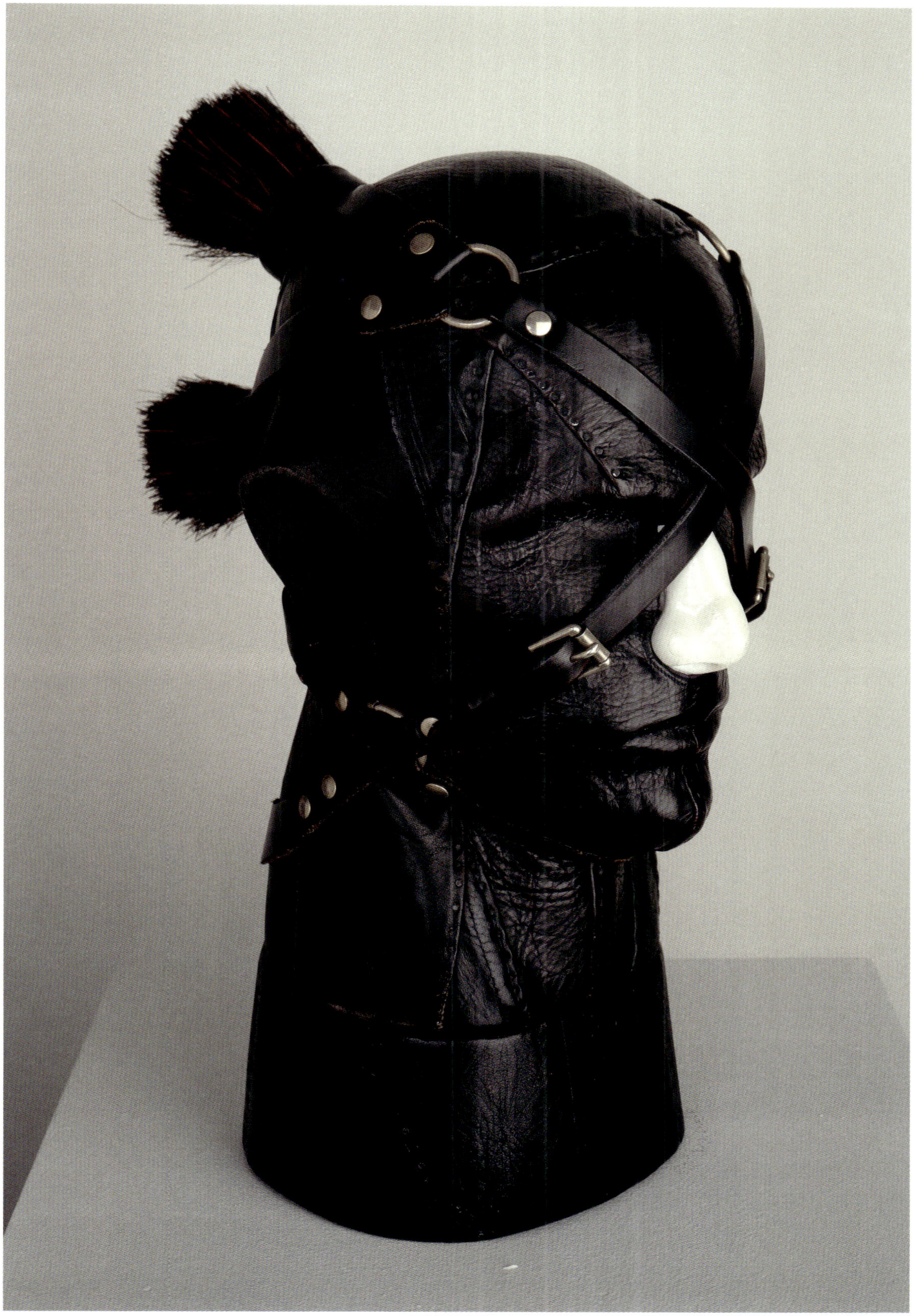

AL HELD American, 1928–2005

IN THE 1950S AL HELD was attracted to both the formless chaos of Jackson Pollock's drip paintings and the clear, hard-edged paintings of Piet Mondrian. By the end of that decade, Held had synthesized these seemingly mutually exclusive impulses into large-scale works that featured broad, expressive brushstrokes within an architectural framework of interlocking parts. In time, Held came to feel that Abstract Expressionism was too ambiguous, too lacking in the formal structure he sought, and his work moved toward a monumental geometry. Structure, as he said years later, was what he was looking for.

In an early series of paintings in which Held began his search, he magnified, cropped, and capitalized on the design of individual letters of the alphabet as the subject of the work. Another series, the Taxi Cab paintings, most closely put Held in the camp of Pop art; these works were brightly colored interpretations of the signs and symbols of urban New York. But, as the art historian Irving Sandler has noted, "By 1967, Held felt limited by the simplicity of his images and suffocated by their flatness. . . . he felt the need to introduce complexity, space, and volume into his painting."[1]

The visual vocabulary of Held's geometric paintings consists of straight lines of varying thickness, circles, triangles, rectangles, and innumerable overlapping combinations of these elements. In a series of large-scale black-and-white paintings from the 1970s, of which *East-Northeast* is an example,[2] Held moved toward increasing complexity and ambiguity: certain shapes seem to advance into the viewer's space while others appear to move back into the distance. None of these shapes is modeled to look three-dimensional, but the illusion of volumetric forms derives from Held's interest in Renaissance perspective. In general, the boldly outlined rectangular forms recede in space, while those that are more delicately delineated hover closer to the picture plane. Nonetheless, a boxlike shape in the upper right corner seems to protrude forward into the circular form there, and three fine lines that do not describe particular shapes weave in and out across the canvas.

In *East-Northeast*, the oversize forms typically push against the edges of the canvas, as if the frame cannot contain their size or directional force. Held's abstraction was pictorial in nature; that is, his forms act as characters on a stage: they are "complex networks of open cubes, spheres, and pyramids" pieced together "as if they were masonry."[3]

Over a career spanning five decades, Held obsessively explored the possibilities of structure in space, and his style changed along with his restless ambition. He painted only in black and white from 1967 to 1975, then returned to color as his compositions became increasingly spectacular in their complexity. From 1962 to 1980 Held—though a high school dropout himself—was a professor of art at Yale University, where he influenced students to explore ideas and painterly strategies simultaneously, instilling in them the great notion that an ongoing synthesis of sources could continue to expand the language of art.

WS

Notes
1. Irving Sandler, *Al Held* (New York: Hudson Hills Press, 1984), 39.
2. The Weatherspoon holds several other works by Al Held in its collection, including an earlier black-and-white painting, *B/W VX*, from 1968.
3. Sandler, *Al Held*, 39.

East-Northeast, 1973. Acrylic on canvas, 84⅛ × 96⅛ in. Museum purchase with funds from Burlington Industries and the Ciba-Geigy Corporation, 1975

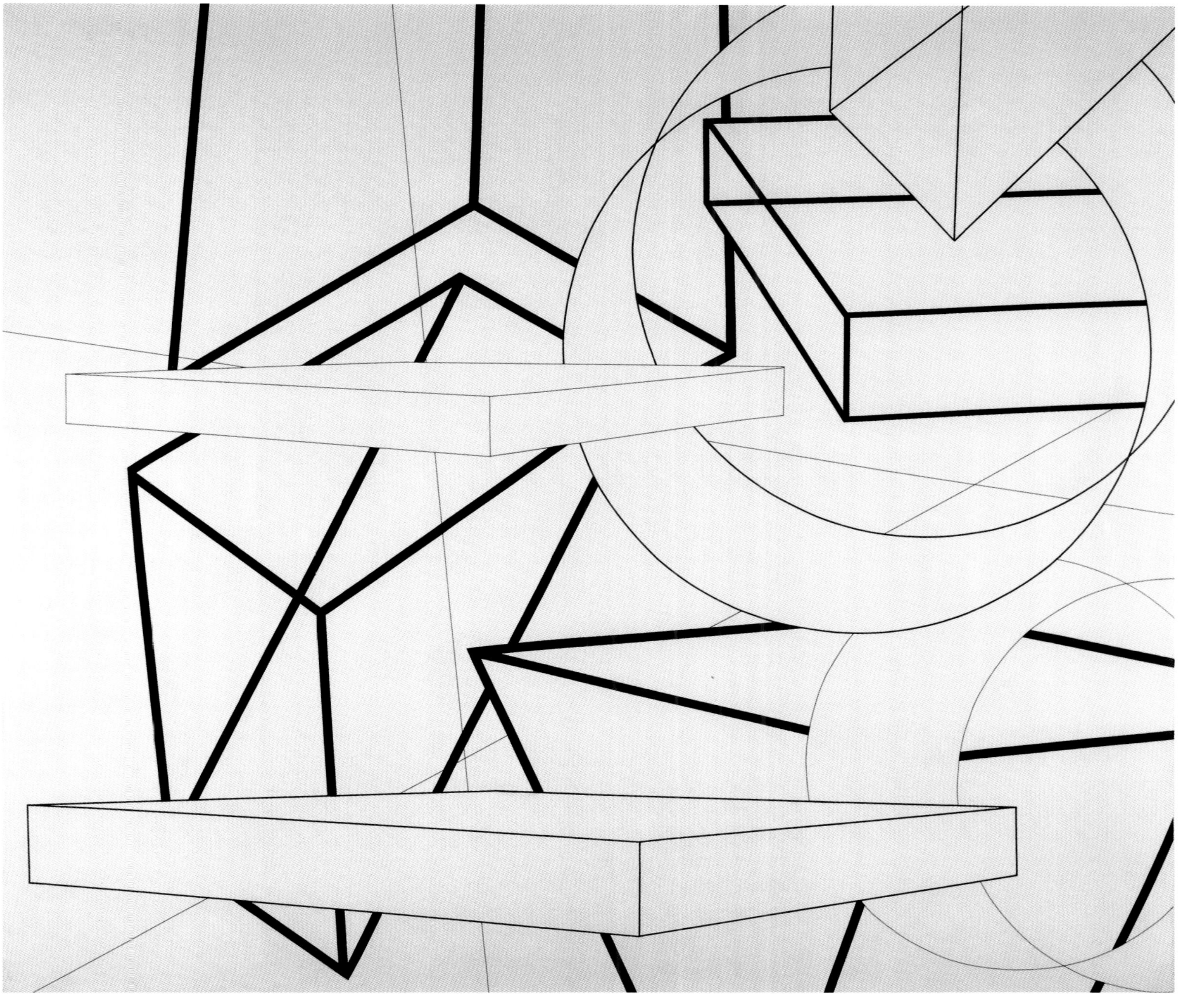

RONALD BLADEN American, born Canada, 1918–1988

RONALD BLADEN IS REMEMBERED as a Minimalist sculptor whose works figured prominently in such landmark exhibitions of the mid-1960s as the Jewish Museum's *Primary Structures* (1966) and a show with Tony Smith and Barnett Newman at the Corcoran Gallery of Art, Washington, DC, a year later, the latter dominated by his giant two-story-high painted wood *X*. (The full-size piece, built for the show and later dismantled, no longer exists.) The wonder is that at this time he had only recently made the transition from painting to sculpture.

Born in Vancouver in 1918, Bladen, like Tony Smith, was a generation younger than most of the artists associated with Minimalism. He began as a painter, studying first in the Vancouver School of Art and then the California School of Fine Arts (later the San Francisco Art Institute) from 1939 to 1945. His early paintings, from the 1950s on, rooted in Abstract Expressionism, are large in scale and heavily impastoed. Later in the 1950s, the geometric paintings of Al Held became important to him, as did the artist himself, who encouraged Bladen to move to New York City. In New York, in 1957, still thinking of himself as a painter, he produced plywood reliefs and folded paper collages that he exhibited at the Brata Gallery with such artists as George Sugarman—also remembered primarily as a sculptor—Nicholas Krushenick, and Held. By 1962 his bas-relief paintings had become still more sculptural, and by 1965 he moved into sculpture as such.

Bladen's earliest freestanding sculptures are explorations of the relation between mass and space, among them *Rockers* (1968), included in the exhibition *Concrete Expressionism* in New York University's Loeb Center, and consisting of a set of twenty-foot-tall L-shaped pieces with rounded bottoms in which the space between the masses was made an important and integral component of the work. The sculptures that followed exploited these spatial possibilities, while further reducing and simplifying the forms. His best-known work, *Three Elements* (1965), included in the *Primary Structures* exhibition at the Jewish Museum, consists of three identical freestanding rhomboid forms spaced approximately eight feet apart and leaning precipitously backward, as though defying gravity. Other freestanding sculptures restricted to minimal geometric shapes and, like *Three Elements*, painted black and related to the sculptures of that other Minimalist, Tony Smith, followed. *Untitled Prototype (Study for "V")* is, as the title suggests, a study that might have been—though was not—developed further, perhaps on a larger scale. (Bladen's claim that he never made preliminary drawings or small-scale models is contradicted by the Weatherspoon work.)

Constructed of plywood and painted black, *Untitled Prototype (Study for "V")* consists of a V form nestled within a notched rectangular box. (The V might be seen, alternatively, as a partial and open rectilinear form oriented to one of its points and supported by a closed, more complete rectangular box.) The box or base stabilizes and grounds the V, relating it to Bladen's work *X* of 1966. An alternative, gravity-defying conception is behind *Three Elements*, whose bottom edges are cut at an angle of sixty-five degrees, and the ten-foot-tall *Black Triangle* (1966) that stands on one point, as does an untitled levitating box included in the 1966 Whitney Annual. On the evidence of these last works, Bladen seemed a sculptor preoccupied with the kind of precarious balance for which Richard Serra later became known. That this was not his sole concern, however, is proven by *Untitled Prototype (Study for "V")* and *X*, which are perfectly balanced arrangements of forms.

Never a doctrinaire Minimalist, Bladen was receptive to a variety of approaches of the 1960s, including what was called the Process art of Robert Morris and Serra. During the 1970s and 1980s, his work opened up to a range of ideas, some still grounded in geometry, though of a more complex kind, others completely fantastic. In his last works, thin pieces of pine are bolted together to create elaborate cages incorporating buffed aluminum sheets. The geometric forms of sculptures such as *Untitled Prototype (Study for "V")* have completely given way to razor-sharp edges. If one goes back to the beginnings of Bladen's career as a painter and follows its trajectory through his Minimalist sculptures, it is obvious that the latter tell only part of the story of a rich and restless sensibility.

CG

Untitled Prototype (Study for "V"), 1973. Painted plywood, 60½ × 106 × 8 in. Museum purchase with funds provided by friends in memory of Herbert S. Falk; additional funds provided by the National Endowment for the Arts, 1976

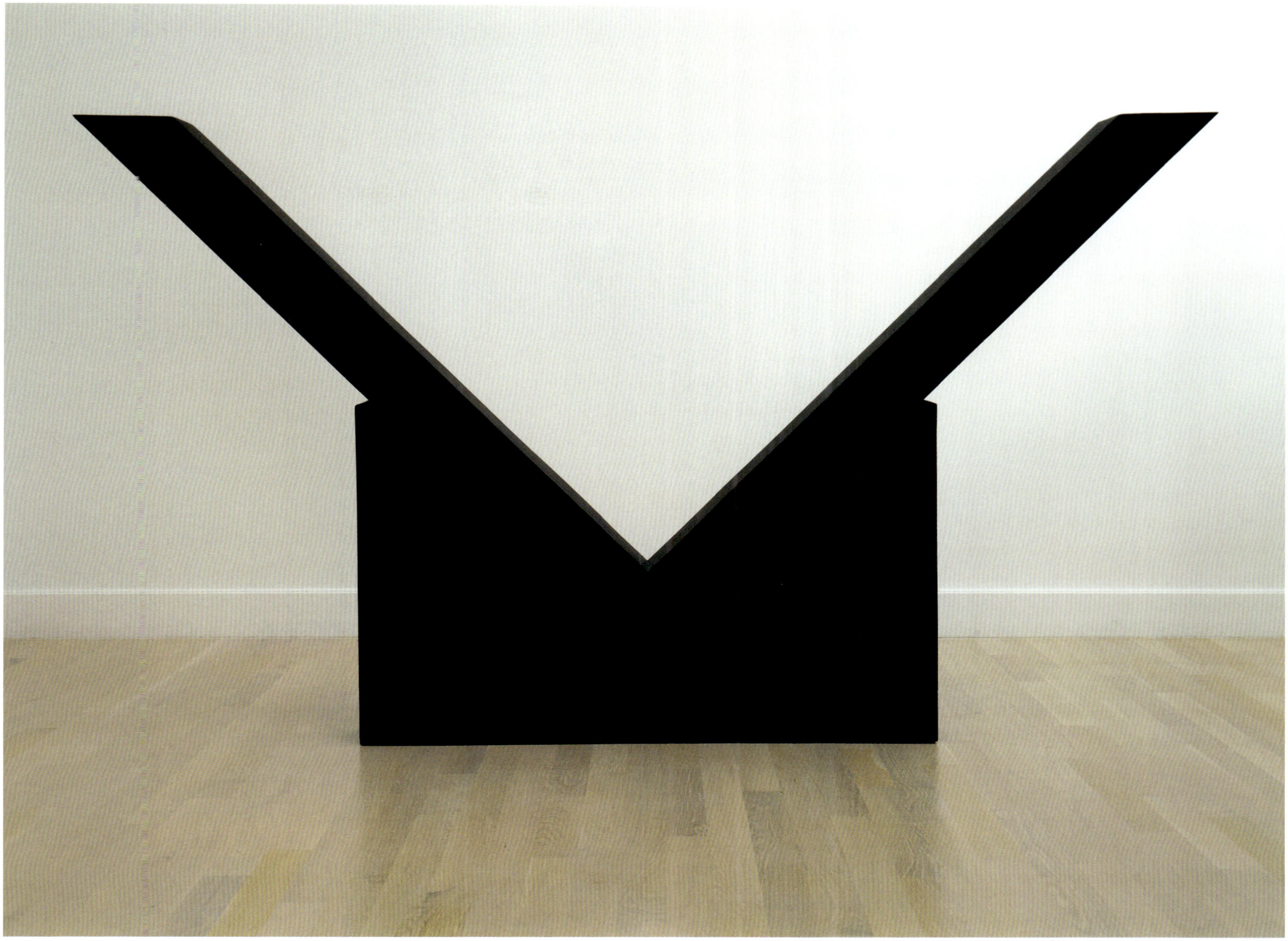

SOL LEWITT American, 1928–2007

CONCEPTUAL ART, by definition, interweaves idea and object. It is a physical manifestation of a mental process. The idea in Conceptual art, whether derived from random associations or systematic structures, takes precedence over the completed art object. Sol LeWitt's Incomplete Open Cube series, begun in 1974, exemplifies a logic-based methodology that characterized much Conceptual art of the time. It was an approach that LeWitt fostered through the beginnings of Minimalism in the mid-1960s and practiced throughout his career.

The Incomplete Open Cube series comprises 112 individual structures, each a freestanding white aluminum cube delineated solely by its edges. LeWitt devised a system whereby removing one or more of the cube's edges—there are twelve in a complete cube—resulted in the creation of a unique structure. The integrity of the cube is retained, however, even when as few as three edges or axes remain.

The Weatherspoon Art Museum's *Incomplete Open Cube 7-11* and *Incomplete Open Cube 8-24* (also 1974), acquired in 1987 and 1988 respectively, are two of the 112 permutations of LeWitt's open-cube system. The title of each work is designated by the number of edges it contains and by its place in the chronological progression of the series. LeWitt replicated the series on a smaller scale in wood and also documented it through schematic drawings and photographs illustrating each possible open-cube configuration.

Although mathematical rules abound in LeWitt's work, he was careful to suggest that logic may merely be a way to "camouflage the real intent of the artist, to lull the viewer into the belief that he understands the work."[1] In other words, the object may not be as simple as it appears. The viewer must negotiate the contradictory area between logic and illogic, order and disorder, and intellect and sensation in order to elicit meaning from the work. The Incomplete Open Cubes, for instance, compel viewers to imagine the structures as whole forms while creating ambiguity by assuming a geometric rationale.

For LeWitt and other Minimalist artists in the 1960s, this essential participation by the viewer coupled with the removal of the artist's ego and hand provided a needed alternative to the overtly psychological and emotionally invested work of the Abstract Expressionists who had preceded them in the 1950s. While Abstract Expressionism had seemingly taken traditional painting to its climax, Minimalism and, subsequently, Conceptualism offered new directions and recourse for what many artists thought were the failings of modernism.

LeWitt's early experiences in graphic arts and modern architecture in I. M. Pei's architectural firm, along with personal interests in the serial music of Arnold Schoenberg and the Minimalist compositions of Philip Glass, paved the way for the artist's experimental three-dimensional paintings and eventual open modular cubic structures that, like an architectural drawing or musical score, could be fabricated or performed by someone other than the artist. Even until shortly before his death in 2007, LeWitt delegated the actualization of his works, including large mural drawings and fiberglass structures, to studio assistants and manufacturers. This machine-made, factory-based approach to object making, also shared by Pop artists like Andy Warhol, defied the individualistic qualities that had been hailed in American art during the first half of the twentieth century.

AG

Note

1. Sol LeWitt, "Paragraphs on Conceptual Art," *Artforum* 5, no. 10 (June 1967): 79–83; reprinted in Gary Garrels, ed., *Sol Lewitt: A Retrospective* (San Francisco: San Francisco Museum of Modern Art, 2000), 369–71, at 369.

Incomplete Open Cube 7-11, 1974. Baked enamel on aluminum, 42 × 42 × 42 in. Museum purchase with funds from the Benefactors Fund in honor of Editha Carpenter, 1987

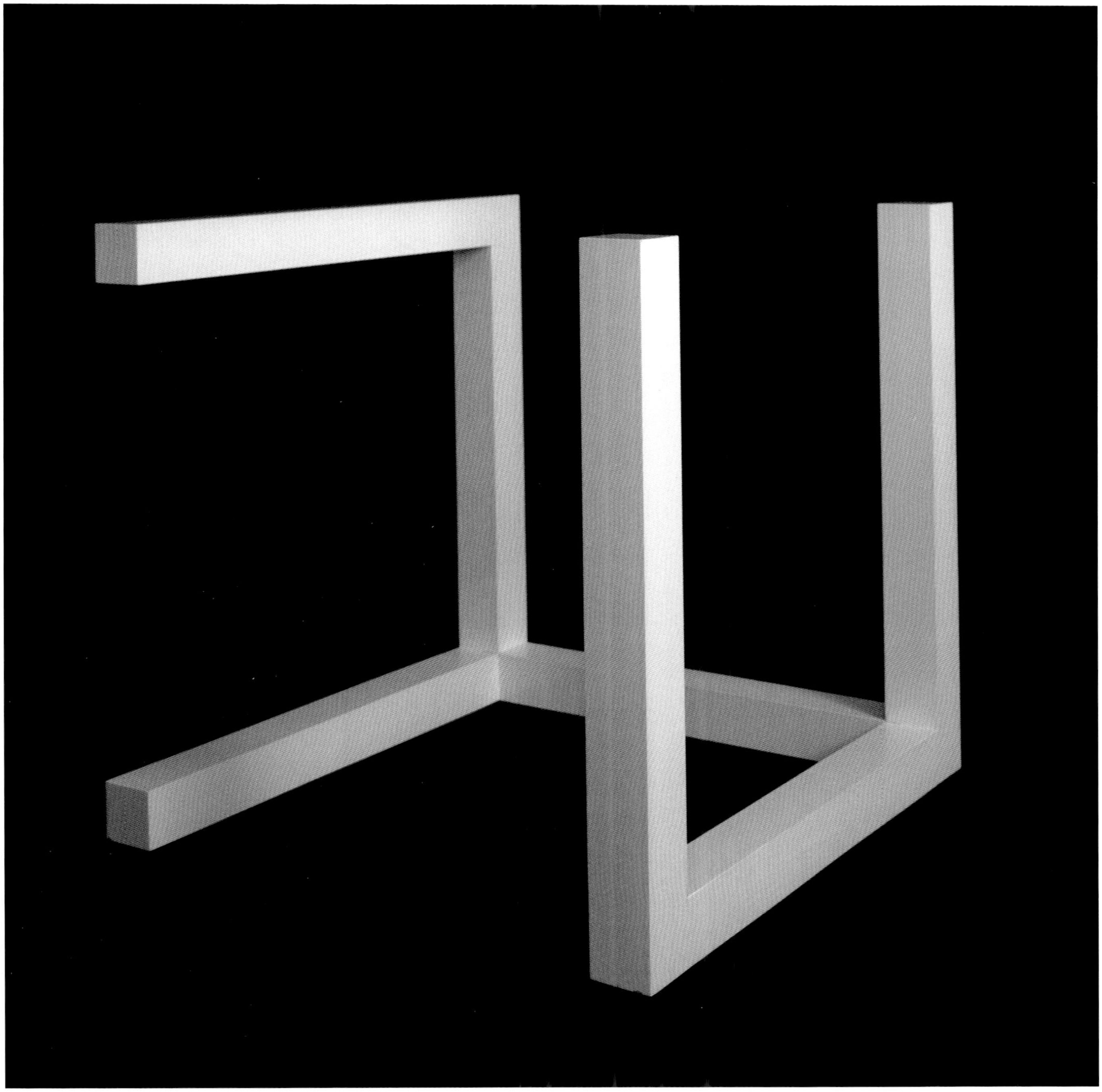

RAY JOHNSON American, 1927–1995

GERTRUDE STEIN LOOKS ON while Judy Garland goes domestic. Really? Collage was Ray Johnson's medium of choice. He cut paper bearing images and patterns and assembled the pieces into compositions. Often Johnson augmented the results with drawing or painting. The juxtaposition of images and fragments created new wholes, realities of apparent probability that never existed. Sometimes associated with Pop art, Johnson maintained that he had instead invented Chop art.[1]

The creative hothouse of Black Mountain College, near Asheville, North Carolina, which Johnson attended from 1945 to 1948, gave him the permission, withheld in his parents' strictly disciplined household, to invent his life as an artist. His subsequent move to New York City provided the stage for his new creation. Johnson was famously reluctant to sell his works or to conform to the expectations of the art world. At the same time, the denizens of that world—artists, critics, curators, and collectors—have unambiguously stated their profound respect for his work.

Gertrude and Judy never met.[2] In *Untitled (Gertrude Stein with Judy Garland's Kitchen)*, "Dad" (butch "mother of us all" of the avant-garde) comes home and says (in "her" blue balloon), "Cock, cock." The "Little Woman" ("The Man That Got Away" fem) responds (in her pink balloon) with "Hen, hen"—if her duck is female, that is. Johnson has given them speech through the decorative signifiers that each woman chose as her emblem. Stein clamps shut any possible view of her feminine attributes, her breasts and cleavage, with a rooster pin (guarding the henhouse), while Garland ducks into her cozy role by donning her fowl-figured apron—a gendered garment signifying woman's work and place.

Gertrude Stein and Judy Garland are among the contract players in Johnson's pantheon that he assembled as his own studio system. If Garland's studio, MGM, could boast "more stars than there are in heaven," Johnson could easily match its luminosity. Movie stars, celebrities, writers, and artists abound in his collages. Stein was a methodological lighthouse. Wendy Steiner remarks of Johnson's art, "There has not been such an unsentimental exploration of dis/connection since Gertrude Stein, postmodernism's great precursor."[3] Johnson used a photograph of Stein by the photographer George Platt Lynes, who had been drawn into Stein's circle when he traveled to Paris in 1925. Using a photograph by Lynes, who also was gay, Johnson in turn joined the circle around Stein and ensured that the sources and content of *Untitled* firmly remained within the gay cosmos.

Judy Garland was a diva whose tremendous talent and troubled life are still revered by gay men today. Here she seems caught in the kitchen by a photographer from the publicity department in one of the studio's usual efforts to explain the paradox that Hollywood's goddesses were also "just real people." Judy was so "real" that before her kitchen could be professionally photographed (as if a photographer were another applicance), MGM had to change her name from Frances Ethel Gumm.

Stein is not the only one who is looking at Garland. She is also observed by a skull that peers up at her from the underworld below the linoleum at her feet. Perhaps this is a reference to her death or the manner of her death, which was ruled to have been a suicide. Life and death are classic themes in the history of art, and Johnson once made an artist's book on the subject of death. This skull is so very close; the living Judy stands on it, its grin ready to devour her. We recall what we avoid: in our lives, death is always there, part of the crowd, unnoticed until it claims our time for a private conversation.

On Friday, January 13, 1995, Ray Johnson took a fatal swim. He had called his performance art events "nothings"; his dive into the waters of oblivion was his last performance. In typical Ray Johnson language, the "nothing" in his works produced "no thing." The commonplace "it's nothing" means "no big deal," a stoic regard for death as part of the natural order. "A nothing" is a "nobody," a meaning that recalls Johnson's ambiguity about fame and celebrity—his and that of others. Yet on that Friday, something did happen to a somebody, and the art world registered it. Reflecting on Johnson's life and death, the sculptor Richard Lippold, who had been one of his teachers at Black Mountain and his lover for twenty-seven years, said, "Now that I think of him more after his death, I don't think that I really knew who he was. Very hard for me to say that, but who was this man? . . . His whole life was a kind of game like his work."[4] Johnson, always constructing ciphers, had called a friend only days before his last Friday to hint that he was working on the "biggest work of his life."[5]

RG

Notes

1. Ray Johnson Estate, "Ray Johnson Biography," at http://www.rayjohnsonestate.com/biography.php.
2. Among the interesting possible intersections that link Stein and Garland is one that Johnson, with his penchant for associative collisions, would probably have greatly enjoyed. The website Who's Dated Who? postulates a close connection of only four degrees of separation by "dating"—Judy Garland to Marlene Dietrich to Mercedes De Acosta to Alice Toklas to Gertrude Stein; http://www.whosdatedwho.com/dating/six-degrees.asp?ID1=6408&ID2=31311 (accessed August 9, 2009).
3. Wendy Steiner, "The Webmaster's Solo: Ray Johnson Invites Us to the Dance," in *Ray Johnson Correspondences*, ed. Donna De Salvo and Catherine Gudis (Columbus: Wexner Center for the Visual Arts, Ohio State University, 1999), 72.
4. *How to Draw a Bunny*, DVD, directed and edited by John Walter (New York: Palm Pictures, 2002).
5. Ibid.

Untitled (Gertrude Stein with Judy Garland's Kitchen), 1975. Collage on Masonite, 16 × 23 in. Museum purchase with funds from the Lynn Richardson Prickett Acquisition Endowment and the Weatherspoon Art Museum Acquisition Endowment, 2007

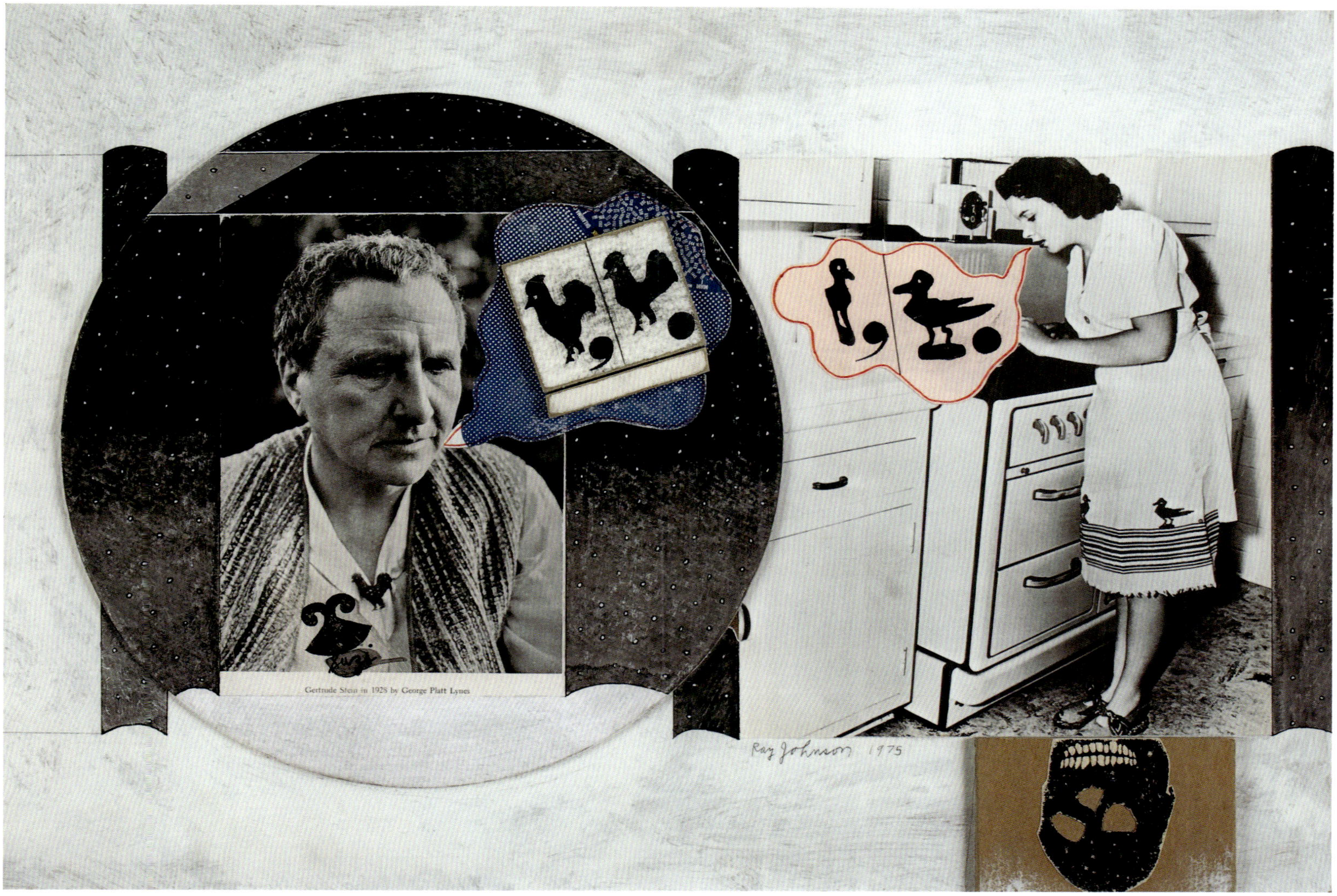
Gertrude Stein in 1928 by George Platt Lynes
Ray Johnson 1975

ANA MENDIETA American, born Cuba, 1948–1985

COMBINING CONCEPTS related to performance, feminist, and land art, Ana Mendieta used her own body as both form and medium. She inscribed her body into the natural world by burning or carving its shape into landscapes or digging the contour of it out of the earth. She is best known for her Silueta (Silhouette) series, ephemeral performances that she termed "earth-body" sculptures, which she made between 1973 and 1980. Mendieta was prolific, creating hundreds of Siluetas within this seven-year period. Her understanding of issues related to social alienation, feminism, and cultural displacement greatly informed her work.

As a young girl living in Havana, Cuba, she personally experienced the fallout of the political upheaval of Fidel Castro's rule. Her father was accused of, and later imprisoned for, counterrevolutionary activities, and in 1961 Mendieta and her sister were airlifted out of Havana as part of Operation Peter Pan, a United States–assisted effort to evacuate nearly fourteen thousand Cuban children. Alone and with no American relatives to turn to, the two sisters lived in refugee shelters and orphanages, before finally settling into a foster home in Iowa. Their mother and brother eventually were permitted to join them there in 1966. Mendieta attended the University of Iowa, where she developed a strong interest in video and performance art. Although she came to consider her identity to be transnational, Mendieta experienced feelings of difference and dislocation throughout her life.

For her Silueta series, Mendieta rendered the shape of her body by molding it in relief, digging it out in a shallow depression, assembling it from twigs and leaves, or inscribing it on the landscape. She experimented with a vast array of natural materials, including blood, earth, flowers, and grass. Her works from this series are documented in black-and-white and color photographs as well as film and video. While it is now common for artists to use photography and video to document temporal works, Mendieta was one of the pioneers of this practice. For the performance represented in the black-and-white photograph *Untitled (Silueta Series)*, Mendieta traced the shape of her body with gunpowder, then ignited the trail of powder to leave a dark outline of singed grass and earth. She took this photograph immediately following the burn, evidenced by the cloud of smoke that hovers at the upper center of the image. This cloud and the imprint of an iconic female form seared into the earth suggest that a mysterious ritual has just taken place.

Mendieta was extremely interested in ancient representations of the female form as a symbol of nature and fertility. She was particularly influenced by Santería, a spiritual belief of her native Cuba that combines aspects of both Yoruban religion and Roman Catholicism that has a long tradition of performing rites within the landscape. The Santeros view nature as the source of all things in the universe and believe that therefore all things are connected. Mendieta expressed her desire to achieve this union on the most basic level—her body present and at one with the landscape.

In her short life, Mendieta gave voice to a variety of pressing and important issues related to feminine identity and multiculturalism. Her works created an alternative to the monumental land art of her male contemporaries, such as Michael Heizer or Robert Smithson. Hers was a much more intimate and personal way of integrating the landscape into her work. As Olga Viso writes, "Acting as a metaphorical, and at times a metaphysical agent between the ancestral past and present, between memory and history, biology and society, sculpture and performance, nation and culture, human drives and social discourses, her active presence suffuses her art with a mesmerizing energy and palpable aura."[1] But while Mendieta's inscription of her body directly onto the earth expresses a desire to connect to nature and the world, conversely, in the Silueta images, her body is extracted and displaced, implying the impossibility of finding a consistent refuge or context from which to define oneself. An artist at the forefront of Conceptual performance-based practice, Mendieta made work that continues to resonate with viewers and inspire artists.

XE

Note

1. Olga Viso, "The Memory of History," in *Ana Mendieta: Earth Body* (Washington, DC: Hirshhorn Museum and Sculpture Garden, Smithsonian Institution, 2004), 134.

Untitled (Silueta Series), ca. 1978. Gelatin silver print, 16 × 20 in. Museum purchase with funds from the Weatherspoon Art Museum Acquisition Endowment, 1998

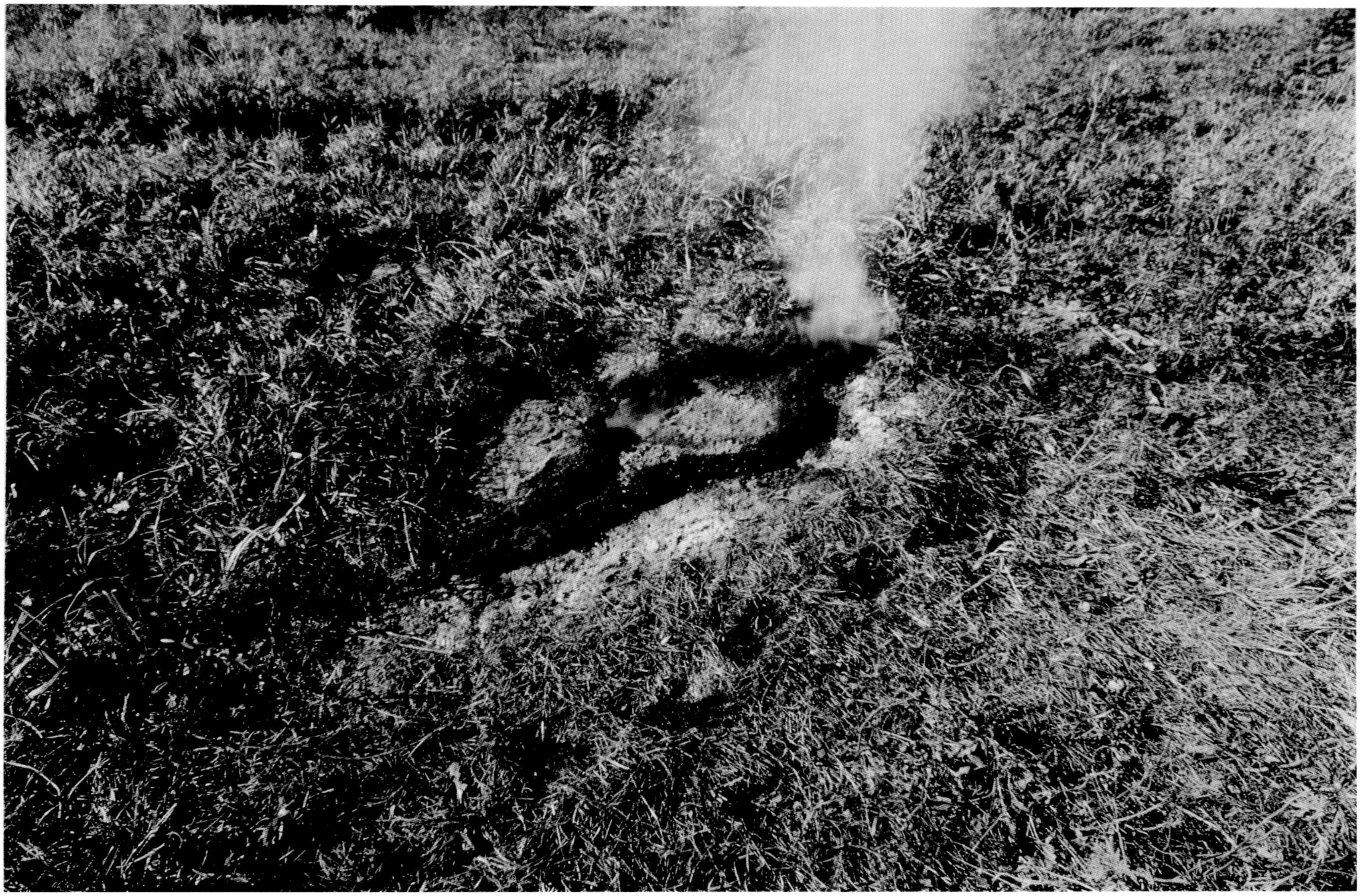

SYLVIA SLEIGH American, born England, 1916

ALTHOUGH SHE DOES NOT ENJOY the same name recognition as other figurative artists from the mid-to-late twentieth century, Sylvia Sleigh is celebrated for her large-scale portraits showcasing the many rising female artists of the 1970s as well as for her figurative paintings that depict men, rather than women, as odalisques. Born in Llandudno, Wales, and trained as a realist painter at the Brighton School of Art in Sussex, England, Sleigh immigrated to New York with her husband, the art critic Lawrence Alloway, in 1961. Despite having been told as a student at Brighton in the 1940s, "You have no talent. You're just here to waste time until you get married,"[1] Sleigh did, in fact, continue to paint after her marriage. But rather than align herself with the Conceptual artists and formal abstractionists who dominated New York's art scene in the 1960s and early 1970s, she joined the burgeoning women's art movement.

Begun on the West Coast in the late 1960s, the feminist art movement gathered steam in New York in the early 1970s with the emergence of two of the first feminist cooperative galleries in the United States: A.I.R. (Artist-in-Residence) in 1972 and SOHO 20 in 1973. Female artists who desired to assert an identity and to promote art forms that were neither subordinate to nor dependent on the authority of men were pivotal in founding these co-ops. The members wanted to establish a gallery system that allowed women artists to create work that reflected women's lives and experiences and to have a platform to exhibit and sell these works as well. Sleigh's interest in gender issues naturally aligned her with these groups.

Over the course of her career, Sleigh has focused on exploring issues of power and sexuality in her nude figurative paintings. Subverting conventions and expectations, the artist looks at the human form with the same frank and appreciative eye that male artists traditionally reserved solely for their female models. *Maureen Connor with Water Lily* presents the sculptor Maureen Connor, one of the twenty founding members of SOHO 20 and a personal friend of Sleigh's, as a reclining nude in a nondescript space.[2] The painting emphasizes both Connor's distinct identity as an artist and her sexuality. Surprisingly, Sleigh adhered to art-historical tradition and depicted Connor looking away from the viewer/artist, thus minimizing her power. Yet this pose allowed Sleigh to critique the assumed male gaze and to imbue her painting with a new level of self-expression.

Working from direct observation rather than photographic sources, Sleigh paid considerable attention to Connor's face and mood. Although not overly expressive, the sculptor appears pensive as she looks toward the large water lily form that dominates the painting's foreground. Prominent both in scale and placement, this structure represents one of Connor's large sculptures made of silk, a material considered at the time feminine. The conflicting scale and perspective with which sculpture and figure are rendered make it difficult for the viewer to make sense of the space. Yet obviously the sculptor and her artwork are closely linked. The curling fibers on the soon-to-open pods echo the texture and shape of Connor's pubic hair, while the pinkish coral skin tones of her face and body duplicate the flower blossom's palette. Whereas Connor is portrayed as erotically alluring, if detached, the depiction of the sculpture is sketchy and simplified, particularly the petals that make up the lily's blossom. The surrounding nondescript space does little to help the viewer understand the spatial arrangement: Is the water lily on the floor with Connor or elevated and closer to the viewer/artist? While these questions go unanswered, it is evident that Sleigh included the large sculpture to impart an art-historical–metaphorical dimension to the portrait.

Although the definition of feminist art continues to evolve, as do its forms and methods of art making, its political and social message of empowerment and egalitarianism remains constant, due in part to the creative talents and spirit of such early practitioners as Sleigh. Paintings like *Maureen Connor with Water Lily* changed the attitudes of many critics and raised both awareness of and appreciation for women artists among its audiences.

EDG

Notes

1. Quoted in a press release for *Sylvia Sleigh: Portraits and Group Portraits*, Newhouse Center for Contemporary Art, Snug Harbor Cultural Center, Staten Island, NY, June 2–October 2, 2005, and referenced in Michael J. Fressola, "In the Sunshine of Her Love," *Staten Island Advance*, September 11, 2005, E-2.

2. In fact, SOHO 20's first exhibition showcased work by Connor and Sleigh, although, according to Sleigh, this was mainly because the two artists had work ready to exhibit. Sylvia Sleigh, personal statement dated September 18, 2008, Weatherspoon Art Museum object file.

Maureen Connor with Water Lily, 1979. Oil on canvas, 48 × 72 in. Museum purchase in honor of the Weatherspoon Guild with funds from the Weatherspoon Guild Acquisition Endowment and with gifts given in memory of Mary Lee Copeland, 2008

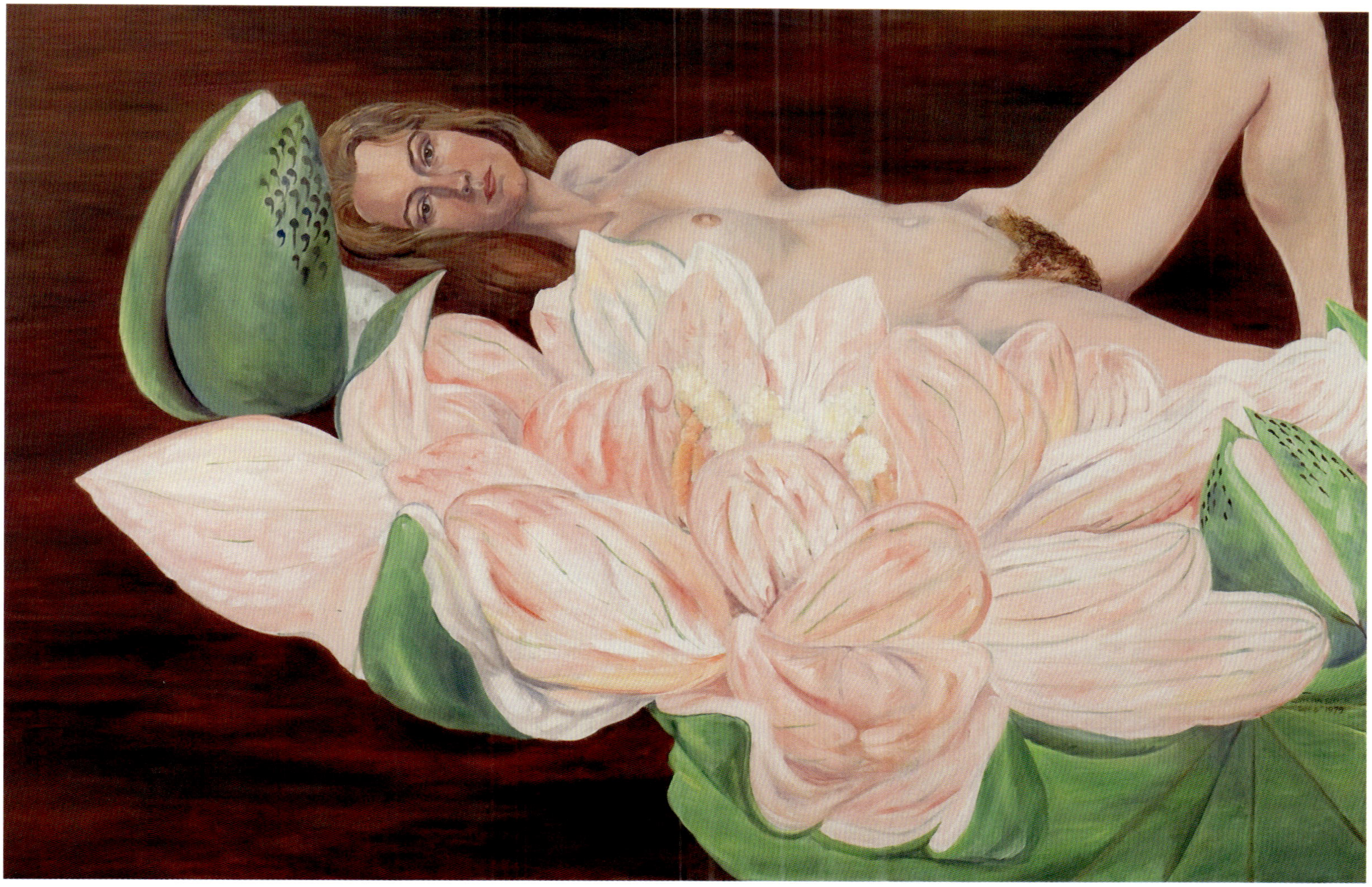

CINDY SHERMAN American, born 1954

OVER THE YEARS, Cindy Sherman has represented herself as a range of female stereotypes and characters to examine the construction of identity within Western society. In her provocative "film still" photographs, she appears in the guise of female heroines in Hollywood movies. She uses pose, costume, lighting, framing, and makeup to produce a believably filmic still image, creating a tension between the artificiality of theater and personal identity. Sherman's works should not be construed as self-portraits, however; they have more to do with how we understand and construct our own identity than any idiosyncratic tendencies of the artist herself. She invites us to dissect the influence of fictive identities on our lives and to examine the anxiety produced between inner perceptions and the outer representation of the self.

Sherman originally gained notoriety for her series of black-and-white photographs collectively titled *Untitled Film Stills* (1977–80), in which she staged herself as an actress playing stereotypical female roles in 1950s films. *Untitled #85* is part of a series that followed for which she created large, full-color, horizontal photographs. Although the horizontal format simulates the 16:9 ratio of the standard film screen, Sherman's inspiration came from a commission to produce a series of double-page spreads for *Artforum* magazine.[1] Often termed the Centerfold series, these photographs depict women in vulnerable situations who often convey a level of fear or anxiety.

For the images, she fabricated simple sets and selected her wardrobe from thrift and costume shops to portray scenes that appear to be pulled from recent films. However, the works are not modeled directly from actual films; rather, they represent generic types. In *Untitled #85*, Sherman wears a mussed, long-haired wig and a girlish gingham dress. The set consists of a rustic wooden floor and dramatic lighting that sweeps across the image. An antagonist is implied by Sherman's stark gaze (she seems almost blinded by fear): Is the character a victim of physical aggression or someone in hiding, about to be discovered? Sherman positions the camera such that we are placed in the position of a voyeur, hovering above a subject vulnerable to our gaze. As Peter Schjeldahl writes of this series, "The hypnotic women of the 'horizontals' strike beneath personality and gender, almost beneath humanity. Their reveries are like so many viewpoints on the darkest sensations, and the terror, of existing."[2] Her wardrobe, makeup, and the set suggest the scene could be taking place in a country homestead, attic, or barn. By leaving the work untitled, Sherman gives viewers room to make their own interpretations, creating yet another fiction within a fiction.

Today, Sherman is one of the most highly regarded American artists to emerge from the New York art scene of the 1980s. She numbers among the generation of artists, which includes Barbara Kruger and Robert Longo, who took the media-saturated culture within which they were raised as subject matter. Sherman's early work played an important role in the analysis of issues related to gender representation and sexual desire within visual culture. By directing, shooting, and starring in images of various female types, she draws our attention to the pervasiveness of the patriarchal gaze in film, television, and magazines. In addition, she asks us to marvel at the myriad fictional characters that infiltrate our image-saturated commercial culture, and to take a step back to analyze how we perform a self to others in our everyday lives.

XE

Notes
1. Sherman's *Artforum* commission was never published.
2. Peter Schjeldahl, "The Oracle of Images," in *Cindy Sherman* (New York: Pantheon Books, 1984), 9.

Untitled #85, 1981. Cibachrome photograph, edition 10/10, 23½ × 48½ in. Gift of Donald Droll in honor of Anne Wortham Cone, 1983

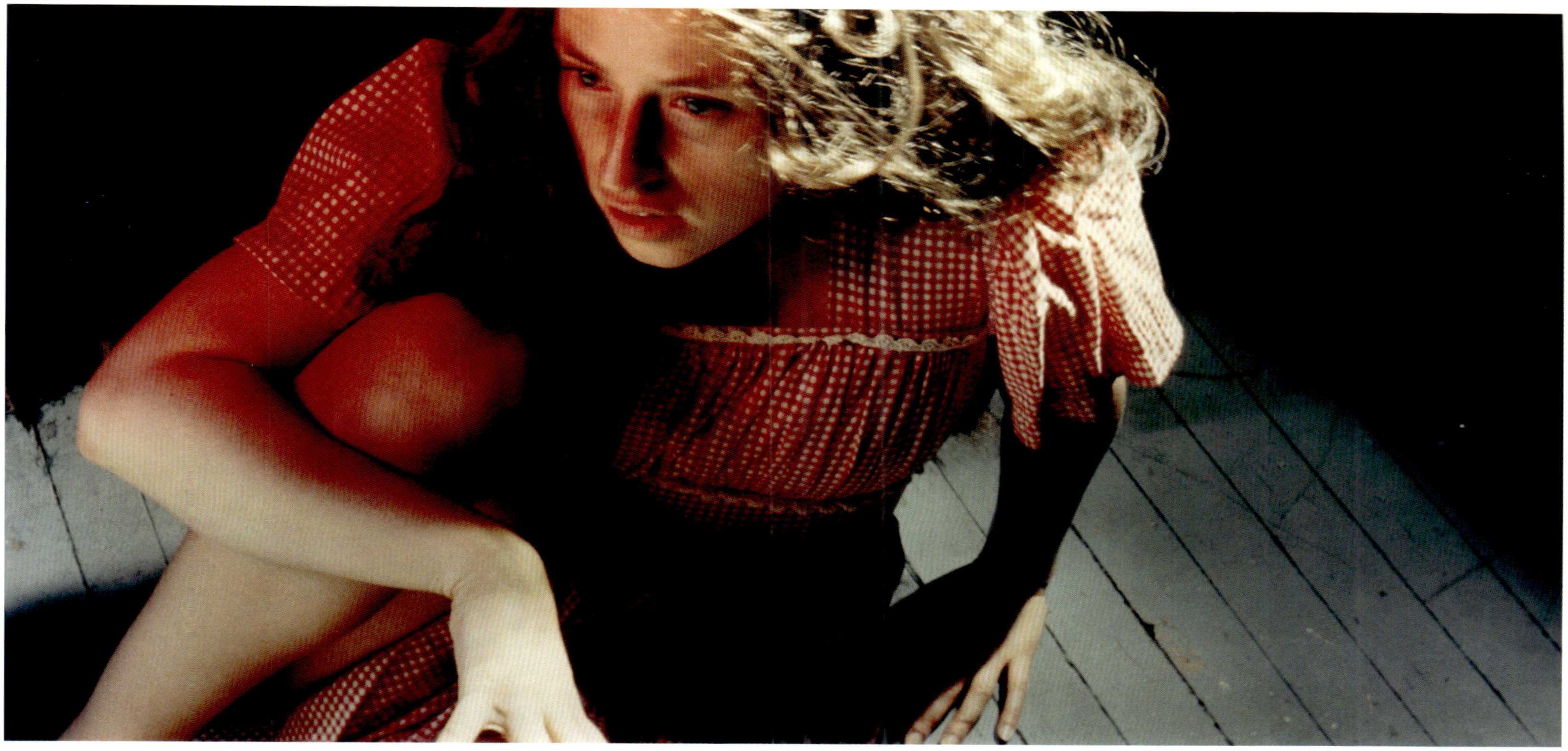

TOM OTTERNESS American, born 1952

TOM OTTERNESS'S *The Frieze* illustrates in approximately 121 linear feet a satirical story of human civilization from its dawn to its destruction. Depicted in the classical tradition of storytelling on the Parthenon and the Arch of Titus, this contemporary narrative is told through the artist's iconic plump white figures who look more like the Pillsbury Doughboy than warring soldiers. Otterness's characters work, play, wage battle, revel in their achievements, and ultimately reach a gruesome end, only to be born into the life cycle once again.

The narrative begins with a panel Otterness titles "Paradise," in which a male and a female figure join hands standing atop an inverted cone. From there the story immediately divides into two distinct gender-based paths: clockwise for the female version, and counterclockwise for the male. The early evolutionary stages are represented by what Otterness calls "Bad Boys" and "Bad Girls," in which boys break things and girls expose their posteriors. Both genders, distinguishable by their genitalia, labor physically and mentally by hauling large sacks of "weighty thoughts."[1] For the women, a "Boating Party" becomes a respite from work, while the men enjoy a "King's Parade."

The symbolic wrestling of the snake from the Garden of Eden seen in "Female Heroics" leads to "Female Revolution," where the female workers topple a phallic monument and instate one of their own amid the graphic dismemberment of the male king and an act of bestiality. In comparison, the "Male Revolution," represented by a cracked world shattered by a worker's hammer, foretells the "Fall of the King," in which the king's motorcade is overturned as he is led away, bound and shackled, and made to kiss an elephant's rear end. Neither gender, of course, fares well in Otterness's final section, entitled "Judgment." Despite the artist's consigning the figures to an ugly demise at the hands of a Goya-esque Saturn, who devours and gives birth to its young, Otterness maintains a lightheartedness that gives *The Frieze* its appeal.[2]

Throughout his career, Otterness has approached the human condition through satire, politics, humor, and appropriation, often simultaneously employing multiple art-historical references. As one of the founders in the mid-1970s of Colab (Collaborative Projects, Inc.), Otterness, along with other communally minded artists, staged public performances and exhibitions in New York City to protest the lack of gallery representation and support for artists who were working outside the prevailing style of Minimalism. It was Otterness's interest in making affordable art for the public that initially inspired him to cast sculptures in plaster that he then sold on the street for $4.99.[3]

Otterness first exhibited *The Frieze* at the Brooke Alexander Gallery, New York, in 1983. Seeking to recoup costs for the elaborate installation and to make the work economically affordable, he allowed the gallery to sell sections of the narrative by the running foot.[4] In 1991 the Weatherspoon Art Museum commissioned Otterness to re-create and permanently install *The Frieze* around the perimeter of the atrium ceiling in its newly constructed Anne and Benjamin Cone Building. *The Frieze* is one of three versions that exist as complete narratives, the others being located at Palm Beach Community College in Lake Worth, Florida, and the Los Angeles Federal Plaza in California.

AG

Notes

1. Tom Otterness, in *Print Collector's Newsletter* 14, no. 1 (March–April 1983): 14.
2. Hayden Herrera, "Tom Otterness," in *Tom Otterness* (Santa Monica, CA: James Corcoran Gallery; New York: Brooke Alexander Gallery, 1990), not paginated.
3. Tom Otterness, interview by Douglas Dreishpoon, Weatherspoon Curator of Collections, May 17, 1996, New York City.
4. Ibid.

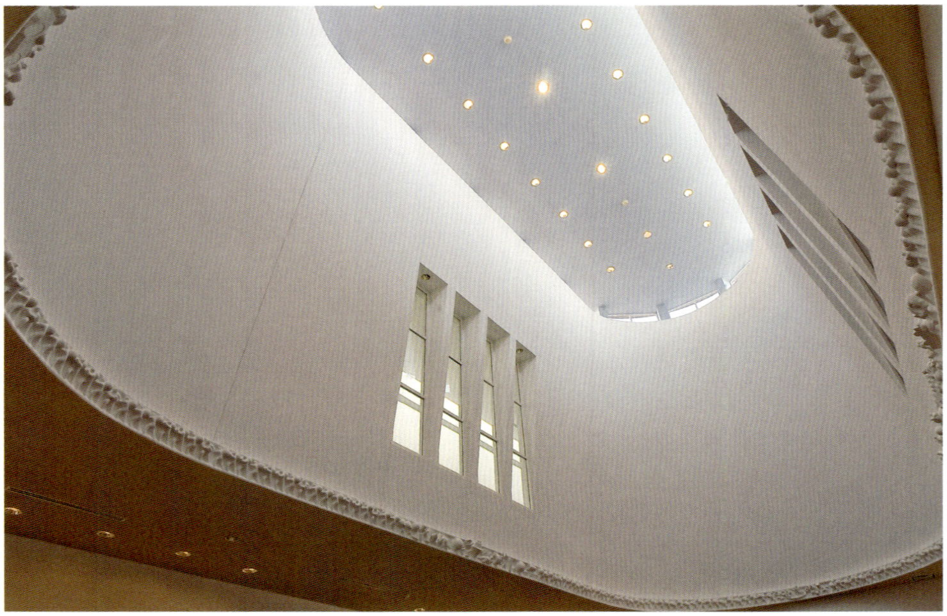

The Frieze, 1982. Cast plaster and paint, 121 ft. 6 in. × 10 in. × 6 in. Gift of Sarah and Jack Warmath in honor of her parents, Sarah Ford and Henry Worsham Dew, 1991

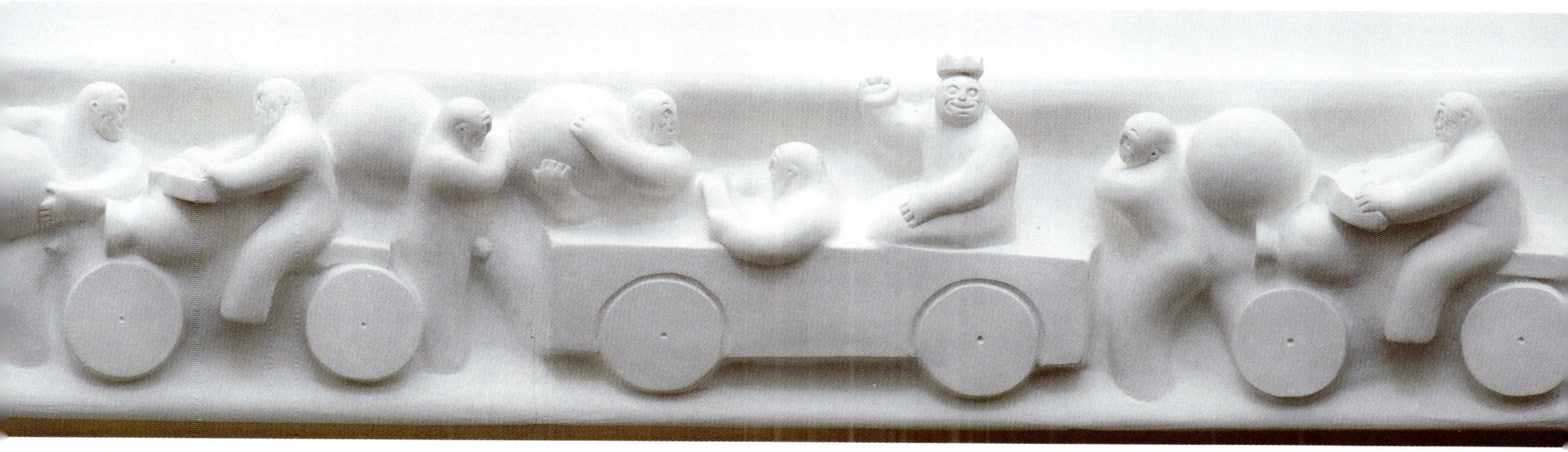

King's Parade

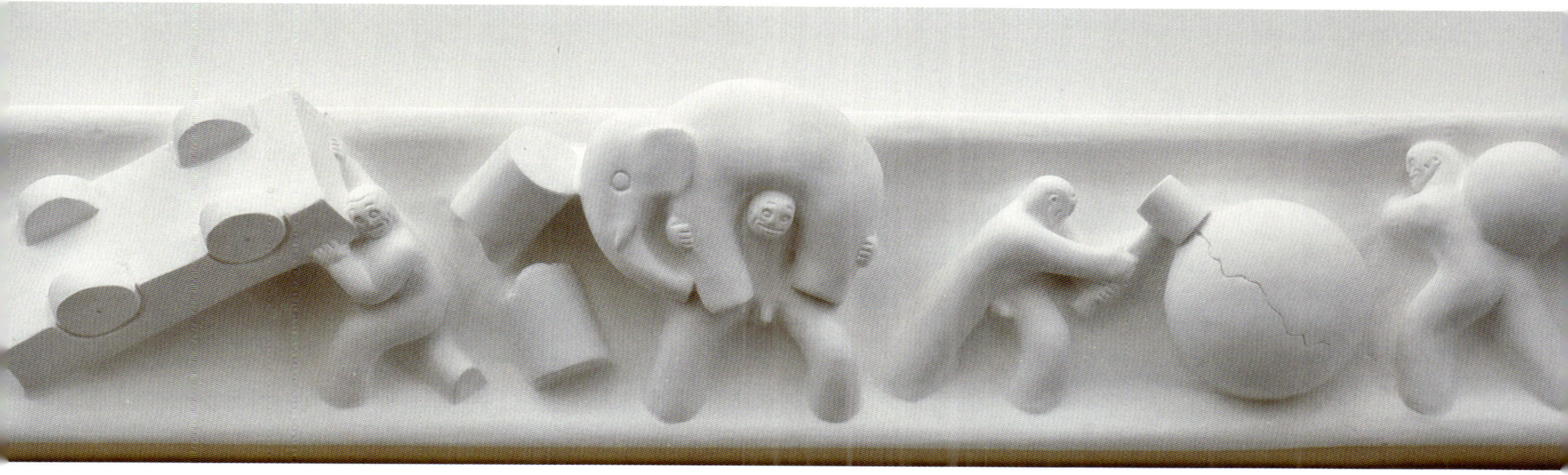

Male Revolution

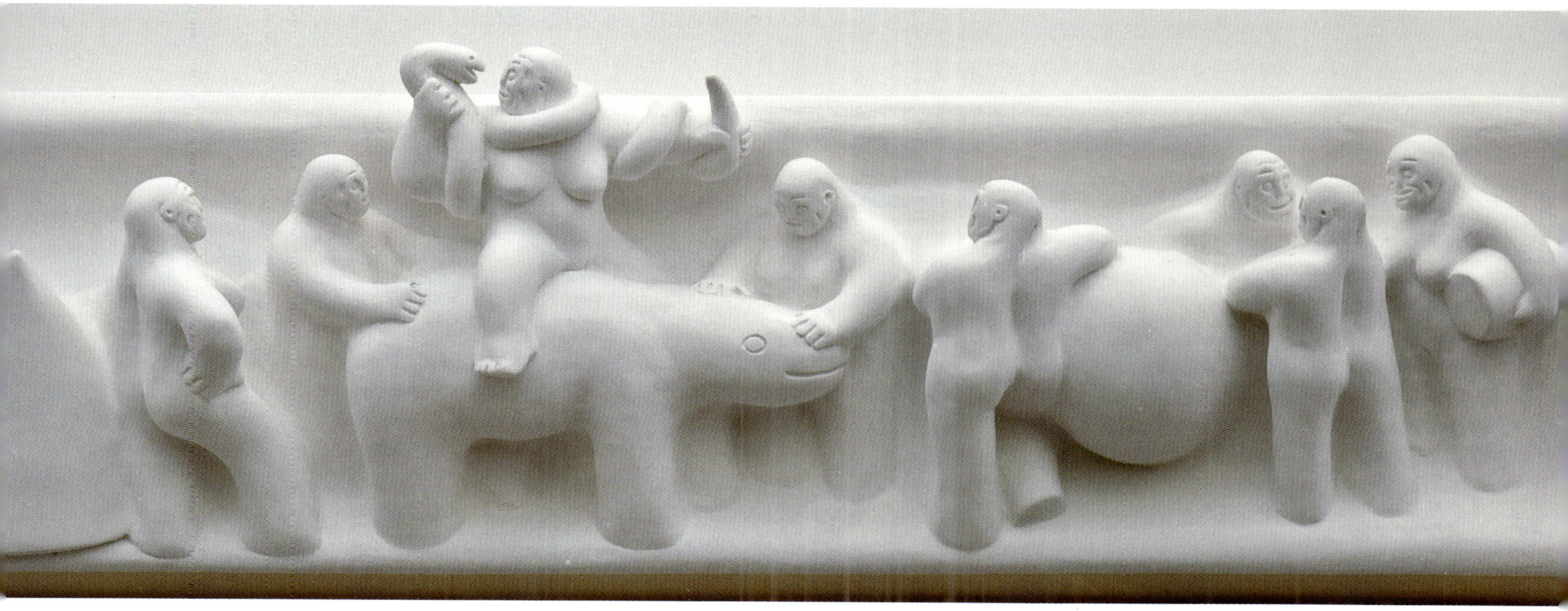

Female Heroics

JASPER JOHNS American, born 1930

FOR MORE THAN HALF a century now, Jasper Johns has made work that stubbornly resists a fixed place in the narrative of modern and contemporary art. *Untitled (Red, Yellow, Blue)*, like the rest of his oeuvre, simultaneously begs decoding even as it frustrates the possibility of coherent meaning. It achieves, in Susan Sontag's terms, a virtuosic "flight from interpretation."[1] His objects present a hermeneutic impasse, in that his refusal "to mean" something other than what he has made is composed literally of the various signs—words, symbols, images—that constitute the basis on which human beings create understanding.

In the course of the Weatherspoon's acquisition of these three prints (2006–7), Johns sent a letter of clarification that resolutely refuses to do any such thing even as it gives primacy to process:

> *Usually the three etchings are hung together—Red-Yellow-Blue—and, I suppose, are considered a triptych. Based on these etchings, I made three paintings which were hung together in that order. Over time I decreased the width of the spaces between the paintings, finally connecting the three canvases to make one rectangle. In 1991 I reworked three of the etching plates and printed them together as a single image.*[2]

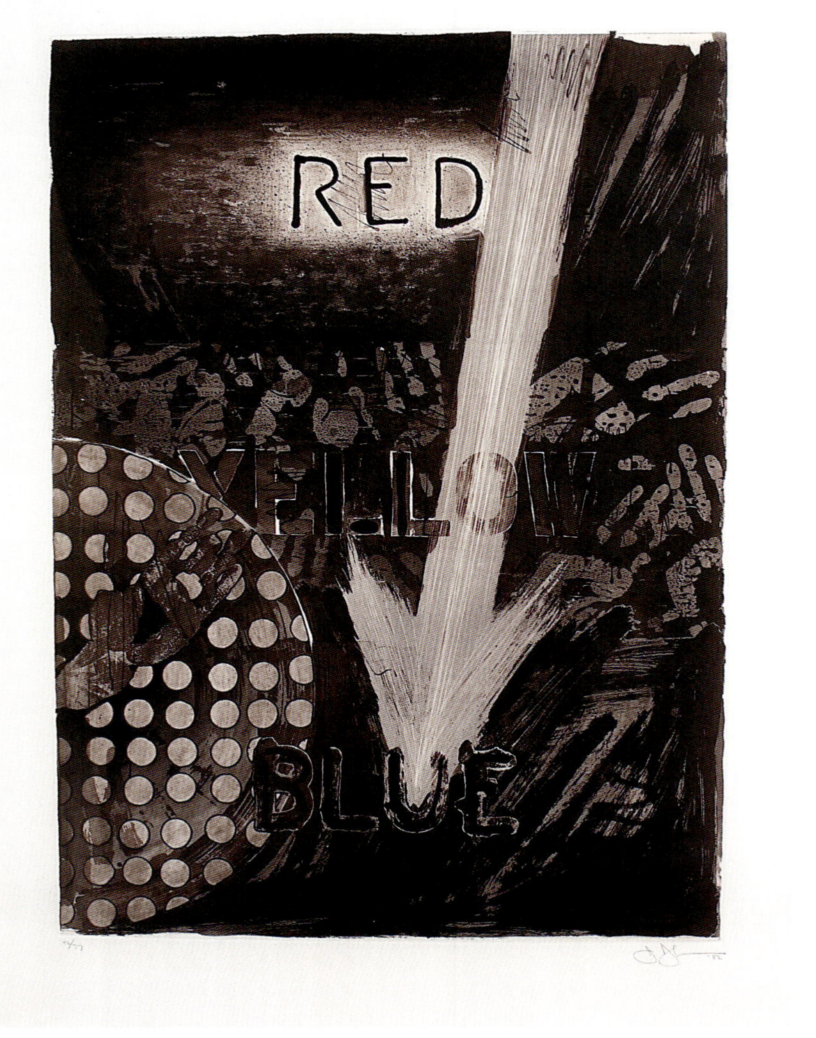

Johns's characteristically antidogmatic "I suppose" keeps faith with an attitude toward art making formulated five decades earlier: "At every point in nature there is something to see. My work contains similar possibilities for the changing focus of the eye." Kirk Varnedoe observed that Johns's "references to the 'eye' and to 'focus' involved a metaphoric ideal of agilely shifting mental attentiveness, and his ambition was to present reality not as more integrally complete, but as more fragmented and discontinuous."[3]

Untitled (Red, Yellow, Blue) remains staunchly irresolute, a tripartite assemblage of recurring motifs dating back to such paintings of the early 1960s as *Land's End*, *Periscope (Hart Crane)*, *Device*, and *Diver*. The names of the primary colors appear parenthetically in the title even while the print remains "untitled." Red, yellow, and blue are, at least in theory, foundational as the basis for art education and the painter's palette. Yet this system fails the practical needs of most painters, since many colors cannot be obtained by the mixing of these three primaries alone. Red, yellow, and blue provide, in other words, the perfect subject matter for Johns's ongoing meditations on the gaps between what the world is, what the eye sees, and what the mind knows.

Johns's prints name for us the primary colors in a certain order while simultaneously withholding them as sensory experience. The literal "color" of these three prints remains resolutely somber and muted, confined to a narrow range of rust brown and slate gray. The mutedness is itself a product of tainted mixture, the very incarnation of impurity as hybridity. On the verbal side of things, the letters that compose the names of the primary colors are at least as interesting as visual form as they are as conceptual content. They are to be looked at rather than simply decoded. The "red" of the first panel glows with the illusionistic legibility of a neon sign. If the "yellow" of all three prints takes the form of standard industrial stencils, the "blue" of the third panel is scripted in grade-school cursive on an illusionistically rendered folded cloth that is tacked at its upper corners in a manner clearly meant to invoke early Cubism. By the early 1980s Johns was willing to allow mimesis back into his pictorial field, if only to

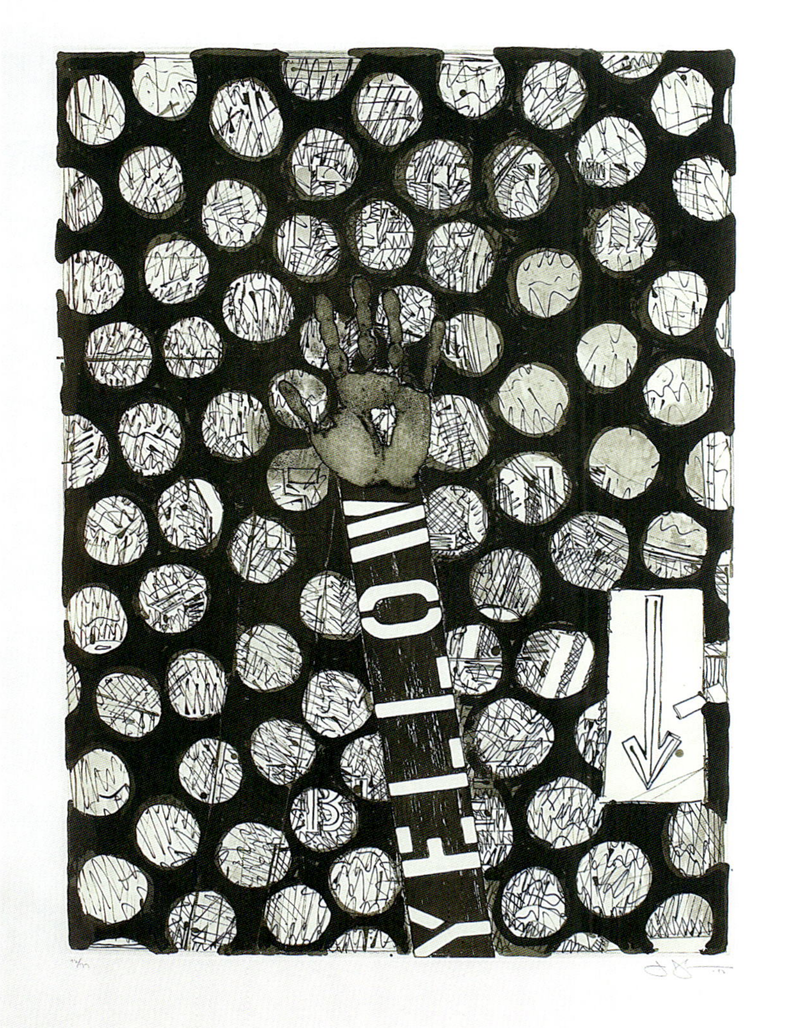

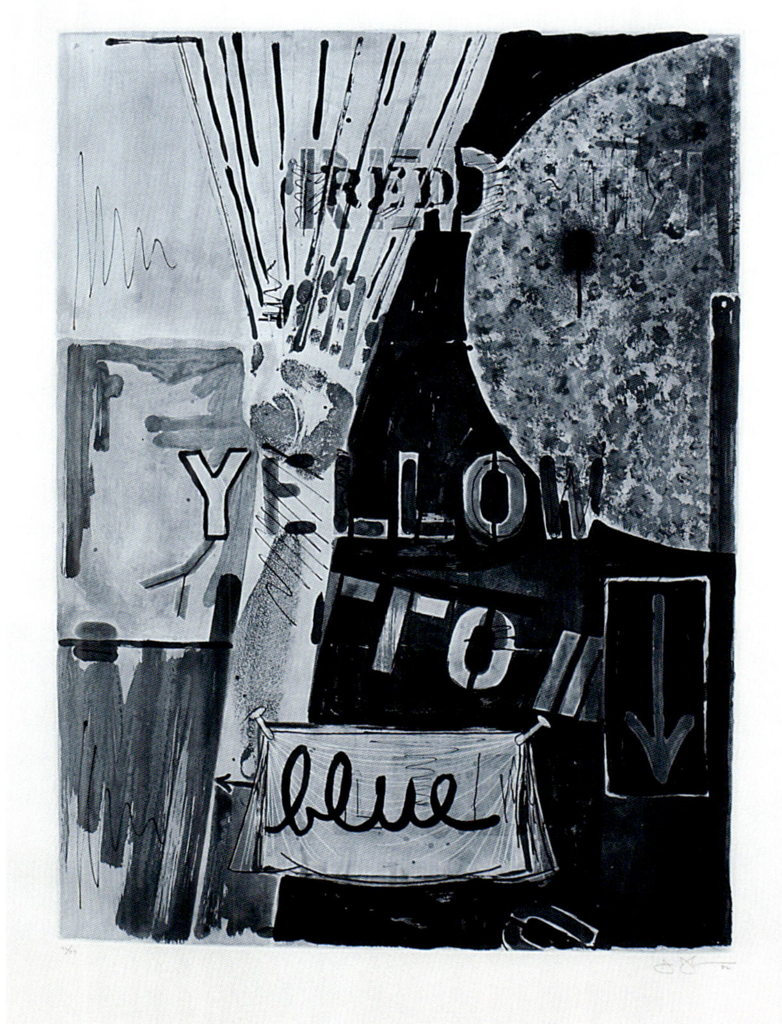

qualify and complicate postmodern proclamations concerning the demise of painting.

The recycling of older motifs in this work reminds us of Johns's lifetime preoccupation with the history of art and the philosophical quandaries of sign, language, and representation. The gravitational pull toward meaning and interpretation is palpable in this work. Yet "art" for Johns must ultimately resist and refuse the closure of the mind's will to understanding. This three-in-one print functions like a Zen koan, in keeping with Johns's long friendship with John Cage. It is a visual equivalent to "the sound of one hand clapping," a catalyst to an enlightened form of perception beyond the limitations of logical thought. An object of visual contemplation, it is designed to mirror the pleasures and frustrations of human intelligence. It functions as a model for experience in flux, where the gaps between what the world presents, the eye takes in, and the mind conceives remain pregnant with possibilities and contradictions.

Untitled (Red, Yellow, Blue) is an elegantly composed field of semiotic red herrings, a set of propositions that ramify endlessly. It succeeds in translating into visual form that intensity of being and perplexity of feeling that accompany that strangest and most characteristically "human" of moments, when the eye affords glimpses into a mind caught in the act of engaging with the world.

GD

Notes

1. Susan Sontag, "Against Interpretation," in *Against Interpretation and Other Essays* (New York: Farrar, Straus & Giroux, 1966), 10.
2. Jasper Johns to Will South, Curator of Collections, January 22, 2007, Weatherspoon Art Museum object file.
3. Kirk Varnedoe, *Jasper Johns: A Retrospective* (New York: Museum of Modern Art, 1996), 18.

Untitled (Red, Yellow, Blue), 1982. Intaglio prints on paper, each 42⅛ × 29¾ in. Museum purchase with funds from the Benefactors Fund, 2006

ELIZABETH MURRAY American, 1940–2007

WELL KNOWN FOR HER SHAPED, multi-paneled canvases that address topics associated with domesticity, motherhood, and everyday life, Elizabeth Murray came to maturity in New York in the 1980s. Although respected today for reinvigorating the medium of painting, Murray's ascent in the art world was neither guaranteed nor rapid. When she arrived in New York in the fall of 1967, after having studied in her native Chicago and the San Francisco Bay area, the art world was more interested in artists who explored the stylistic, conceptual, and formal ideas associated with Minimalism, Conceptualism, and performance and process art than one with a penchant for painting life's emotional and domestic aspects. In addition, it was not until the early 1980s that Murray mastered her working methods, most notably the use of hand-built shaped canvases, and realized the expressive possibilities of her artistic voice.

Throughout her career, Murray resisted literal readings of her work as narrative or symbolic in favor of ambiguity. In spite of that, *Lost Hat*, notwithstanding its cryptic title and obscure representation, does suggest a story. Analyzing the painting from bottom to top, viewers can discern an upside-down figure with spiky hair, an open mouth, and a triangular torso, followed by a large skirt shape that flares out between the splayed legs of a chair. Two skinny, elongated arms extend from the figure's shoulders and circle around the canvas's edges to meet at the top of the painting as two cartoonlike hands. Such references to comic strip traditions are abundant in Murray's work. The oval form with a central hole/void serves as both the underside of the figure's conical dress and the crown of a hat, the main subject of the painting. Dangling from the hat's crown, in the opposite direction from the arms, are two string ties. Last, two bluish green ovals, perhaps representing teardrops and alluding to the work's title, are affixed to the painting's outermost surface.

Sculptural in form, *Lost Hat* brings together Murray's signature elements: whimsy, ambiguity, abstract and figurative forms, and a painterly application of color. Murray considered her loose, energetic brushwork as essential to her paintings as her choice of colors and dynamic compositions. Labeled a Neo-Expressionist for her emotive content and paint handling, she worked on an instinctual level of consciousness, altering fundamentals as she went along. Throughout her career she reprocessed a compilation of images (coffee cups, figures, chairs, tables, etc.) whose meanings altered somewhat depending on the context. Murray was attracted to Cubism's fractured forms and to Surrealism's suggestive biomorphism and figments of imagination, but she added to her work the scale and loose brushwork of Abstract Expressionism as well as the humor and wittiness of cartoon illustrations. Most often she favored a swirling, active composition punctured by a hole or void at its center. Although typically open-ended, her paintings consistently suggest that something is about to, or already has, happened. Murray simply left it up to viewers to interpret the meaning behind the barrage of information that she thrust at them, believing that more than one interpretation was appropriate. About 2000 she embarked on a new phase in which she combined numerous small, irregular canvases into one work that display more white space than in the past. In addition to paintings, she produced over the course of her career works on paper in all sizes and media as well as illustrated books.

EDG

Lost Hat, 1985. Oil on canvas, 119 × 121 × 10½ in. Museum purchase with funds from the Jefferson-Pilot Endowment, the Weatherspoon Art Museum Acquisition Endowment, the Weatherspoon Guild Acquisition Endowment, the Carol and Seymour Levin Acquisition Endowment, the Louise D. and Herbert S. Falk Acquisition Endowment, and by exchange, 2009

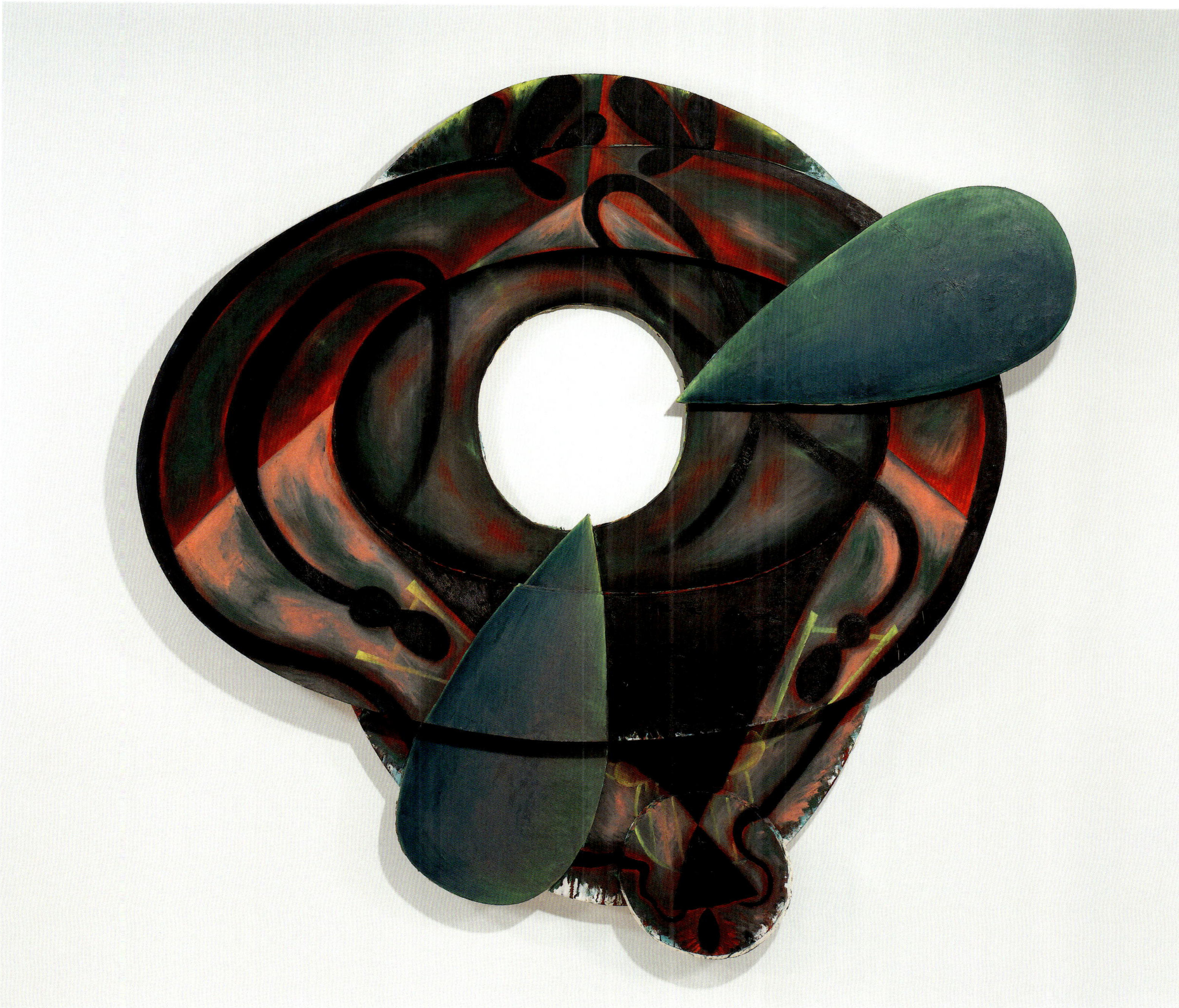

ADRIAN PIPER American, born 1948

A PROFESSOR OF PHILOSOPHY and a foundational artist in the Conceptual and performance art movements, Adrian Piper is a contemporary role model for artists interested in social interaction, philosophy, race, and feminism.

In the 1960s Piper's intellectual dedication to questions of physical and moral existence led to seemingly disparate projects. In 1968, for instance, she undertook both a textual analysis of a square and a documentary work that showed her cooking and serving four hamburgers to her boyfriend. Piper, a philosopher and a vegetarian, was probing the logical bounds of her relationships to the world in every facet of her life. While writing on Emmanuel Kant's *Critique of Pure Reason*, Piper reaffirmed her own existence through the practice of staring into a mirror whenever she became utterly absorbed by her intellectual pursuits and recording her thoughts.[1] Piper's interests in the self and maintaining a connection to the physical or social world were present even during this early phase but were not yet full expressions of her politically engaged art practice.

As her career progressed, Piper explored social interactions, the art world, and political activism. In the 1970s she continued to push social boundaries and norms. For example, she shopped at Macy's department store wearing clothes covered in sticky white streaks and a sign declaring "Wet Paint"; rode public transportation with her mouth stuffed with a rag; and walked through elite arts venues with all of her senses—sight, smell, touch, taste, and hearing—blocked off.[2] These performance pieces, which challenged social behavioral norms, were greatly influenced by the similar work of Vito Acconci, Yvonne Rainier, and Rosemary Mayer. Piper's confrontations with both everyday interactions and the insular practices of the high-art world have become foundational philosophical and artistic inquires into race, gender, and transgression.

During this same period Piper participated in protests against the U.S. invasion of Cambodia and the Kent and Jackson State massacres.[3] During the late 1970s and early 1980s, Piper's work took on an overtly political tone that would become a mainstay of her career. During this period we can see the roots of *Vanilla Nightmares #7*. In 1976 Piper wallpapered the inside of a minimalist white-cube room with newspaper clippings reporting on various acts of violence, stenciled the words "NOT A PERFORMANCE" on the interior of this space, and entitled the whole *Art for the Art World Surface Pattern*. In this work, created a decade before the Vanilla Nightmares series, South Africa appears as one of the places of global unrest and violence to which Piper draws our attention.

Apartheid, the institutionalized racism and government policy that was in effect in South Africa from 1948 to 1990, began the year Piper was born. The personal and political are thus linked; Piper draws visual parallels between South African black violence and African American identity that bring this international issue home. In *Vanilla Nightmares #7* Piper's early interest in formalism comes out in the rhyme she creates between the circular form around a body that was "necklaced," seen in the upper right corner of the page from the *New York Times* that serves as the drawing's support, and the chains around the necks of the slaves who loom behind this news release. "Necklacing," the practice of forcing apartheid collaborators into the center of an automobile tire, pouring gasoline into the tire, and then igniting this deadly ring, was used as a tool of intimidation in South Africa beginning in 1984 and quickly entered Piper's political consciousness.[4]

In this work Piper confronts the viewer with the eyeless specters of slavery, colonialism, and racism—social anxieties or prejudices that loomed behind the slow response of the United States to the violence in South Africa. She is careful to frame her drawing so we can read snippets about the U.S. policy of "constructive engagement," which maintained diplomatic ties with the South African government well beyond the beginning of boycotts by other countries. She also leaves visible a discussion of a U.S. House of Representatives bill that would finally impose full trade embargoes on the South African government and explanations by resistance fighters that "necklacing" was a means to ensure collaborators would "know not to delay the struggle." Through her selective editing, she implies that the United States is part of this delay.

In the Vanilla Nightmares series Piper confronts fears of black sexuality, economic racism, and the continued assumption of whiteness as a norm in American culture. The deliberate confrontation of racism and normative whiteness is also the subject of another artwork by Piper in the Weatherspoon's collection, *My Calling (Card)* (1986). In this series, which lasted from 1986 to 1990, Piper presented calling cards to persons in social situations when racist comments were made. These two works of 1986 highlight Adrian Piper's confrontations of the specter of racism, be it public or private.

EP

Notes

1. Maurice Berger, "Styles of Radical Will: Adrian Piper and the Indexical Present," in *Adrian Piper: A Retrospective*, ed. Berger (Baltimore: University of Baltimore Fine Arts Gallery, 1999), 18.
2. Adrian Piper, "Personal Chronology," in ibid., 188.
3. Ibid.
4. Rodney Davenport and Christopher Saunders, *South Africa: A Modern History*, 5th ed. (New York: St. Martin's Press, 2000), 701.

Vanilla Nightmares #7, 1986. Charcoal on newspaper, $23^{7}/_{8} \times 13^{3}/_{4}$ in. Museum purchase with funds from the Benefactors Fund, 2001

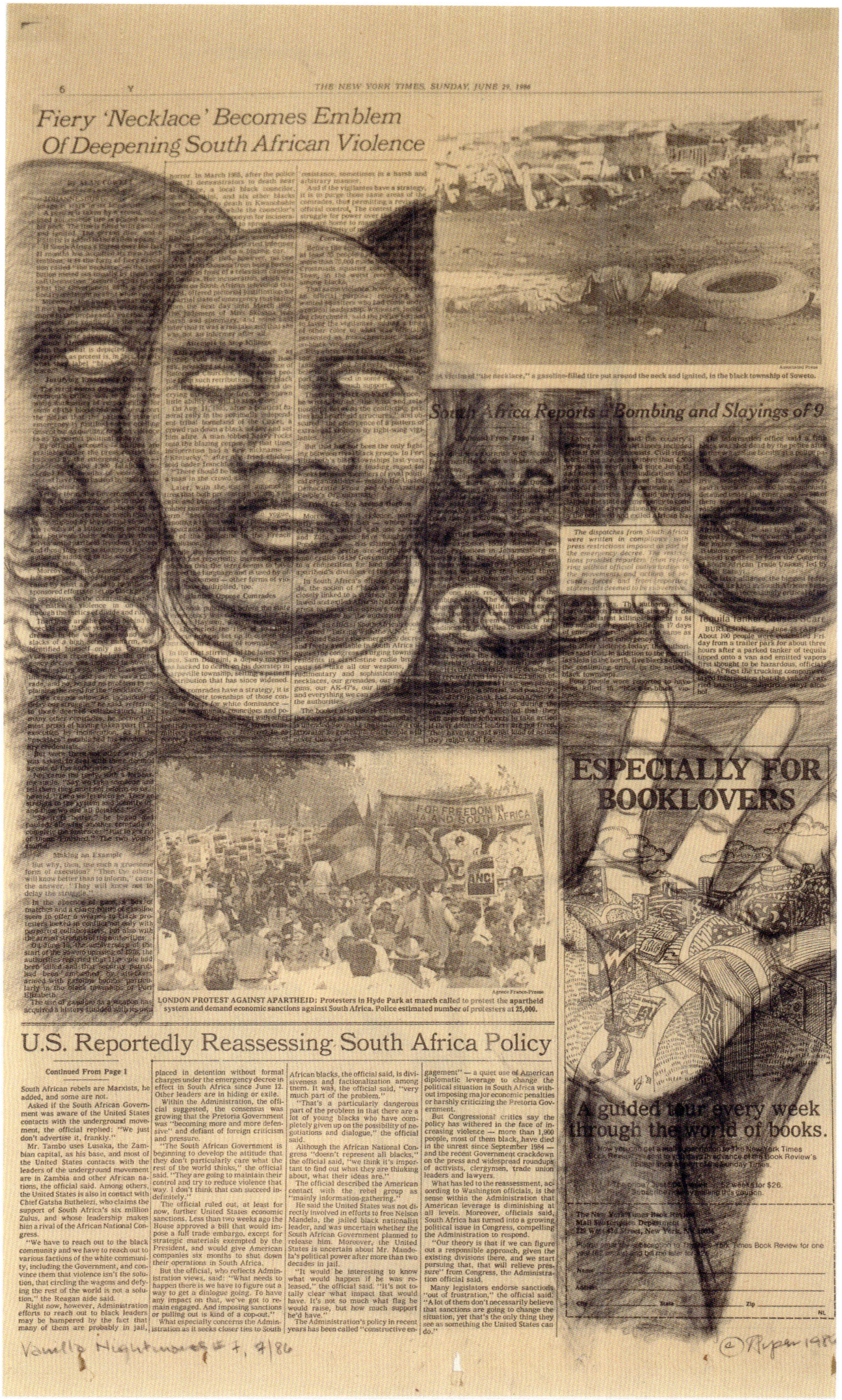
THE NEW YORK TIMES, SUNDAY, JUNE 29, 1986
Fiery 'Necklace' Becomes Emblem Of Deepening South African Violence
A victim of "the necklace," a gasoline-filled tire put around the neck and ignited, in the black township of Soweto.
South Africa Reports a Bombing and Slayings of 9
FOR FREEDOM IN SOUTH AFRICA
ANC
LONDON PROTEST AGAINST APARTHEID: Protesters in Hyde Park at march called to protest the apartheid system and demand economic sanctions against South Africa. Police estimated number of protesters at 25,000.
U.S. Reportedly Reassessing South Africa Policy
ESPECIALLY FOR BOOKLOVERS
A guided tour every week through the world of books.
Vanilla Nightmares #7, 7/86
© Piper 1986

DAVID REED American, born 1946

DESPITE REPEATED PRONOUNCEMENTS of the death of painting, David Reed has remained committed to prolonging its life and to the belief that painting participates in a continuum. He is notable among contemporary painters for his reformulation of elements from the history of painting to address the vicissitudes and conversations of the present.

Reed's hallmark works are large-scale canvases whose sensual beauty belies the rigor of their intellectual grounding. Most characteristic of his paintings are large, rhythmic, wavelike gestures that Reed conceives of as extending beyond the confines of the canvas. His longstanding interest in and admiration of Baroque art is evidenced in the sweep and complexity of these forms. They appear to be exaggerated brushstrokes, but they are representations of brushstrokes, emblems of the gestural mark that has come to define expressive abstraction. As one critic points out, however, Reed's paintings are not abstract in the sense of being cool, removed, expressionistic, or tactile.[1] In his work, the gesture should be seen as the physicality of the painter's body as it makes the mark, reinforcing the sense of movement—and therefore time—within the painting itself. There is little visible evidence, however, of how the mark is made, of how the surface of the painting is created, or of how the dramatic play between light and dark is achieved.

The Weatherspoon's painting, *#252* (numbered rather than titled as are many of Reed's works), exemplifies the initially perplexing ways in which the artist's paintings operate. Tall and narrow, the work is the vertical corollary to his horizontal paintings inspired by the wide-screen Cinemascope of cowboy westerns. Reed is keenly interested in films for their inherent embodiment of time and movement, an idea that he strives to simulate in his paintings. The proportions of his canvases make it impossible for the viewer to take them in all at once: things that happen at the periphery of our vision stop when we fix on a particular spot. As a result, the paintings appear in a state of constant change.

In *#252*, it is only through repeated scannings that one recognizes that an arc at the top of the painting is echoed by one at the very bottom; they cannot be seen simultaneously from a normal viewing distance. The rising, or cascading, brushstroke forms are luscious variations of blues, grays, and yellowish creams that turn to black and gray in the bottom section of the painting. Along the left side are two long rectangles. In the lower one, Reed has scratched through the black paint to the canvas beneath, thereby bringing a mark of the artist's hand to counter the mystery of how the paintings are made; above, he introduced a more vivid blue that one then seeks to find replicated within the blues elsewhere.

These divided sections of varying scale, color, and direction threaten compositional unity in Reed's paintings. While he brings them together by his insistence on color, light, and intense value contrasts, he uses these disruptions to create emotional tension that engages the viewer in the here and now. The viewer's attempt to visually pull the pieces together and to work out their interconnections keep that tension in the present. Paradoxically representational (the images of brushstrokes) and abstract (nonfigurative), Reed's paintings distinguish themselves for taking on some of the toughest challenges of keeping painting alive and well.

David Reed hails from San Diego, which might explain in part his keen interest in films. He attributes his four years at Reed College in Portland, Oregon, from which he graduated in 1968, to an awakening interest in art; he went on to study painting at the New York Studio School under Philip Guston and Milton Resnick. He has had solo exhibitions in New York since 1976, and large exhibitions of his work traveled throughout Europe in 1985 and 2001 and in this country in 1998 and 2005.

NMD

Note

1. Mieke Bal, "David Reed's *#275*: A Story of Erotic Vision," in *David Reed Paintings: Motion Pictures* (San Diego: Museum of Contemporary Art, 1998), 37.

#252, 1987. Oil and alkyd on linen, 108 × 36 in. Gift of Anthony T. Podesta, Washington, DC, 2000

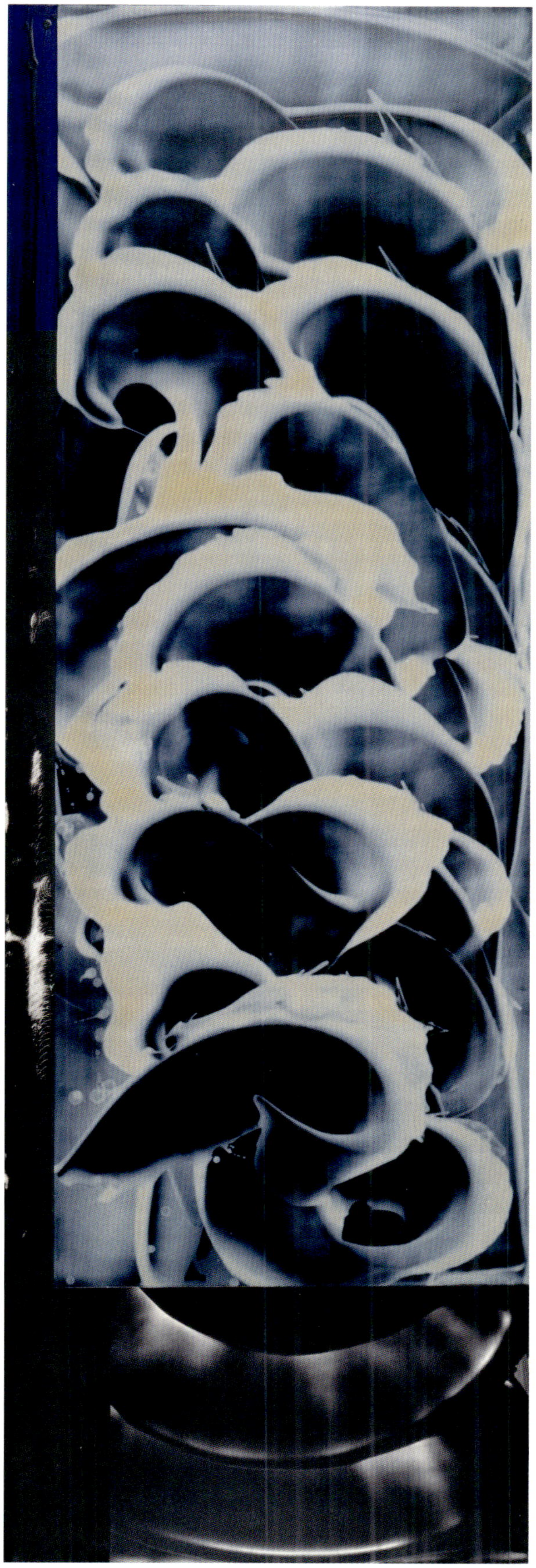

TERRY ALLEN American, born 1943

EVER SINCE GRADUATING from the Chouinard Art Institute in Los Angeles in 1966, Terry Allen has worked in a wide variety of media, including painting, sculpture, musical and theatrical performance, poetry, video, radio, and installation. With all these talents at his disposal, it is not surprising that this versatile artist also has a wealth of narratives that he feels compelled to express, most often by revisiting, revising, or further developing his ideas in serial work.

Aparté (Rat Talk at the Sonic) is a mixed-media assemblage that belongs to Allen's ambitious Youth in Asia series, a decadelong endeavor that focuses on the social and political ramifications of the Vietnam War.[1] The works making up the series are literary and musical as well as pictorial and sculptural. As a whole, the series presents a revisionist history of the United States government's involvement in Vietnam as told by angry war veterans, hippies, and Vietcong prisoners of war. Individually, each piece tells an autonomous portion of the narrative, although certain elements such as characters, settings, and story lines frequently recur.

Aparté (Rat Talk at the Sonic) overflows with personal references, wordplay, metaphors, and symbolism. Its multilayered imagery conveys the complexity of the war as well as the disillusionment and destruction left in its wake and the loneliness, despair, dislocation, guilt, and betrayal felt by its veterans. Although it is impossible to know completely why every component was included, each element serves an important role in the telling and understanding of the story line.

Adhered to a trophy plaque on the exterior of the work's shadowbox frame, the taxidermied rat and parrot serve as gruesome reminders of the death and atrophy experienced in Vietnam. The appalling and conspicuous stuffed rat is also an oblique reference to Walt Disney's legendary character Mickey Mouse and to the absurd never-never land that the war seemed to embrace. To make this point more vivid, Allen depicted the actual Mickey Mouse character in the painting's upper left corner. Wearing a smock and a beret and holding a palette and brush, the grimacing Mickey represents the youth who went to war as well as the folly and unrealities of the war in general. Allen intuits that the children raised on Disney in the 1940s and 1950s grew up on the battlefields of Southeast Asia in the 1960s and 1970s.[2] And, like Mickey's entirely fabricated world, Vietnam turned out to be a world built on illusions. Moreover, none of the promises implicit in Disney's fairy tales came to pass.

The upside-down framed painting of a female figure in the center of *Aparté (Rat Talk at the Sonic)* is an indirect reference to the French precursors of the Vietnam War. The image is a detail taken from a painting by the eighteenth-century French artist Jean-Baptiste Greuze, *The Wicked Son Returned* (1778). Greuze's painting appears to depict the story of a son who returns too late to reconcile with his dying father. The gesturing, distraught woman to the left of the bedridden father expresses the anguish and dismay felt by his family—and by Vietnamese and American families alike. Symbolizing France's longtime involvement in Southeast Asia, the inverted painting also denotes the upside-down madness of the Vietnam experience. In addition, the word *aparté* in the painting's title is French for "aside," which signifies the experience of returning veterans.

Equally obvious in the painting are the images of the dining table and its attendant booth seating. The tableau and the word *Sonic* in the painting's title may refer to the quick service, drive-in restaurant chain established in 1953 and still in existence today. Simulating the inside of a café, diner, or bar, the setting may symbolize a site for honest, face-to-face discourse on the war and its effects. It also recalls the Kitty Kat nightclub and other such places for rest and relaxation that were frequented by soldiers on leave in Hong Kong and Bangkok.[3]

The painting's rough surface texture evokes both camouflage netting and pocked and weathered stucco walls. The characterlike lettering in the painting's upper register suggests actual words, while the bright yellow, conical form worn by a cartoonlike green parrot recalls hats worn by Vietnamese farmers. Although difficult to discern, this bird is repeated behind the taxidermied animals wearing a cane hat and holding a cane or umbrella, but still representing the foolishness of the war.

Complex in nature and overflowing with references and information, *Aparté (Rat Talk at the Sonic)* tells a somber story. Although various parts of the composition call out and fight for the viewer's undivided attention, the overall story it tells reminds us of the need to come to terms with this critical segment of American history.

EDG

Notes

1. The impetus for the Youth in Asia series was Allen's being asked in 1982 to work on the soundtrack of a film by Wolf-Eckart Bühler entitled *Amerasia*. *Terry Allen: Youth in Asia* (Winston-Salem, NC: Southeastern Center for Contemporary Art, 1992), 3.
2. *Terry Allen: Youth in Asia Series* (Pittsburgh: Pittsburgh Center for the Arts, 1988), 8.
3. *Terry Allen: Youth in Asia* (Winston-Salem), 11.

Aparté (Rat Talk at the Sonic), 1988. Taxidermied rat and bird, wood, spackle, pastel, oil, gouache, and Plexiglas, 48¾ × 48¾ × 9¼ in. Gift of Peter Norton, 2001

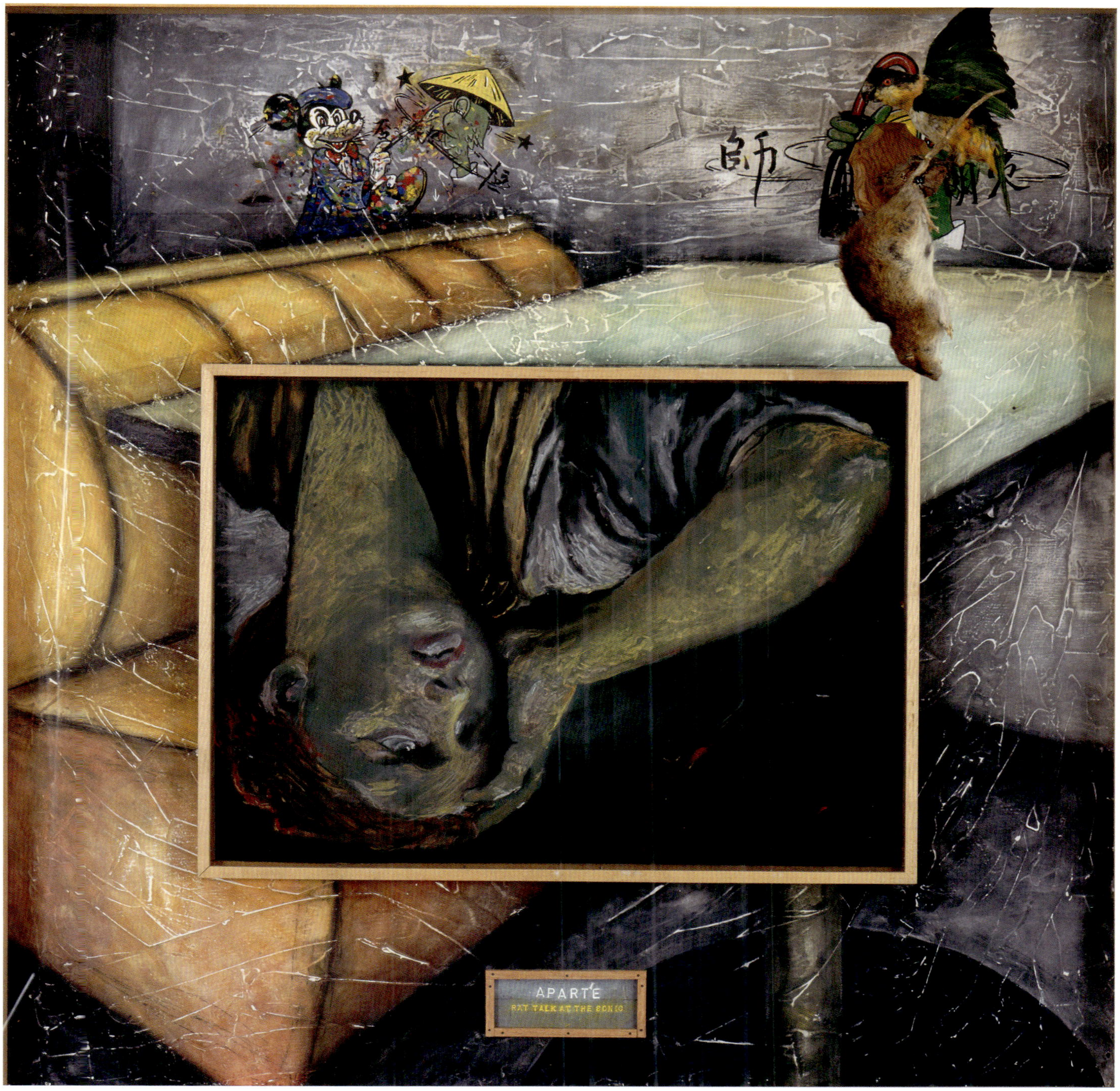
APARTÉ
RAT TALK AT THE SONIC

ANTONY GORMLEY British, born 1950

"CAST IRON AND AIR." With a decision as basic as what media to place on a didactic label, Antony Gormley reminds viewers that a sculpture is not merely iron, wood, or clay, a few of the media that can denote a form, but it can also describe the space within or surrounding an object, what art students first learn about as negative space.

During the early 1980s Gormley's work sought to illuminate what he has described as "the hidden syntax of the human body," including such basic postures as standing, sitting, kneeling, and crouching.[1] Gormley's classical education at the University of Cambridge and the Slade School of Art, London, is paired with a deep interest in Buddhist philosophy, and his artworks are metaphysical reflections on bodily existence, human interactions, and community.

The artist frequently made casts of his own body in his early work. This experience, during which he felt the pressure of the mold and was aware of the volume that his body displaced, led him to contemplate the inner spaces of the body.[2] Gormley describes his interest in the casting process by stating, "I think you could identify my project as a whole as a return to the body not as object but as place."[3] By interpreting the body as a place, Gormley reminds viewers that the body is inhabited; it is a space from which human beings define their experience of the world.

To make *Landing III*, two embracing figures, Gormley welded together twenty pieces of cast iron. One figure lies atop the other as they press their bodies together so firmly they create a single form. At the bottom, the four feet merge in a cross shape that comes together at a point. This contact between two mirrored figures reflects Gormley's goal of undermining dualistic thinking and his belief that the cross, a cross-cultural symbol, is part of human bodily syntax.[4]

The cross references the cardinal directions and Emmanuel Kant's ideas of human occupation of space, in which "our geographical knowledge, and even our commonest knowledge of the position of places" is understood in relation to our bodily experience of up and down, right and left, front and back.[5] Gormley's sculptures explore the directions in which bodies move and encourage philosophical reflection on our corporeal existence.

The humanist geographer Yi-Fu Tuan explains that, in Kantian and Eastern traditions, when our bodies are in the supine position, we "accept our biological condition," as opposed to an upright stance, which implies "achievement and order."[6] Tuan's combination of Western and Eastern philosophy finds resonance in Gormley's own training and helps us see that *Landing III* draws attention to a human acceptance of position and orientation. The mirrored figures either imply the sense of place and position in relation to one another or are a reference to the mirroring of the self.

Gormley's later figural works take the exploration of bodily existence and inner space beyond the literal scale of the artist's body. *Angel of the North* and *Havmann*, both of 1994, instead refer to human beings' larger-than-life inner space, the internal worlds of human existence and emotions. These works, measuring sixty-six and thirty-six feet high respectively, face out into the wind or the sea. Their grand presence seeks to engage the public and ask viewers to meditate on their inner life. These monumental works stand in stark contrast to Gormley's *One & Other* (2009), one of the Fourth Plinth Projects installed in Trafalgar Square, London. Instead of erecting a monumental sculpture, Gormley granted 2,400 members of the public a one-hour slot on the Fourth Plinth. Although it may seem the antithesis of his large-scale sculptures, Gormley's Fourth Plinth work nonetheless is an extension of his philosophical reflections on the human construct by using bodies and spaces. He continues to explore the boundaries of human experiences, both corporeal and conceptual, both within and without the skin of our individual bodies.

EP

Notes

1. Stephen C. Levinson, "Space and Place," in *Some of the Facts* (Cornwall: Tate St. Ives, 2001), on Gormley's website, http://www.antonygormley.com/.
2. Ibid.
3. Quoted in ibid.
4. Annette DiMeo Carlozzi, "An Interview with Antony Gormley by Annette DiMeo Carlozzi," in *New Works: 95.3* (San Antonio: Artpace, a Foundation for Contemporary Art, 1996), 5.
5. Emmanuel Kant, quoted in Yi-Fu Tuan, *Space and Place: The Perspective of Experience* (Minneapolis: University of Minnesota Press, 1977), 36.
6. Ibid.

Landing III, 1988–89. Cast iron and air, 20 × 82½ × 23½ in. Museum purchase with funds provided by the Weatherspoon Art Museum Association, Jefferson-Pilot Corporation and Burlington Industries, 1993

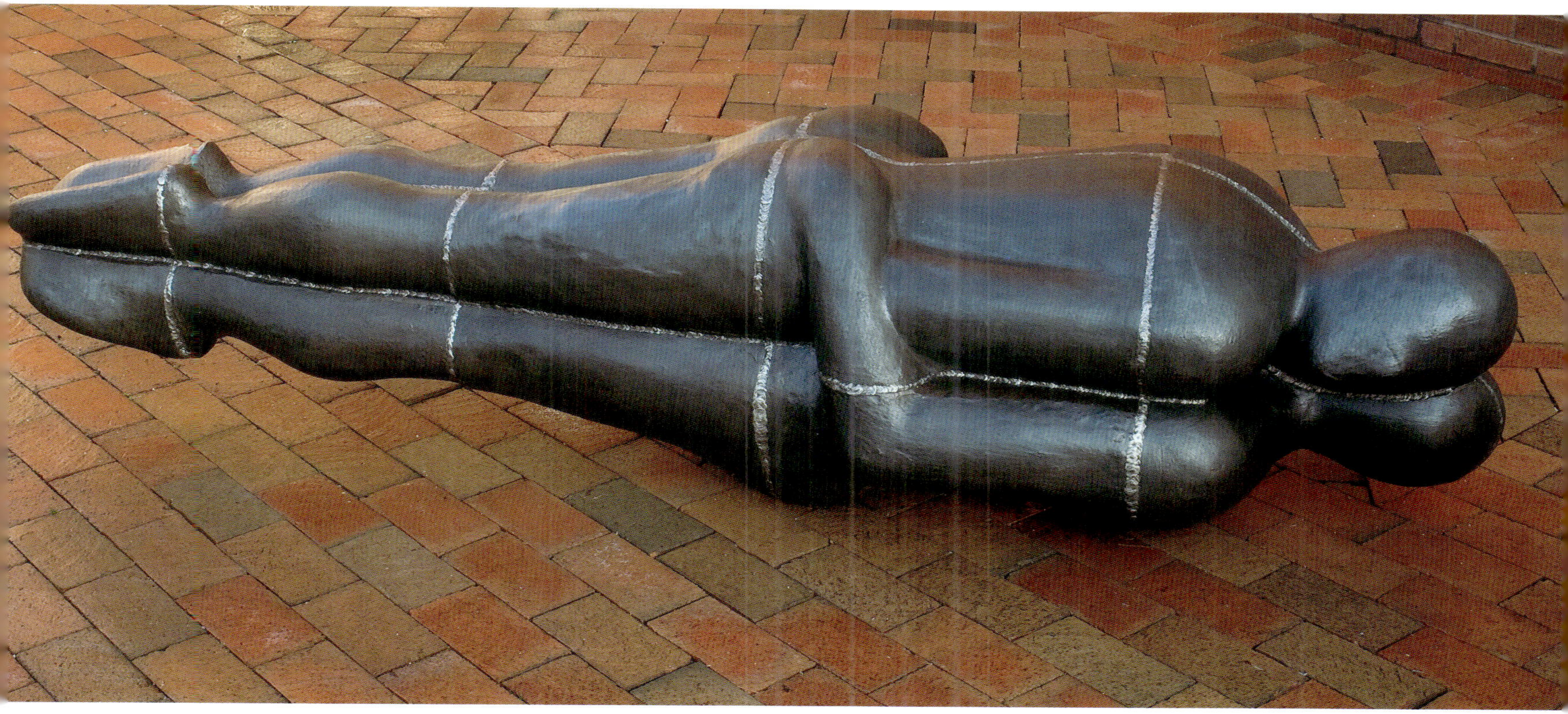

DAN GRAHAM American, born 1942

DAN GRAHAM'S CAREER has been diverse, to say the least: he was an early performance and video artist, commercial gallery director, photographer, sculptor, installation artist, and rock music critic. But his trademark works are his interactive glass structures, which appear in sites around the world.

Graham's life as a gallery director was short-lived, but it gave him the opportunity to show architecturally inspired work by the likes of Sol LeWitt and Dan Flavin. When the gallery folded after a year, he became an artist himself, part of the vanguard of Conceptual art and critical art writing in the 1960s. Graham was particularly interested in matters of perception and the ways that viewers experience works of art and the spaces they occupy.

He constructed his first pavilion in 1978, although the Weatherspoon's is the first to have a triangular form. Graham's pavilions are usable spaces that have their precedents in gazebos, temporary exposition halls, and even bus shelters. Their use of glass relates to the ideal of modernist architecture of breaking down distinctions between interior and exterior space. Minimalist in form, they are, however, loci for social and psychological interaction.

Triangular Solid with Circular Inserts is an equilateral triangle in three dimensions. One side has a central circular opening through which a spectator-participant can enter. Circles of glass and/or mirror of equal circumference are centered in each of the other two vertical sides of the pavilion. The side through which one enters is clear glass; the left side is a two-way mirror with a circular insert of plain mirror on both the exterior and interior; and the right side is transparent glass with the circular inserts on both sides being a two-way mirror. One's position relative to the pavilion creates multiple perspectives. At a distance, the piece can both flatten out and repeat itself infinitely; from inside, the experience of each of the three facets differs; and from outside, looking in, the viewer has any number of experiences—seeing all the way through the sculpture, being able to view only the feet and head of a person inside whose torso is blocked by reflective mirror, or seeing one's torso clearly mirrored while only feet and head are reflected by the glass.

As with all of Graham's glass pavilions and no matter from which view they are seen, each becomes specific to its site. The Weatherspoon's work is united with the environment of the museum's sculpture courtyard. Its human scale reinforces the fact that, in Graham's work, perception is grounded in bodily experience and is social in character. The viewer is made keenly aware of his or her self-image and role in activating the piece and interacting with whoever else may be viewing it.

Dan Graham has had no formal artistic training; his knowledge and experience of contemporary art began with his yearlong directorship, from 1964 to 1965, of the John Daniels Gallery in New York City. Even more conceptually grounded than many of the artists whose art he showed there, Graham at first moved away from the gallery context altogether, producing text works and short films and videos, and writing from a critical perspective about his own work and that of some of his contemporaries.

Graham has had solo exhibitions and commissions throughout the United States, Europe, and Asia, and the bibliography on his work is extensive. His seventh retrospective, coordinated by the Museum of Contemporary Art, Los Angeles, and the Whitney Museum of American Art in New York, was presented in 2009. *Triangular Solid with Circular Inserts* was commissioned by Nexus (now the Atlanta Contemporary Center in Georgia) in 1989 and remained on display there until the Weatherspoon purchased it in 2006.

NMD

Triangular Solid with Circular Inserts, 1989. Two-way mirror, clear glass, and aluminum, 84 × 84 × 84 in. Museum purchase with funds from the Jefferson-Pilot Endowment, the Burlington Industries Endowment, the Weatherspoon Art Museum Acquisition Endowment, the Frances Stern Loewenstein Acquisition Endowment, the Louise D. and Herbert S. Falk Acquisition Endowment, the Lynn Richardson Prickett Acquisition Endowment, the Jane and Richard Levy Sculpture Fund, the Judy Proctor Acquisition Endowment, the Melanie H. and Robert C. Ketner Family Acquisition Endowment and the Weatherspoon Guild Acquisition Endowment, 2006

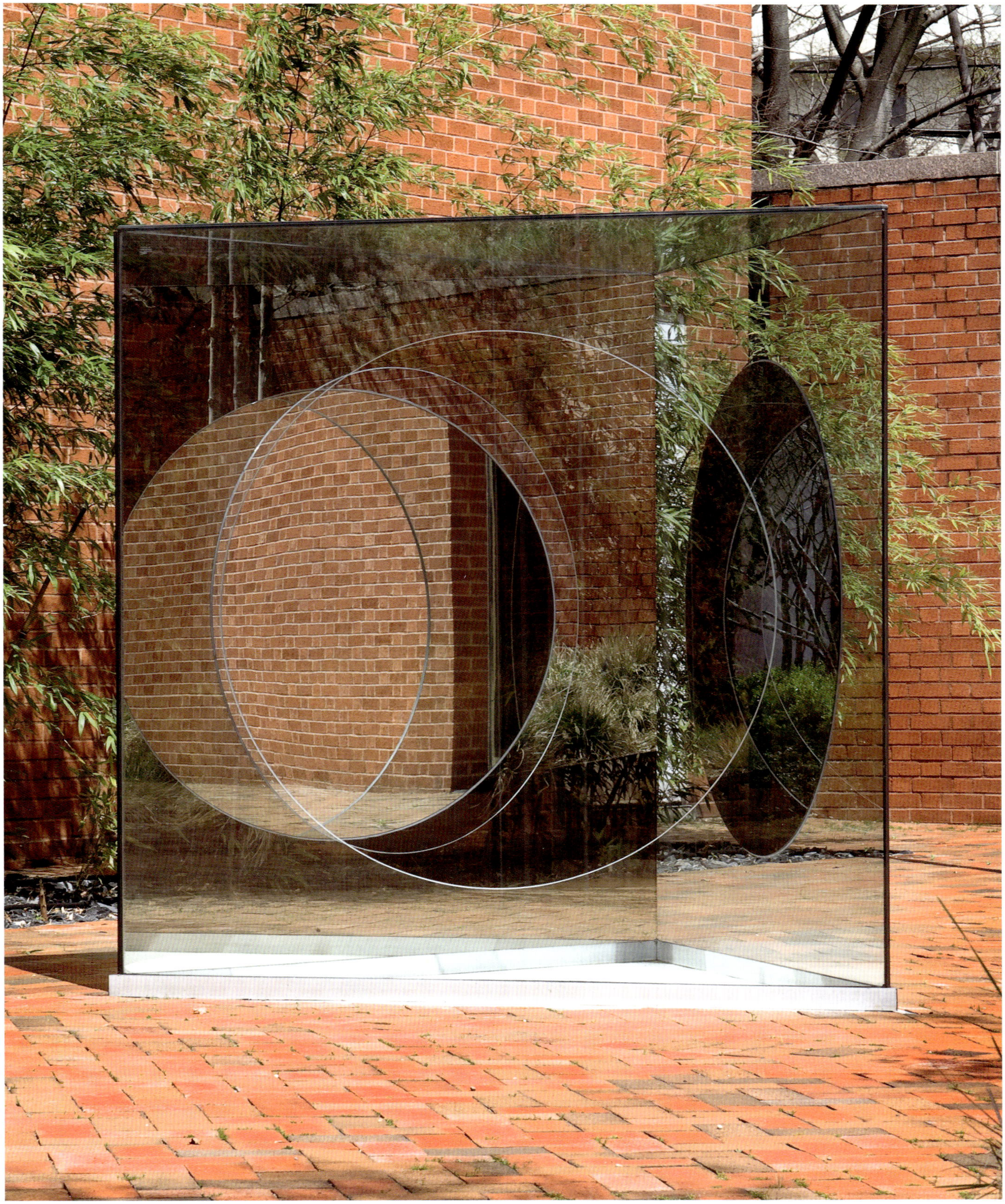

ED PASCHKE American, 1939–2004

THE SUBJECT OF ED PASCHKE'S *Mono-Pareja* is Diego Velázquez's portrait of Juan de Pareja, painted in about 1650. When the Velázquez work was purchased by New York's Metropolitan Museum of Art in 1970, Paschke had just earned his MFA degree from the School of the Art Institute of Chicago and was emerging as a leading member of the Chicago Imagists. Throughout his career Paschke drew inspiration from popular culture, often reinterpreting images popularized by exposure in print and electronic media. His *Mono-Pareja* is one in a series of paintings that expand on the media fame of Velázquez's portrait.

Few people had heard of Juan de Pareja, let alone seen his portrait by Velázquez, until it was acquired by the Metropolitan Museum. Even now, far more people know reproductions of the portrait than the work itself. The painting made front-page news in the *New York Times* on May 13, 1971, when museum officials confirmed that it had been purchased for more than $5.5 million, setting a record for paintings sold at auction. Controversy over the purchase price soon gave way to curiosity about the historical context of the portrait and the identity of the sitter, both explored in a television special aired in 1984. Since then *Juan de Pareja* has been featured in Sister Wendy's televised museum tours and promoted in ads offering commercial reproductions of museum masterpieces as seen on TV.[1] With intentional irony, Paschke likewise depicted Velázquez's portrait as if it were being viewed on television.

Paschke's *Mono-Pareja* revisions *Juan de Pareja* in both obvious and subtle ways. Instead of replicating Velázquez's portrait format, Paschke used a horizontal canvas that dwarfs the dimensions of most widescreen televisions. Framed by an opening that resembles the shape of a smaller, midcentury television screen, Paschke's cropped image reduces Velázquez's half-length figure to a bust portrait, perceptibly altering the relation between the figure and its setting. Like Velázquez, Paschke used oil paint, and he even restored the yellow of the varnish that had given Velázquez's painting a greenish cast before it was cleaned. Ramping up the restricted palette of *Juan de Pareja*, Paschke added hues that have the intensity and vibrancy of colors transmitted through the cathode ray tubes of vintage color televisions. Whereas Velázquez applied paint in loose, transparent strokes to create the illusion of three-dimensional depth and substance, Paschke layered dry-brush stippling and short, flat strokes over a multihued ground that looks as if it was painted with an airbrush. The resulting color patterns and surface textures mimic the visual distortions of electronic static that was common during the era of analog television.

Less immediately apparent than differences of format, composition, color scheme, and technique are changes Paschke made in the appearance and accessories of Velázquez's subject. Close scrutiny of *Mono-Pareja* reveals that the figure's skin tone reinforces the racial identity of Velázquez's Moorish sitter. In Paschke's painting, Juan de Pareja has a slightly broader face, less prominent eyebrows, and a fuller upper lip, which is reiterated in a ghost image to the right of his mouth. Yet another ghost image creates the illusion that Paschke's figure is peering through a wire-rimmed monocle. Although Paschke retained the lace-trimmed collar worn by Juan de Pareja, all the subtle changes in his repainting of a subject identified as Velázquez's studio assistant make Paschke's figure look like someone who might have been his own studio assistant.

The title *Mono-Pareja* could allude to a type of television set, to the monocle Paschke added to Velázquez's portrait, or to monovision, which is technically a method for correcting vision with two different contact lenses. Figuratively, this term aptly characterizes Paschke's singular artistic vision. By creatively repainting and renaming the portrait of Juan de Pareja, Paschke reversed the mass media's process of commodification that had transformed a seventeenth-century painting into the Metropolitan Museum's multimillion-dollar Velázquez. In doing so, Paschke reclaimed the aura that Walter Benjamin had predicted would be lost in an age of mechanical reproduction.[2] Acquired by the Weatherspoon in the year it was painted, *Mono-Pareja* now challenges the digital generation to consider how contemporary artists can continue to renew the art of the past.

KPA

Notes

1. For documentation of media exposure, see Nadine Covert, ed., *Art on Screen* (Boston: G. K. Hall, 1991), 176; and http://1st-art-gallery.com, item number 10281709.
2. Walter Benjamin, *The Work of Art in the Age of Its Technological Reproducibility and Other Writings on Media* (Cambridge, MA: Belknap Press of Harvard University Press, 2008), 19–55.

Mono-Pareja, 1990. Oil on linen, 60 × 78 in. Museum purchase with funds from the Benefactors Fund, 1990

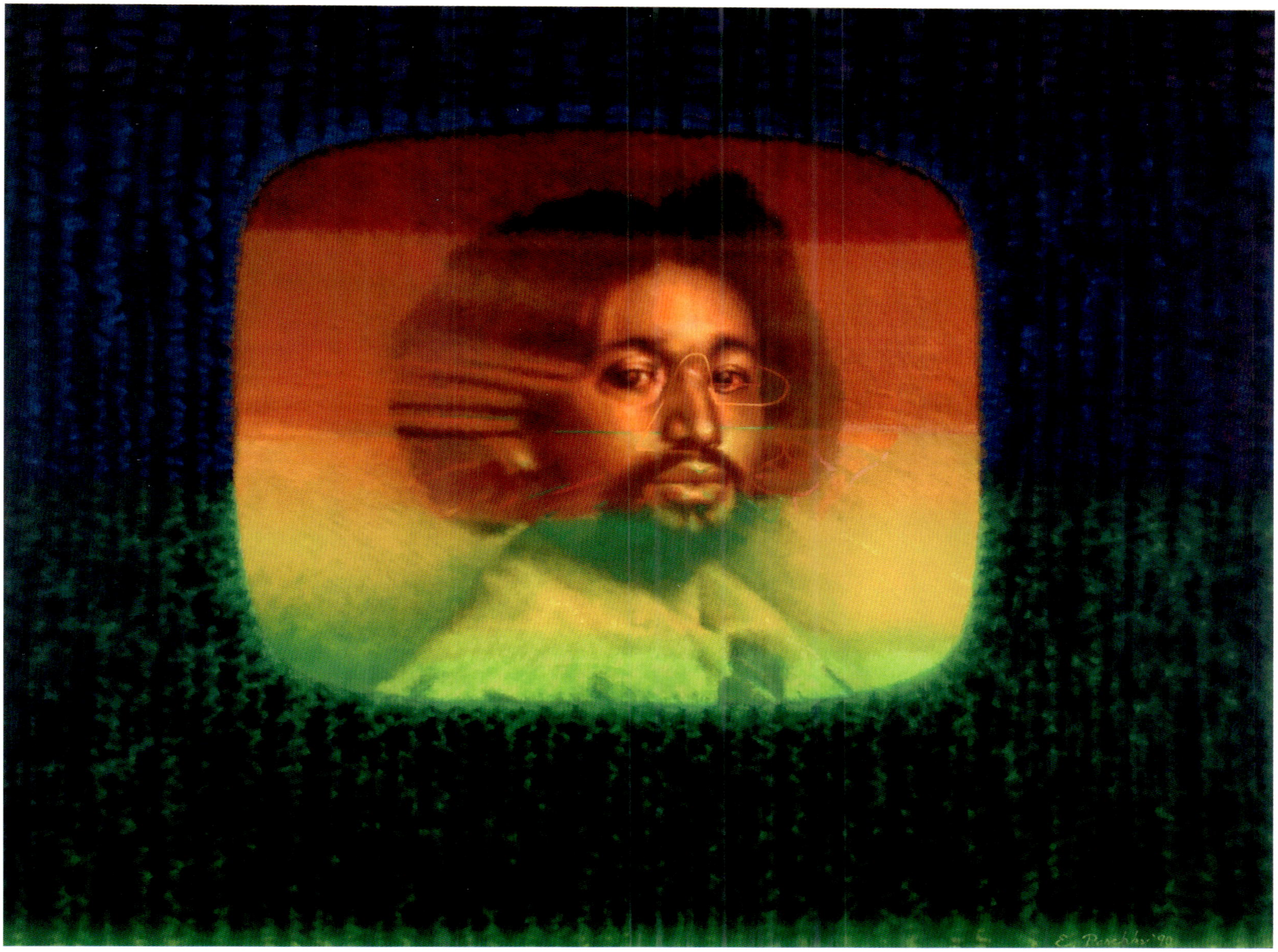

JOYCE SCOTT American, born 1948

NO MORE THAN TWENTY-TWO inches tall, *Big Mama* nevertheless has a funky, exotic presence that commands attention. Composed of tiny, shimmering beads of glass and plastic, she is an exotic creature. We don't quite know what to make of her, whether to respond with humor, celebration, derision, pathos, or dismay. Part fetish object, part caricature, she inhabits the space of art on the boundaries of the familiar and recognizable, where perception begins to unravel and associations proliferate. She holds together in her protean strangeness a mix of possible references: black Venus, bathing beauty, racist stereotype, votive offering, kitsch artifact, and child's doll. Yet clearly she is also none of these, a profoundly idiosyncratic creature synthesized from the artist's social experience, cultural heritage, and creative imagination.

The beads are so dark a shade of purple that they register as black. The delicacy of their satiny sheen brings to mind a line from Alice Walker's *The Color Purple*, advocating a sensuous as well as a spiritual relationship to the universe: "I think it pisses God off if you walk by the color purple in a field somewhere and don't notice it."[1] Scott's freestyle female idol poses with one arm akimbo, the other raised; she takes the stance of a beauty pageant contestant with a bright blue sash draped from right shoulder to left hip. She is far too lumpy and schematic to qualify as an eroticized nude, yet as a sculptural figure she is much too playfully conceived and inventively executed to be written off as a one-liner. (For example, her eyes, breasts, lips, nose, and teeth are all exquisitely differentiated by different sizes and colors of bead.) She stands on her pedestal in grandiloquent fashion. Her base, a tour de force of beadwork, depicts a complex cityscape. With close scrutiny, we can make out (with some difficulty) a miniature swimmer in blue water along with an urban terrain inhabited by towers, cars, human heads, vegetation, and highway. Perhaps *Big Mama* provides mock-epic commentary on the Statue of Liberty. Then again, it may be that she bestrides the landscape like a black female folk equivalent (in mock miniature) of that masculinist wonder of the ancient world, the Colossus of Rhodes. The work possesses all the freedom of a child's imagination while reflecting the sardonic wit of adult understanding. Finally, the viewer's attempts at narrative and figurative coherence must give way to the artist's own exuberant agnosticism when it comes to sources and meanings: "I just want to keep making work that confounds me. I want to be confused, ignited, knocked down by my own work."[2]

Joyce Scott still lives in the Baltimore neighborhood of her childhood. The daughter of the eminent fiber artist Elizabeth Talford Scott, she is both art school–trained and the descendant of three generations of quilters, storytellers, basket makers, and artisans who worked in fabric, wood, metal, and clay. Like *Big Mama*, she refuses traditional categories. She occupies, serially and in combination, the roles of sculptor, jeweler, printmaker, installation artist, performance artist, and educator. Her work across these diverse media agitates for a radical reevaluation of social relations. Race and gender, those domains of contestation and sources of human suffering, are at the heart of her cultural and political agenda: "Humans have a really long way to go on any evolutionary ladder to get to anything close to civilization. . . . Nobody is immune to violence or sexism or racism."[3] At the heart of her capacious and multifarious practice is her identity as an African American woman sustained by her connections, both spiritual and practical, with the indigenous, artisanal practices of her African ancestors and her New World forebears.

Big Mama is informed by both postmodernism and postcolonialism. The viewer is licensed, therefore, to assign to the beadwork a broad range of reference—from Yoruba orisha to Dutch currency (the purchase price of the island of Manhattan), from ritual fetish to fashion accessory, from cultural critique to childhood delight. The figure embodies the irreverence, exuberance, and unruliness of an African American female persona long relegated to the margins of high art and polite society. Most immediately and prosaically, *Big Mama* must be, in some measure, a tribute to her namesake, Willie Mae (Big Mama) Thorton, whom Scott portrayed in the 2007 movie *Hounddog*. Thorton was among the greatest of blues legends, a self-taught drummer and harmonica player whose strong voice, defiant attitude, and incandescent stage presence can be taken to be emblematic of the tradition that Scott continues.

GD

Notes

1. Alice Walker, *The Color Purple* (New York: Harcourt Brace Jovanovich, 1982), 203.
2. Joyce J. Scott, George Ciscle, and Leslie King-Hammond, *Kickin' It with the Old Masters* (Baltimore: Baltimore Museum of Art and Maryland Institute, College of Art, 2000), 88.
3. Ibid., 49.

Big Mama, 1991. Glass and plastic beads, wire, fabric, and thread, 21⅝ × 13¾ × 12¼ in. Museum purchase with funds from the Benefactors Fund, 1997

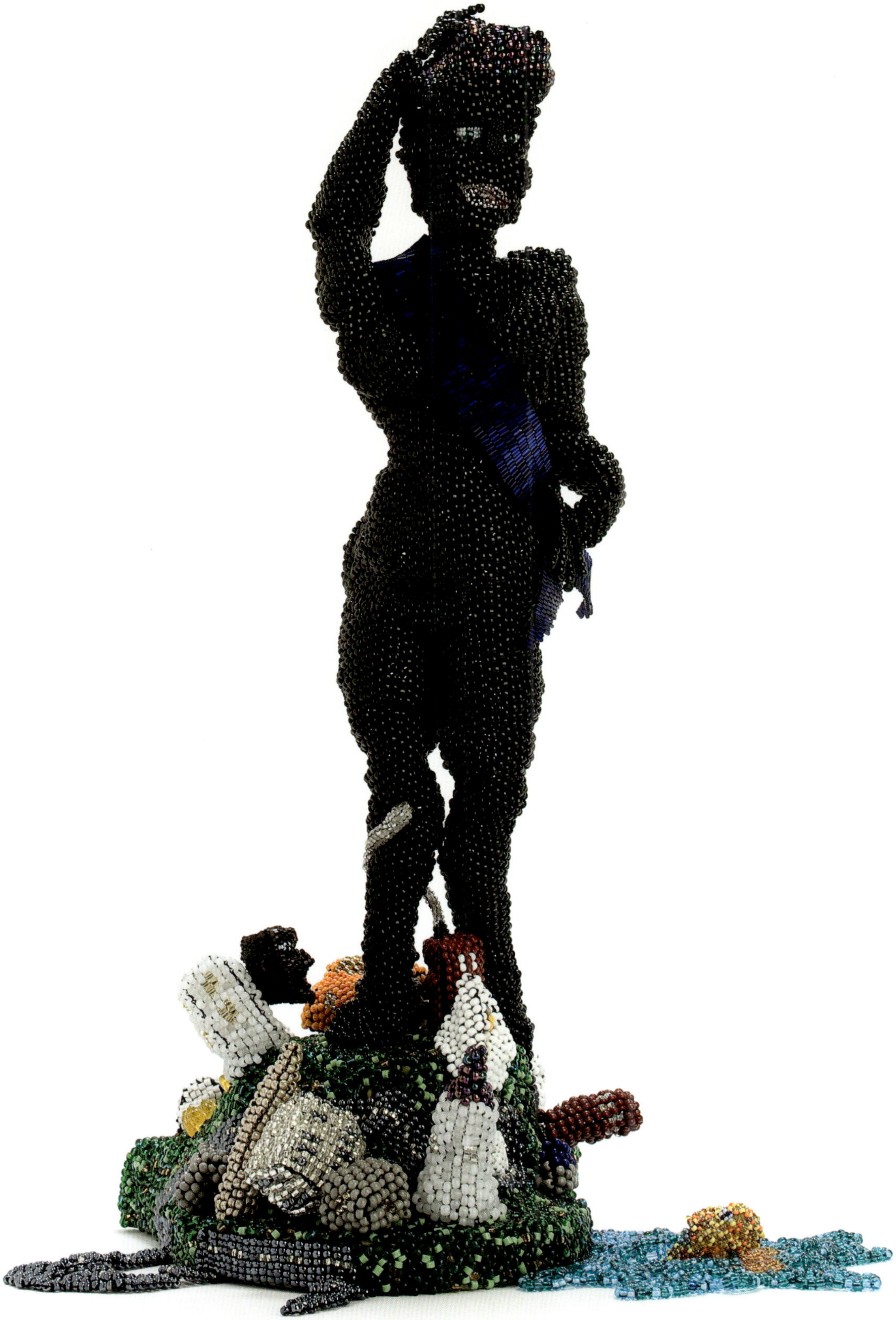

MAGDALENA ABAKANOWICZ Polish, born 1930

FROM ITS PROMINENT POSITION on the first floor of the Weatherspoon Art Museum, Magdalena Abakanowicz's sculpture *DYBY* quietly commands attention. According to the artist, this work from 1993 is intended to evoke an atmosphere of suffering,[1] a human condition about which the Polish sculptor is an unfortunate expert, having lived under two oppressive regimes, Nazism and Stalinism. Her haunting, metaphorical art, of which *DYBY* is an excellent example, is drawn from the personal experiences of the sculptor's life, yet it constantly eschews the specific in favor of the universal.

Abakanowicz was born in Falenty, Poland, in 1930 to an aristocratic family of ancient lineage. Her peaceful childhood at her family's isolated country estate east of Warsaw was abruptly shattered by the onset of World War II. As a volunteer at a local hospital, Abakanowicz witnessed the toll the war took on individuals, and she also saw her mother shot and maimed by German soldiers in 1943.[2] A year later the family left for the Polish capital, where yet another hellish experience awaited. Ultimately, the Abakanowicz family lost their property and wealth in the war and its aftermath.[3]

Working odd jobs and selling her blood to make money, the artist studied at the Academy of Fine Arts in Warsaw from 1950 to 1954, when she began her career, not as a sculptor, but as a painter.[4] Not many years passed, however, before Abakanowicz was working in three dimensions. She took the stereotypically "feminine" process of weaving and redefined its possibilities through her revolutionary monumental hanging forms of the 1960s, titled *Abakans*.

As evidenced by *DYBY*, Abakanowicz's innovative use of fiber has remained a constant in her nearly fifty years of work, as has the human body, which the artist introduced into her oeuvre in the early 1970s and directly associates with her material. "The fiber which I use in my works, derives from plants and is similar to that which we ourselves are composed. . . . Our heart is surrounded by the coronary plexus, the most vital of threads."[5] Here, within a rectilinear construction made of rough-hewn wood, sits a life-size figure made of burlap and resin. The fabric is coarse and frayed along the edges, looking surprisingly brittle. In areas, masses of thinner fibers snake back and forth like veins on the surface of this hollow figure, which is missing a head, back, and arms below the elbow. The immediate impression is of a body that has been subjected to violence and is now decaying or mummified and without an identity, as is characteristic of Abakanowicz's human forms, which she displays alone or in groups.

The figure of *DYBY* and the process by which it was made are akin to the eighteen forms of Abakanowicz's famous series from 1974, known as Seated Figures, where she first explored the human form at life size. For these forms, as for the Weatherspoon work, the artist made a plaster cast, which, when waxed, functioned as a mold. To it she glued pieces of burlap. The result was a thin, hard shell that can be pulled from the mold.[6] Each of the casts produced a form that was slightly different in appearance from the others, making each form unique.

Unlike her earlier Seated Figures, which were placed on minimal steel supports, the figure of *DYBY* is seated on a substantial horizontal wooden beam and centered between two posts supporting another wooden beam, all the same size. Two wooden braces, set at a forty-five-degree angle to the uprights, complete the symmetrical construction. The title confirms the perceptibly grim aura created by the work. As the artist explained, the Polish word *dyby* means "the special wooden construction used to expose a law-breaker to humiliation. My sculpture . . . doesn't represent a real construction . . . but an atmosphere of suffering."[7] Indeed, even the slouching posture of the figure reinforces this emotional tone.

Abankanowicz, who works and lives in Warsaw, is widely recognized as the foremost living sculptor treating the human form today. Not surprisingly, she has won numerous prestigious awards, and her works are preserved in more than four dozen museums and public collections internationally.

HH

Notes

1. Phillip A. Bruno to Nancy M. Doll, July 5, 2000, Weatherspoon Art Museum object file.
2. Magdalena Abakanowicz, *Portrait × 20*; reprinted in *Magdalena Abakanowicz: Recent Sculpture* (Providence: Museum of Art, Rhode Island School of Design, 1993), 23–31.
3. Nancy Princenthal, "Abakanowicz: Memories and Monuments," *Art in America* 78 (March 1990): 179–82.
4. Barbara Rose, *Magdalena Abakanowicz* (New York: Harry N. Abrams, 1994), 12.
5. Ibid., 21–22.
6. Ibid., 49.
7. Bruno to Doll.

DYBY, 1993. Burlap, resin, and wood, 63 × 82⅝ × 25⅝ in. Museum purchase with funds from the Tannenbaum-Sternberger Foundation in honor of Leah Louise Tannenbaum, 2000

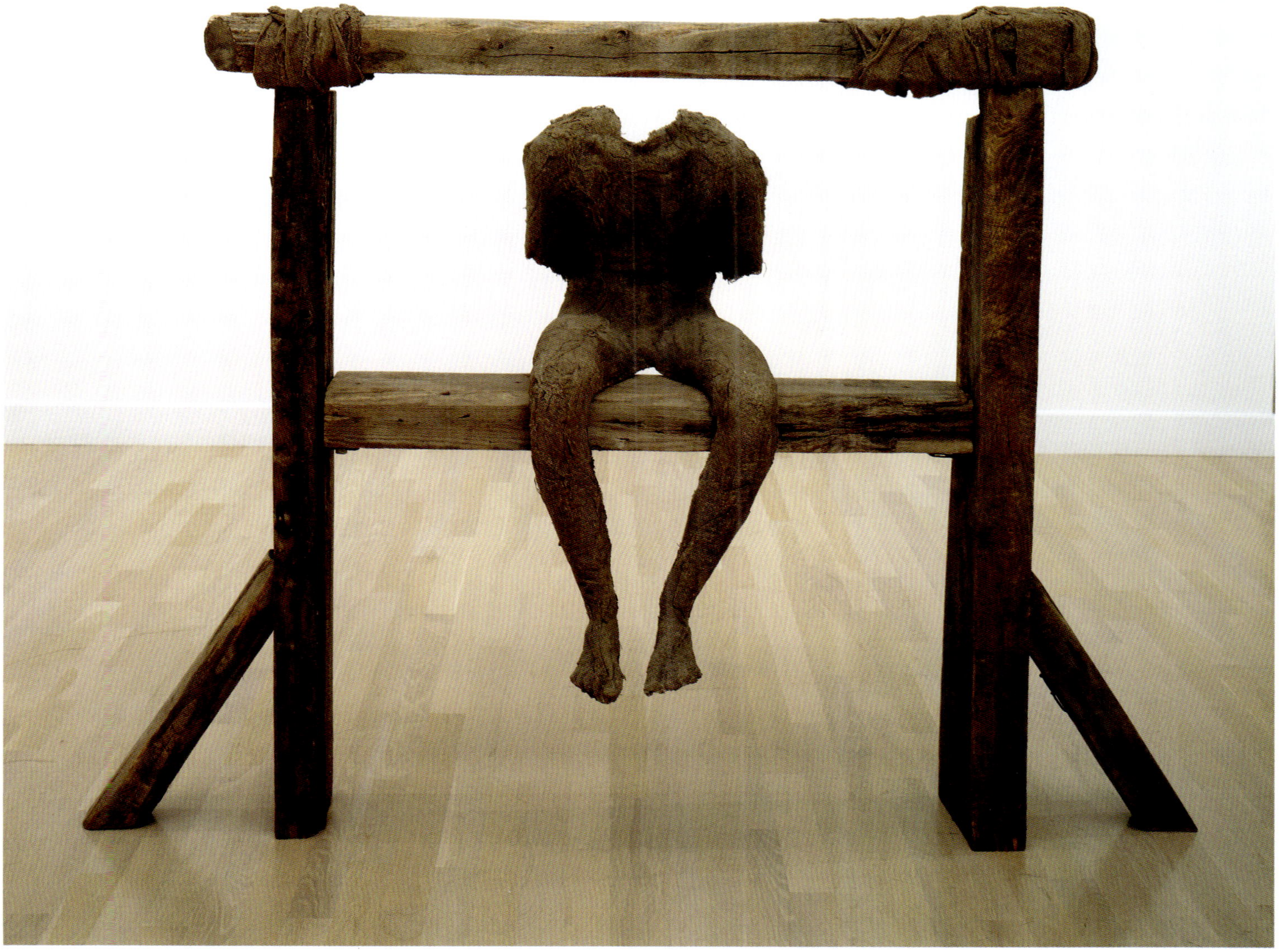

JESSICA STOCKHOLDER American, born 1959

TRAINED AS A PAINTER, Jessica Stockholder has a remarkable ability to work with color. She uses both applied color, as is characteristic of most painting in two dimensions, and the color inherent in the plastic, glass, fabric, and other ready-made elements she introduces into her three-dimensional forms. Her wild and wildly imaginative works are strictly neither painting nor sculpture, but hybrids of both. Few sculptors have reveled in color as a formal element more than Stockholder. And few with painterly concerns of color have been able to make it feel so utterly at home in three-dimensional form. Unwilling to categorize or classify her works, Stockholder has made a profound impact on many younger artists who now eagerly embrace the crossovers among media, materials, and formats.

Stockholder cites among her artistic influences the work of Henri Matisse and Paul Cézanne, Robert Rauschenberg and Frank Stella, Minimalism and Richard Serra. She first became known in this country, and more so in Europe, for her large installations: combinations of materials and forms seemingly impossible to reconcile into a coherent whole. They alter our assumptions about space and how it is occupied; our perceptions of dimensional form; and certainly any of our preconceptions about what a work of art can be, do, and mean.

As curious as her works are on first encounter (and maybe second and third), her titles equally catch us off guard. *Recording Forever Pickled Too*, *Growing Rock Candy Mountains in Canned Seed*, or *TV Tipped Toenails & the Green Salami* seem like nonsensical riddles or random groupings of words pulled from a dictionary. But, if one enters into the free fall of the work (and there is little point or possibility of not doing so), the titles begin to make perfect *non*-sense. They are superb foils for the works themselves in their shared refusal to be one thing or another, in their offer of unbridled possibility, and, quite simply, in their sense of humor and fun.

While engaged in the mammoth productions of some of her installations, Stockholder was making self-contained studio works that more closely approximate traditional sculpture. Like the Weatherspoon's *#204*, many of these are almost freestanding, save their decided connection to the wall via electrical cords or wall-hung elements, and reinforce Stockholder's intent that her work not be interpreted as one thing or another, but rather both, or many. As one writer put it in discussing the first of these studio works, *Kissing the Wall*, "Kissing breaks a formal boundary between two parties and carries the potential for deeper engagement. It is no coincidence that Stockholder's art does this as well."[1]

#204 first was exhibited at the Weatherspoon in *Pink Lady*, a 1994 exhibition of Stockholder's work, and the museum purchased it at auction in 2002. Comprising a typical array of objects—some suggesting home, others Home Depot—the work is an excellent example of Stockholder's hybrid forms. Formal and color correlations jump about from one plane to another: yellow and purple vie for the viewer's attention; a painterly swath of that same purple melds into various pinks above it; and an orange garbage can introduces a new jolt of color, while a number of cords meander from it to the wall and add a linear aspect of drawing to the already multigenre work.

Jessica Stockholder was born in Seattle in 1959 and grew up in Vancouver, British Columbia. When her parents divorced, her father encouraged her to take drawing lessons from the artist Mowry Baden, whose performances, sculptural works, and participatory environments were important influences on Stockholder later in her career. She earned a BFA in 1982 from the University of British Columbia and an MFA from Yale University in 1984. This was one of those times at Yale when its art department was energized by an amazing group of faculty artists such as Ursula von Rydingsvard, Judy Pfaff, and George Trakas—all risk takers who, like Stockholder, were helping to forge new definitions for art in a postminimalist world.

NMD

Note

1. Katie Robinson Edwards, "Annotated Chronology," in Nancy Doll and Terrie Sultan, *Jessica Stockholder: Kissing the Wall; Works, 1988–2003* (Seattle: Marquand Books, 2003), 70.

#204, 1993. Garbage pail, galvanized sheet metal, bolts, string, wooden furniture, paper, pastel, oil, acrylic, linoleum tile, electric wires, and hinge, 38 × 62 × 60 in. Museum purchase with funds from the Judy Proctor Acquisition Endowment, 2002

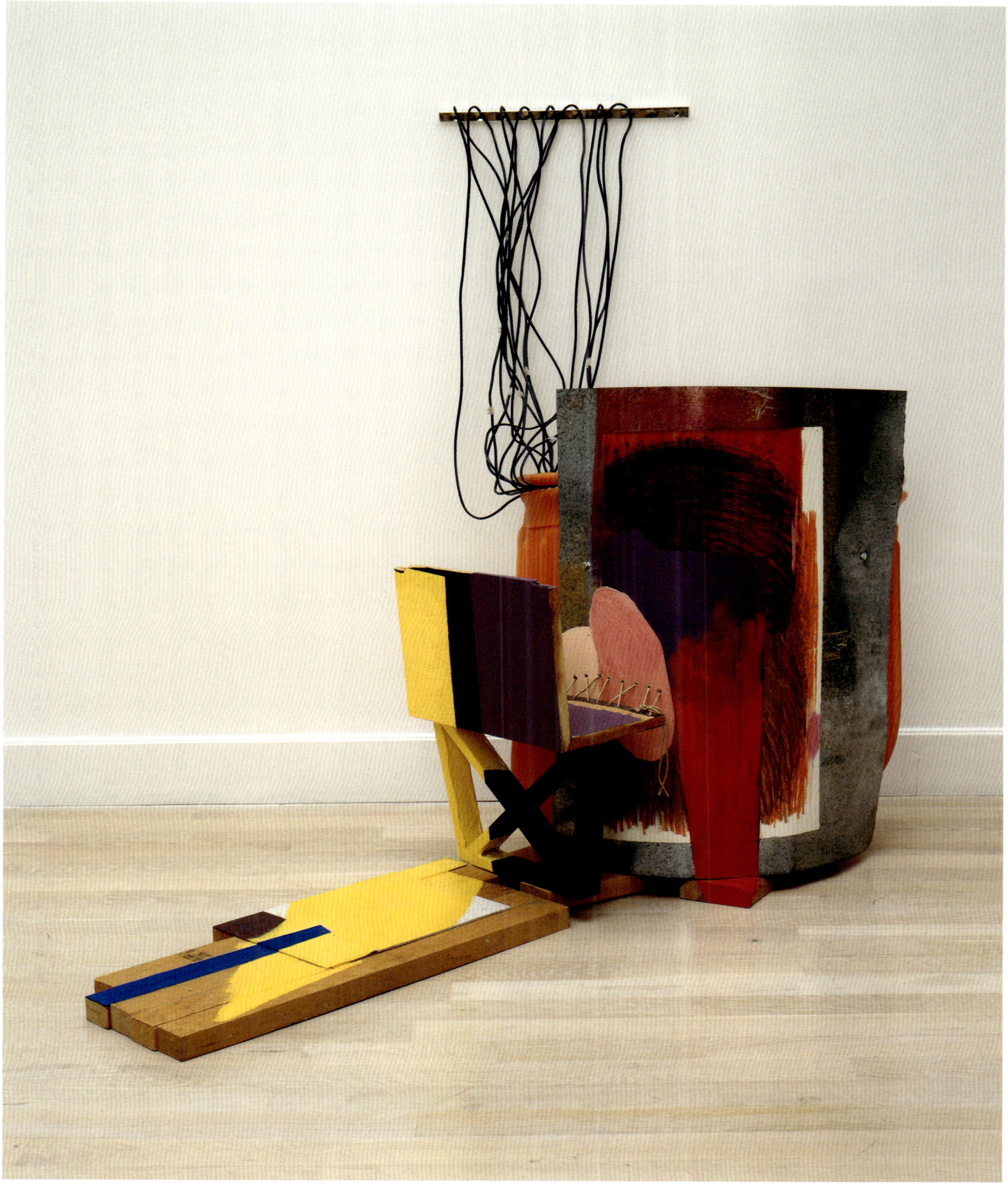

PAT STEIR American, born 1938

PAT STEIR'S DRAMATIC CANVAS *Melancholy Painting I/Red Waterfall* from 1994 is part of a series that occupied the American painter and printmaker for more than a decade, beginning in 1989. Here, as in other paintings from the Waterfall series, Steir explores the process of painting itself, while physically removing herself from that process as much as possible, "in pursuit of the moment of communion between herself and the cosmos," a goal of Far Eastern meditation.[1] Indeed, the artist's multiple trips to Asia have become an informative element in her work, perhaps most detectable here in Steir's self-less process, which is rooted in imposed limitations, careful planning, and paint application, and is realized, finally, by gravity. Steir's method has been interpreted as a search for a way of making that is not bound up in the ego or as a recognizable or characteristic artist's mark.[2] However, Steir's Waterfall paintings have, perhaps despite her efforts, become intimately linked to the artist as her most important series to date.[3]

In its dichromatic palette, *Melancholy Painting I/Red Waterfall* is akin to Steir's 1990 Waterfall canvases, which feature white paint on a black background. Here, as in those slightly earlier works, Steir began by applying diluted, matte black paint with a large brush. This application is easily visible in *Melancholy Painting I/ Red Waterfall*, where her wide, horizontal brushstrokes meet along the work's vertical axis. On top of the black background, and a few inches from the upper edge, Steir then made a single stroke with a paint-filled brush, loaded with diluted oil paint. This single brushstroke, "the simplest thing you can do with paint,"[4] according to the artist, is part of the limitations she imposes on herself within this group. In addition, she restricts her physical contact with the picture, especially once the paint begins to flow down its surface. "The thing that I always have to force myself to do is let the paint hit the canvas, walk away and let it do its thing. . . . If I watch, I'll meddle with it," said Steir.[5] And yet, she does exert control over the paint. This is accomplished by diluting the medium, which affects both its color and how it flows.

After the initial mark is made, Steir adds what she calls a "splashback," which she creates by flinging paint onto the surface.[6] This particular technique is evident in the lower half of *Melancholy Painting I/Red Waterfall*, where it adds a layer of depth. In the finished work, Steir's creative gestures are permanently frozen in a kind of suspended animation, recording her physical act of painting in a manner reminiscent of the Abstract Expressionists. However, Steir is not an Abstract Expressionist, as she is quick to point out.[7] Rather than born of rapid, seemingly spontaneous action, her paintings grow from "a very long and slow process that gradually progresses from the combination of concentration and precisely targeted action. I work with a particular plan in mind, although I may change it in the process," Steir has said.[8]

Despite its seemingly nonrepresentational nature, *Melancholy Painting I/Red Waterfall* is not viewed that way by the artist. "Quite the opposite, in fact. These are not only drips of paint. They're paintings of drips, which form waterfall images—pictures."[9] To use her words, Steir is also "walking a thin line between image and not image,"[10] and to traverse this artistic tightrope successfully she not only draws from Conceptual art, Asian art, and abstract painting but also relies on a deep knowledge of art history and its stylistic development, as revealed in her earlier output like the famous Breughel series.

Born in 1938 in Newark, New Jersey, Steir studied painting and comparative literature at Boston University and graphic art at the Pratt Institute in Brooklyn, where she received her BFA in 1961. Today she works in New York and Amsterdam and is represented in more than two dozen major museums and public collections. *Melancholy Painting I/Red Waterfall* is one of several examples of post-painterly abstraction preserved in the Weatherspoon Art Museum, by such artists as Dona Nelson, Harriet Korman, Sue Williams, and Philip Taaffe.

HH

Notes

1. Doris von Drathan, "Rhythm of Silence," trans. Matthew Partridge, *Pat Steir: The Rhythm of Silence* (Philadelphia: Locks Art Publications, 2003), 13.
2. Ibid.
3. Ibid., 5.
4. Brook Adams, "Conversation with Pat Steir, September 15, 1992," in *Pat Steir: Elective Affinities* (New York: Robert Miller Gallery, 1992), not paginated, in Weatherspoon Art Museum object file.
5. Anne Waldman, "Pat Steir," *Bomb*, no. 83 (Spring 2003): 36.
6. Adams, "Conversation."
7. Doris von Drathan, "Within the Interspace between Reality and Reality," in *Pat Steir, Paintings* (Milan: Charta, 2007), 15.
8. Ibid.
9. Adams, "Conversation."
10. Waldman, "Pat Steir," 33.

Melancholy Painting I/Red Waterfall, 1994. Oil on canvas, 48 × 48 in. Museum purchase with funds from the Jefferson-Pilot Endowment, Burlington Industries Endowment, Weatherspoon Guild Acquisition Endowment, and the Louise D. and Herbert S. Falk Acquisition Endowment, 2002

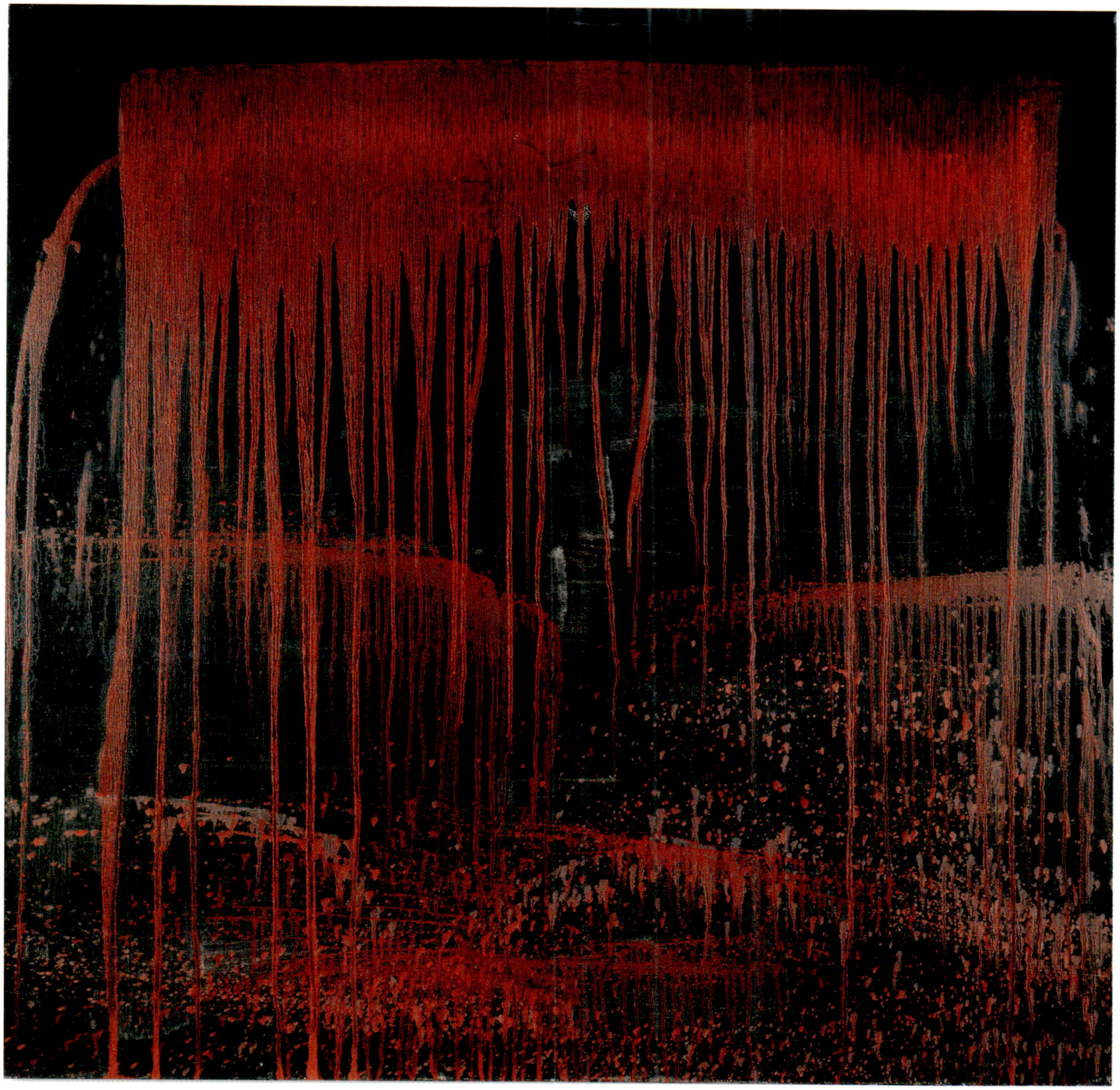

MEL CHIN American, born 1951

PERFORMANCE ARTIST, political activist, socially engaged philosopher—all of these describe Mel Chin. Yet these labels fail to convey the subtlety of this artist's work and the continuous undercurrents that run through his oeuvre. Namely, Chin revels in wordplay, social engagement, and the symbolic potential of materials. Even his early work, such as *Six Tennessee Turnips* of 1974, plays with words and the selection of materials. Born in Tennessee to immigrant Chinese parents, Chin plays on the idea of his "roots" by reproducing a turnip version of *Six Persimmons*, a famous painting by the thirteenth-century Chinese artist Mu Chi.[1]

In the case of *Fan Club,* Chin's puns and interest in materials take on a macabre tone. This work commemorates the Chinese American engineer Vincent Chin, who died at the hands of American autoworkers in 1984. During the rapid decline of the American auto industry, Vincent Chin was mistaken as Japanese and beaten to death with a baseball bat by disgruntled autoworkers, who saw Japan as the source of their growing vulnerability in a globalizing market.

The literal club here is a baseball bat that the artist has sliced into sections and used to form the ribs of this larger-than-life fan emblazoned with the Japanese flag. The silk of the fan is sewn into sleeves that each accommodates a flat section of wood. Vincent Chin was not a direct relation of the artist, but, in a symbolic act of solidarity, Mel Chin used his own blood to paint a sun at the center of this image of the Japanese flag. The dark dried blood is applied to the surface of the silk fan thinly toward the top, but toward the bottom of this circle, a thick application of shiny blood accentuates the fact that this is not merely paint.

The artist also commissioned his father, Den B. Chin, to paint the dedication that accompanies the fan: "Something to whip up the baseball fans—a setting sun fan. / In memory of Vincent Chin and all victims of racial violence."[2] Although accessible to English speakers only through translation, this dedication in Chinese calligraphy explicitly addresses the racial violence that caused Vincent Chin's death.

During 1994 Chin also created *Spin Control*, a work that features maps of cities in which race riots had occurred: Detroit, Miami, Brooklyn, and south-central Los Angeles. This sculpture, in the shape of an electric fan, looks as though it could fracture apart. Both *Fan Club* and *Spin Control* are continuations of a theme Chin explored in 1992. He created a vending machine entitled *DISpense/DIStribute*, which dispensed pieces of the American flag dipped in various flavors in exchange for one dollar. Chin referred to this as "junkfood patriotism," a play on America's various ethnic and cultural flavors.[3]

Chin's work consistently demonstrates a dedication to pushing conceptual content. This artistic passion and vision were made famous in 1991, when Chin received and almost lost a National Endowment for the Arts (NEA) grant for *Revival Field*, a work that used plants to extract heavy metals from polluted land. John Frohnmayer, the then NEA chairman, threatened to veto Chin's prize because he deemed its political content too overt.[4] The inspirational outcome of this conflict is that Chin began discussions to diffuse the tension, the grant was reinstated, and *Revival Field* has been expanded to other venues and countries and continues to revitalize landscapes to this day.

Chin has never been represented by a commercial gallery and works as an artist and public intellectual on social and environmental issues. He now lives in North Carolina and collaborates with a variety of artists, scientists, and communities worldwide.

EP

Notes

1. Benito Huerta, *Inescapable Histories: Mel Chin* (Kansas City: Mid-American Arts Alliance, 1997), not paginated.
2. Ibid.
3. Ibid.
4. Tom Finkelpearl, *Dialogues in Fublic Art* (Cambridge, MA: MIT Press, 2001), 385–86.

Fan Club, 1994. Ash wood, blood on Chinese silk, and ink on paper, 38 × 60 in. Museum purchase with funds from the Weatherspoon Art Museum Acquisition Endowment, 1999

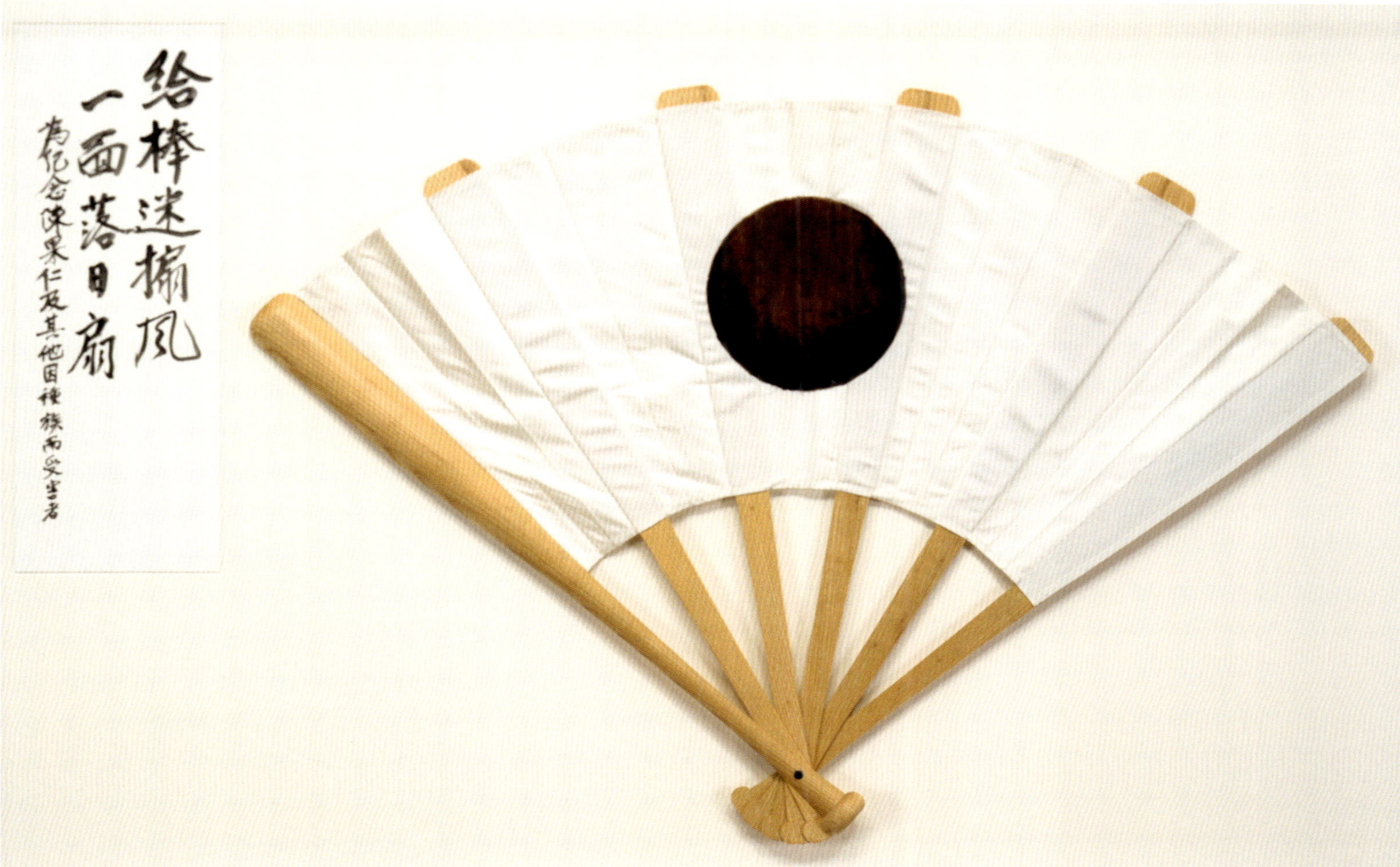
给棒迷搧風
一面落日扇
為紀念陳果仁及其他因種族而受害者

ROBERT COLESCOTT American, 1925–2009

A VISIT FROM UNCLE CHARLIE is a typical example of Robert Colescott's highly satirical, emotionally charged paintings that mine history, literature, and social frameworks in pursuit of an alternative narrative. Colescott uses this less seen, less heard counternarrative to speak for the oppressed and powerless.[1]

Colescott's interest in art and music began at a young age. His parents, both musicians, moved from New Orleans to Oakland, California, where Colescott remembers watching Diego Rivera working on his mural *Pan-American Unity* in the 1940 Golden Gate International Exposition.[2] Following his service in the army in World War II, Colescott enrolled as an art student at the University of California, Berkeley, but it was during a yearlong study in Paris with Fernand Léger that he developed a modernist approach to figuration and narration.

Colescott returned to graduate school, receiving his MFA from Berkeley in 1951, at a time when Abstract Expressionism was gaining a foothold in the United States. Colescott's early works, like those of other younger Bay Area artists of the time, emphasized color, surface, and pattern. Yet Colescott sought to merge the personal with the abstract. This awareness of identity and emotional subjectivity would remain in his work throughout his career of six decades.

By the mid-1970s Colescott's brand of narrative figuration fully developed under the influences of Pop, West Coast funk, and feminist art. His earliest works, such as *George Washington Carver Crossing the Delaware: Page from an American History Textbook* (1975) and *Les Demoiselles d'Alabama ("desnuda" and "vestida")* (1986), challenged ingrained Western cultural ideals by inserting African Americans into historically white roles.

Colescott's appropriation of famous art-historical subjects eventually gave way to more personal narratives about sex, race, and equality, yet these works were no less controversial. His use of racist stereotypes to challenge and comment on social norms was seen by some critics as a triumphant step toward reclaiming history, whereas to others it was shockingly offensive. Colescott acknowledged these responses: "I never painted them with that in mind, that I was offering somebody salvation or offering somebody something to laugh at or to be sad about or anything. I just did it as an expression of myself."[3]

By the late 1980s and 1990s, paintings like *A Visit from Uncle Charlie* marked Colescott's move to looser, more gestural, and complex formal compositions and to a deliberate use of visual puns and literary allusion. Take, for example, Uncle Charlie, the black male figure at the center of the painting who, save for his socks and saddle shoes, is completely naked and yet is almost invisible. He is framed on the right by a skeleton in a closet and on the left by a rosy-cheeked white couple in fur coats. Uncle Charlie's head and torso are almost lost within the ruff of the man's coat, implying that it is his skeleton that has come out of the closet. Cartoon text bubbles float above the couple's heads as they begin to imagine the implications of the unexpected visitor. They ask themselves, ". . . and the children?" and simply reply, "don't tell 'em!!"

In recalling the painting, Colescott said, "During the great migration North, a lot of people from Louisiana moved up to Chicago and other places. That's why you see the snowflakes in the background of the painting. People were passing for white. But Uncle Charlie is as black as the ace of spades, and when ol' Uncle Charlie shows up the s——t hits the fan and the cat's out of the bag."[4]

Colescott commonly filled the edges of his canvases, and one might presume the edges of society, with caricatures of outcasts and stereotypes. In this instance, a burglar, a boy with a gun, a native African, and a faceless female figure with exaggerated features and crudely painted bicolored skin accentuate the couple's or our own fears of miscegenation conjured by Uncle Charlie's visit. Compositionally, the painting succeeds in almost erasing Uncle Charlie from view through the push and pull of garish colors and repetitive patterns, in much the way the red and green of the checkerboard quilt are indistinguishable to those who are color-blind.

At seventy-one years of age, in 1997, Colescott was the first African American artist to represent the United States in the prestigious Venice Biennale. *A Visit from Uncle Charlie* was included in this exhibition soon after its acquisition by the Weatherspoon. Despite the narrative aspect of his work, Colescott claimed he was not a writer. For him, the story that unfolds is determined by the viewer. In this way, Colescott managed to subvert the very views and perceptions he sought to challenge and rewarded viewers by giving them a view they can understand if they look carefully at themselves.

AG

Notes

1. Miriam Roberts, "Robert Colescott: Recent Paintings," in *Robert Colescott Recent Paintings* (Santa Fe: SITE; Tucson: University of Arizona Museum of Art, 1997), 20.
2. Ibid., 12.
3. Robert Colescott, quoted in Sharon Fitzgerald, "Robert Colescott Rocks the Boat," *American Visions* 12 (June–July 1997): 16.
4. Colescott, quoted in Douglas MacCash, "Pushing Buttons: The Dark Comedy in Master Painter Robert Colescott's Bright Canvases Has Roots in the Big Easy," *New Orleans Times-Picayune*, February 11, 2000, Lagniappe sec., L20.

A Visit from Uncle Charlie, 1995. Acrylic on canvas, 84 × 72 in. Museum purchase with funds from the Benefactors Fund, 1997

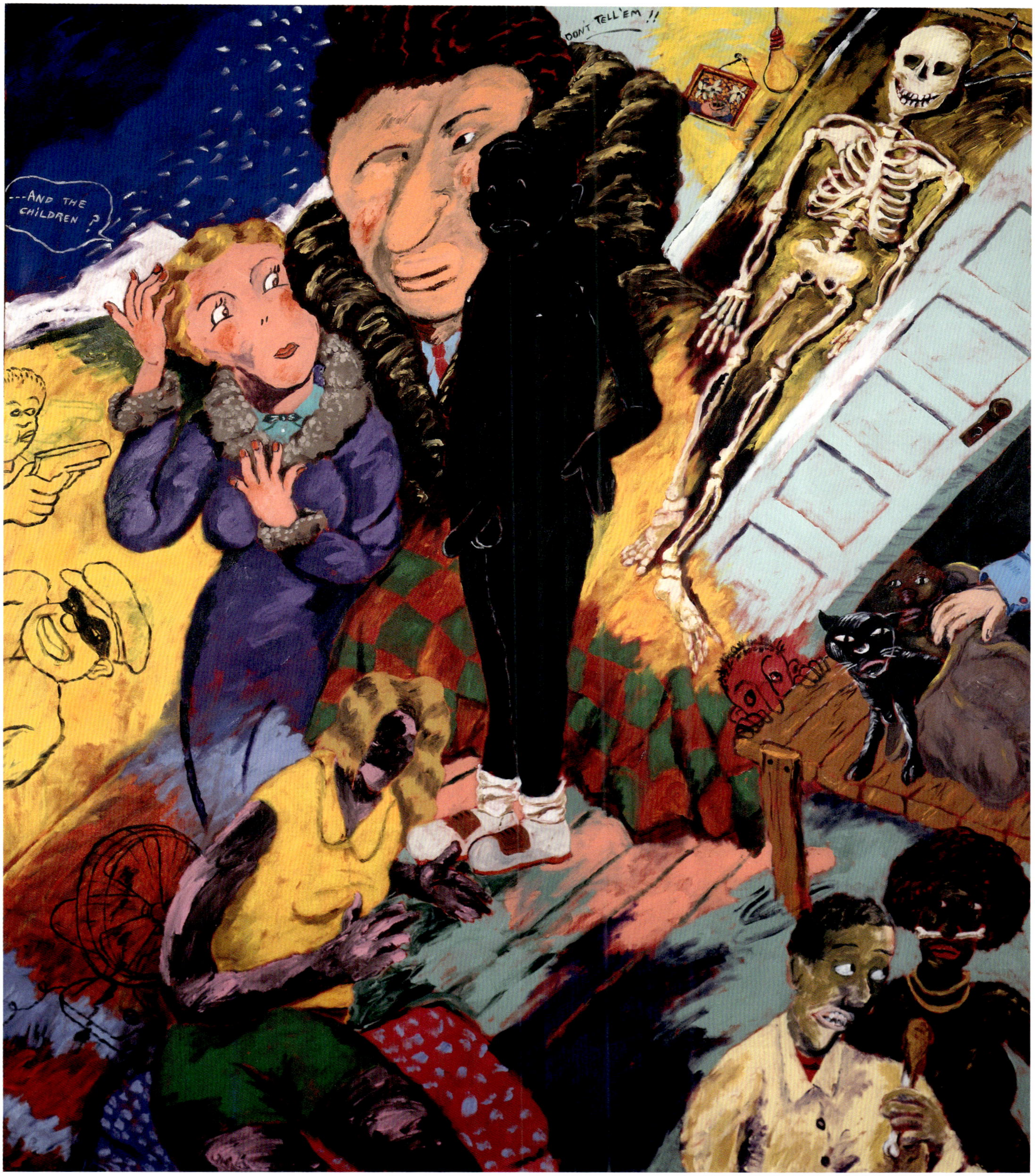
---AND THE CHILDREN ?
DON'T TELL'EM !!

DEBORAH KASS American, born 1952

DEBORAH KASS CAME OF AGE during the years when Andy Warhol was the most celebrated artist in America. Kass completed her BFA degree at Carnegie-Mellon University in Pittsburgh in the early 1970s, the decade when Warhol expanded his repertoire of celebrity portraits to include the fabled Chinese revolutionary and Communist party leader Mao Zedong, as well as such pop divas as Liza Minnelli. These and other portraits by Warhol served as models for Kass's Warhol Project, a series of works begun in the early 1990s and subsequently featured in an exhibition that traveled from 1999 to 2001. The Weatherspoon purchased *Cindy Sherman* from that exhibition in 2001. The acquisition of Kass's double portrait of the photographer Cindy Sherman posing as Warhol's Liza Minnelli was a fitting addition to a collection that already included Warhol's *Double Mao* and an untitled work by Cindy Sherman, both discussed in this publication.

Kass's *Cindy Sherman* consists of two paintings that are shown together as a diptych. Although the diptych is a common format for paired icons and portraits, the subjects of the two images are usually different. Kass followed Warhol's example in using the diptych for two portraits of a single iconic subject. The diptych format introduces doubling as a theme that informs multiple aspects of Kass's portrait of Cindy Sherman. Except for variations in skin tone and shades of blue eyeshadow, the two images of Sherman are doubles. This doubling in turn alludes to Sherman's dual role as subject and artist in her own photographic impersonations. As Kass's subject, Sherman donned a jet black wig with a saucy pixie cut to double as Warhol's depiction of Minnelli. Directing and recording this staged masquerade was Kass, who, like her subject, engaged in role-playing.

In her role as celebrity portrait painter, Kass convincingly mimicked the visual impact and appeal of Warhol's Pop art. For her double portrait of Sherman, she chose canvases that are identical in size to those used by Warhol for his portraits of Minnelli. She also replicated Warhol's signature technique, painting over silkscreen transfers of a photograph. Her style is as bold and her palette as vibrant as Warhol's. Only her choice of colors registers as an immediately perceptible sign of difference. Whereas Warhol set his subject against expanses of hot pink and blue-green, Kass opted for contrasting grounds of lipstick red and chalky white. Even before the viewer notices subtle differences in the head shape and facial features, the ground colors announce that Kass's *Cindy Sherman* is not Warhol's *Liza Minnelli*.

Not coincidentally, Kass's subject is an artist whose work is about disguise and identity. *Cindy Sherman* is likewise a work that uses the strategy of disguise to explore multiple facets of identity. The portrait actually represents Sherman, yet it reveals as much about Kass as it does about her sitter. The choice of Warhol's image of Minnelli as Sherman's disguise doubles as an allusion to Kass's professional and sexual identities. While unapologetically declaring her professional affinity for the language of Pop art, Kass made a conscious effort to extract new meaning from that language. In remaking Warhol's portrait of Minnelli, an icon of the gay culture Warhol himself embraced only covertly, Kass created an image that indirectly affirms her self-professed lesbian identity.[1]

Like other artists of her postmodern generation, Kass positioned herself in relation to art history and contemporary culture by appropriating and reformulating artistic traditions. In *Cindy Sherman* and the other portraits that make up the Warhol Project, Kass acknowledged Warhol's legacy even while distancing herself from his cult of movie-star glamour and media fame. For Kass, Warhol's work and reputation constituted a conceptual screen through which she filtered her experience and the heroines she claimed as role models. Despite the fact that she admired Warhol's ability to transform the familiar imagery of popular culture, she was also keenly aware that his unique style concealed his personal identity. In simultaneously celebrating and critiquing Warhol's creative practices, Kass proved herself adept at constructing witty parodies of his work that double as multireferential images of her self-identity.

KPA

Note

1. On images of lesbian identity and desire in Kass's work, see Michael Plante, "Screened Identities, Multiple Repetitions and Missed Kisses: Deborah Kass's Warhol Project," in *Deborah Kass: The Warhol Project* (New York: D.A.P., 1999), 55–57.

Cindy Sherman, 1995. Silkscreen ink and acrylic on canvas, 2 panels, each 40 × 40 in. Museum purchase with funds from the Benefactors Fund and an anonymous donor, 2001

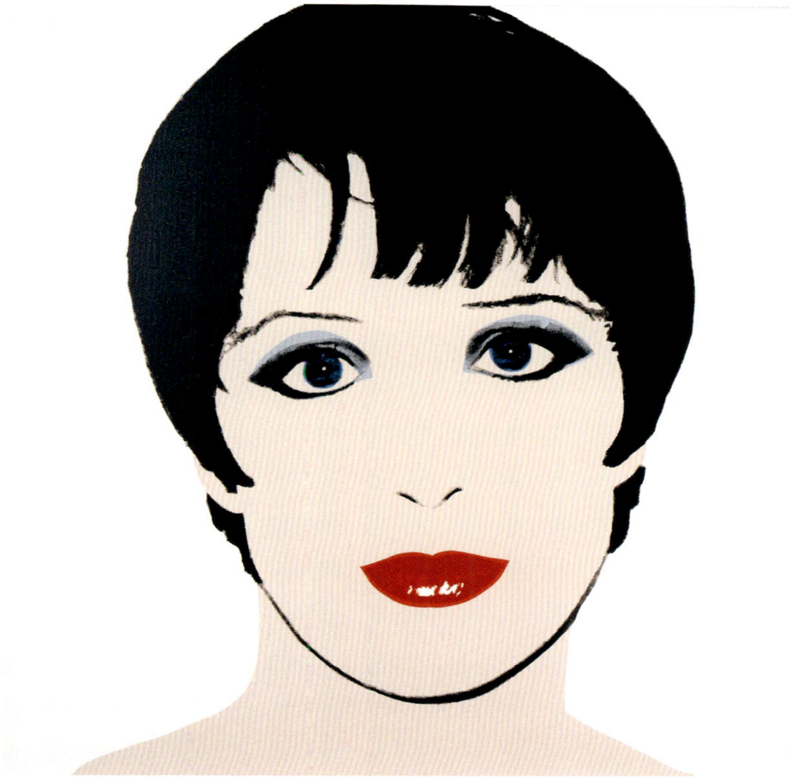

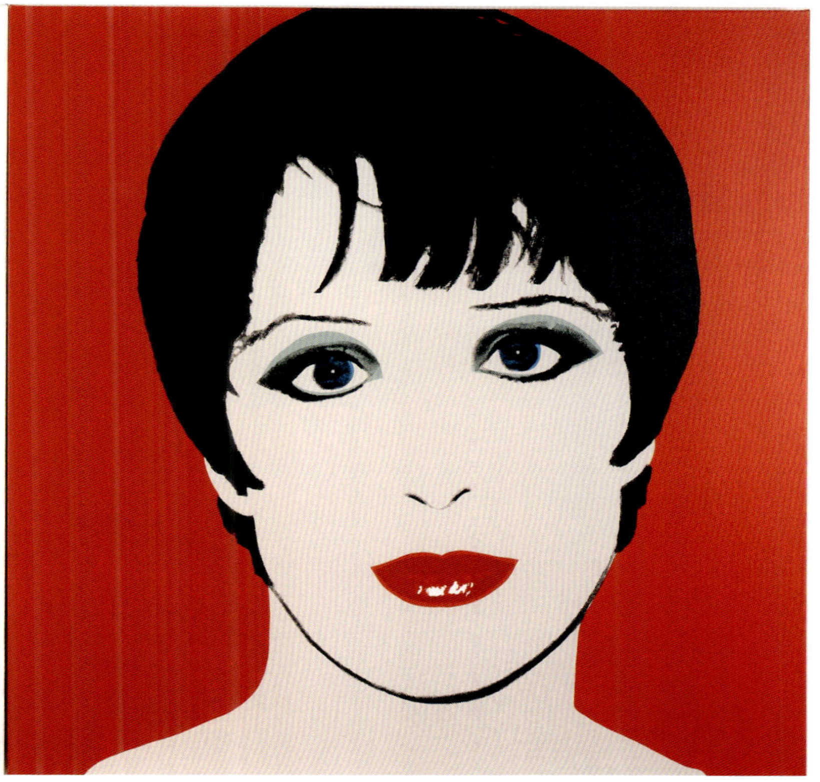

JOHN AHEARN American, born 1951

DURING THE SUMMER OF 1995 the sculptor John Ahearn was in residence at the Weatherspoon Art Museum. At the time Ahearn was already known as an artist who preferred working in vibrant urban neighborhoods. He did the same in Greensboro. Following a practice established fifteen years earlier when he moved to the South Bronx, Ahearn opened a workshop in a storefront next to Carolina Tattoo on the south side of Lee Street. Curious passersby and casual visitors were as welcome in Ahearn's temporary studio as the Greensboro residents who sat for portraits—sometimes with a bit of trepidation. Six of the seven works by Ahearn in the Weatherspoon's collection were cast in the Lee Street workshop. Only *Ed Whitfield at the Caldcleugh Community Center* was cast on-site at what is now the Caldcleugh Multicultural Arts Center. Ahearn cast the sculpture in an edition of three: one each for the sitter, the center, and the Weatherspoon. The museum's version is unique in that it is flanked by framed photocopies of newspaper clippings that document significant events in Whitfield's life.

Ahearn made contact with Whitfield after reading an article he had written for the *Carolina Peacemaker*. They discovered they had two things in common: they were (and still are) engaged in community outreach, and both attended Cornell University. Ahearn, who earned a BFA degree at Cornell in 1973, had enrolled shortly after Whitfield left the university to teach in Greensboro. To convey the idea of three stages in Whitfield's life story, Ahearn combined sculpture with photographic images and text. One documentary fragment of Whitfield's past is a photograph from 1967 showing President Lyndon Johnson presenting him with a Presidential Scholar Award shortly after his graduation from Little Rock Central High School. The caption beneath the second photograph, which illustrates an article published on the front page of the *Arkansas Gazette*, April 21, 1969, identifies Whitfield as the leader of a group of armed black students who had occupied a building on the Cornell campus. By the time he met Ahearn, Whitfield had long since moved beyond militant activism to community and labor organizing. He is represented in Ahearn's sculpture as a Caldcleugh Community Center volunteer and a role model for children enrolled in a summer program at the center.

Whitfield and his young friends learned that modeling for Ahearn meant something other than holding a fixed pose. Together, Ahearn and Whitfield decided that the sculpture would incorporate children's hands. Whitfield stretched out, looking down at seven children who each placed a hand on his chest. As onlookers gathered around to observe the life-casting process, Ahearn poured molding gel over the children's hands and Whitfield's head. Next he added layers of plaster surgical bandages soaked in water, chatting amiably as he worked to maintain an atmosphere of calm and trust. Drinking straws inserted into Whitfield's nostrils assured that he could breathe while the plaster set. About twenty minutes later, Ahearn carefully removed the hardened bandages, which became the mold from which he later cast plaster reliefs. After carving into the plaster to give shape to the eyes and ears, Ahearn applied acrylic paint to differentiate skin tones and define Whitfield's hair and facial features. To recapture the immediacy of a temporal moment in the finished portrait, Ahearn consulted Polaroid snapshots taken as preliminary studies and visual records of a personal relationship. The eyeglasses, scratched from use, were one of Whitfield's contributions to this collaborative project. Perched just so on his nose, they add a final touch of individuality to the portrait.[1]

In works by a hyperrealist sculptor like Duane Hanson, the eyeglasses would have contributed to the illusion of a disconcerting, fool-the-eye naturalism. That is not the effect produced by Ahearn's portrait sculpture, nor was that the artist's intention. Like all of Ahearn's figurative sculptures, *Ed Whitfield at the Caldcleugh Community Center* communicates meaning by effectively balancing the language of art with human body language. Color thinly applied to the plaster cast enlivens the forms without replicating actual skin tones and texture. Similarly, Whitfield's partially open mouth and the children's protective gestures are vividly expressive, while never letting the viewer forget that this multimedia portrait is, after all, an ensemble of disembodied sculptural fragments and photocopies.

KPA

Note

1. For information on Ahearn's working process, I am indebted to the artist and two of his models, Edward Levy and Ed Whitfield.

Ed Whitfield at the Caldcleugh Community Center, 1996. Acrylic on plaster and two framed documents, 20 × 28 in. Gift of Richard and Jane Levy in memory of Frances S. Loewenstein, 1996

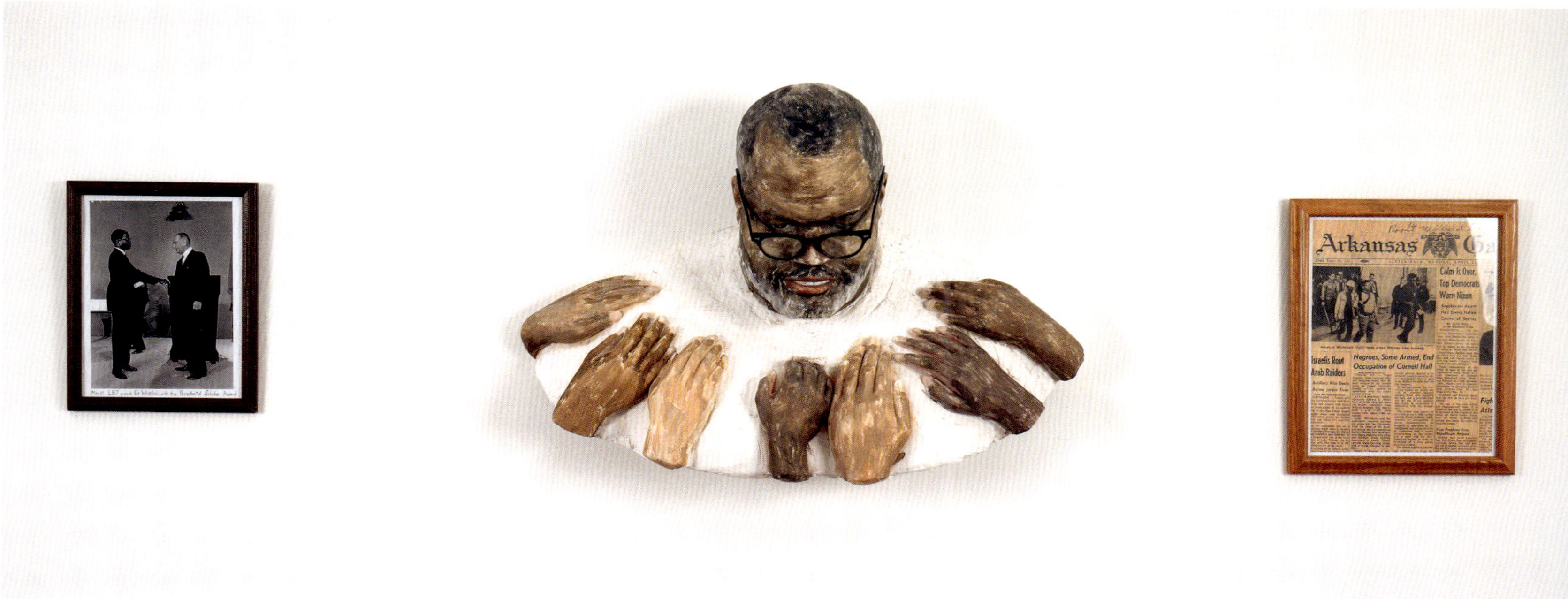
Arkansas
Calm Is Over, Top Democrats Warn Nixon
Israelis Rout Arab Raiders
Negroes, Some Armed, End Occupation of Cornell Hall

MAUD GATEWOOD American, 1934–2004

MAUD GATEWOOD is arguably North Carolina's best-known painter. Born in Yanceyville in Caswell County, she lived there most of her life. At age sixteen she entered Woman's College (now The University of North Carolina at Greensboro), where she studied under the Art Department's first chair, Gregory Ivy. After earning her BFA, she received an MFA from Ohio State University.

Ivy believed that students should combine a firm grounding in art history with exposure to and study of the experimental art of their time. Gatewood thus benefited from critiques and lectures by such visiting artists as Philip Guston and Franz Kline, as well as from two summers spent at Ivy's school in Burnsville, North Carolina. The proximity of Black Mountain College and the exchange of faculty between the two schools further exposed Gatewood to some of the most vanguard art and artists from New York.

While a good deal of Gatewood's work captures life in and around Caswell County, she was by no means simply a local or provincial artist painting figures and landscapes. She digested the lessons of modernism and postmodernism and translated them into a unique style.[1] She also brought to bear on her work a strong awareness of the history of art, sometimes quoting important artists from the past. Her widespread travels, first on a Fulbright Fellowship to study in Vienna, and later to China, Iraq, Australia, Africa, Indonesia, and elsewhere, also inspired a significant amount of her work.

The Bungles from the Creek Bed is a prime example of Gatewood's love of structured composition. Working from photographs only as visual notes, she represented landscape scenes while turning them into colorful abstractions and negotiated a complex interplay between illusionistic space and flat patterns. The Bungle Bungle National Park is a World Heritage site in remote northwestern Australia. The Bungles are a massive group of towering sandstone formations that rise from a gorge and cover an area of some 4,500 acres. Certainly Gatewood was taken by their alternate striping in bands of orange and deep bluish gray and how these striations visually flattened out the enormous volume of the rocks: in the Weatherspoon's painting, some of the bands leap from one rock to another, across the intervening space. She combined colors directly on the canvas and achieved unusual surface textures and patterns by using combs, scrapers she made from plastic palette knives, tape, and tools such as an automotive striper and a coarse paint sprayer.

Gatewood had a long and deep relationship with the Weatherspoon Art Museum and The University of North Carolina at Greensboro, which awarded her an honorary doctorate in 1999. During her last two years as a student at Woman's College, she worked as an assistant at the Weatherspoon and helped to uncrate Willem de Kooning's *Woman*—and loved to tell the story of how she almost stepped on it. In her penchant for organization, she left a detailed will listing the order in which various museums around the state could select a specified number of paintings and drawings from her house and storage. Second in line to choose, after the North Carolina Museum of Art, the Weatherspoon had *The Bungles* at the top of its list.

NMD

Note

1. For an excellent appraisal of Gatewood's work, see Robert Hobbs's essay in *Maud Gatewood: Re-visions* (Greensboro, NC: Weatherspoon Art Museum, 1994).

The Bungles from the Creek Bed, 1996. Acrylic on canvas, 60 × 72 in. Bequest of Maud F. Gatewood, 2004

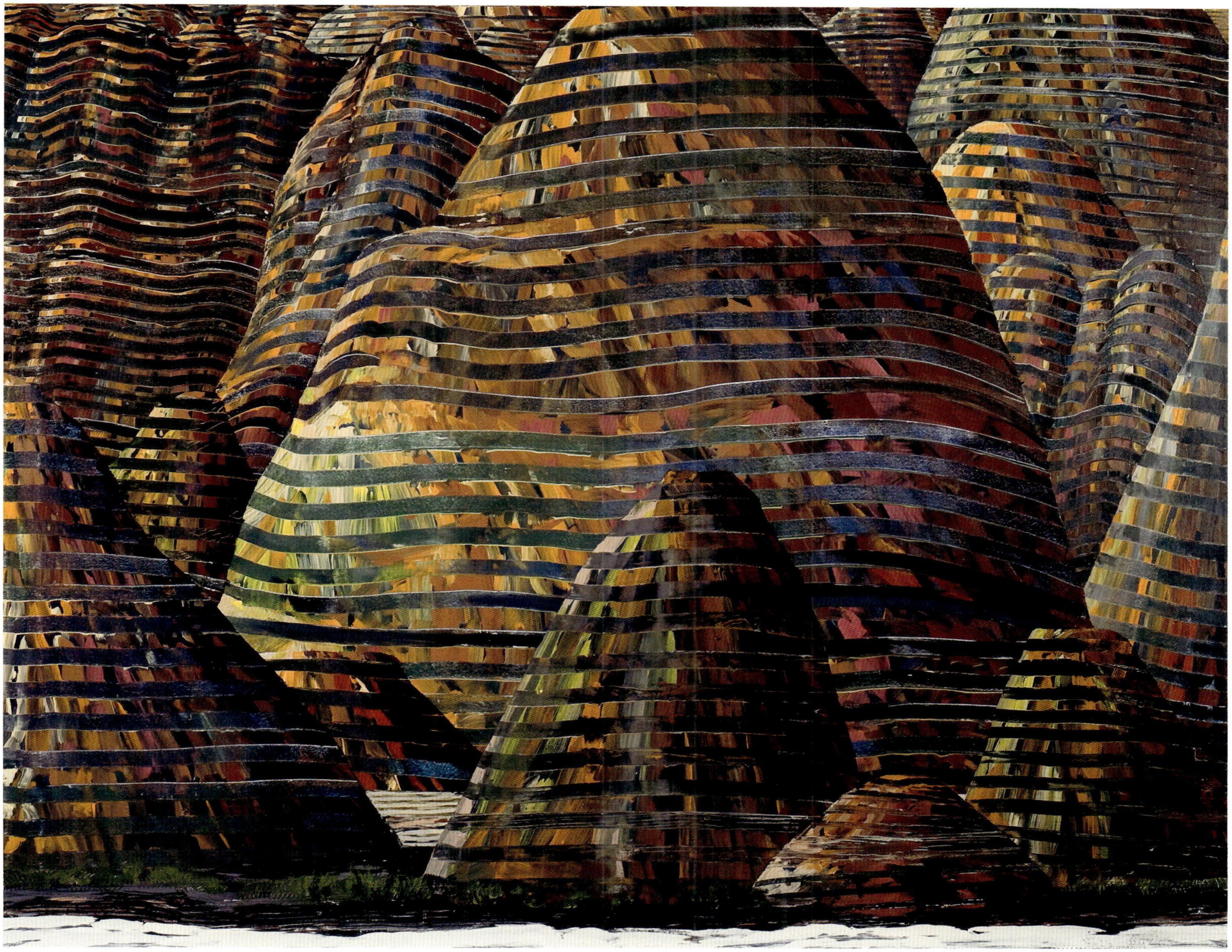

MARK DI SUVERO American, born China, 1933

MARK DI SUVERO has often been called a "man of steel," a reference to the fact that he has mastered the medium at a scale and to an extent that few other sculptors have achieved. Particularly notable is his ability to animate industrial materials and process with graceful form and movement. From his time in junkyards and shipyards, where he learned to weld and use cranes, di Suvero holds in high regard the skills necessary to make the kind of work he does, demanding the utmost from both himself and his crew members. He is involved at every step in the production of his work and uses no plans as specific as blueprints or factory-order components. Remarkably, even with the largest of his works, which can measure as much as seventy or eighty feet in height, intuition and improvisation are part of di Suvero's process.

Whether of enormous scale or small enough to be called tabletop sculptures, di Suvero's work is always monumental. *To Be* demonstrates the artist's interest in salvaging: the stationary base is made of parts from an earlier piece, *One Oklock*, and the upper mobile element is the positive shape removed from *Tyne Anew*. Poised on a knuckle at the top of the vertical pole, the upper piece spins around and rocks up and down; as little as a touch of the hand puts it into motion. The two sections—one vertical and one horizontal—are thus literally balanced, almost like a figure skater with one foot on the ice while the other leg stretches out parallel to the ground. The differences in the materials—steel and stainless steel—result in variations in the patina.

Di Suvero followed an unusual path on his way to becoming an artist. He was born in Shanghai to Italian parents, who moved to the United States in 1941. He left high school in San Francisco before graduation and spent a few years painting houses, building boats, and traveling solo by sailboat and bicycle. This inevitably reflective time spurred his return to college as a philosophy major, but he later switched to sculpture and graduated from the University of California, Berkeley in 1956. The next year, he moved to New York and had his first one-person exhibition there at the Green Gallery in 1960.

As he was preparing for that exhibition, di Suvero suffered critical injuries while moving lumber on top of an elevator that did not stop when it should have. He broke his back and, after two years of staying off his feet, defied odds to walk again with the use of canes and crutches. It was after the accident and his recovery that the use of cranes came to be so critical to his work. He moved massive beams and steel plates just as an artist creating smaller sculpture from found pieces would. Di Suvero could orchestrate movement at dizzying heights, using the crane to move, shift, turn, and otherwise try out forms in space.

Mark di Suvero is the first living artist invited to exhibit his sculptures in Paris's Tuileries Gardens in 1957. Countless exhibitions, publications, commissions, and awards have followed, including fellowships from the National Endowment for the Arts and a Heinz Award. Always interested in helping other artists, in 1986 di Suvero established the Socrates Sculpture Park, near his riverfront studio in Long Island City, as a place where both emerging and established artists can present outdoor sculpture. His Athena Foundation helps fund the park's operations and provides several studios for artists. Celebrating its twenty-fifth anniversary in 2011, Socrates Sculpture Park has grown into a multidisciplinary program that brings artists and community together.

NMD

To Be, 1996. Steel and stainless steel, 89 × 111 × 97 in. Museum purchase with funds from the bequest of Anne Wortham Cone, 2002

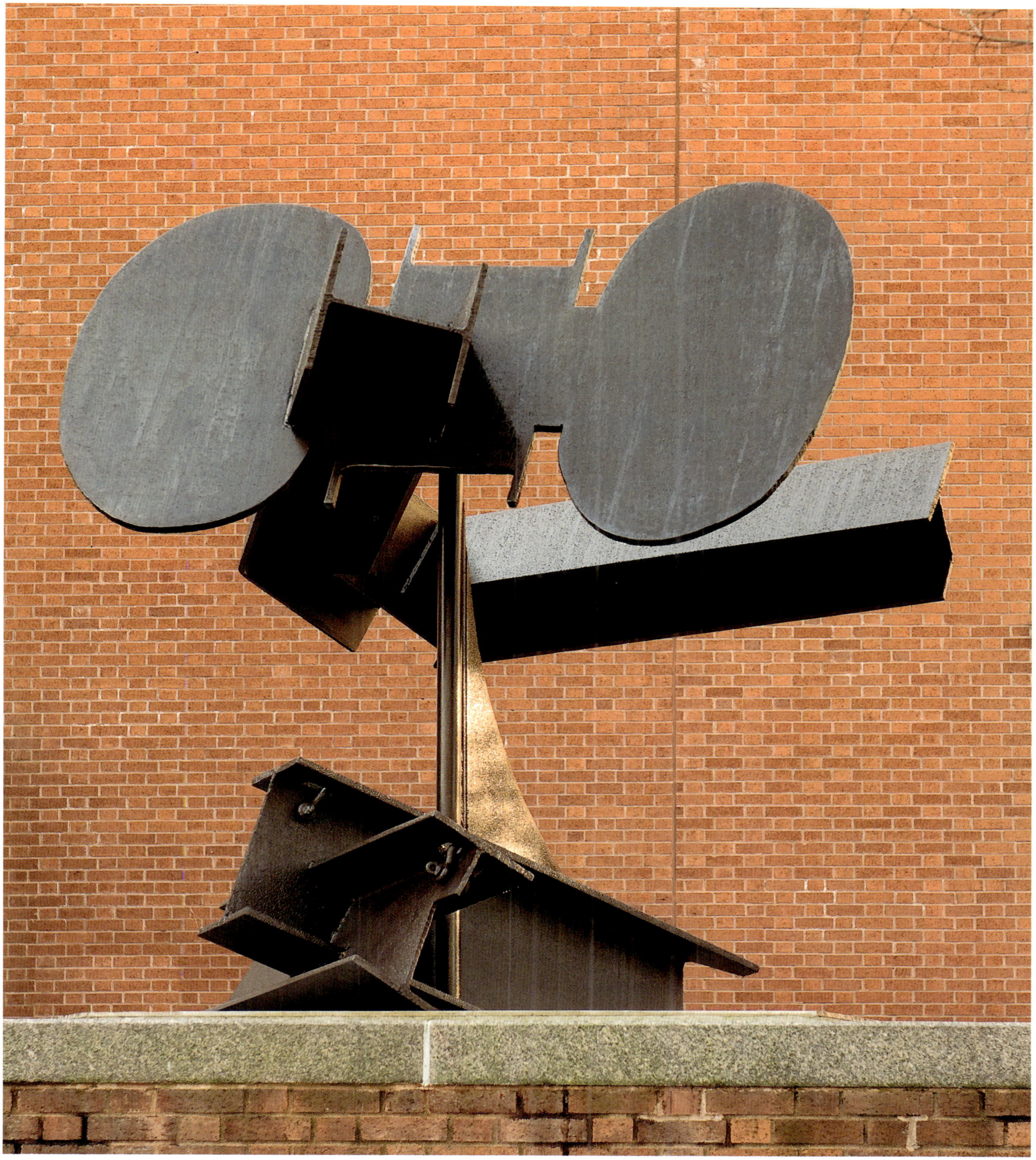

YASUMASA MORIMURA Japanese, born 1951

THE PHOTOGRAPHIC SELF-PORTRAITS of Yasumasa Morimura invariably elicit double takes. The Weatherspoon's *Self-Portrait (Actress) / after Jodie Foster 2* is no exception. Even the knowledge that Morimura's subject is a self-portrait does not diminish the shock value of seeing a middle-aged Japanese man disguised as the teenaged Jodie Foster in the role of Iris Steensma, a preteen prostitute from Martin Scorsese's film *Taxi Driver*. *Self-Portrait (Actress) / after Jodie Foster 2* is from a series in which the photographer posed in elaborately contrived costumes and settings as iconic film stars. This work expands the Weatherspoon's holdings in contemporary photography with an image that refers not only to a twentieth-century film but also to multiple aspects of the eighteenth- and nineteenth-century Japanese prints donated to the museum by Lenoir Wright.

A 1978 graduate of Kyoto City University of Arts, Morimura has spent three decades experimenting with appropriated images from a variety of sources to create what he has called "open" self-portraits.[1] By the late 1980s Morimura had established an international reputation with photographs that are uncannily faithful representations of famous paintings from the history of Western art. In addition to directing and producing these staged photographs, he also posed as impersonations of the principal figures, many females among them. In 1996 Morimura temporarily shifted his focus from painting to film, assuming the personas of veteran actresses as well as the ingénue Jodie Foster. For Morimura, role-playing is a vehicle for exploring multiple aspects of his self-identity. His artful disguise as Foster in the role of Iris challenges the viewer to consider the possibility that every aspect of self-identity—even gender—is a cultural construction.

If impersonating actresses underscored Morimura's self-perceived artistic role as a performer, so too did his reprisal of the Japanese theatrical tradition of the *onnagata*. *Onnagata* are male actors who historically performed the parts of women in Kabuki plays and are often depicted in Japanese woodblock prints. Not coincidentally, the Kabuki plays were as popular a form of mass entertainment in Edo Japan as Hollywood films were in the global culture of the twentieth century. Whereas the halter top, short pants, and platform sandals Morimura sports in *Self-Portrait (Actress) / after Jodie Foster 2* replicate an outfit worn by Foster in *Taxi Driver*, his heavily made-up facial features are reminiscent of the Kabuki *onnagata* pictured in their roles as courtesans in Japanese actor prints.

Morimura's penchant for cross-cultural references is also apparent in the setting of *Self-Portrait (Actress) / after Jodie Foster 2*. The first version of this image shows Morimura posed against a neutral ground. In the Weatherspoon's version, the artist restored the urban surroundings of his film source but changed the locale. Signage indicates that the setting is a bar-lined back alley in the artist's native Osaka rather than the streets of Manhattan. Littering the pavement are packets of tissue with notes that serve the same purpose as personal ads in the mass media. These advertisements have a history that is documented in one of the Japanese prints in the Weatherspoon's collection. An early-nineteenth-century print by Utagawa Kuniyasu shows a courtesan with a roll of tissue clenched between her teeth to signify her sexual availability.[2] As props in Morimura's *Self-Portrait (Actress) / after Jodie Foster 2*, the visually coded tissue packets carry much the same meaning.

Morimura's self-portraits subvert traditional assumptions about photography as well as personal identity. His skillful command of photographic processes, from traditional darkroom printing to computer manipulation, leaves no doubt that photographs are visual constructions as opposed to unmediated records of reality. The Weatherspoon's *Self-Portrait (Actress) / after Jodie Foster 2* is an Ilfochrome, successor to the Cibachrome print, and recognizable as such by the black border and glossy surface, both of which contribute to the illusion that this is a framed publicity shot. By manipulating color balances to envelop the setting in a bluish haze and to heighten the saturated intensity of the red, Morimura singled out one of Foster's signature costumes as the visual focus. This visible evidence of technical manipulation makes the viewer keenly aware that Morimura's medium is as essential to his fictions as his disguises.

KPA

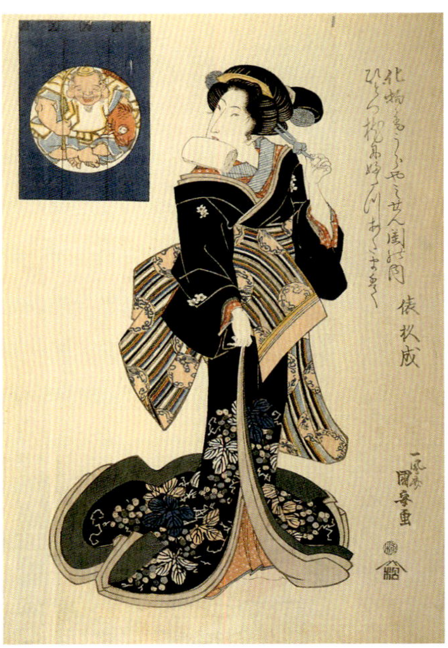

Utagawa Kuniyasu (Japanese, 1794–1832), *Ebisu*, ca. 1820. Woodblock print on paper, 14⅝ × 9⅜ in. Gift of Dr. Lenoir C. Wright, 1998

Notes

1. Interview with the artist, cited in Dana Friis-Hansen, *Yasumasa Morimura: Actor/Actress* (Houston: Contemporary Arts Museum, 1997), 2.
2. Information communicated by Allen Hockley, Associate Professor of Art History, Dartmouth College, and curator of the Weatherspoon Art Museum's *Inside the Floating World: Japanese Prints from the Lenoir C. Wright Collection*, 2002.

Self-Portrait (Actress) / after Jodie Foster 2, 1996. Ilfochrome photograph on acrylic sheet, 47¼ × 37½ in. Museum purchase with funds from the Joseph R. Morton Acquisition Endowment and the Weatherspoon Art Museum Acquisition Endowment, 2002

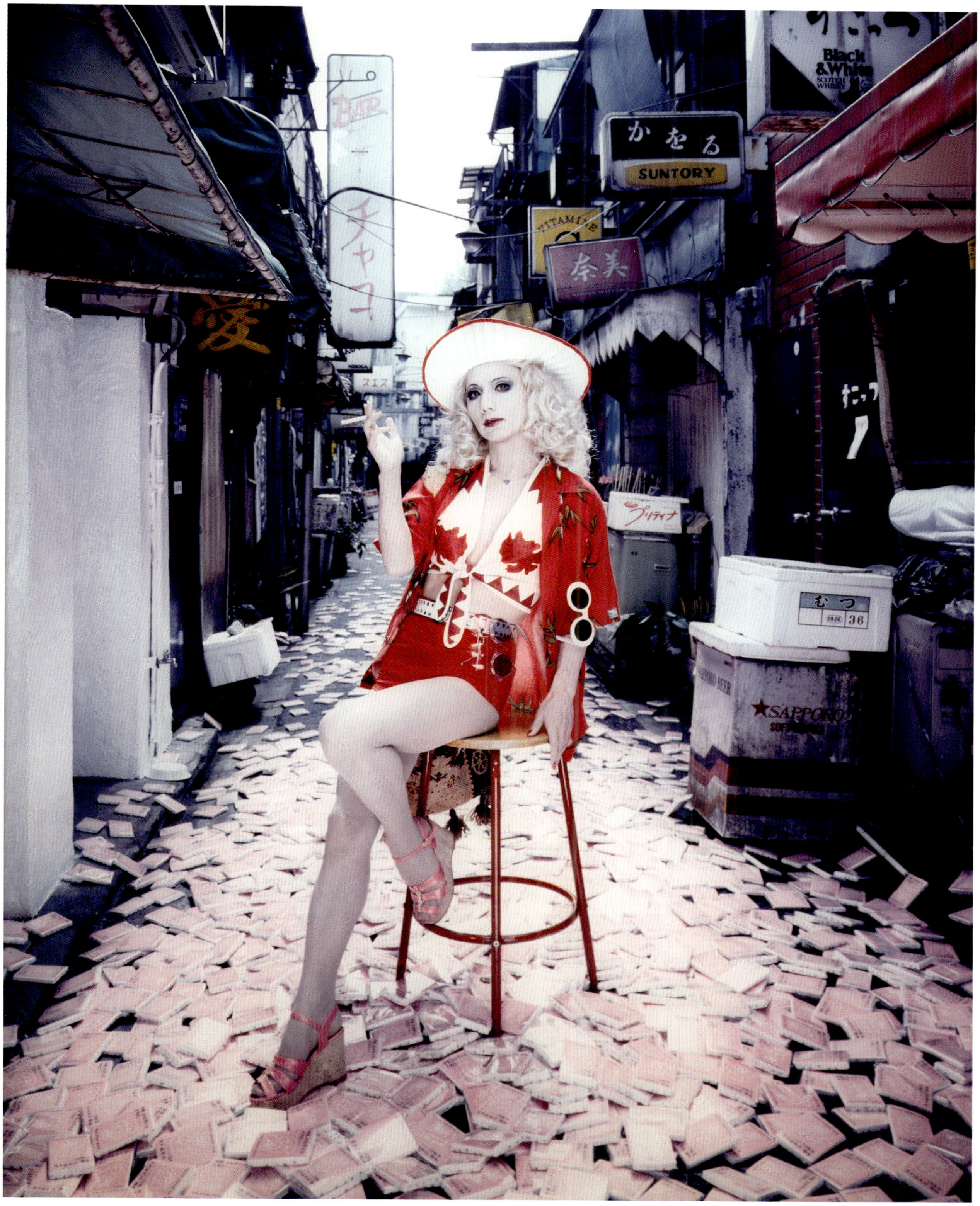
BAR
チャコ
愛
かをる
SUNTORY
奈美
Black & White
むつ
36
SAPPORO

VIK MUNIZ American, born Brazil, 1961

WITH AN ABIDING INTEREST in foraging through our collective visual memory, the Brazilian-born artist Vik Muniz has interpreted everything from Leonardo da Vinci's famous *Last Supper* and archetypal images of Robert Morris's Minimalist sculpture to publicity photos of Marilyn Monroe. He depicts these and other well-known works of art and images from popular culture using unconventional materials such as chocolate syrup, dust, and diamonds. He photographs his sculptural drawings and then destroys them; thus, photography is the final medium of his work.

In *Youth, Gaspar*, Muniz plays on the artifice of photography while paying homage to another artist, in this case, Edward Weston, whose 1925 portraits of his nine-year-old son Neil served as Muniz's inspiration.[1] The work is part of Pictures of Soil, a series that consists of photographs of drawings the artist made on a large light table covered with soil. The use of soil has a fascinating correlation to the image represented. Muniz often references Ovid's *Metamorphoses* as a major influence on his thinking. The poem begins with a beautiful line, "My mind is bent to tell of bodies changed into new forms." Indeed, in *Youth, Gaspar*, the body is greatly transformed, for what at first appears to be a monochromatic image of a young boy's torso is soon revealed as an unstable field of tiny specks of soil, small pebbles, and decomposing leaves and branches. On close examination, we find the keys to the illusion: a collarbone is rendered of small twigs; a belly button is formed from delicately placed bits of earth; and the scale of the work is revealed through the artist's inclusion of a single black ant in the lower right-hand corner. As we look, the representation of the body seems to disintegrate into the soil.

The invocation of soil as the substance from which life emerges and to which it will return recalls the long art-historical genre of the memento mori. By carefully rendering an image of his young son, Muniz communicates the age-old desire for immortality (similar to Weston's image and recalling Ovid's poem), but because the image is made from earth, it simultaneously puts forward the reverse concept: that human existence is of a fleeting nature.

Youth, Gaspar is a complex and visually engaging work that operates on multiple formal and conceptual levels. The work delights us with its sheer ingenuity while compelling us to delve deep into our psyches to decipher its meaning. The use of unusual materials informs the work, but Muniz also says he seeks to achieve "the worst possible illusion," by which he means an illusion so obviously contrived that the viewer must acknowledge the image as a deception.[2] This statement gets at the root of Muniz's project, which is humorously to marry subject matter with material to reveal what we often overlook: that photography itself is an interpretation of the thing represented.

XE

Notes

1. *Youth, Gaspar* is based on a photograph of Muniz's own son, Gaspar, who was about the same age as Neil when the work was created.
2. Vik Muniz, quoted in Marguerite Feitlowitz, "Vik Muniz: Between Illusion and Memory," *Americas* 53 (July 2001): 7.

Youth, Gaspar, 1998. Gelatin silver print, 56¾ × 45¹⁄₁₆ in. Museum purchase with funds from the Jefferson-Pilot Endowment and Burlington Industries Endowment with additional funds provided by Geoff Wall, 2008

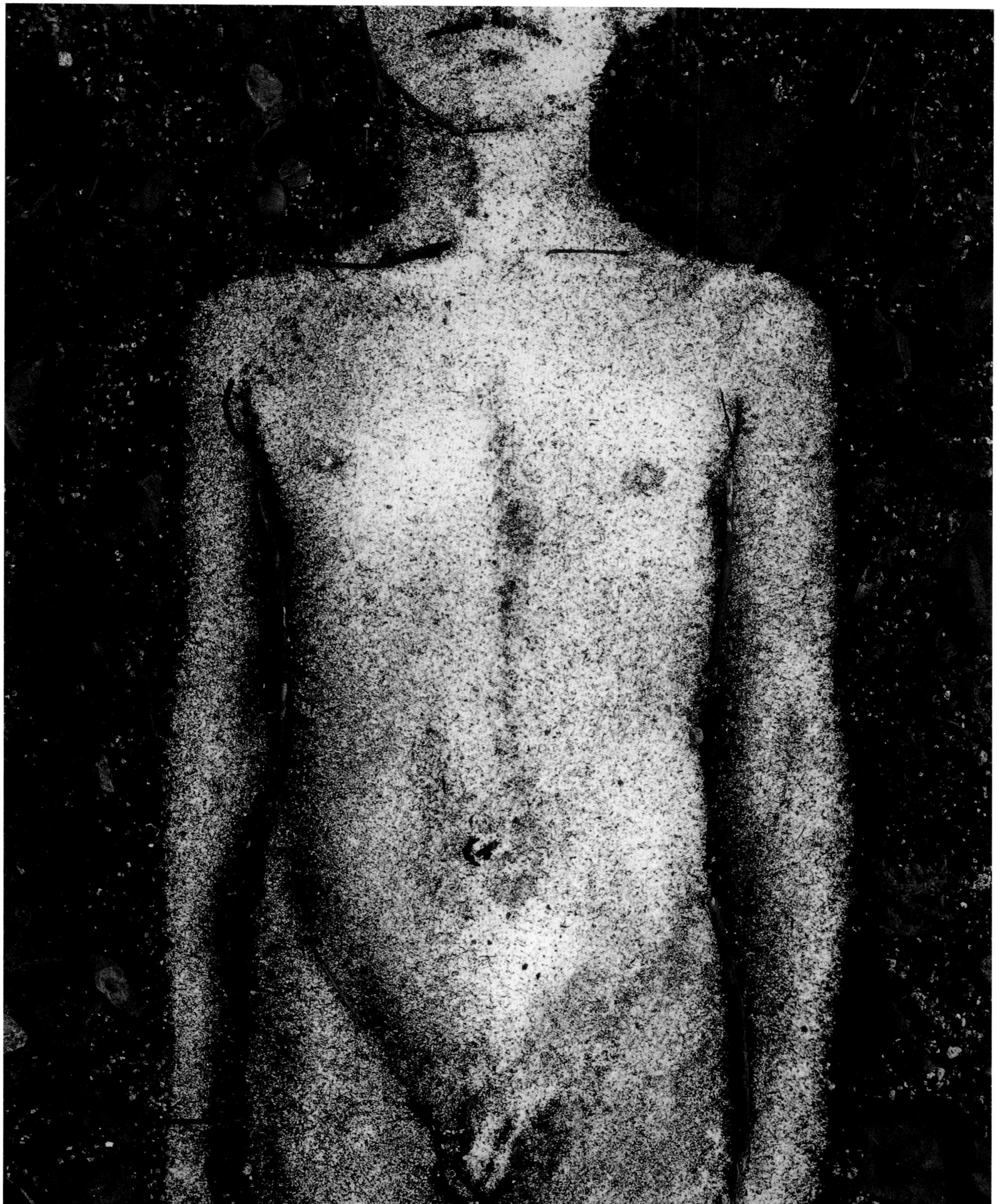

ALISON SAAR American, born 1956

IT WAS ALMOST INEVITABLE that Alison Saar become an artist, given that as a child she was immersed in the arts. Her father was a conservator and an artist, and her mother, Betye, is widely recognized for her collages and assemblages. The couple frequently took Alison and her sisters, Lezley (also a visual artist) and Tracye (a writer), to museums and art openings, and their home was filled with art and objects they brought back from their far-flung travels.

Saar's formal training in art includes a BA from Scripps College and an MFA from the Otis Art Institute, but the strongest influences on her work came from her background. She was the child of an early interracial marriage: her father was white, and her mother came from an unusual mix of African American, Irish, and Native American heritages. Saar always has felt a strong affinity to her mother's side of the family and its Southern and African Caribbean roots. Laurel Canyon, the Los Angeles neighborhood in which she grew up, was the site of recurring natural fires, and Saar witnessed the cycle of sacrifice—or death—and regeneration. Rummaging through the remains of destroyed homes, she found fragments of their histories, items that took on a talismanic quality. Throughout her career, Saar has continued to reinvest found objects with ritualistic significance and power.

Compton Nocturne brings together many hallmarks of the artist's mature work in an empowered black female body embedded with the artist's feminist politics, cultural critique, and references to her varied background and other world cultures. The city of Compton, California, is today, even after the dismantling of segregation, a predominantly African American community that borders on the neighborhood of Watts, the site of the famous Watts Tower, created over decades by the visionary artist Simon Rodia. Saar's family visited the site when she was nine; its magic and beauty, wrought from the discards of daily life, made an enormous impression on her.

Compton Nocturne is a quintessential example of Saar's ability to combine multiple, even contradictory, sources into works of compelling interest. It is one of a number of her stylized figures that reference magical and spiritual practices in traditional cultures. The medicine bottles atop the tree branches forming the figure's hair refer to the spirit bottle tree, once a staple of the Southern landscape. This practice of hanging bottles from tree limbs was spread by hoodoo rootworkers, conjurers with the ability to capture in the bottles evil spirits who were enticed by the dazzle of sunlight reflecting off them. In the Santería religion, "prescriptions" for repelling evil spirits include placing medicinal herbs in bottles to enhance the properties of the medicine and speed up recovery.

The earthy, self-contained figure of *Compton Nocturne* is, at the same time, part of a long art-historical tradition of the recumbent female nude, dating back at least as far as Titian and Giorgione. The odalisque—as many of these figures are labeled—was a woman at the lowest scale of a Turkish harem, often a slave to the concubines. This image was popularized during the orientalizing trend in art of the nineteenth century: the woman was posed for male gratification, often watched over by an African attendant. Saar, however, has turned that premise fully on its head with a black woman taking the place of the desired white female, asserting herself as an empowered and sensual being.

Saar has clad the figure in tarnished tin ceiling tiles, selected and formally arranged to emphasize such body parts as the knees and the spinal column. These embossed tiles were the Victorian commoners' effort to replicate the elaborate carved plaster ceilings found in homes of the wealthy. Now, in their second-class status as discarded and damaged material, the artist has found beauty and elegance as well as the means to further elaborate on the complicated issues of race, power, and personal agency.

NMD

Compton Nocturne, 1999. Wood, tin, bottles, paint, and tar, 35¼ × 84 × 30 in. Museum purchase with funds from the Benefactors Fund, 1999

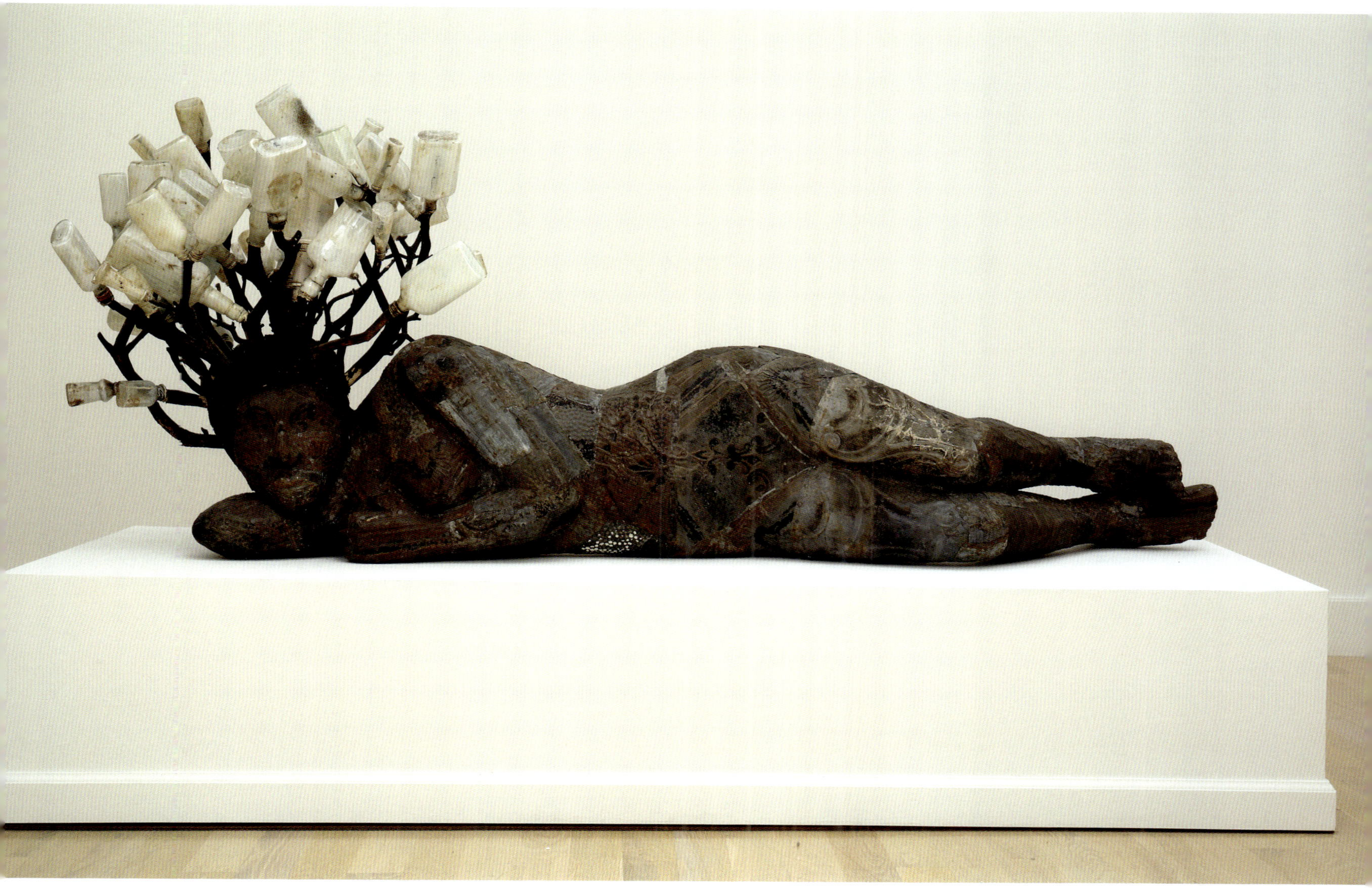

GREGORY CREWDSON American, born 1962

What I'm after, what I've always been after, . . . is a picture that tells a story. I see it all in my head beforehand, and I set out obsessively, maybe even narcissistically, to make it. . . . In part I see what I'm doing as exploring the American psyche through the American vernacular landscape, much as [Edward] Hopper did.

—Gregory Crewdson[1]

GREGORY CREWDSON'S large color photograph arrests our attention. An adolescent girl and a younger boy are engaged in some kind of occult, nighttime ritual while two canine creatures (wolves? coyotes?) bear enigmatic witness just outside the door of a nondescript, working-class, American home. The picture has the lush color and atmospheric lighting of a first-run Hollywood film yet retains sufficient documentary verisimilitude to give the viewer pause. What is going on here? What happens next?

Crewdson, born in 1962, is a Yale MFA graduate who has become an influential teacher there. His images inhabit ambiguously a middle ground between Surrealist tableau and narrative cinema, a postmodern domain where lens-based pictures need not take sides in the century-old civil war over the question of whether photography and its progeny should be championed as redemptive fine art or condemned as crass popular entertainment. Crewdson's strategy is to commandeer the highest production values available from the film and television industries and place them at the service of a single, very large, supersaturated, pictorial image possessed of a visual portentousness reminiscent of nineteenth-century history painting. A Crewdson picture is every bit as much of a Salon machine as was Théodore Géricault's *Raft of the Medusa*. Accounts of his work often pay as much attention to the elaborate staging—his costly use of actors, lighting crews, set dressers, art directors, and makeup people—as to the final photograph.[2]

At the same time, this image is deeply indebted to a "pictures" generation of conceptually based, postmodern artists—Cindy Sherman and Jeff Wall, especially—who pioneered the practice of the staged photographic tableau as a rich vein for exposing the role of representation in reproducing and reenforcing the established social order. Crewdson's domain is more psychological and less political than the work of either Sherman or Wall. His pictures repeatedly pierce the uneasy facade of small-town life in America to realize (i.e., to stage and thereby make visible as an image) specific terrors, fantasies, and confusions originating in a young person's imagination.

Untitled weds the interpretative richness of Sigmund Freud's theories of dream work (Crewdson's father was a psychoanalyst) with the collective unconscious of an American film culture whose shared references include *American Graffiti*, *Blue Velvet*, *The Exorcist*, and *Close Encounters of the Third Kind*. Crewdson's method entails complete control over every aspect of the image's production in the manner of an auteur film director devoted to the portrayal of the uncanny when it erupts amid scenes of working-class life. The "uncanny," in Freud's definition, is that pervasive sense of foreboding resulting from the complex and divided apprehension of something that is, at one and the same time, both intimately familiar and disturbingly strange. Lighting, pose, and composition conspire to underscore an atmospherics of titillating domestic apprehension.

The "scene" being enacted in this picture invites all the complexities of a Freudian dream interpretation and all the narrative possibilities of a Hollywood film plot. (It is probably worth asking what kind of film this image might have come from: horror, sci-fi, film noir, teen-coming-of-age?) Central to the image's effect is the withholding of any reliable frame of interpretation. The viewer is not the subject of psychoanalysis, nor is this a film still, no matter how much it looks like one. Crewdson's gift is to elide his personal memories, dreams, and preoccupations with those of the larger social order. His identifications and projections are themselves caught up in the myths and icons of contemporary media culture. This image owes as much to David Lynch and *The Twilight Zone* as it does to postmodern, art-world photography. It enacts that strange combination of voyeurism and Puritanism that attends current media contemplations of adolescent sexuality. Yet it also remains true to a modernist tradition of self-reflexivity. The time-honored culture war between painting and photography has ended here with a decisive victory on behalf of the camera, as evidenced by the cameo appearance of John Constable's *Haywain*. The pride and glory of English Romantic painting is reduced here to a kitsch reproduction placed indifferently between window and light switch, its original aura surrendered up to the visual seductions of a digital age.

GD

Notes

1. Annette Grant, "Lights, Camera, Stand Really Still: On the Set with Gregory Crewdson," *New York Times*, May 30, 2004, at http://www.nytimes.com/2004/05/30/arts/design/30GRAN.html#.

2. Adrian Searle, "Too Much Information," *Guardian*, April 19, 2005, at http://www.guardian.co.uk/artanddesign/2005/apr/19/photography.

Untitled, 1998. Cibachrome photograph, 47 3/8 × 59 3/8 in. Museum purchase with funds from the Weatherspoon Art Museum Acquisition Endowment, 2000

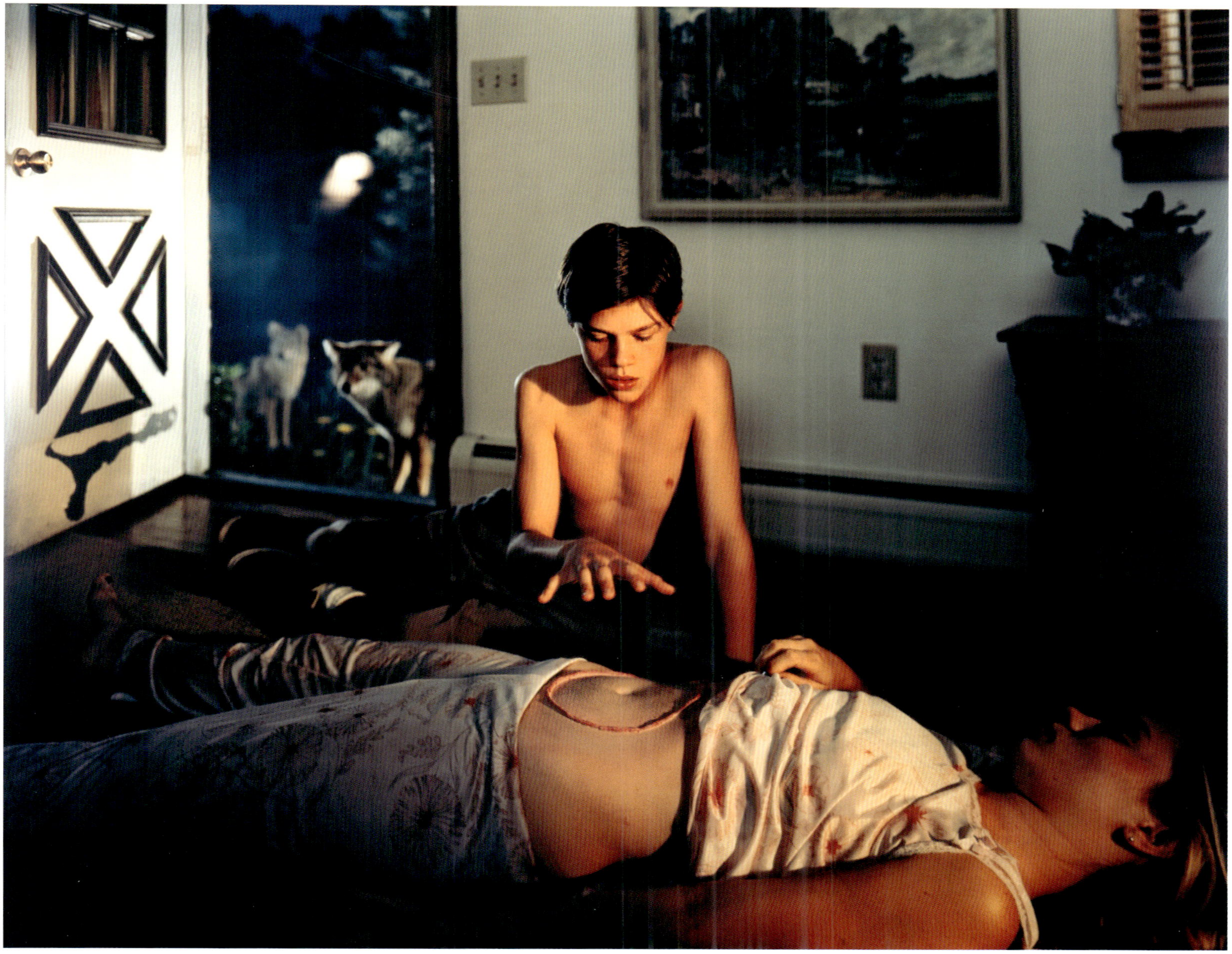

KIKI SMITH American, born 1954

THE EXPLORATION OF MATERIALS and processes is one of the most noted and notable aspects of Kiki Smith's art. She crafts sculpture in glass, paper, bronze, plaster, and ceramic; her prints push the possibilities of the medium, often mixing multiple print techniques in a single work; and she probes an extensive range of drawing materials. No matter the medium or technique, Smith's work consistently exhibits the mark of her hand, the sureness of her touch, and, most of all, deep engagement with her subject matter. The remarkable results of Smith's interrogation and her dedication to the female body and to nature have become her signature. At once delicate and strong, seemingly tentative and powerful, her work resides in a realm of beauty and profoundly felt emotion.

When she moved to New York in 1976, Smith joined a generation of young artists interested in the body as a physical being and a socially constructed site of identity. She used *Gray's Anatomy*, the famous record of anatomical structures and systems, as a source for works depicting internal organs and body fragments and, in the early 1990s, produced a series of figurative sculptures that often were mediations between fragile media and gripping emotional states.[1] Smith has been strongly influenced by feminist concerns while refraining from arguments for particular points of view. Rather, her "feminism" resides in her humanist sensibilities and refusal to abide by any preconceived notions of gender and sexuality.

Alongside her abiding interest in the human form has been her engagement with animals as subjects, not as our surrogates but in their own right and in the relations we forge with them. The subjects of *Two Mirror-Eyed Lambs* are drawn with great delicacy in white ink on a black ink ground. The black ink has caused the handmade Japanese paper that is the drawing's support to crinkle, and its density suggests a starless night sky. Both the paper and Smith's careful rendering reinforce the metaphoric interpretations of lambs as gentle, patient, and innocent creatures. Raised a Roman Catholic, Smith has long been interested in the rituals and beliefs of that faith. Lambs appear frequently in the Bible, at times offered as gifts, at other times as sacrifice. One of the earliest domesticated animals, they symbolized gods in the early religions of both Egypt and Mesopotamia. They also are one of the earliest symbols of Christianity, over time coming to represent Christ himself, the Lamb of God.

The two lambs in this drawing gaze at the viewer with what seems to be trust devoid of fear. A small but important element—the mirrors of the animals' eyes—points to Smith's wide-reaching studies and source materials that include art history and visual cultures around the globe. Just as mirrored eyes symbolize the spirit world in some African figurative sculpture, here they also may represent the artist's interest in the spiritual connections between humans and animals. Like all of her artworks, *Two Mirror-Eyed Lambs* derives its compelling character from Smith's sensibilities and freely associative responses to the world around her.

The daughter of the architect and sculptor Tony Smith and the opera singer Jane Lawrence, Smith grew up in New Jersey in a milieu of artists and their work. In 1992 she presented a one-person multimedia installation, *Life Wants to Live*, at The Kitchen in New York City, the first in a remarkable roster of exhibitions around the world. In 2005, at one of the off-site locations of the Venice Biennale, Smith presented *Homespun Tales*, a large installation incorporating numerous media and forms at the sixteenth-century palazzo housing the Fondazione Querini Stampli.

NMD

Note

1. In one of the most powerful of these works, *Train* (1993), several long strings of red beads trail on the floor behind a body-cast wax figure of a slouched-over woman. The alluring beauty of the wax surface and the sparkle of the beads celebrate the work as an image of menstruation, the cycle of feminine energy in its dissipation and renewal.

Two Mirror-Eyed Lambs, 1999. Ink and mirrors on handmade Japanese paper, 19½ × 53 in. Museum purchase with funds from the Judy Proctor Acquisition Endowment, 1999

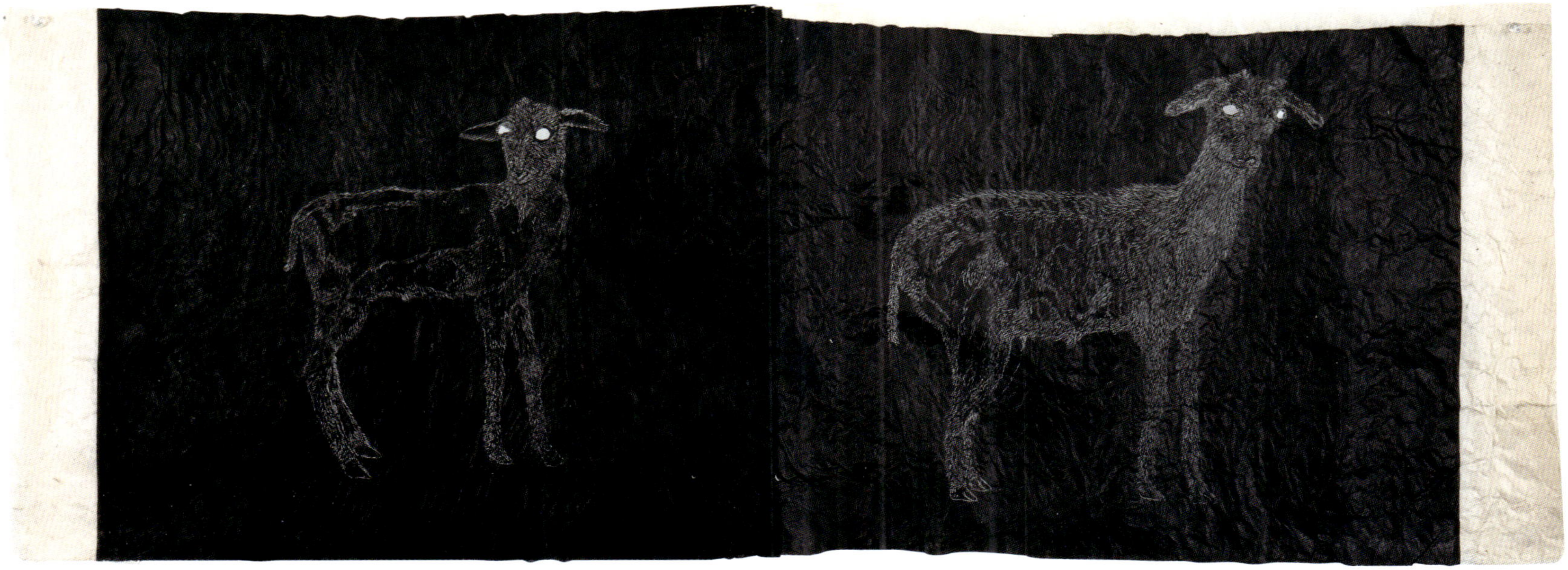

RICHARD MISRACH American, born 1949

RICHARD MISRACH FIRST encountered the Mojave Desert as a child on family vacations. Returning many years later, he found the desertscape a site of remarkable power and beauty. Misrach's photography of this terrain, printed exclusively in color and made with a large-format camera, led to the creation of a series of images entitled the Desert Cantos. In poetry or song cycles, a canto is a part of a larger whole. Misrach's early cantos included the Terrain, the Event, the Flood, and the Fires. The Battleground Point series represents the twenty-fourth installment in the ongoing Desert Cantos project. Using a large-format 8-by-10-inch camera has enabled Misrach to capture a remarkable amount of detail in these works.

Committed to interpreting the desert in both artistic and political terms, Misrach is fascinated by the important role played by place in the cultural life of those who inhabit it. When the area of Battleground Point, for example, was excavated in the mid-1980s, archaeologists discovered the graves of 416 of the area's inhabitants from a period extending over three thousand years. The area is the site of a legendary battle between the Toidikadi (also known as the Stillwater Paiute) and an enemy tribe of red-headed giants. Regardless of whether this story is truth or fiction, the human remains found at Battleground Point give evidence of some type of major catastrophe. The graves surfaced when waters receded from the flood-prone area; in 1998 it again was underwater. Misrach took his photographs there the following spring on a commission from the Nature Conservancy after the waters had evaporated.

Of course, the Weatherspoon's *Battleground Point #5* does not visually impart this detailed background information. It does, however, draw attention to the still-spectacular physical setting and, by revisiting the natural grandeur of the American West, inspires us to become aware of the environmental and social issues associated with its seriously threatened ecological balance. The viewer reacts to the epic beauty of the scene and is compelled to wonder: Is this land protected? Is there water? Does anyone still live here? Misrach's political advocacy is silent but commanding. This land, his photographs subtly but emphatically suggest, is worth preserving.

Misrach believes the value of the beautiful is in its power to convey difficult ideas: that the sensually attractive image draws the viewer into complex propositions—such as preservation—that he or she otherwise easily might ignore. Beauty is certainly seductive in *Battleground Point #5*, where rows of sinuous wind-carved lines in the desert lead to a sweep of hill poised against a flood of clouds. How could this majestic environment be the same as that we always hear is under human assault? It is precisely this deep irony—that such majestic environments are so often under human assault—that Misrach identifies in the making of his photographs.

Richard Misrach in a native of the West, born in Los Angeles. He credits numerous spiritual pursuits prevalent in California for his interest in the desert—yoga, meditation, and the whole earth movement among them. In addition to his series on the desert, he has completed bodies of work based on his travels to Greece, Hawaii, and Africa. In all cases, the artist is motivated by the tension between an assumed natural purity and relentless human encroachment. "It's the way the story is told," Misrach says, "that makes us reexamine life afresh."[1]

WS

Note

1. Quoted in Philip Gefter, "Beauty as a Firebomb in the War on Nature," *New York Times*, February 19, 2006, Arts sec.

Battleground Point #5, 1999. Chromogenic dye coupler print, edition of 25, 48¼ × 61⅛ in. Museum purchase with funds from the Benefactors Fund, 2003

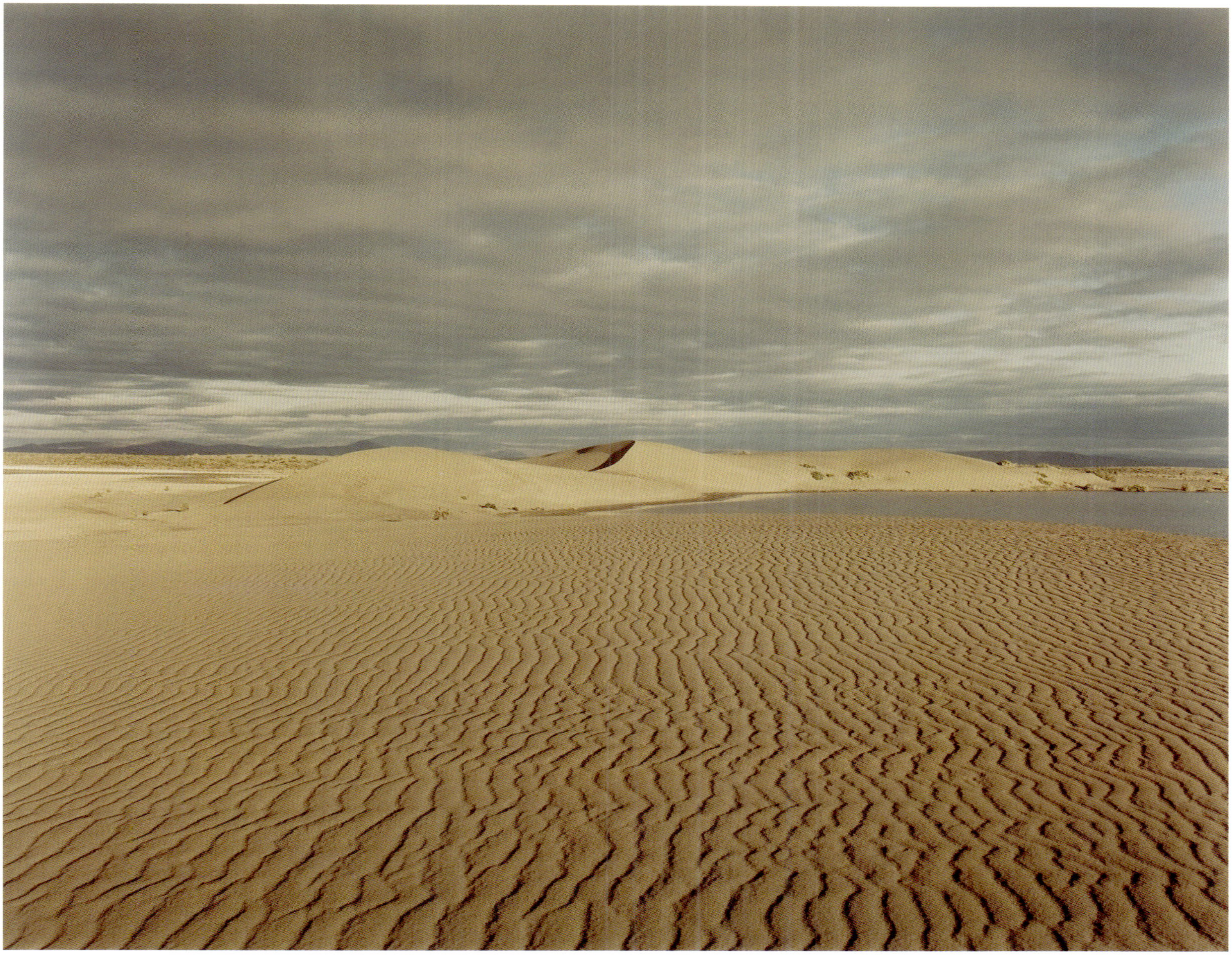

LINDA BESEMER American, born 1957

AFTER ONE HUNDRED YEARS of brightly colored modern paintings—from the joyous brilliance of Henri Matisse through the sound-inspired compositions of Piet Mondrian to the shaped canvases of Frank Stella—it would seem as if there were no new strategy to contribute to this historic stream of creativity. However, this is precisely what Linda Besemer did when she began making paintings out of paint *only*, using no traditional support such as paper, panel, or canvas.

Besemer makes her curtainlike paintings by layering gallon after gallon of thin skins of acrylic onto a large sheet of glass in overlapping grids of color, and then using pin-striper's tape to create stripes and plaids. When the work is finished, she peels from the glass these stacked layers of pure paint—shiny, smooth, and flexible. Works like *Fold #8: Baroquesy* are hung over an aluminum rod with the back side lower than the front so that both sides are seen, thereby charting their evolution from one pattern to another.

This fold, however, is not variable. The shape one sees against the wall is a square, but if the entire painting were flattened out, the ratio of the overall length of *Fold #8* to the square dimension is roughly the same as the square to the fold. In short, Besemer has used the classical golden ratio (also known as the divine section or golden proportion). This mathematical ratio stretches back to antiquity and has fascinated artists ever since. Besemer's contemporary adaptation of it is a testament to her immersion in aesthetic theory and its applications.

Her use of the golden ratio, her intelligent interrogation of what has become a long history of geometric abstraction, and her fully unconventional and painstaking mode of creating a painting set Besemer's work apart from that of younger artists still mining a kind of minimal abstraction. By using the golden ratio and then simultaneously losing it in the fold, the artist subtly questions the primacy of any given formula—ideal formats, she suggests, are there to be experimented with, to be literally folded into another format.

Besemer honors the tradition of precise, reductive abstraction. In their final form as relatively thick sheets of plastic mounted over rods, the paintings resemble blankets or lengths of fabric. They acknowledge their presence in a world of synthetic materials and one in which boundaries between the high art of modernist painting and the world of crafted goods have been conflated. The manufactured appearance of Besemer's paintings is belied by their painstaking creation.

WS

Fold #8: Baroquesy, 1999. Acrylic paint over aluminum rod, 46 × 46 in. Museum purchase with funds from the Benefactors Fund, 2000

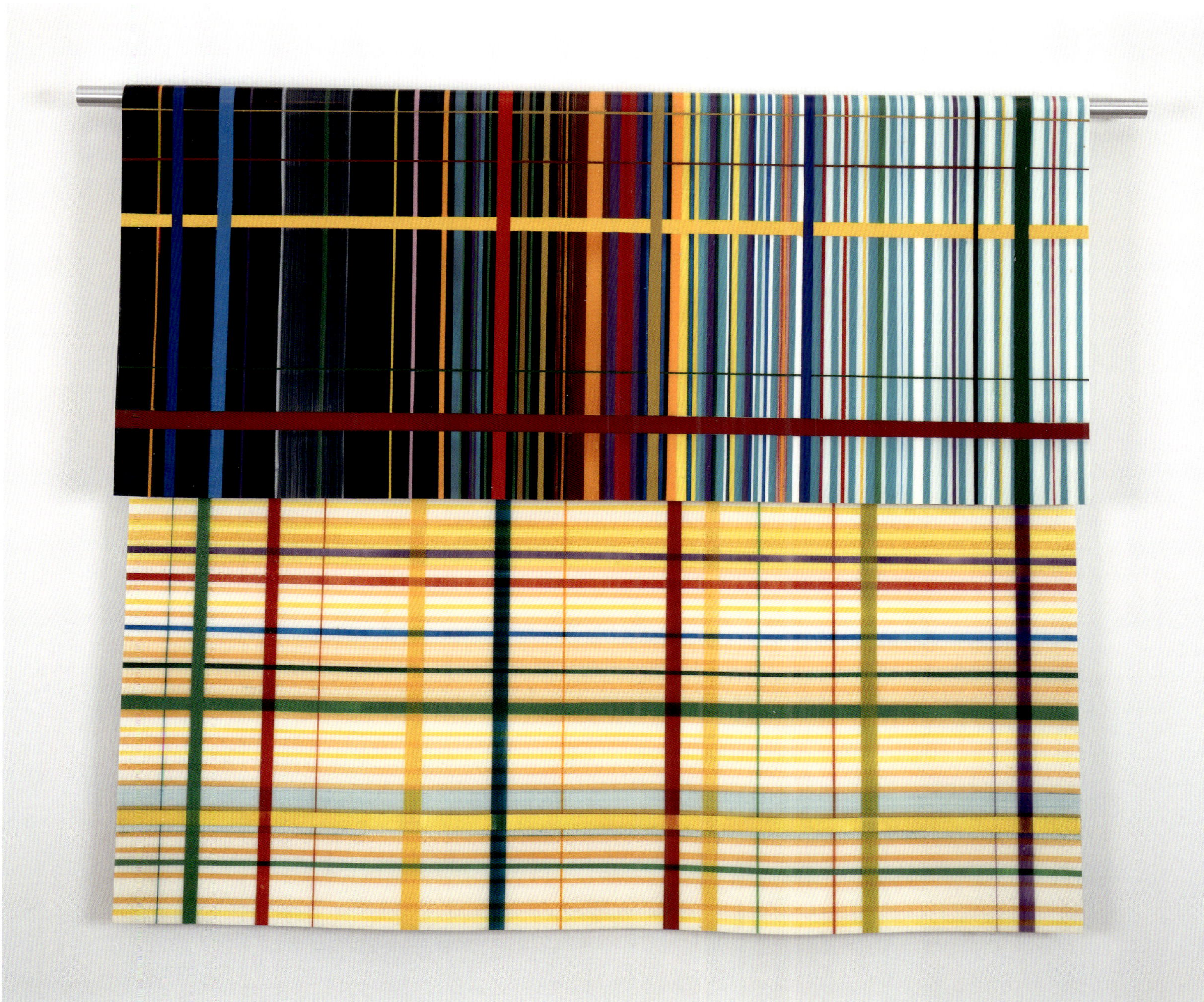

ANN HAMILTON American, born 1956

Making visible that which is usually invisible is one of Hamilton's principal strategies for drawing attention to what we are blind or insensitive to, and for upsetting inherited hierarchies of perception which privilege sight over other forms of sensory knowledge.

—Katy Kline and Helaine Posner[1]

TRAINED IN TEXTILES, design, and sculpture, and mostly self-taught in photography and video, Ann Hamilton is known for her process-oriented installations that link elements of perception, knowledge, and experience. Interested in verbal and written language as much as she is in the visual, Hamilton begins the creative process by reading a broad range of literary, anthropological, and sociological texts. Then, drawing on these sources, she creates site-specific installations of intense sensory experience. Since most of her projects are temporary, the majority of her work endures only in documentary photographs, sketches, and individual components.

In 1999 Hamilton was chosen to be the United States' representative for the 48th Venice Biennale, for which she created an installation entitled *myein* (the Greek root of the word *mystery*) that responded to the American pavilion's Neoclassical architecture. The artist addressed issues of suffering and oppression in America's social history by embossing excerpts from the poem "Testimony" by Charles Reznikoff in Braille along the pavilion's interior walls. A fine red powder continuously drifted down from the ceiling, making the words along the bare white walls literally and figuratively visible. A whispered recording of Hamilton reciting words about slavery and healing, taken from Abraham Lincoln's second inaugural address, added to the poetic aura. Outside the pavilion, as another component of the artwork, Hamilton installed a freestanding, textured glass wall that distorted the view of the building. Seen through it, the Neoclassical architecture appeared as though reflected in the surface of the surrounding water.

Made on the site of the American pavilion during Hamilton's installation of *myein*, *Reflection (12:45)* serves as a means of exploring perceptual awareness as well. The artist had herself photographed looking through the stacks of glass before they were installed for the exterior wall. One in a suite of twelve images that were taken every five minutes over the course of an hour, beginning at noon, *Reflection (12:45)* incorporates the elements of light and time that are so fundamental to Hamilton's oeuvre.[2] The audience views the artist's "portrait" as if through a screen or veil, another common element in Hamilton's work that alternately reveals and obscures the subject, to dematerialize it and make it known. Paradoxically, the textured glass screen draws further attention to itself, both drawing us in and heightening our awareness of separation from the figure. Evoking a quiet but mysterious presence, the individual is visually alluring but ultimately inaccessible.

The Weatherspoon owns two other works by Hamilton. *slaughter* is a glass-covered box containing a silk-organza work glove that was hand-embroidered with lines from Susan Stewart's poem "Slaughter." *scripted* consists of two metal thimbles, one gold, one silver, juxtaposed in a glass-covered wooden box. The gold thimble stands vertically and is photo-engraved in open filigree with words from "Cinder," another of Stewart's poems, while the silver one rests horizontally with long gray horsehairs extending from its scalplike pores. Once again, in both sculptures, the artist has given form to language, seeing the two as interchangeable.

EDG

Notes

1. Katy Kline and Helaine Posner, *Ann Hamilton myein* (Venice: United States Pavilion, 48th Venice Biennale, 1999), 7.
2. The prints were published in 2000 by the Institute of Electronic Arts and the artist as a way to thank those who helped in the production of *myein*.

Reflection (12:45), 1999–2000. Iris print on Arches watercolor paper, edition 3/10, 46¼ × 34⅛ in. Gift of Gail Boulton Miller, 2003

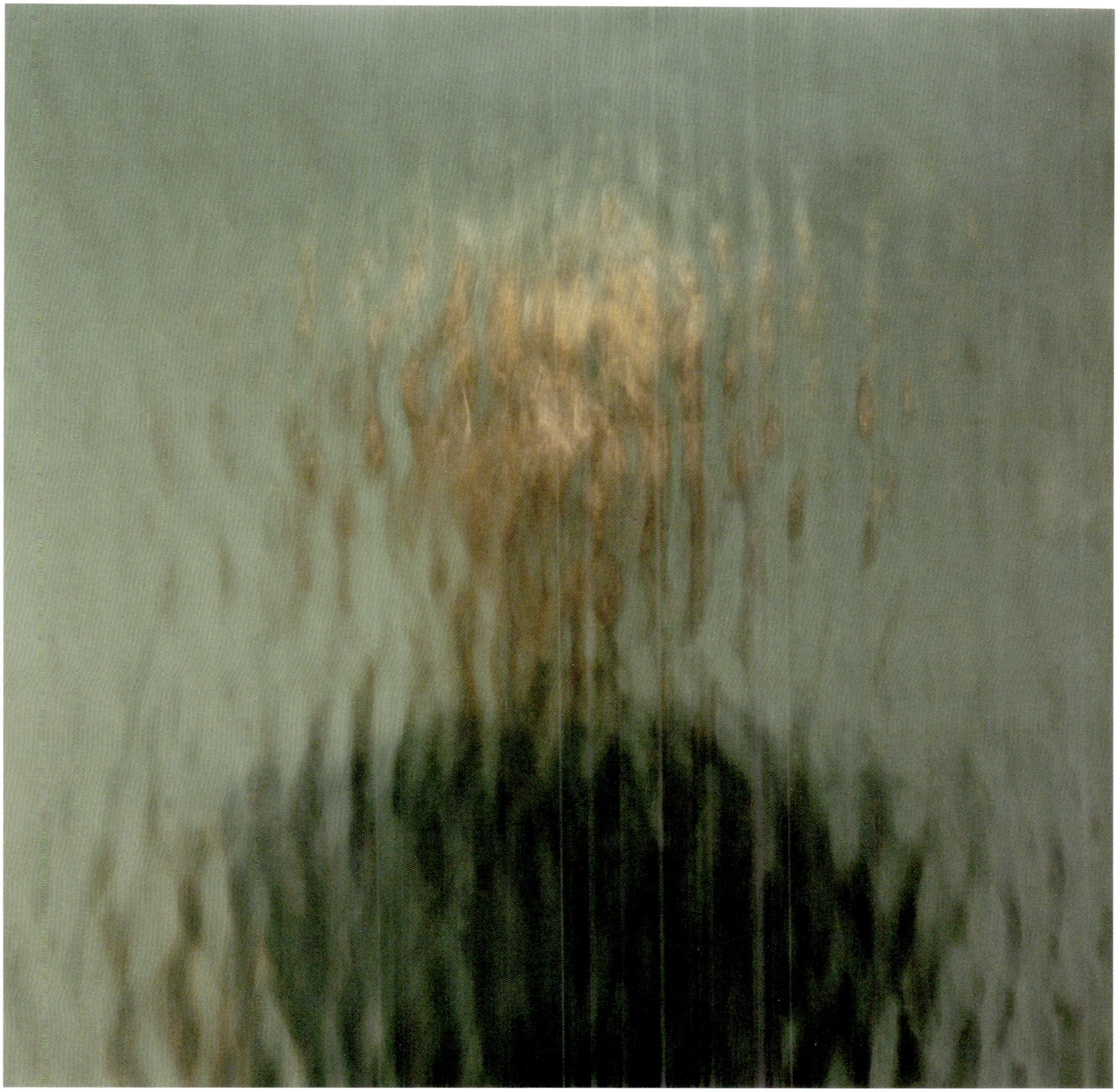

JUDITH SHEA American, born 1948

FROM HIS POSITION OUTSIDE, in the Weatherspoon's sculpture garden, Judith Shea's *Urban Francis* gazes upward. What he is truly seeing, however, remains purposely elusive and open to interpretation, like so many elements of this sculpture. As Shea intended, the viewer asks, is it heaven he perceives, or is it the Holy Spirit approaching to inflict the stigmata? Does he watch his traditional avian friends, which hop from tree to tree around him, or is his focus on something else entirely—something otherworldly, unperceived, and even unfathomable to humans? The answer truly is in the eye of the beholder.

Shea, an American sculptor who is perhaps best known for her powerful works centering on clothing as icon, receptacle of memory, and signifier of gender, noted in 2008 that after more than seventeen years of implying the form of a body, it was time for her to "return" the actual figure to her work.[1] *Urban Francis*, which dates from 2000–2002, is part of that refocusing.

The Weatherspoon's *Francis* is the third in a series of three hollow, bronze, life-size representations of the famous Italian saint and the museum's first acquisition of an example by Shea. His appearance, modern dress, and virtual lack of attributes make the subject initially difficult to identify. Only the figure's tonsured head points in a general direction to his holy identity, which is then specified by Shea's title.

The saintly subject of Shea's sculpture was born into privilege in 1181, in Assisi. After being called by God to "repair my house," the young Francis renounced his inheritance and worldly possessions and dedicated himself to a life of poverty, ministry to the sick, and preaching.[2] He wandered the Italian countryside for several years before acquiring followers and founding the Franciscan Order.

Shea notes, however, that when she first began working on the figure that would become *Urban Francis*, she was not thinking of the humble saint. Rather, Shea's inspiration was a man she glimpsed standing on the street at the corner of Chambers Street and West Broadway, New York, where she lives. Shea recalls his appearance as both "ascetic looking" and "aesthetic," with a shaved head, huge overcoat, and two enormous bags slung over his shoulders. Standing where tourists routinely snapped photos of the sun setting between the towers of the World Trade Center, this individual, like them, seemed to be transfixed by the light falling between the structures. To Shea, he appeared to grasp something unseen, and, in retrospect, given the horrific events that followed on September 11, 2001, the individual on the street that day even seemed prophetic.[3]

Eventually this individual evolved into *Urban Francis*, a modern Everyman version of Italy's patron saint, and the first in a series of contemporary saints, which developed from Shea's intense dialogue with Roman religious sculpture during her yearlong residence at the American Academy in Rome, in 1994–95, when she was the winner of the Rome Prize.

Urban Francis is dressed simply. He wears Shea's trademark large, collared overcoat with pants that are too long and pool at his ankles. The fabric of both garments, rough and frayed at the hems, evokes the humble cowl of the Franciscans. He is barefoot and stands on an unassuming base of cast wooden planks, his hands hanging by his sides. *Francis*'s head is tilted upward and slightly to his left, and his lips are parted, further animating the face. The texture of his closely cropped hair and clothing contrasts with the smoothness of his skin. Rivulets of white patina run over the surface, activating the entire sculpture. The artist's choice of white, rather than the green, patina, found on her other works (such as *Without Words* from 1988), is meaningful to her, and it loads the element with seemingly particular portent. And yet, when asked, Shea noted that there is not one intended interpretation, but instead a desire to evoke for the viewer that which is absent, whether that is birds, rain clouds, the source of spiritual illumination, or even a jeering crowd.[4]

Much like the patina, Shea's figure of *Urban Francis* himself eludes precise identity. He is both everyone and no one, Italian saint and New York vagrant, contemporary and timeless, distracted and riveted. *Urban Francis* quietly poses questions of the viewer but gives few direct answers, appropriately eliciting contemplation instead.

HH

Notes

1. Judith Shea, artist's talk, Weatherspoon Art Museum Association Annual Meeting and Members' Night, May 14, 2008.
2. David Hugh Farmer, *The Oxford Dictionary of Saints*, 3rd ed. (New York: Oxford University Press, 1992), 186.
3. Shea, 2008.
4. Judith Shea, interview by the author, Greensboro, NC, May 16, 2008.

Urban Francis, 2000–2002. Cast bronze, edition 3/3, 76 × 41 × 32 in. Museum purchase with a bequest from Leah Louise Tannenbaum and funds from the Tannenbaum-Sternberger Foundation given in her memory; additional funds provided by the Burlington Industries Endowment and the Weatherspoon Art Museum Acquisition Endowment, 2007

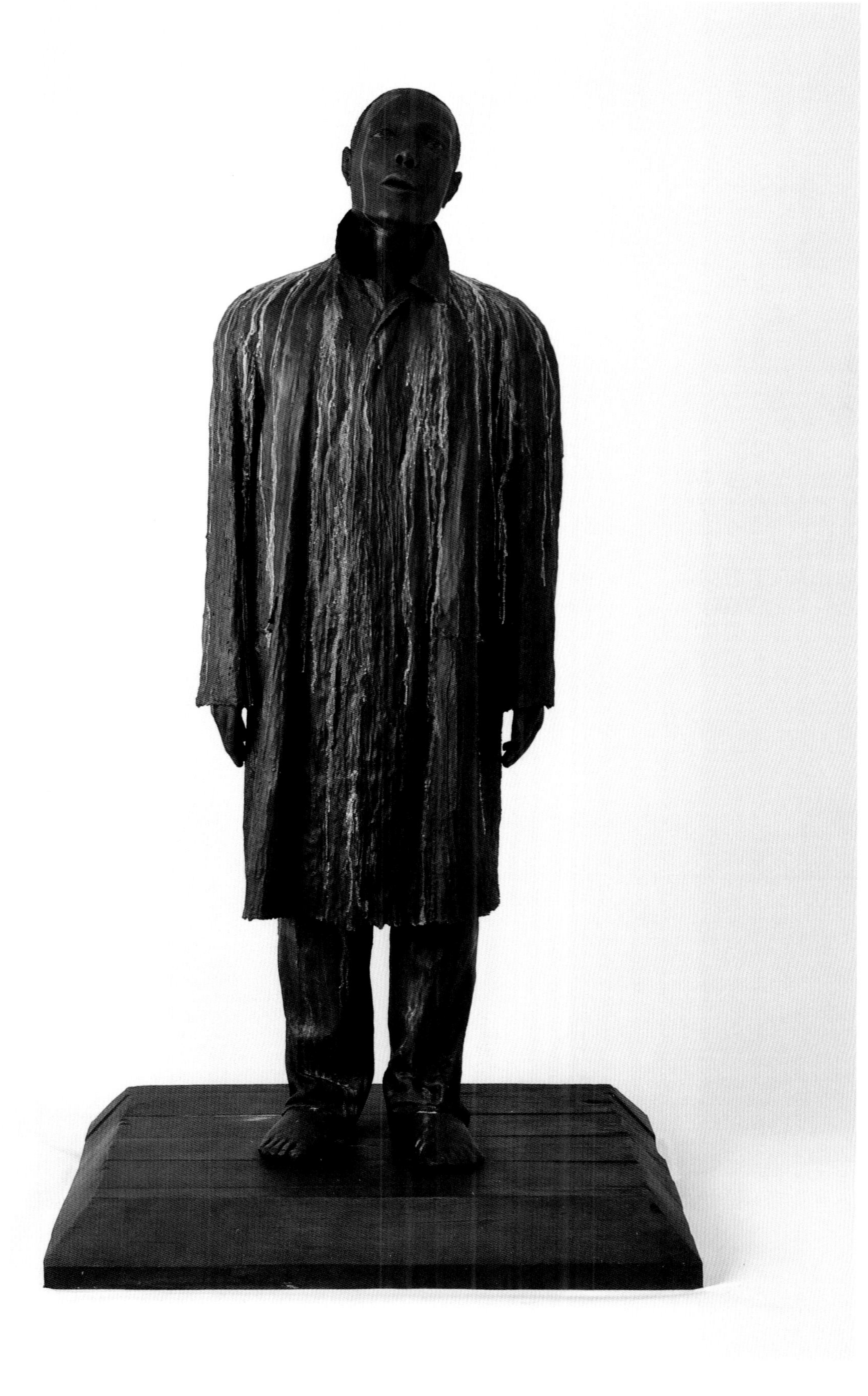

RONI HORN American, born 1955

IN PLAYING ON THE TENETS of repetition and seriality laid out by Minimalism, Roni Horn investigates the emotive possibilities of geometric form and brings issues of time and personal identity into the fold. Her photographic works address duality and ambiguity through juxtaposed sequences of images of facial expressions and natural phenomena. They encourage us to examine the relation between the camera's ability to capture instantly one moment from many and the change in the appearance (and our perception) of things over time. The artist places similar images side by side to bring attention to the space in between.

The clown appears in a number of Horn's works as an ephemeral and shifting personality whose facial expressions always appear blurred and multiple. *Clowndoubt (Us)* combines two almost identical images of a clown's face. On first encounter, the work appears a seamless whole, but, on closer inspection, we find it is assembled from eight parts that have been collaged together. To create this work, Horn shot a number of one-minute-long exposures of a clown posing in her studio. She then worked with two prints from the series, cutting them up and reconfiguring them before mounting them on paper. The notations in graphite that are faintly visible on the edges of the cuts are the means by which she pieced the parts together. Drawing is a central component of Horn's practice, and she uses the term *photographic drawing* to describe this process. Since the mid-1980s Horn has also made pigment drawings that are similarly constructed of cut-up, repeated forms.

A mercurial character throughout the centuries, the clown is at times a figure of circus hilarity and at others, dark and threatening. The mask of the clown in *Clowndoubt (Us)* is created with the typical white grease paint covering the face, large red lips and nose, blackened brows, and a white plastic cap that covers the hair. The two images of the clown appear to mirror each other, but they also seem to blend together, forcing the viewer's eyes to oscillate between them in an attempt to find fixed pairings. A search for points of recognition of the person beneath the mask is fruitless—there is little to be learned about the identity of the player, as both gender and age have been completely obscured by makeup and the blurring of the image.

Horn has stated, "I have always felt androgyny as central to my relationship with both myself and the work. As far as an individual's experience of a given work goes, I throw the issue of self-identity back out to the viewer."[1] By blending masculine and feminine traits, the androgyne integrates difference to form an identity that is not easily named. In a sense, it is a looser and much more expansive expression of self since it is not governed by conventional gender roles. The motif of the genderless clown in this work toys with our insecurities about identity, while its doubling articulates the process through which we begin to define difference, which, Horn reveals, can be effected only through the act of comparing similarities.

Note

1. Roni Horn, in an interview by Collier Schorr, "Weather Girls: Interview with Roni Horn," *Frieze*, no. 32 (January–February 1997): 44.

Clowndoubt (Us), 2001. Photographic drawing (graphite and collage), 32 × 39 in. Museum purchase with funds from the Dillard Fund, the Weatherspoon Art Museum Acquisition Endowment and the Jefferson-Pilot Corporation Endowment for the Dillard Collection, 2002

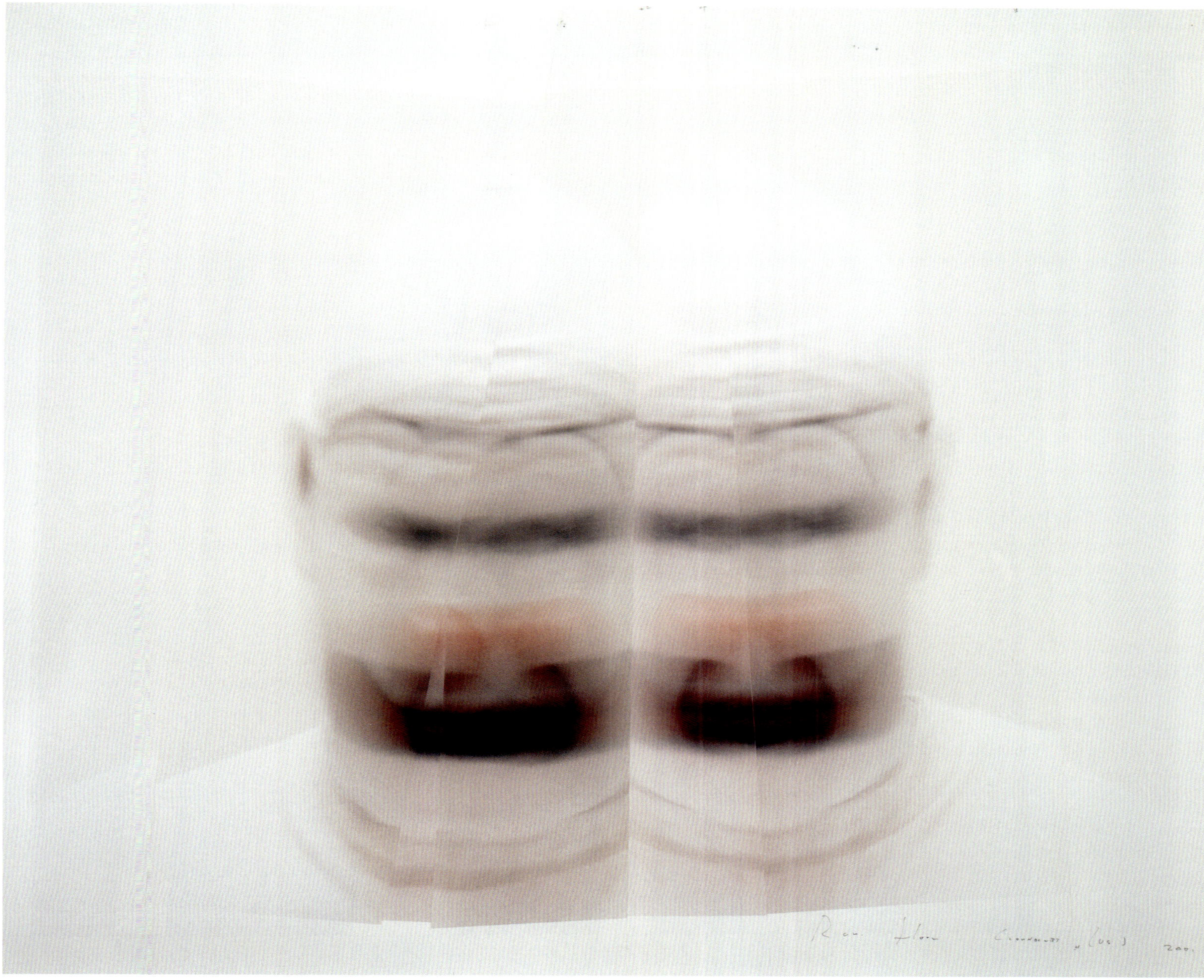

AMY CUTLER American, born 1974

SADDLEBACKED TAKES ITS NAME from a term often used to describe the curved back of an old horse, worn by years of labor. Yet, in a humorous and bewitching twist, Amy Cutler has literally inverted the relation between her beasts of burden and their owners. We are presented, not with hardworking curved-backed horses carrying heavy loads, but with a delightful visual pun. Two women appear in an open white space and are literally saddled with seemingly bearable but nonetheless weighty horses. Although one woman has bent over to rest and put down the feedbags and rope she may have been carrying, these sturdy figures seem capable of carrying their load. The woman to the left bears her horse, packages, and bags with a quiet stoicism.

This tension and humor are typical of the artist's visions. Moreover, the delicacy with which Cutler depicts her scenes enthralls and charms viewers. Each vignette creates in the beholder both the desire to create a narrative that explains the action and a feeling of contemplative observation. Cutler's audiences probe her inspired draftsmanship and the manner in which she makes even the most absurd situation somehow believable.

Drawing from observations of human behavior and subtle misunderstandings,[1] Cutler creates entire worlds that seem to have sprung from the pages of Grimm's fairy tales. Indeed, the subtly dark imagination with which she infuses her work is more in keeping with the original tone of the Brothers Grimm. Her work relies on the uncanny, that which is unsettling because it reminds us so poignantly of familiar objects or circumstances.[2] Cutler's narratives most often feature women confronting a situation or participating in a ritual that takes place in a world with rules of physics or behavior that are similar to those of but that are not of this world. This tension leaves the viewer with an incomplete narrative thread and a slight discomfort.

For instance, the effort of the woman resting in *Saddlebacked* is difficult to explain in light of her companion's stalwart expression. As we delve into the work, details are revealed that only enrich the experience. One can see that the figure on the left has a knife in a holster attached to her saddle; its purpose is a mystery. The almost absurdly calm expression of the two white horses the women carry assure us that these beasts are used to this mode of transportation, but why are they being carried? Why are they so serene and docile?

These questions of content are intimately related to Cutler's technique. Through relationships Cutler draws viewers in to analyze her application of paint and attention to detail. The delicacy of line and attention to composition in her gouaches enliven the act of viewing. In *Saddlebacked* the rope, cast somewhat loosely aside in the lower right, provides a point of interest that plays against the visual weight of the packages held in the arms of the figure to the left. Cutler's attention to each twist of rope encourages the exploration of further details and rewards the viewer who stops to observe the way in which the light blue box has been tied in a square pattern to complement the pattern of its wrapping. The texture of the women's boots, the light blue outlining of an indigo dress, and even a silver glimmer of a dangling necklace affirm the artist's expectation of the viewer's visual pleasure and inquiry.

Cutler's study of everything from Japanese woodblock prints and Persian miniatures to military survival manuals and nature studies can be seen in these details. Perhaps it is this nuance that has impressed both critics and the public alike. Since her graduation from the Cooper Union School of Art in 1997, Cutler has been featured in *Elle* magazine as well as the Whitney Biennial.[3] Part of a new generation of two-dimensional artists revitalizing the use of the human figure in narrative contexts, Cutler has been compared with David Rathman, Shahzia Sikander, and Kara Walker.[4] Though this return to figuration is, as of yet, unresolved as a movement, it is clear that Cutler has tapped into a sensibility that resonates with contemporary viewers and her fellow artists alike.

EP

Notes

1. Alison Ferris, *Fantastical Fables* (Brunswick, ME: Bowdoin College, 2008), 5.
2. Sigmund Freud, *The Uncanny* (New York: Penguin, 2003), 195–200.
3. Lisa D. Freiman, "The Marvelous World of Amy Cutler," in *Amy Cutler: Paintings and Drawings* (Indianapolis: Indianapolis Museum of Art, 2002), 10.
4. Ibid., 13; and *Dialogues: Amy Cutler/David Rathman* (Minneapolis: Walker Art Center, 2002), at http://www.walkerart.org/archive/4/B0730558332A58C76132.htm.

Saddlebacked, 2002. Gouache on paper, 30 × 22¾ in. Museum purchase with funds from the Dillard Fund for the Dillard Collection, 2002

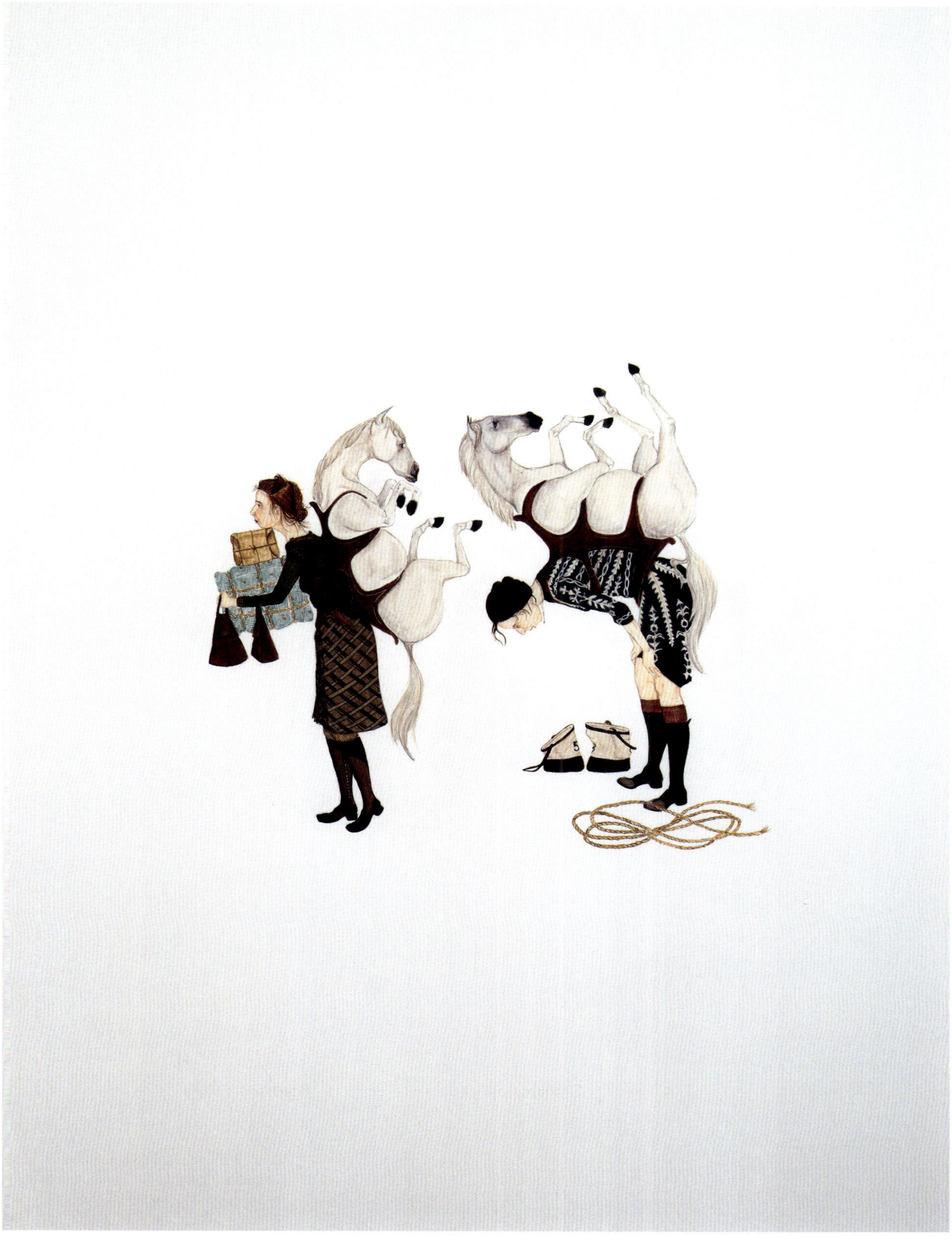

JENNIFER STEINKAMP American, born 1958

THROUGH HIGHLY REALISTIC, digitally animated works, Jennifer Steinkamp creates illusionistic spaces within which the viewer becomes physically and perceptually absorbed. Her haunting representations of the natural world are generated entirely from computer software. Often they take the form of swaying trees and flowering vines that seem to bend and twist as if in umbrage. Light, space, and color are combined with perpetual movement to create an intense sensory experience.

Hurdy Gurdy Man (Dahlia) is a digitally generated animation of gyrating dahlia plants. The title of the work comes from a Donovan song of the same name and refers to players of a pleasant-sounding stringed musical instrument invented in the Middle Ages. The instrument became associated with deviant behavior in the nineteenth century because of its alleged encouragement of exotic dancing, and then became a symbol of psychedelia in 1968 through the droning melody of Donovan's hypnotic hit. Steinkamp revives this long history by digitally rendering animations of beautiful dancing flowers that bend and cavort at the artist's command. The captivating movements of the flowers seem natural at first, but when looked at more closely, their movements convey a sense of the uncanny. This transition clouds our perception of the images as innocent spring flowers, replacing it with a darker view of a nature thoroughly manipulated by man. Steinkamp's seemingly benign version of nature is rooted in the grotesque.

A pioneer in the use of digital technology, Steinkamp has received critical acclaim for her extraordinary and mesmerizing interpretations of nature and large-scale abstract works. While her work often takes the form of installations consisting of multiple floor-to-ceiling projections that envelop the viewer in a transformative architectural space, *Hurdy Gurdy Man (Dahlia)*, although small in scale, is equally powerful. Through this series of flowers, Steinkamp contributes to the ongoing challenge of exhibiting new media within the museum context. The work is presented in a lit room as a four-foot-wide projection using a bright, high-definition DLP projector connected to a computer hard drive. The computer runs a software program that creates the image in real time. The work does not require a separate, darkened room, as is the case with many projected works, and stands as one of the first light-projected new media works designed to be shown along with other, more traditional works of art, such as paintings, sculpture, and photography.

Steinkamp's studio has devised a system that allows it to archive the animation as hard copy, such that it can be re-created if (or when) the original technology for the work becomes so outdated that it cannot be replaced or if new technology makes it impossible for the work to operate properly. However, in terms of concept, Steinkamp is clearly invested in the ephemeral quality of her work: "It's all code to create [the] images. I like that world, nonreality putting itself into reality and transforming reality. If the power goes out it doesn't exist anymore."[1] With *Hurdy Gurdy Man (Dahlia)*, Steinkamp hones her interest in the "nonreality" created by technology, the influence of which is felt throughout contemporary culture, to create works that engage viewers in an intimate perceptual and sensory experience.

XE

Note

1. Quoted in Scott Timburg, "Tangling with Technology? It's an Art," *Los Angeles Times*, December 19, 2004, E-6.

Hurdy Gurdy Man (Dahlia), 2005. Projected digital animation, edition 5/6, dimensions variable. Museum purchase with funds from the Carol and Seymour Levin Acquisition Endowment, the Louise D. and Herbert S. Falk Acquisition Endowment, the Judy Proctor Acquisition Endowment, and the Melanie H. and Robert C. Ketner Family Acquisition Endowment, 2006

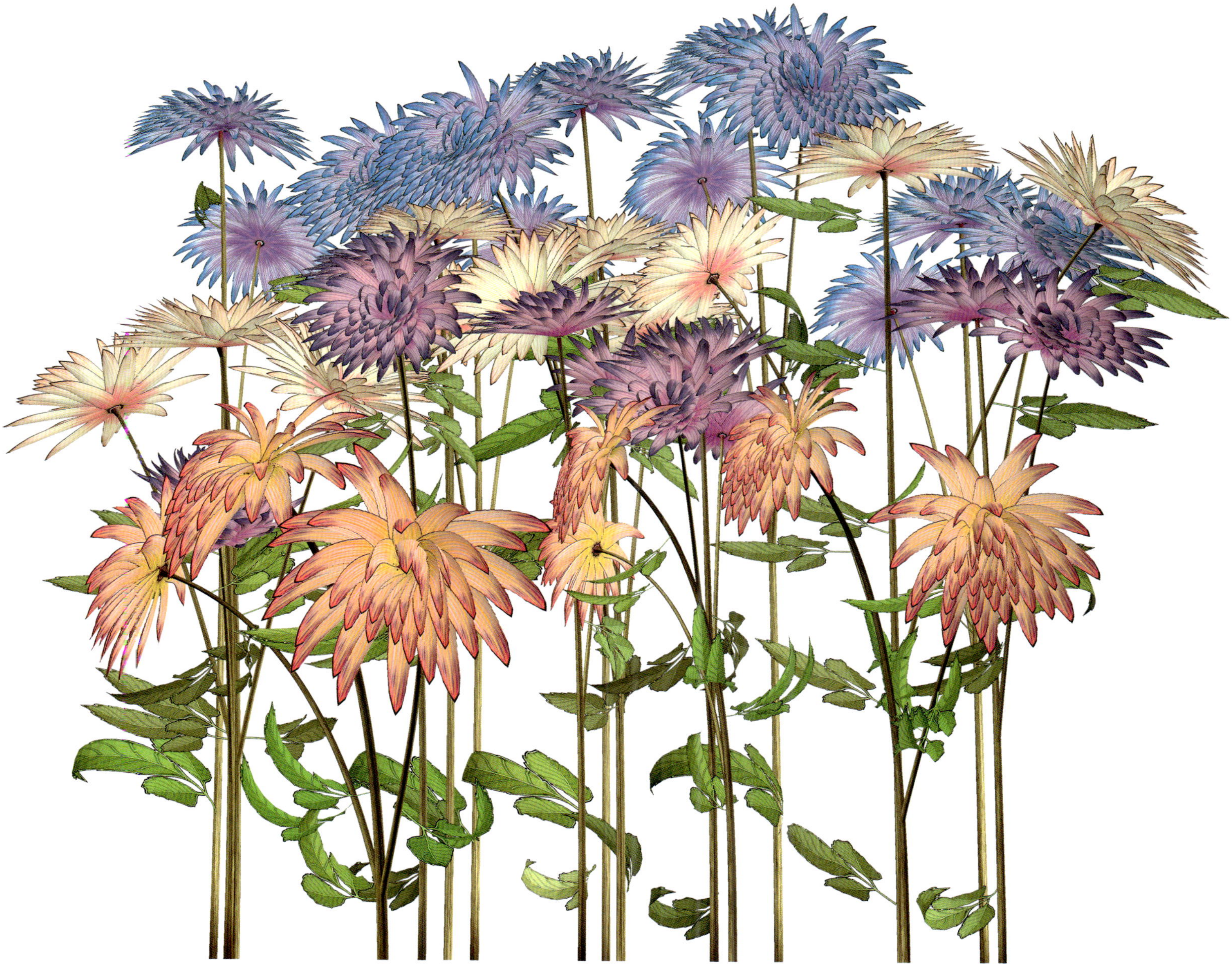

AMY SILLMAN American, born 1956

IN HER PAINTINGS IN OIL on canvas, Amy Sillman explores the tension between figuration and abstraction. She revives the concerns of abstract painting by examining the rich formal relations found in juxtaposing levity and weight, drawing and painting, outline and color plane; however, a major focus of her work is the back-and-forth between different modes of looking and communicating through painting. Through gesture, color, and form, Sillman simultaneously concerns herself with defining the limits of painting in the tradition of abstraction and infiltrating it with various tactics of pictorial image making.

After working in a cannery in Alaska, a feminist silkscreen factory in Chicago, and training to become a Japanese interpreter for the United Nations at New York University, Sillman entered the painting program at the School of Visual Arts in New York. Graduating in 1979, she spent the 1980s content to devote herself to studio practice and had little interest in getting work into exhibitions. In the late 1990s, after she graduated from Bard College's MFA program, she began to show her work and has, since then, received substantial critical success.

Untitled (yellow w/bird) projects a playful use of color and style. The use of bright yellow and red and the suggestion of an armlike appendage reaching out toward an object of desire are emblematic of Sillman's work. Vertical blocks of gradated blue and a brilliant yellow divide the image into parts, while the bold, yet sparingly drawn lines of dark gray, brown, and red move energetically across the canvas. A figure holding a small bird emerges from these lines. This rather forlorn-looking, abstract form—on the right side of the canvas and in a shape that recalls the elephant found in some of Sillman's other works—gazes out at a very simple representation of a white-breasted songbird. This existential figure seems to exist purely for the delight of this moment of observation.

Reflecting the influence of the artists Willem de Kooning, Richard Diebenkorn, and Philip Guston, abstract and figurative aspects vie for dominance in Sillman's work. She deftly combines uninhibited gestures with areas of comparative restraint and clarity. The simplification of form in her work forces us to focus on the manipulation of paint and the varied textures and tones of the medium, yet our eye shifts from the flat surface of the canvas to engage with a vaguely narrative scene. Such back-and-forth may leave the viewer with a feeling of doubt. But much of Sillman's work deals precisely with this doubt, particularly as it relates to the possibilities for contemporary painting. She challenges herself and, in turn, the viewer to question what painting offers as a medium after so many years of exploration and to wonder at its potential to be endlessly reinvented.

XE

Untitled (yellow w/bird), 2007. Oil on canvas, 45 × 39 in. Museum purchase with funds from the Benefactors Fund, 2009

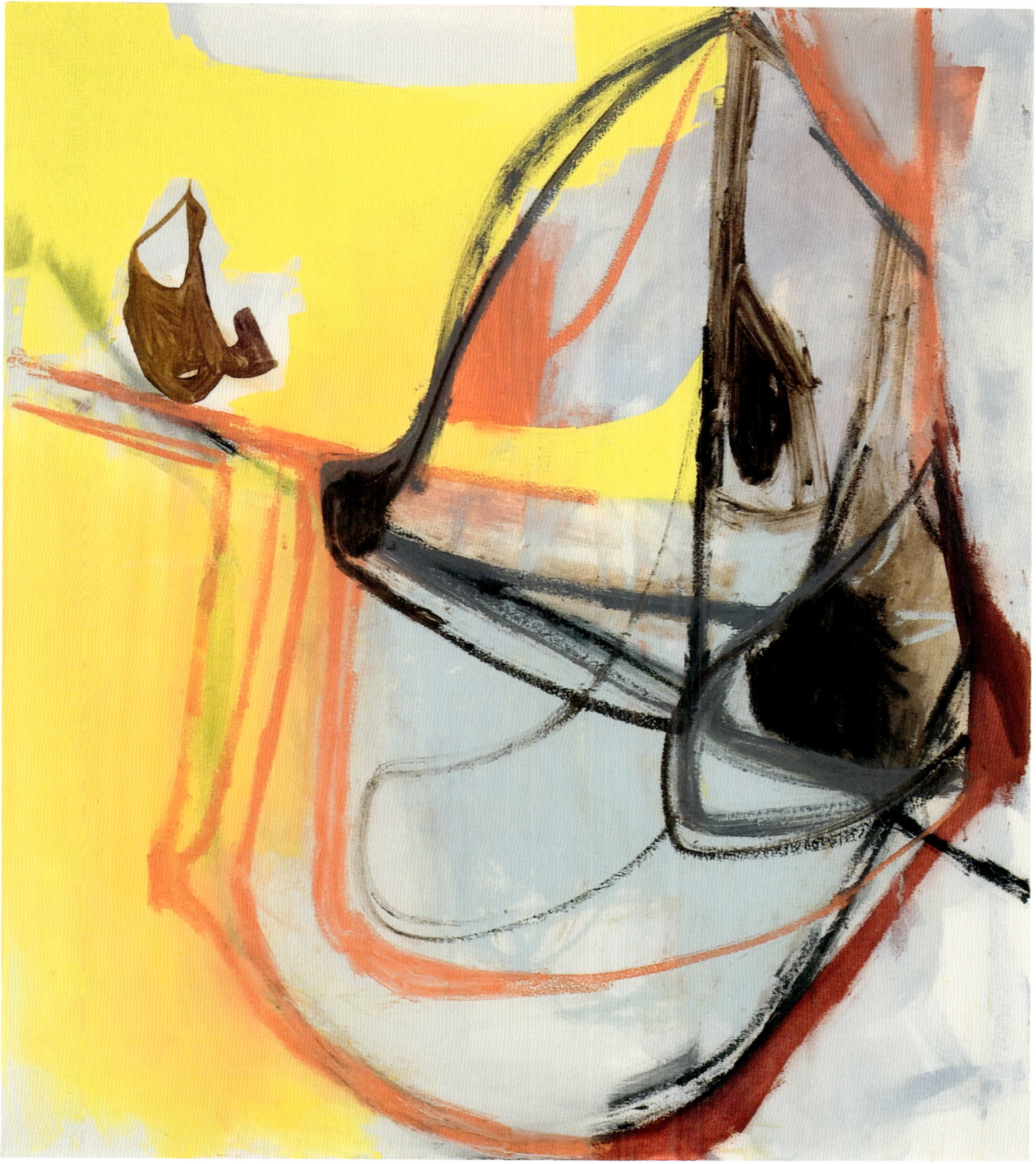

ELLIOTT HUNDLEY American, born 1975

ELLIOTT HUNDLEY CREATES sculptural collages that combine drawing, painting, performance, and photography into mythological tableaux. He uses eclectic materials, assembling his works from cut-up magazines, personal photographs, drawings, and a variety of found objects such as feathers, strings, and twist ties. With titles that often refer to classical drama and mythology, each of Hundley's works represents a fantastical world full of cryptic imagery and meaning.

Hundley finds many of his materials at thrift stores or in the street, recalling the work of other artists working in assemblage, most significantly Robert Rauschenberg's Combines, which also intertwine painting, sculpture, and collage. To create his work, Hundley engages with dramatic performance on two levels. First, he stages photographs and inserts those images within the work, and, second, he transmutes the emotive qualities of Greek theater into a static sculptural form.

The Body of Polydoros is one of a series of works Hundley made in his Los Angeles studio between the summer of 2008 and the spring of 2009 that were inspired by the Greek tragedy *Hekabe* by Euripides. A native of Greensboro, Hundley created this sculpture for the Weatherspoon's *Art on Paper* biennial exhibition in 2008. This early work in the series expands on the sad story of Polydoros, the youngest son of Hekabe and Priam. The story begins shortly after the Battle of Troy, during which Polydoros had been entrusted with the family's gold under the protection of the Thracian king, Polymestor. When Troy falls, appallingly, Polymestor murders Polydoros and dumps his body at sea, then claims the family's entire fortune. *The Body of Polydoros* is specifically derived from the scene in which Polydoros's mother, Hekabe, is presented with her son's lifeless body. Red letters pasted across the front-most surface of Hundley's work include five lines taken from parts of Hekabe's dialogue with Agamemnon:

> *A sea-thrashed thing. And look how he hacked at the flesh.*
> *Then didn't even think the body worthy of a grave!*
> *Call this shameful! Respect me!—and take pity.*
> *Or else stand back like a painter and contemplate me, the evils I suffer.*
> *I do not exist. There is nothing left. Not even evils.*[1]

Bits of coral and shell, part of a broken ship model, tangled masses of string (that look like seaweed), and dangling lengths of glass disks (foraged from the remnants of a cheap room divider) convey the semblance of something washed ashore. Gold and copper leaf applied to the surfaces of other objects symbolize the treasure that Polydoros held and that Polymestor was entrusted to protect.

This inventive adaptation of Greek tragedy in a contemporary art form can be seen to operate as set, script, *and* player. The work includes several cutout, black-and-white, staged photographs that are collaged onto paper. To create these images, Hundley invited friends to act out the scenes and characters in the play using improvised costumes and props. The photographs, cut letters, and found, cast-off objects form a dense network of detail, and the lightweight wood armature from which everything is suspended resembles a large, unwieldy kite. Life-size, *The Body of Polydoros* dangles precariously at a height that confronts the viewer directly.

XE

Note

1. *Grief Lessons: Four Plays by Euripides*, trans. and with an introduction by Anne Carson (New York: New York Review Books Classics, 2006), 135–36.

The Body of Polydoros, 2008. Paper, wood, bamboo, string, wire, metal, ceramic, coral, shells, spray paint, oil paint, plastic, epoxy putty, cardboard, glue, rag, and gold and copper leaf, 100 × 40 × 23 in (variable). Museum purchase with funds from the Dillard Fund and a partial gift of the artist and Andrea Rosen Gallery for the Dillard Collection, 2008

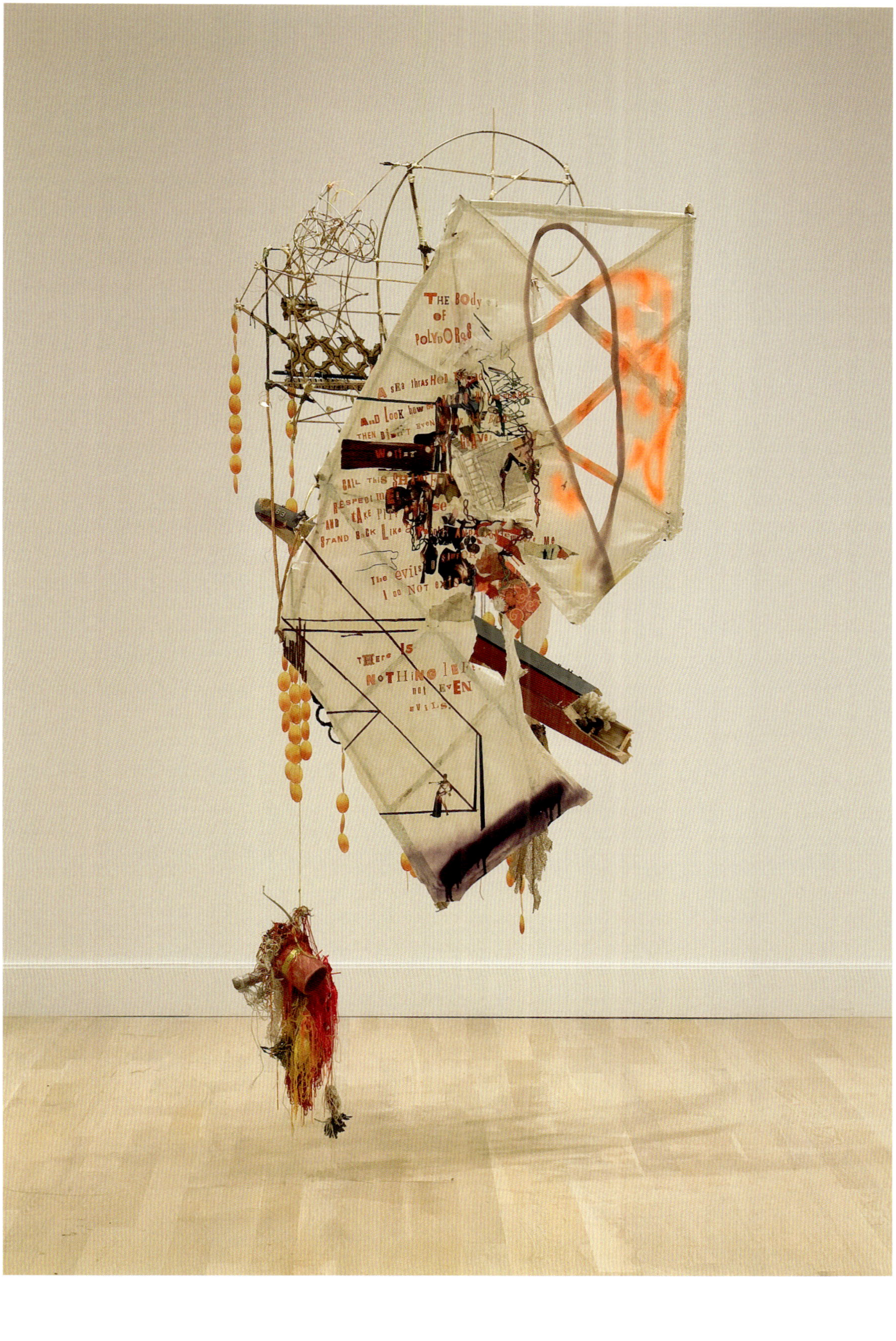
THE BODY
OF
AND LOOK how
CALL THIS
STAND BACK LIKE
The evils
I DO NOT
THERE IS
NOTHING
not EVEN
EVILS.

DEBORAH BUTTERFIELD American, born 1949

WHILE EARNING HER MFA DEGREE at the University of California, Davis, Deborah Butterfield was interested in the human form and figural explorations of mental states. Her mentors at Davis, Roy De Forest, Robert Arneson, Wayne Thiebaud, and Manuel Neri, were both professors and practicing artists. The dynamism of this art department inspired a generation of West Coast artists in the 1960s and 1970s. For Butterfield, their professional ambition provided the inspiration for her leap into professional art production.[1]

Some of Butterfield's early, ephemeral horses were constructed of mud and sticks that represented metaphorically vulnerable self-portraits. Though her work today is not nearly as transitory, Butterfield still sees her sculptures as a form of self-portrait. Although her sculptures sometimes bear masculine names, such as Lunalilo, a male member of the historic Hawaiian royal family, she always envisions these stalwart figures as mares.[2] The feminine is implied in the figures' stillness and strength. *Lunalilo* was created from Hawaiian wood, gathered by Butterfield during her annual residence in Hawaii away from the harsh Montana winters.

As her career advanced, Butterfield's horses moved beyond literal self-portraiture into sculptural reflections on internal gesture, the relation of human beings to the natural world, and serene contemplations on the nature of horses. She does not stray far from her source of inspiration. When in Montana, where she lives from the early spring to autumn on her ranch, Butterfield rides horses daily and sees a strong parallel between her artwork and the manner in which she builds the musculature of her horses as she trains them in the discipline of dressage riding.[3] This riding style demands that the rider and horse perform a set of prescribed movements with precision. The subtle signals of the rider guide the horse through trotting, canters, and even pirouettes that are the result of rigorous training and are commonly referred to as a horse ballet.

This same sense of lyricism comes through in Butterfield's sculpture. Circumambulating *Lunalilo* can result in the contemplation of internal mood and gesture. At a distance viewers can appreciate the way in which Butterfield assembles what seems to be worn wood to compose the curve of *Linalilo*'s jaw or hindquarters; they can see the way she utilizes branches to guide the viewer's eye through the internal space and accentuate the still power of this mare. As one approaches the form, another layer of Butterfield's artistic mastery comes to light. The original wood from which this piece was made has been replaced with carefully patinated bronze.

When she composes works of steel, Butterfield completes equine sculptures in found materials. Worn paint and rust reveal the influences of time on the old machinery and building materials that make up her works. A painterly aesthetic of line and texture goes into selecting each twisted piece of metal. For her bronze sculptures, the completion of the assemblage process requires acts of inspired and technically demanding trompe l'oeil casting.

Butterfield and a team of assistants first cast her bronze sculptures in clay, burn away the original wood, fill this cast with wax, and then replace this wax with bronze. The metal is then treated with pigments and chemicals to re-create the subtle grays and browns of weathered wood. This process is so effective that many people are tempted to touch the delicate surfaces of these sculptures.

In both the strength of her forms and their attention to detail, Butterfield encourages viewers to contemplate the weathering and forming processes that create both her raw materials and inspire her final products. Butterfield has discussed that the wood she gathers in the hills of Hawaii is charged with *mana*, the Hawaiian word for spiritual energy.[4] She has studied Asian, African, and indigenous American art and draws on her spiritual connection to the land as she works on her sculptures. Both her full-size and smaller-scale works prove that, in the hands of a gifted artist, a single subject can capture the attention of casual viewers and critics alike.

EP

Notes

1. Deborah Butterfield and Lawrence Weschler, "Metamorphoses: Horse Branch Bronze, a Conversation between Deborah Butterfield and Lawrence Weschler," in *Deborah Butterfield*, ed. Lisa Jann (Venice, CA: L.A. Louver Gallery, 2009), 136.
2. Kimberly Davis, L.A. Louver Gallery, e-mail correspondence with Ann Grimaldi, Curator of Education, Weatherspoon Art Museum, December 17, 2009.
3. Marcia Tucker, "An Interview with Deborah Butterfield," in *Horses: The Art of Deborah Butterfield* (San Francisco: Chronicle Books, 1992), 51.
4. Butterfield and Weschler, "Metamorphoses," 143.

Lunalilo, 2008. Bronze, 40¾ × 50¾ × 14¼ in. Museum purchase with funds from the Weatherspoon Acquisition Endowment, the Lynn Richardson Prickett Acquisition Endowment, the Frances Stern Loewenstein Acquisition Endowment, the Jane and Richard Levy Sculpture Fund, the Louise D. and Herbert S. Falk Acquisition Endowment, and the Judy Proctor Acquisition Endowment, 2009.

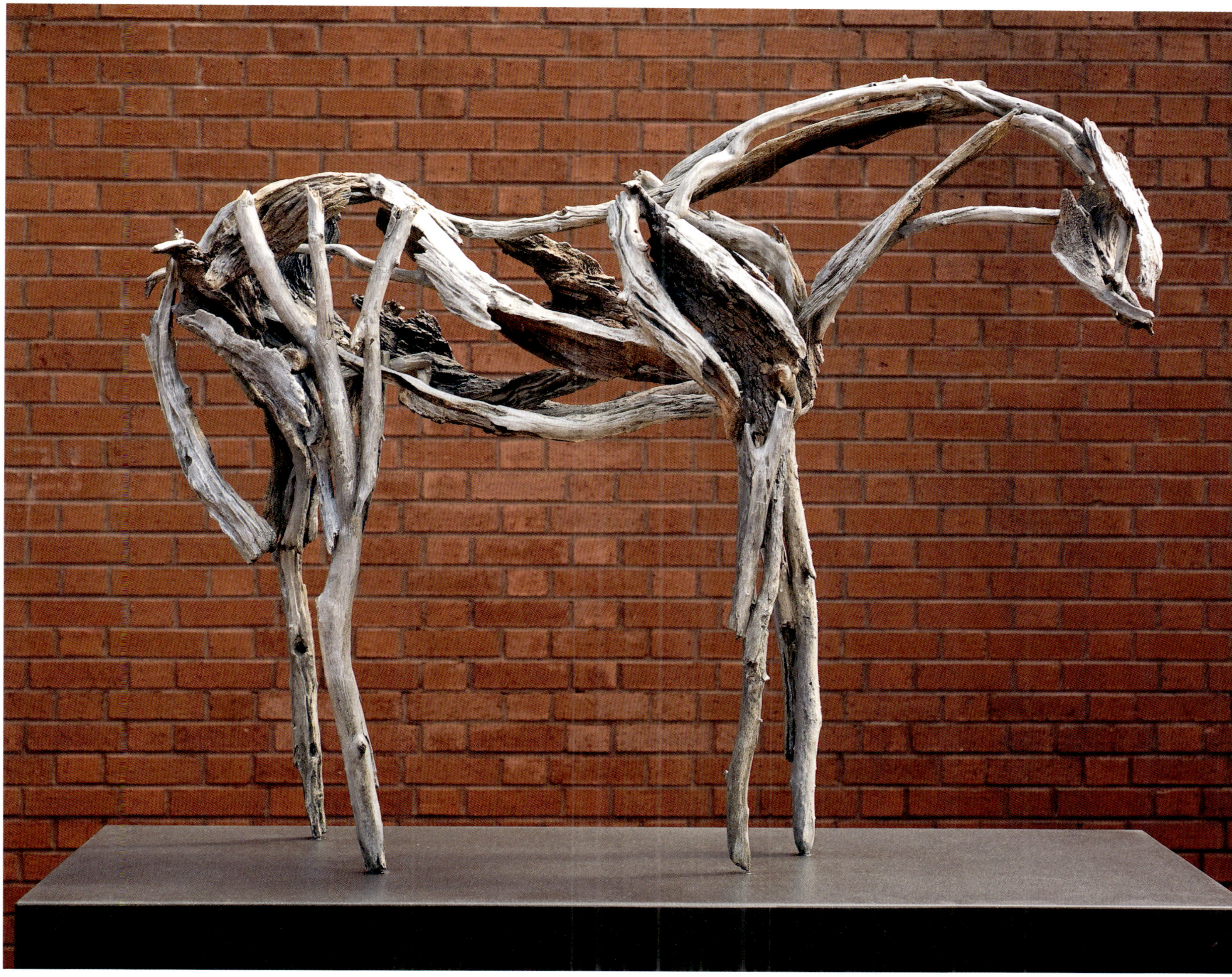

Index of Artists

Photography Credits

All images are the property of the Weatherspoon Art Museum and are in the public domain or reproduced with permission of the artist, with the exception of those noted below.

© Terry Allen, 171

© 2010 The Josef and Anni Albers Foundation / Artists Rights Society (ARS), New York, 99

Art © Carl Andre / Licensed by VAGA, New York, NY, 141

© Eleanor Antin, Courtesy Ronald Feldman Fine Arts, NY, 135

Art © The Estate of Ronald Bladen, LLC / Licensed by VAGA, New York, NY, 149

Art © Estate of Ilya Bolotowsky / Licensed by VAGA, New York, NY, 77

© Louise Bourgeois, 91

Harry Bowden, 84

Art © Deborah Butterfield / Licensed by VAGA, New York, NY, 227

© 2010 Calder Foundation, New York / Artists Rights Society (ARS), New York, 87

Art © Elizabeth Catlett / Licensed by VAGA, New York, NY, 89

© Robert Colescott, 1995, 189

detail, Courtesy of the artist and Luhring Augustine, 4

Courtesy of the artist and Luhring Augustine, 205

© Amy Cutler, Courtesy Leslie Tonkonow Artworks & Projects, NY, 219

Courtesy of Washburn Gallery, New York, 83

© 2010 The Willem de Kooning Foundation / Artists Rights Society (ARS), New York, 85

© Mark di Suvero, 197

© 2010 Stephen Flavin / Artists Rights Society (ARS), New York, 121

detail, © 2005 Estate of Maud F. Gatewood, 129

© 2005 Estate of Maud F. Gatewood, 195

Art © Estate of Leon Golub / Licensed by VAGA, New York, NY / Courtesy Ronald Feldman Fine Arts, 117

© 2010 The Arshile Gorky Foundation / Artists Rights Society (ARS), New York, 81

© Antony Gormley, 173

Courtesy of the artist and Michael Rosenfeld Gallery, NY, 145

Courtesy of the artist and Sean Kelly Gallery, NY, 213

detail, Art © Al Held Foundation / Licensed by VAGA, New York, NY, 3

Art © Al Held Foundation / Licensed by VAGA, New York, NY, 147

© The Estate of Eva Hesse, Courtesy Hauser & Wirth, 122, 123

© Roni Horn, 217

© Elliott Hundley, 225

detail, © 2010 The Jess Collins Trust, 79

© 2010 The Jess Collins Trust, 97

Art © Jasper Johns / Licensed by VAGA, New York, NY, 162, 163

© Ray Johnson Estate, Courtesy Richard L. Feigen & Co., 153

detail, Art © Alex Katz / Licensed by VAGA, New York, NY, 78

Art © Alex Katz / Licensed by VAGA, New York, NY, 115

© 2010 The LeWitt Estate / Artists Rights Society (ARS), New York, 151

detail, © The Estate of Lee Lozano, Courtesy Hauser & Wirth, 2

© The Estate of Lee Lozano, Courtesy Hauser & Wirth, 111

© 2010 Robert Mangold / Artists Rights Society (ARS), New York, 137

© 2010 Estate of Reginald Marsh / Art Students League, New York / Artists Rights Society (ARS), New York, 59

© 2010 Succession H. Matisse / Artists Rights Society (ARS), New York, 23

© The Estate of Ana Mendieta, Courtesy of Galerie Lelong, NY, 155

© Richard Misrach, 209

© Estate of Joan Mitchell, 107

© Yasumasa Morimura, 199

Art © Vik Muniz / Licensed by VAGA, New York, NY, 201

© The Murray-Holman Family Trust, Courtesy of The Pace Gallery. Photo by G. R. Christmas, 165

Courtesy Sperone Westwater, New York / © 2010 Bruce Nauman / Artists Rights Society (ARS), New York, 125

© 2010 Estate of Louise Nevelson / Artists Rights Society (ARS), New York, 95

detail © Ed Paschke, *Mono-Pareja*, 1990, 6–7

© Ed Paschke, *Mono-Pareja*, 1990, 177

© APRA Foundation, Berlin, 167

© 2010 The Pollock-Krasner Foundation / Artists Rights Society (ARS), New York, 75

detail, Art © Estate of Robert Rauschenberg / Licensed by VAGA, New York, NY, 5

Art © Estate of Robert Rauschenberg / Licensed by VAGA, New York, NY, 105

© 2010 David Reed / Artists Rights Society (ARS), New York, 169

© Estate of Milton Resnick, Courtesy Cheim & Read, New York, 103

Art © Estate of Larry Rivers / Licensed by VAGA, New York, NY, 101

detail, © Ed Ruscha, Courtesy Gagosian Gallery, 128

© Ed Ruscha, Courtesy Gagosian Gallery, 133

© Cindy Sherman, Courtesy of the artist and Metro Pictures, cover

© Cindy Sherman, Courtesy of the artist and Metro Pictures, 159

© Amy Sillman, 223

© The Slobodkina Foundation, 65

Art © Estate of David Smith / Licensed by VAGA, New York, NY, 69

Art © Estate of Robert Smithson / Licensed by VAGA, New York, NY, 126, 127

© Nancy Spero, Courtesy of Galerie Lelong, 119

Courtesy Zabriskie Gallery and the estate of the artist, 93

© Jennifer Steinkamp, Courtesy Lehmann Maupin Gallery, NY, 221

© Pat Steir, 185

© Jessica Stockholder, 183

detail, © 2010 The Andy Warhol Foundation for the Visual Arts, Inc. / Artists Rights Society (ARS), New York, 8–9

© 2010 The Andy Warhol Foundation for the Visual Arts, Inc. / Artists Rights Society (ARS), New York, 143

Collection Center for Creative Photography, © 1981 Arizona Board of Regents, 63